Religion and Political Culture in Jefferson's Virginia

Religion and Political Culture in Jefferson's Virginia

EDITED BY
GARRETT WARD SHELDON
AND DANIEL L. DREISBACH

ROWMAN & LITTLEFIELD PUBLISHERS, INC.
Lanham • Boulder • New York • Oxford

ROWMAN & LITTLEFIELD PUBLISHERS, INC.

Published in the United States of America
by Rowman & Littlefield Publishers, Inc.
4720 Boston Way, Lanham, Maryland 20706
http://www.rowmanlittlefield.com

12 Hid's Copse Road
Cumnor Hill, Oxford OX2 9JJ, England

British Library Cataloguing in Publication Information Available

Library of Congress Cataloging-in-Publication Data

Religion and political culture in Jefferson's Virginia / edited by Garrett Ward Sheldon and Daniel L. Dreisbach.

p. cm.

Includes bibliographical references and index.

ISBN 0-7425-0774-2 (alk. paper) — ISBN 0-7425-0775-0 (pbk. : alk. paper)

1. Christianity and politics—Virginia—History—18th century. 2. Church and state—Virginia—History—18th century. 3. Virginia—Church history—18th century. 4. Jefferson, Thomas, 1743–1826. 5. Madison, James, 1751–1836. I. Sheldon, Garrett Ward, 1954– II. Dreisbach, Daniel L.

BR555.V8 R45 2000
322'.1'0975509033—dc21 99-044090

Printed in the United States of America

™ The paper used in this publication meets the minimum requirements of American National Standard for Information Sciences—Permanence of Paper for Printed Library Materials, ANSI/NISO Z39.48–1992.

For Wilson Carey McWilliams, mentor and friend, who taught me the importance of religion to American politics.

— G.W.S.

For Keller Cushing Freeman, a teacher of vision; and for Robert and Virginia Cowley, who gave me much for which to be thankful.

— D.L.D.

Contents

Editors' Preface

This book is about the religious influences on Jefferson's Virginia. It is difficult to overstate the contributions of Thomas Jefferson and James Madison to the founding of the American republic and its institutions. It is similarly difficult to exaggerate the role of religion in shaping the political culture of the founding era. This book examines the religious concepts and communities that influenced Jefferson and Madison and may have informed their political and religious thought, the political culture of their time, and the development of a distinctive American approach to church-state relations.

Most of the chapters in this volume came from a symposium held on 19-20 January 1996 in Mr. Jefferson's "academical village"—the University of Virginia in Charlottesville. A comment by political historian J.G.A. Pocock of Johns Hopkins University was the inspiration for this symposium. At a 1984 conference celebrating the bicentennial of Jefferson's "Statute for Establishing Religious Freedom," Professor Pocock opined that "the historical study of the statute [for religious freedom] is incomplete" if we ignore the religious traditions, experiences, and perspectives of, among others, the "Baptist revivalists in Revolutionary Virginia."[1] Pocock, the leading scholar of the "Classical Republican" paradigm in early American historiography,[2] lamented that religious perspectives have been all too frequently neglected in scholarly analyses of Jefferson and Madison. Although this book does not confine itself to the Baptist historical perspective (if, indeed, there is one), we do think it takes some steps toward rectifying the omission Pocock identified. Many chapters in this book challenge long-held assumptions and conventional orthodoxies about the role of Christianity in early Virginia politics. They bring fresh perspectives and innovative research, as well as a critical reassessment of the existing scholarship, to the study of Jefferson and Madison.

The story of religion and politics in Thomas Jefferson's Virginia is an important chapter in the American experience. The Old Dominion, Thomas E. Buckley observed,

> provided the most critical experiment of the Revolutionary era, for Virginia served as a politicoreligious microcosm in which the whole nation could study the alternatives for a church-state relationship and then choose from among them. . . . [A]ll sides of the church-state controversy were ably represented: the

> traditional religionists who clung to the establishment ideal and insisted upon civil support for religion; the rationalists who believed religion to be an entirely personal affair and fought for an absolute separation of church and state; and dissenters of every stripe who, despite their own differences in polity and theory, wanted equal religious rights and a church freed from state control. For over a decade these Virginians developed the full range of arguments over the various alternatives presented for consideration: the retention of a single establishment, its replacement by a multiple system with state aid for all churches, the removal of religion from any relationship with civil authority, and the equality of religious groups without governmental assistance but free to influence society's morals and values.[3]

Jefferson's beloved Commonwealth was the most populous, prosperous, and influential of the former British colonies. Events in Virginia inevitably impacted developments in other states. Thus, when Virginians debated whether or not to redefine the church-state arrangements inherited from colonial times, citizens up and down the Atlantic seaboard and as far west as the Appalachian range took notice. This debate concerning the legitimate and prudential role of religion in public life was vital to a profoundly religious people. The church-state question assumed an urgency with the overthrow of the colonial order, with its ecclesiastical establishment, and the spread of religious revivals that were particularly vibrant in Jefferson's native Virginia Piedmont. Gordon S. Wood, in *The Radicalism of the American Revolution,* described the Second Great Awakening, a religious revival that began around the end of the eighteenth century, as the movement that made the United States the most evangelical Christian nation in the world.[4] Virginia was a leader in developing and testing a distinctive approach to religious liberty, denominational pluralism, and church-state relations. What emerged in Virginia and, indeed, in the new nation, was truly unique in the annals of Western civilization.

The dramatic disestablishment of the Church of England in Jefferson's Virginia captured the attention of the founding generation and continues to intrigue us more than two centuries later. We are drawn to this story because the struggle—in which Jefferson, Madison, and other venerated statesmen of the era played decisive roles—was important and dramatic. The church-state debates of revolutionary Virginia produced George Mason's seminal Article XVI of the Virginia Declaration of Rights, James Madison's trenchant "Memorial and Remonstrance against Religious Assessments," and Thomas Jefferson's eloquent "Statute for Establishing Religious Freedom"—some of the most impassioned and influential declarations ever penned in defense of religious liberty. This debate also produced scores of poignant and moving petitions for religious liberty from congregations and hamlets from the Tidewater to the Blue Ridge. Although not as learned and polished as Jefferson's tracts, these petitions, perhaps more than any other source, reveal the heart and mind of ordinary citizens on the vital concerns of religious faith and liberty. The great documents of the Virginia church-state debate arguably informed the intellectual milieu that produced a national policy on church-state relations in the U.S. Constitution. The story of politics and religious culture in Jefferson's Virginia is thus in many respects the story of religion and politics in the nascent American republic. The lessons of this story we ignore at our peril.

Church-state relations and religion in American political culture have been a source of controversy since the first settlement in the New World, and they continue to generate vigorous debate. Indeed, rarely in American history has the relationship between religion and politics been more widely discussed and warmly debated than it is today. Few topics in American public life are more appropriately informed by a thorough understanding of history. The Virginia contribution to the pursuit of religious liberty is especially pertinent to contemporary church-state debate. As Supreme Court Justice Wiley Rutledge opined in *Everson v. Board of Education* (1947): "No provision of the Constitution is more closely tied to or given content by its generating history than the religious clause of the First Amendment. It is at once the refined product and the terse summation of that history. That history includes not only Madison's authorship and the proceedings before the First Congress, but also the long and intensive struggle for religious freedom in America, more especially in Virginia, of which the [First] Amendment was the direct culmination."[5] The *Everson* Court and virtually all subsequent courts, in their efforts to articulate the constitutional relationship between religion and politics, have turned frequently to the thoughts and deeds of Jefferson and Madison not only because they led the dramatic disestablishment struggle in revolutionary Virginia, but also because their idea of the proper church-state relationship is thought to be expressive of the purposes of the First Amendment nonestablishment provision.[6]

This book is divided into three sections. In the opening section on religious culture in Jefferson's Virginia, Mark A. Beliles vividly profiles the religious communities of central Virginia and considers their impact on selected political issues. A chapter by Thomas C. Thompson focuses on sectarian perceptions of Virginia deists and the impact of deism on organized religion in the last half of the eighteenth century. Various theological and philosophical influences on Jefferson and Madison are explored in a second section. Charles B. Sanford offers a nuanced and concise description of Jefferson's religious beliefs. Garrett Ward Sheldon examines the philosophical and theological influences on Jefferson's political thought, and Douglas L. Wilson discusses the ambivalent influence of Bolingbroke on Jefferson. The influence of Presbyterianism on Madison's political thought is explored by Mary-Elaine Swanson. Church-state themes are the subject of the third section. The section begins with a chapter by Daniel L. Dreisbach that describes the bitter legislative debates to redefine church-state relations in Virginia in the tumultuous decade following independence. Robert L. Cord makes the revisionist case that Jefferson espoused a "nonabsolute" wall of separation between church and state. Daniel L. Dreisbach builds on Cord's chapter in an examination of Jefferson's celebrated "Bill for Establishing Religious Freedom" and four companion bills on religion in the revised code of Virginia also framed by Jefferson and sponsored by Madison in the Virginia legislature. Madison's views on the constitutional relationship between religion and politics as evidenced by his role in crafting the First Amendment establishment of religion clause are explored by Donald L. Drakeman.

We are happy to acknowledge the many institutions and individuals whose generous contributions and assistance made this book possible. We want to thank the Providence Foundation and Virginia Foundation for the Humanities and Public Policy for organizing and sponsoring the 1996 symposium from which most of these essays were drawn. The Providence Foundation is a not-for-profit Christian educational organization devoted to the study of a Christian philosophy of life and the role of religion in American history. The Virginia Foundation for the Humanities and Public Policy is a not-for-profit organization dedicated to developing and supporting research, education, and public programs in the humanities. It was fitting to hold the symposium at Mr. Jefferson's University. We thank the University of Virginia for the use of its facilities, including the dome room of the Rotunda. We also thank our editor Stephen Wrinn and his colleagues at Rowman & Littlefield Publishers for their encouragement and assistance.

The symposium brought together eminent scholars representing many disciplines and diverse perspectives for a spirited conversation. All shared an interest in the role of religion in American public life. Among the conference presenters and discussants were Gary Amos, David Bearinger, Richard Brown, Thomas Buckley, S.J., Carl Diemer, Martin Doblmeier, Alan Heimert, Fred Hood, David Holmes, Ralph Ketcham, David Little, David Mattern, Stephen McDowell, Robert M. O'Neil, A. James Reichley, Ronald Rosenberger, Roger Schultz, Herbert Titus, and Jennings Wagoner. We regret that, due to space limitations, we were unable to include in this volume several excellent papers and commentaries presented at the symposium. Also among the conference participants were clergymen, lawyers, journalists, and other informed citizens whose contributions through stimulating questions and insightful discussion are reflected in the final version of the book. We are grateful to all these individuals, named and unnamed, for their part in exploring the themes of this book and challenging and refining the ideas discussed.

We hope this book makes a useful addition to the literature on American intellectual history. We believe it makes a contribution to the study of religious influences and themes in the political culture of Jefferson's Virginia. An examination of the religious influences on the lives of Jefferson and Madison, given their continuing impact on political and legal thought, casts light not only on the past but also on the future role of religion in American public life.

Garrett Ward Sheldon
Daniel L. Dreisbach
Alexandria, Virginia
January 2000

Notes

1. J.G.A. Pocock, "Religious Freedom and the Desacralization of Politics: From the English Civil Wars to the Virginia Statute," in *The Virginia Statute for Religious Freedom: Its Evolution and Consequences in American History*, ed. Merrill D. Peterson and Robert C. Vaughan (New York: Cambridge University Press, 1988), 61.

2. J.G.A. Pocock, *The Machiavellian Moment: Florentine Political Thought and the Atlantic Republican Tradition* (Princeton, N.J.: Princeton University Press, 1975).

3. Thomas E. Buckley, *Church and State in Revolutionary Virginia, 1776-1787* (Charlottesville: University Press of Virginia, 1977), 6.

4. Gordon S. Wood, *The Radicalism of the American Revolution* (New York: Alfred A. Knopf, 1992), 328-334.

5. *Everson v. Board of Education*, 330 U.S. 1, 33-34 (1947) (Rutledge, J., dissenting).

6. See generally Daniel L. Dreisbach, "*Everson* and the Command of History: The Supreme Court, Lessons of History, and Church-State Debate in America," in *Everson Revisited: Religion, Education, and Law at the Crossroads*, ed. Jo Renée Formicola and Hubert Morken (Lanham, Md.: Rowman & Littlefield, 1997), 23-57.

Part I

Religious Culture in Jefferson's Virginia

Chapter 1

The Christian Communities, Religious Revivals, and Political Culture of the Central Virginia Piedmont, 1737-1813

Mark A. Beliles

The Central Virginia Piedmont is the area of pleasant rolling hills that stretches westward from the fall line of the James and Rappahannock Rivers to the edge of the Blue Ridge Mountains, and then reaches southward to Bedford County. In the heart of this territory is Albemarle County (a county that once extended all the way south to Bedford). This study examines the Evangelical religious communities of Albemarle County and the surrounding regions. The settlement of the Piedmont differed in two significant ways from the settlement of the Shenandoah Valley and Tidewater regions of Virginia. The first difference was in regard to nationalities. Whereas other regions were settled predominantly by one ethnic or national group, whether it was English, Scotch-Irish, or German, Albemarle County and the surrounding areas were settled by a blend of these groups.[1] Second, it was different in regard to religion. Regions other than the Piedmont were settled predominantly by one religious sect (e.g., the Presbyterians in the Valley and the Anglicans in the Tidewater area). But in Albemarle County and environs, these groups grew up side by side during the first settlement period, producing a unique tradition of religious diversity, tolerance, and interdenominational cooperation. This chapter focuses on the religious communities, leaders, and movements in the Central Virginia Piedmont where native sons Thomas Jefferson and James Madison lived most of their lives.

Early Religious Communities and Tutors in the Central Virginia Piedmont

The Anglican Church was the first Christian community to be established in the Piedmont in the 1720s as settlers moved into the area. As rector of St. James Parish, Anthony Gavin began preaching in the Piedmont (in present day Albemarle, Amherst, and Nelson counties) twice a year in 1738.[2] Gavin relied heavily on laymen, the most significant of whom was Dr. William Cabell.[3] In 1742, Cabell began lobbying for the creation of the new St. Anne's Parish; and he, more than any other layman, was responsible for establishing the Anglican faith on the frontier. He built five Anglican church buildings—the first in 1748.[4] He also built chapels for dissenters, setting an example of interdenominational tolerance that was continued by subsequent Anglican laymen in the area, such as Jefferson and Madison.

Robert Rose was selected by the vestry to be the first resident minister of St. Anne's Parish in southern Albemarle County. Their second minister was chosen by the governor instead of the vestry, and his immoral behavior was a source of great division within the parish. At about the same time, in the Fredericksville Parish in the northern half of Albemarle County, James Fontaine Maury served as minister from 1751 to 1769. In the famous Parson's Cause case, Maury sued his vestry for the balance of his salary which he thought they owed him. Likewise, in Orange County's St. Thomas Parish, two early ministers were fired. Most problems were with ministers chosen by the governor; therefore, between 1738 and 1790, in the southern half of the Piedmont, six of the fifteen ministers were chosen by their vestries without waiting for the customary gubernatorial recommendation. Significantly, one-third of these cases occurred in St. Anne's vestry of Albemarle County. This suggests that St. Anne's Parish was more independent and self-governing than most in the Commonwealth.[5] In 1769, the vestry chose Charles Clay, a cousin of Henry Clay, as its third minister without waiting for the governor's appointment. Thomas Jefferson became a member of St. Anne's vestry at about this time.

Clay was an Evangelical. Evangelicals emphasize the authority of the Bible and the necessity of a personal conversion known as the "new birth." Only between three and eight percent of the Anglican clergy in Virginia were Evangelical,[6] but in the Central Virginia Piedmont region it was the norm. Between 1761 and 1768, the Parish of St. Thomas in Orange County had an Evangelical minister, James Marye, Jr.[7] After his departure, the vestry chose a young Presbyterian-trained clergyman, Thomas Martin, to become its new minister. Martin came directly from the revivals at the Evangelical and Presbyterian College of New Jersey (Princeton) and moved into Montpelier, the Madisons' home. Later in the 1780s, St. Thomas Parish invited two Evangelicals, Methodist Henry Fry and Presbyterian James Waddell, to work together with an Evangelical Episcopalian minister, Alexander Balmaine.[8] James Madison was a member of this parish. This reveals that distinctions between Presbyterians and Anglicans were not very important in the Piedmont, and that interdenominational cooperation was common. This was also true in Augusta County, just to the west, where dissenters actually controlled the Anglican vestry until 1769.[9]

The Anglicans were dominant in the eastern portion of Orange County, although there were a few German Lutherans in the western parts. In Albemarle County, the Anglicans were dominant in the southern and eastern portions around the Southwest Mountain range, but the western and northern sections of the county were settled by Scotch-Irish Presbyterians, otherwise known as the Covenanters, who had migrated to Virginia by the thousands in the early 1700s.

They started an Albemarle County church in 1737, and by 1745 had built the Mountain Plains Meeting House.[10] Their first permanent pastor, Samuel Black, began ministering there in 1747.[11] Another congregation named Rockfish Church organized further to the south (in present day Nelson County). In the Piedmont, the Anglicans and Presbyterians were the dominant religious communities in the formative period. (There are no records of Lutheran, Roman Catholic, or Jewish worship services in Albemarle County until around the time of the Civil War.)

Religious groups had an enormous impact on the early culture of the Piedmont. Their influence was not only on the soul through worship, but also on the mind through education. Tutors were especially influential in this formative period. Gaillard Hunt observed: "One reason why the ruling class in Virginia acted with such unanimity [during the Revolution] . . . was that a large proportion of them had received the same kind of education. This usually came first from clergymen."[12] Even if most people worshiped in Anglican buildings, many of the tutors and schoolmasters were Scotch-Irish Presbyterians. George M. Marsden writes that "it is not much of an exaggeration to say that, outside of New England, the Scots were the educators of eighteenth-century America."[13] This was especially true in the Central Virginia region. The experiences of Thomas Jefferson and James Madison provide excellent examples of this influence. One of Jefferson's early teachers was a Scottish clergyman, William Douglas. Later, at the College of William and Mary in Williamsburg, the Scottish professor William Small had a profound influence on him.[14] Madison was also tutored by clergymen, including the Evangelical James Marye, minister of St. Thomas Parish in Orange County, and Donald Robertson, a Scotch-Irish tutor/minister.[15] The Presbyterian-trained Reverend Thomas Martin tutored Madison just prior to his matriculation at the College of New Jersey. At College, Madison came under the influence of the College's Scottish-born president and Presbyterian minister John Witherspoon.[16] Both Jefferson and Madison, in varying degrees, were instructed by teachers who employed Common Sense philosophy, Classical Republicanism, and Lockean Liberalism; however, because their tutors were predominantly Scotch Presbyterian ministers, the sources used were for the most part "not . . . the deist variety," but "specifically Christian."[17]

The First Great Awakening in the Central Virginia Piedmont, 1743-1780

In addition to the educational influence of Scotch-Irish tutors, the Piedmont experienced consecutive phases of religious revival over a seventy year period. A national revival, known as the Great Awakening, began with Jonathan Edwards in New England in 1734, and spread throughout the colonies. It was encouraged by Anglican evangelist George Whitefield, who first traveled through the colonies in 1739 and spoke to perhaps eighty percent of the American people. Whitefield never came to the Piedmont, but other evangelists ministered in the area. Anglican preacher Anthony Gavin reported that on his first trip to preach in the sparsely-populated mountains of Albemarle County in 1738: "I baptized white people, 229; blacks, 172; Quakers, 15; and Anabaptists, 2."[18] The spiritual hunger in this frontier region was strong. It was during this awakening, in April 1743, that Thomas Jefferson was born and baptized, perhaps by Gavin who preached at the Mountain Chapel near the Jefferson home.

The Presbyterian Phase of the First Great Awakening, 1743-1760

A second phase of the Great Awakening, led by the Presbyterians, was much more influential on Virginians. James H. Hutson writes that the characteristics that marked the Great Awakening actually "originated with Presbyterians and emerged from marathon outdoor 'Communion seasons,' which were a feature of Presbyterian practice in Scotland." Hutson adds that "[r]ecent investigations of the Scotch-Irish have revealed [that] . . . [l]arge-scale, passionate revivals . . . occurred with regularity . . . in both Ulster [Ireland] and in Scotland itself."[19]

The Scotch-Irish brought these revival traditions with them to Virginia. According to recent scholarship, the "Scotch-Irish Presbyterians now appear to have introduced as much religious energy into the eighteenth-century middle and southern colonies as the Puritans did in seventeenth-century New England. . . . [However,] Scotch-Irish religious fervor was less visible and more poorly recorded than that of the New England Puritans because much of it was shrouded in the wilderness of western Pennsylvania and points south."[20] The Scotch-Irish revivalistic influence was felt in Central Virginia. Presbyterian churches were organized in Albemarle County during this phase and, unlike those in other parts of Virginia, most were aligned with the Awakening and had Evangelical pastors. These "New Side" Presbyterians began the second Presbyterian church in Albemarle County called D. S. (or Dee Ess) in 1741.[21] The Presbyterian phase of the Great Awakening spread throughout the Commonwealth following Presbyterian evangelist William Robinson's 1743 visit to Virginia, including to Albemarle County. Samuel Davies, although living in Louisa County, also ministered at the D. S. Meeting House as early as 1747. The Hanover Presbytery was formed in 1755, with Davies serving as the first moderator. He continued to travel into Albemarle County, and in 1756, his preaching gave birth to two more "New Side" churches: one in North Garden, south of Charlottesville, and one in Covesville, even further to the south.[22] Davies' primary assistant in the revival was John Todd of Louisa County who frequently preached in the courthouse in Charlottesville (built in 1762).

The impact of the Presbyterian revival on Albemarle County is best illustrated by the experience of a young tutor named Devereaux Jarratt who moved to the county in 1752 to find work. Mrs. John Cannon, the matron of the estate in the southeastern part of the county where Jarratt taught, was one of these newly awakened Presbyterians. Through her reading aloud sermons each night, Jarratt was converted in 1753 and then attended the Presbyterian churches in the county. Jarratt eventually became "chaplain in Mr. Cannon's family," and he recorded that "[c]onsiderable congregations used to attend those meetings" he led in the area until about 1760 or 1761, when he moved away.[23]

Although the Presbyterian phase of revival activity waned after 1760, their membership continued to increase over the next decade (inclusive of Blacks as well).[24] One of John Todd's disciples, William Irvin, moved from Louisa County in 1769 to become the first resident pastor of the Cove Church in Albemarle. He also led the D. S. and North Garden churches until late 1776.[25] In Orange County, in 1773 and 1774, itinerating Presbyterians Caleb Wallace, Nathaniel Irwin, George Luckey, Moses Allen, and Samuel Stanhope Smith preached in the Anglican parish church and sometimes at James Madison's Montpelier.[26] Madison wrote in 1773 of "Mr. Erwin" visiting there and said that "praise is in every mans mouth Here for an excellent Discourse he this Day preached for us."[27] In 1775, Smith returned twice to preach at Montpelier. Church historian William B. Sprague wrote of Smith that "[p]ersons, without distinction of sect or of rank, flocked to hear him; and those who had been entranced by the eloquence of Davies, seemed to feel as if another Davies had arisen. So powerful an impression did he make."[28] Because of Presbyterian strength in the area, these counties often hosted the Hanover Presbytery meetings in the 1770s, which Todd moderated.[29]

The Baptist Phase of the First Great Awakening, 1765-1777

In the mid-1760s, about the time that Jefferson moved back into the area, the Baptists came to the northern half of the Central Virginia Piedmont. The Separate Baptists, who were more revivalistic, anti-confessional, and Arminian (although not rejecting Calvinism completely) than the Regular Baptists, increased greatly in number in the area. They also emphasized separation of church and state so as to protect complete freedom of conscience.[30] They believed that it was against their conscience to ask the civil government for permission to preach (i.e., obtain a license) since God already had authorized them to be ministers of the Gospel.

Blue Run Church, organized in late 1769 and led by pastor Elijah Craig, was the first Separate Baptist church in the area, and it was located in Orange County close to James Madison's home, Montpelier. Craig also preached in Albemarle County in either the courthouse or homes, as did his brother Lewis Craig, John Waller, and David Tinsley. Baptist itinerant Samuel Harris preached in the Charlottesville area in 1767 and 1776, and John Williams preached there in 1771 to two hundred and fifty people. In 1773, they officially established the Albemarle Baptist Church and built the "Lewis Mountain Meeting House" on the land of one of its members.[31] In addition, Goldmine Baptist Church was founded in 1770, near Ellisville in Louisa County.

Andrew Tribble began coming from Louisa County to preach in Albemarle County and help moderate congregational business meetings. During 1774, the Albemarle Baptist Church deliberated the possibility of calling Tribble as their pastor, and he was eventually ordained to do so in June 1777 by Lewis Craig. William "Baptist Billy" Woods, an elder since 1773, became its second pastor from about 1780 to 1798.[32] One of the church's early members, Martin Dawson, started another Baptist congregation named Totier Creek Church in southern Albemarle County in 1775. Dawson was a popular patriot preacher during the Revolution and served his congregation until 1809.[33] Another church in Orange County began in 1774, led by Pastor Aaron Bledsoe.

Between 1768 and 1774, the Separate Baptists were persecuted severely in the more traditional parishes of the northern Piedmont. In Albemarle and counties to the south, however, persecution was rare or non-existent. Orange County (some accounts say Culpeper County) put Elijah Craig in jail for preaching without a license, but for a month he continued preaching to large crowds through the bars of his cell window. After his release, Craig, Samuel Harris, and others called a meeting for the purpose of setting up the first voluntary Virginia Separate Baptist Association of churches. Attendance swelled to perhaps five thousand people at this 1771 open-air meeting near Blue Run Church.[34]

Hutson writes that up to this time, "First Great Awakening audiences usually came from towns and cities and convened on short notice. [However,] in . . . frontier areas, audiences came from great distances by wagon, packed with provisions to sustain families for several days. When assembled, usually in clearings in the wilderness, these conventions of frontier farmers became camp meetings—a unique American contribution to religious history."[35] The open-air camp meeting technique of evangelism was first developed by Baptists Samuel Harris and James Read about this time (although this phenomena is first noticed by most historians about thirty years later in Kentucky). Baptist historian Robert B. Semple records that "many hundreds of men [would] camp on the ground, in order to be present the next day. . . . Sometimes the floor would be covered with persons struck down under conviction of sin."[36] Evangelist John Waller, around 1776 or 1777, was the first in America to actually use the term "camp-meetings."[37]

Around 1776, John Leland moved from Massachusetts to the Piedmont and became pastor of Goldmine Baptist Church in Louisa County and a traveling evangelist in the region. He emerged an energetic denominational leader, and his preaching contributed greatly to Baptist growth in the area.[38]

The Anglican/Methodist Phase of the First Great Awakening, 1764-1780

At the same time that the Baptist revival occurred in the mid-1760s, the Anglicans also began to experience great renewal and ingathering in the Piedmont. The Albemarle County Presbyterian, Devereaux Jarratt, began to study sermons by George Whitefield and decided that instead of pursuing ordination as a Presbyterian he would follow in the steps of the Anglican revivalist.[39] Jarratt was ordained and then moved to Dinwiddie County, and after a few years began to lead the Anglican phase of the Great Awakening in Virginia from 1764 to 1772. David L. Holmes writes that Jarratt "rode circuits into almost 30 counties of Virginia and down into North Carolina. He had a powerful, musical voice. He preached in homes and on plantations and in fields and on weekdays. . . . His preaching sparked an extensive revival. His congregations overflowed."[40]

Jarratt's greatest impact on Albemarle County came indirectly through one of his disciples, Charles Clay. Clay was converted during the Anglican Awakening and decided to enter the ministry. But instead of the usual route of studying at the College of William and Mary (which was not known for being very Evangelical), he trained for the priesthood "by private study" with Jarratt.[41] Joan R. Gundersen notes that Clay was the only candidate for the ministry that Jarratt and Archibald McRoberts, the two most prominent Anglican Evangelicals in Virginia, ever mutually approved in the colonial period.[42] It is highly significant, then, that Clay was selected by the vestry of St. Anne's Parish in Albemarle County to be their minister in 1769, without waiting for the customary gubernatorial recommendation. Since Jarratt had lived in Albemarle and preached there for about seven years, the vestry was certainly aware of the kind of ministry his disciple, Charles Clay, would bring to the parish. This suggests that St. Anne's Parish was Evangelical in its leanings at the time Jefferson joined its vestry. Clay lived on glebe land (i.e., church farm) on Totier Creek in southern Albemarle County and preached in the parish's churches for eight years.

Historian Harry S. Stout observes that the "most accurate guide we . . . have to what people actually heard are the handwritten sermon notes that ministers carried with them into the pulpit."[43] Significantly, fifty handwritten sermons by Clay from this period have been preserved. They were donated to the Virginia Historical Society in 1992 by Clay's descendants. Since they have not been published, they have been overlooked in virtually all studies on Virginia's religious culture and Clay's famous parishioner, Thomas Jefferson.[44] Clay's messages are especially enlightening because, as Bishop Meade said in his early history of the Episcopal Church in Virginia, they were "sound, energetic and *evangelical beyond the character of the times*." He also records that one of Clay's sermons "on the new birth [was] most impressive."[45] Clay's preaching reveals a theological orthodoxy and Evangelical style unusual for Anglicans. In a sermon (#12), preached in 1775, which warns that God is the adversary of the sinner, Clay expressed his spiritual compassion with these closing words: "My brethren, your souls, your precious souls are at stake; you hang by a very slender thread over the bottomless pit. O call upon God while it is time; Harden not your hearts against him. Let what I have said have its due weight. Do not steel your hearts against what I have offered. Do not refuse a blessing at my hands, but come to the Lord Jesus Christ, and be at peace with him. Remember, it is not I, but the Lord Jesus Christ himself that speaks and says unto thee: 'Agree with thine adversary quickly while thou art in the way with him. [Matthew 5:25]'"

Another aspect of the Anglican revival was Methodism. Started by John Wesley in England, Methodism was a renewal movement within the Anglican Church, but it deserves its own analysis. Jarratt was closely associated with the Methodists from about 1773 onward. The climax of his ministry was a revival in 1775 and 1776, when he preached in the open air "throughout the Piedmont of

Virginia" and elsewhere.[46] The Methodists' most famous convert from the Albemarle area was Henry Fry who, under the preaching of Robert Williams, had a conversion experience in 1774 that included deliverance from alcoholism. Fry had been Jefferson's neighbor in Albemarle County and a fellow-vestryman in the Fredericksville Parish. He and Jefferson had been colleagues in the House of Burgesses during the Stamp Act crisis (1764-1765). He served as Deputy Clerk of Albemarle County as early as 1761, and then as Clerk (1766-1773).[47] His religious conversion was almost certainly well known among the gentry of the area.

Fry attended Philip Gatch's quarterly meeting of preachers in the fall of 1776 and was appointed to be the leader, or circuit-rider, of the Methodist Society in his own area. He recounted in his autobiography that "I rode about to procure preaching places . . . [and] exhorted sinners to flee the wrath to come, and believers to press into the fulness of God Almighty's love." Fry's "labors as a preacher [were] chiefly as a substitute." The main place where he preached in Albemarle County was Maupin's Meeting House (at Whitehall west of Charlottesville).[48] Francis Asbury, who became the most famous Methodist itinerant preacher in early America, traveled frequently through Albemarle County and, as early as 13 October 1780, mentioned in his journal that he "found Henry Fry preaching to about eighty people" at a place called "Mumpin's [or Maupin's] . . . New Preaching House."[49] Methodist revivalism was now established in Albemarle County.

Charles Clay and the Calvinistical Reformed Church, 1777-1785

The Great Awakening continued in the South during the war years. This fact is often overlooked in studies of American history, especially histories of Virginia. Hutson observes that churches in America "continued to be remarkably robust on the eve of the American Revolution, contrary to the persistent notion that religion in eighteenth-century America was progressively declining. . . . [I]n 1776 between 71 and 77 percent of Americans may have filled the pews on Sunday. . . . 'It is more accurate to characterize the years from 1775 to 1790 as a Revolutionary revival.'"[50]

The most interesting evidence of the revival in Charlottesville was a short-lived independent congregation that apparently existed from 1777 to 1785. At first the new congregation was called the Protestant Episcopal Church, but finding this name unpopular, the Calvinistical Reformed Church became the official name.[51] (The church apparently drew people from both Anglican and Presbyterian communities. This mixture was certainly not unusual for the Piedmont.) The founding members signed a document Jefferson drafted in February 1777, entitled a "Subscription to Support a Clergyman in Charlottesville." The signatories to this document included three members of the vestry of St. Anne's Parish: Thomas Jefferson, Philip Mazzei, and John Harvie.

In the *Papers of Thomas Jefferson*, Julian P. Boyd notes that Jefferson "organized" this new independent church. His ample support for the church afforded Jefferson an opportunity to demonstrate his disestablishment conviction that institutional religion and clerical salaries should be wholly financed by voluntary contributions. The founding document expressed additional convictions. It stated: "We the subscribers, . . . [are] desirous of encouraging and supporting the Calvinistical Reformed church, and of deriving to our selves, through the ministry of it's teachers, the benefits of Gospel knolege [sic] and religious improvement." It cited the source of this knowledge as being "the holy scriptures," and continued: "we expect that the said Charles Clay shall perform divine service and preach a sermon in the town of Charlottesville on every 4th . . . Sunday or oftener if a regular rotation with the other churches . . . will admit a more frequent attendance. And we further mutually agree with each other that we will meet at Charlottesville . . . every year . . . and there make choice by ballot of three Wardens to collect our said subscriptions . . . for the use of our church."[52] (Clay was attractive to Jefferson and his fellow subscribers because of his enthusiastic defense of the patriots' cause at a time when many Anglican clergymen were siding with the British.)

The question has been raised whether or not the new independent church ever really came into existence. The evidence suggests that it did. The Calvinistical Reformed Church apparently worshiped in the Albemarle Courthouse in Charlottesville for about seven or eight years. Clay's preserved sermons reference about forty delivery dates between 1777 and 1785, with some specifically noting that they were preached in the Albemarle Courthouse. The table on the next page shows that all but one of Clay's thirty-three dated sermons were preached in the era of the Calvinistical Reformed Church (1777-1785). This list of sermons is important because St. Anne's Parish vestry records, which extend up to 1785, show that Clay had quit preaching to them by at least 1780.[53] Additional evidence that Clay's departure from St. Anne's was final as of 1779 is found in Governor Jefferson's public letter of recommendation for Clay. This document indicated that Clay's ministry in St. Anne's Parish was in the *past*, not present.[54] Finally, Jefferson's regular contributions recorded in his *Memorandum Book* (such as 15 August 1779: "Pd. Revd. Charles Clay in consideration of parochial services")[55] were in *addition* to his ongoing payment of St. Anne's parish levy.[56]

This independent church apparently disbanded because of wartime financial hardships and the absence of major financial supporters (Mazzei and Harvie both moved away permanently around 1780, and Jefferson went to France in 1783 for about six years). Clay's newly discovered sermons and the historical data regarding the Calvinistical Reformed Church provide new evidence of the strong Evangelical sentiment in the Central Virginia Piedmont at the time of the Revolution. The church was the culmination of the First Great Awakening in the region (especially among Anglicans and Presbyterians), although it has been virtually overlooked by historians because of its brief existence.

Dates and Frequency of Clay's Sermons

The numbering system used to identify the sermons below is based on the order they appear in the folders of the Clay Family Papers. Funerals are in parentheses. Sermons without dates are not included. Fragments of sermons with dates are not numbered.

Year	Sermons # preached for first time	Sermons repeated
1769	18, 25, (32), fragment	
1770	7, 5, 27, 41, 42, fragments	18, 25, (32)
1771	9, 33, 47, fragment	5, 18, (32), 47
1772	23, 43, 45	18, 25, 27, (32), 47
1773	(1), 21, 31, fragment	5, 25, 27, (32), 43, 45, 47
1774	4, 14, (17), 37, 39, 48	4, 23, 25, 31, (32), 42, 43, 47, 48
1775	12, 13, 22, (50), fragment	(1), 25, 27, 31, 42, 43, 45, 48
1776	fragments [probably #10]	(1), (17), 22, 23, 27, 31,(32), 42, 45, 46
1777	19, 29, (35), fragment	(1), (17), 23, 25, 31, (32), 42, 45, 47, (50)
1778		19, 25, 27, 31, (35), 42, 45
1779		(17), 28, 29, (35), 41, 42, 43, 47
1780	fragment [probably #2]	12, 13, 25, (35), 41, 42, (50)
1781		(1), 19, 25, 29
1782		5, 7, 9, (17), 19, (50)
1783		25, 27
1784		(1), 5, 7, 18, 19, 27, (35)
1785	38, fragment	(1), 19, 21, 25, 29, (32), (35)
1786		29, 37, 45
1787		(1), (17), 18, 38,
1788		(17)
1789		19

The Second Great Awakening in the Central Virginia Piedmont, 1785-1806

The Central Virginia Piedmont was the last scene of the First Great Awakening and the first scene of the Second Great Awakening—preceding the revival that affected the rest of the nation by at least a dozen years. Even with the disruption caused by the War for American Independence, revival in this region was virtually continuous between the First and Second Great Awakenings.[57] The Second Great Awakening in Virginia was also known as the Great Revival. The Episcopal Church in Virginia was not as involved in the Great Revival as other denominations. The church was severely weakened after the Revolution. Virginia's Bishop James Madison was not an Evangelical; and the Anglican revival leader, Devereaux Jarratt, died in 1801. Another factor was a lack of ministers. There were none in southern Albemarle (i.e., St. Anne's Parish) after Clay left in 1777. Matthew Maury was minister in Charlottesville, northern Albemarle, and Orange counties (with Jefferson's financial support) until his death in 1807.[58]

Though rare, there were some Episcopalians who joined in the Second Great Awakening, but mainly in Orange County and in an interdenominational setting. One was Alexander Balmaine, a Scottish minister who was educated at the University of St. Andrews and the University of Edinburgh, licensed in 1772, and eventually settled in Augusta County. After service in the war, Balmaine became minister of Frederick Parish, but he often preached in Orange County as well.[59] Other Episcopalians who supported the revivals will be noted in the sections that follow.

The Presbyterian Phase of the Second Great Awakening, 1786-1788

In Virginia the revival began as early as 1786 among Presbyterians at Hampden-Sydney College in Prince Edward County, about fifty miles southeast of Albemarle County. The college president, John Blair Smith (brother of the founder, Samuel Stanhope Smith), and teacher Drury Lacy supported the revival, and it began spreading to counties as far west as Augusta.[60] Lacy later preached in Piedmont counties around Albemarle, such as Buckingham (1788) and Orange (1795), together with the Methodist preacher Philip Gatch and the Baptist minister James Saunders.[61] The revival in these areas went largely unreported in Presbyterian records because it was interdenominational in character (associated most strongly with Baptists and Methodists).[62] But that does not mean it did not exist. In Orange County, for example, Colonel Francis Taylor, a cousin of James Madison's father, kept a diary that covered the 1780s and 1790s. At least three times during the Great Revival years of 1786 to 1788, Taylor, an Episcopalian, records that Episcopalian minister Alexander Balmaine, visiting from Culpeper, and Presbyterian minister James Waddell conducted joint services in the Orange County Middle (or "Brick") Church. "The congregation," according to Taylor, "[was] more numerous than I have seen there for several years," and he tells of the new "singing school" in the fall of 1788 that he and many others attended (singing schools were a characteristic of the Great Revival in Virginia).[63]

Waddell's preaching contributed mightily to the Second Great Awakening. Waddell had previously taught school in Philadelphia, and one of his former pupils was Benjamin Rush. He then moved to Virginia and studied for the ministry under John Todd and Samuel Davies. He served churches in the Tidewater area during the First Great Awakening, and was a host for George Whitefield during his visits to Virginia in 1755 and 1763. Waddell moved to Augusta County in 1776 and then to Albemarle County in 1785. By 1798, he was completely blind, but he continued to pastor churches in Albemarle (meeting at D. S. Meeting House, Milton, and the courthouse) and Orange counties (meeting at Gordonsville and Orange courthouse). His son-in-law recollected one occasion when Waddell "preached at Milton [east of Charlottesville near Monticello]. . . . I am satisfied that I never witnessed such a torrent of eloquence before or since."[64] Likewise, an attorney named William Wirt, who moved from Madison County to Charlottesville in 1795, described the eloquence of Waddell's preaching at an unspecified location: "every heart in the assembly trembled in unison. His peculiar phrases had that force of description that the original scene appeared to be, at that moment, acting before our eyes. . . . The effect is inconceivable. The whole house resounded with the mingled groans, and sobs, and shrieks of the congregation."[65] This kind of preaching stirred many people in Albemarle and Orange counties.

The Baptist Phase of the Second Great Awakening, 1785-1795

Between 1785 and 1791, the Baptists also experienced a "great revival" in which thousands were converted and baptized. "From this revival," writes Robert B. Semple, "great changes took place among the Baptists. . . . [T]hey were joined by persons of much greater weight in civil society; their congregations became more numerous than those of any other Christian sect."[66] A new Baptist church in northeast Albemarle County named Preddy's (or Prethis) Creek was begun in 1784 and experienced revival in 1788-1789. George Eve was the pastor from 1786-1798. He also served as the pastor of Craig's Blue Run Baptist Church in Orange County since 1781. There were four Baptist churches in Albemarle County by this time. Another new Baptist congregation in western Albemarle was started by strong Calvinist Benjamin Burgher (an early member of the first Albemarle Baptist Church). This church, known then as Whitesides, changed to Mount Ed Baptist Church in 1806. On one occasion in 1788, the congregation came together to fast and pray that God would judge a local distillery. On the day of the prayer meeting, lightning struck the distillery and it burned to the ground. The church purchased the property and built their new building on that very spot.

Among the leading Baptist evangelists were John Waller and John Leland. Waller, who had left the Baptists for a while to be an independent camp meeting evangelist, returned to his Baptist brethren and a "very great revival commenced under Mr. Waller's ministry in 1787. This continued for several years, and spread

country."[96] The effect, Jefferson said, "was like a shock of electricity, arousing every man."[97] In fact, just three days later the freeholders of Albemarle County met at the courthouse, and (1) denounced the violation of their rights by the Parliament of Great Britain, (2) called for a boycott of trade with England, (3) and declared that the only legitimate legislature they recognized was their own. They also indicated a readiness "to join with our fellow-subjects in every part of the [colonial empire], in executing all those rightful powers which *God* has given us." They presented this resolution to the Virginia House of Burgesses, which agreed with it and also denounced Britain's closing of the port of Boston. These events eventually led to a call for the first Continental Congress.[98]

Clay's fifty recently discovered handwritten sermons provide a rare opportunity to study the political preaching in the Piedmont region.[99] His patriotic oratory continued in 1774 and 1775 when he preached from II Chronicles 7:14 on the Divine promise that God would heal the nation if the people would humble themselves and pray and turn from their wicked ways. Clay's sermon, "The Necessity of National Humility and Repentance," is also significant. It is dated twice, 1775 and 1780, and thus represents both the Anglican and independent Calvinistical Reformed phases of his ministry. A concluding prayer noting that they were "now on the eve of a bloody war," clearly applies to the earlier date of delivery in 1775.[100] A further clue indicating the date of delivery is Clay's plea that "the Divine blessing may descend and rest upon all our rulers, and . . . especially on the general Congress *now convened* by divine permission at *Philadelphia*."[101]

Another of Clay's political sermons, "The Governor Among the Nations," has no definite date, but Clay's notations indicate that it was delivered both before and after independence.[102] This particular sermon began with the text: "Psalm 22:28—For the Kingdom is the Lord's, and He is the Governor Among the Nations." In the sermon, Clay explained in detail "the methods of Providence towards societies." After a lengthy treatment of the history of Israel and showing the "superintendency of Divine Providence . . . in public revolutions [and] the rise and fall of empires," such as the Assyrian, Babylonian, Persian, Greek, and Roman empires, Clay exhorted: "Let us check each desponding thought now in the day of our distress and place our confidence in God alone, and though our enemies rage and threaten us with desolation and destruction, yet let us not despond but seek the Lord by prayer and supplication and cast our burdens on him, for when all worldly supports fail us, we may rest satisfied in this, that things are not left to a blind chance. 'The Kingdom *is* the Lord's, and He *is* the Governor among the nations.'" Clay further stated that there are "just and necessary wars," but that they are now experiencing an "unnatural war." He told the people that "the rapes, the thefts and depredations committed upon our Brethren to the northward" should be "sufficient to rouse you up to resist before they come home to your own houses and families." He boldly called on the people to "defend your country and *the sacred cause of liberty* which *is the cause of God*." Given this truth, then, Clay proclaimed: "Cursed be he who keepeth back his sword from blood in this war!" He implored the men to "plead the cause of their country before the Lord with their blood."[103] Beginning in 1779, Clay preached regularly to the Albemarle Minute Battalion and also to the 2,800 British and Hessian prisoners of war detained at Charlottesville.[104]

Clay was not the only patriot preacher in the area. Other local ministers and religious leaders were active in their County Committees of Safety, which were the local governments during the War of Independence. They included Anglican Thomas Hall and Presbyterian John Todd in Louisa County; Anglican Alexander Balmaine in Augusta County; Presbyterian Samuel Stanhope Smith in Prince Edward County; and Presbyterian David Rice in Bedford County.[105] In February 1775, the Reverend Balmaine helped draft Augusta's "instructions to delegates" attending the state convention.[106] He later became chaplain of the 13th Virginia Regiment and then, from 1778 to 1780, a brigade captain. Another minister in Augusta County, the Presbyterian James Waddell, after settling in the area in 1776, inspired many of his congregation to go forth to heroic service in the Continental Army.[107]

In 1775, two other prominent local leaders emerged. George Gilmer and Philip Mazzei were active Anglicans with strong religious motivation. Gilmer founded the local militia and was the county's "Sam Adams" who led the local committee of correspondence and stirred the people with deeply religious, patriotic speeches and pamphlets.[108] Mazzei, an Italian grape-grower and Jefferson's neighbor, became a member of the Albemarle Committee of Safety after Presbyterians asked him to stand for election and opened their pulpits to him during his campaign.[109] In August 1775, the Virginia Baptist Association presented a petition to the Virginia Convention seeking permission to preach to the army troops. The Baptists recommended the services of Elijah Craig, Lewis Craig, Jeremiah Walker, and John Williams because of their "strong attachment to American Liberty."[110] Elder William Woods of Albemarle Baptist Church was heavily involved in the Revolution and, when questioned by his own congregation in April 1779 about his patriotic activity on the Sabbath day, he stated that "in great emergencies he knew no difference between his patriotism and his religion."[111] In the Piedmont, revolutionary activity and religion were thoroughly integrated.

Religious Communities and Leaders in the Fight for Religious Freedom, 1776-1779

The religious communities and political leaders in the Piedmont worked together in the Revolutionary cause; their cooperation was even greater in the cause of religious freedom. As early as 1770, Baptists, Presbyterians, and some Anglicans had begun petitioning and agitating for greater religious liberty for dissenters. James Madison began speaking out against persecution and defending local Baptists as early as 1773.[112] When Madison was elected a delegate to the Virginia Convention in 1776 with the help of the Orange County Baptists, the Reverend Elijah Craig attended the Convention with him and served as his messenger, bringing information back to Orange County. At the Convention, Madison, believing "freedom of conscience to be a natural and absolute right," proposed replacing George Mason's language of toleration in Article XVI of the Declaration of Rights with an unequivocal statement affirming that "all men are equally entitled to the free exercise of religion."[113]

In October 1776, Jefferson was appointed to the General Assembly's Committee for Religion. All nine petitions in favor of religious freedom that were received by the legislature in 1776 were from the Piedmont or South Central Virginia.[114] John Todd, the moderator of the Hanover Presbytery, led the Presbyterian effort to bring in petitions that fall.[115] The first "Memorial of Hanover Presbytery" was presented to the legislature on 24 October 1776, and bore Todd's name along with that of Madison's friend, Caleb Wallace (then pastor of Cub Creek Church in Prince Edward County). These men personally presented their petition to the legislature. It said that "when our blessed Saviour declares his *kingdom is not of this world*, he renounces all dependence upon state power. . . . [T]*he duty which we owe to our Creator, and the manner of discharging it, can only be directed by reason and conviction*. . . . Therefore we *ask no ecclesiastical establishments for ourselves*; neither can we approve of them when granted to others."[116] William Irvin, disciple of John Todd and pastor of the D. S. Presbyterian Church (and North Garden and Cove churches in Albemarle County), presented a "Petition of Dissenters in Albemarle and Amherst Counties," and obtained almost two hundred signatures from leading families to pressure the legislature "to put every religious Denomination on an equal footing, to be supported by themselves."[117] Irvin, who considered Jefferson a "cordial Friend," sent the petition to Jefferson with a cover letter asking: "Please, . . . befriend the Contents, of it, and in so doing you will greatly oblige the greater Part of your Constituants [sic]."[118]

Elijah Craig and John Waller, both of whom were involved in establishing the first Baptist congregation in Charlottesville, served as lobbyists for the Baptists in Virginia and began meeting with Jefferson to give him their petitions that fall. Jefferson had some of their petitions published in the Williamsburg newspaper that year so that people would understand the Baptist position on religious freedom. In December 1776, the General Association of Baptists drafted a declaration urging the disestablishment of the Episcopal Church. The Baptists argued that "it is contrary to the Principles of Reason and Justice that any should be compelled to contribute to the Maintenance of a Church with which their Consciences will not permit them to join." The Baptists continued: "We believe that Preachers should be supported only by voluntary Contributions from the People, and that a general Assessment (however harmless, yea useful some may conceive it to be) is pregnant with various Evils destructive to the Rights and Privileges of religious Society. . . . The Consequence of this is, that those whom the State employs in its Service, it has a Right to *regulate* and *dictate to*; it may judge and determine *who* shall preach; *when* and *where* they shall preach; and *what* they must preach."[119]

In April 1777, the General Association of Baptists met at Sandy Creek Meeting House, and "a law was drawn up in form, and reported, entitled 'An Act for the Establishment of Religious Freedom,' to be presented to the Legislature, with an earnest petition that it might be adopted as a law of the State." This proposal "attracted the attention of several members of the Legislature, and especially of Mr. Jefferson and Mr. Madison, and had led to various private interviews between them," said historian Robert Howell. "Mr. Jefferson," he continued, "had kindly undertaken to prepare the law; make it accord with their wishes; . . . and secure its adoption by the General Assembly as a law of the State."[120] According to Baptist accounts, Jefferson drew on this draft when he wrote the "Bill for Establishing Religious Freedom."[121] This suggests that Evangelicals were not merely political supporters of Jefferson's campaign for religious liberty; rather, the impetus and, perhaps, actual content of the celebrated religious freedom bill emanated from Evangelical sources.

James Madison's Baptist friend, the Reverend Elijah Craig of Orange County, was again sent by the General Association of Baptists to lobby the Virginia General Assembly in October 1778.[122] His Presbyterian friend and college classmate, Samuel Stanhope Smith, began to rise in political influence in April 1777 when he drafted for the Hanover Presbytery a "Remonstrance against a General Assessment." Two months later, Smith drafted another petition against maintaining an established church and personally presented it to the legislature. He argued that "[i]f Christianity is of divine original it will support itself or forfeit its pretensions."[123] In 1778, Smith wrote to Madison that "there seems to be a favourable opportunity to unite some of our religious parties, if their leaders were sufficiently catholic. I should be ready to concur in such a design." Smith then asked Madison to predict "what turn *religious politics* are likely to take in the legislature?"[124] Before Smith was able to organize an interdenominational Christian "coalition" in opposition to ecclesiastical establishment, he was called back to the College of New Jersey in 1779.[125]

On 12 June 1779, the famous "Bill for Establishing Religious Freedom" was submitted to the General Assembly by none other than John Harvie, one of Jefferson's fellow-members of the independent and Evangelical Reformed Church of Charlottesville.[126] When Smith departed Virginia, Jefferson recruited the moderator of the Hanover Presbytery, John Todd, as a key Presbyterian ally in the political struggle for passage of the "Bill for Establishing Religious Freedom." In an August 1779 letter to Jefferson, Todd expressed his support for the bill, saying that "there is a wide difference between religion sinking and some of its miserable Clergy sinking. . . . *Virtue and pure religion* do better without earthly emoluments than with."[127] In 1780, the Hanover Presbytery met in Pastor James Waddell's home in Augusta County and asked one of his elders, Zachariah Johnston (who was also a member of the House of Delegates at the time), to meet with Governor Jefferson and to present their petitions for religious freedom to the legislature.[128]

Although Presbyterians and Baptists primarily led the way in petitioning for the cause of religious freedom, many Methodists in the Albemarle area also signed petitions against an established church. This, Jefferson observed, was unlike most of the Methodists in the state, but typical of the freedom-loving communities of the Central Virginia Piedmont.[129]

Religious Politics and Disestablishment of the Anglican Church, 1784-1786

In 1784, the Virginia legislature began receiving petitions from many people in favor of a general assessment to support all denominations equally. The Anglican clergy, however, were using their political influence to try to maintain a favored status by being officially incorporated by the state. An indirect factor in the eventual defeat of the Anglicans was the fact that in 1784 Methodist Superintendent Francis Asbury finally endorsed the separation of the Methodist Episcopal Church from the Anglican Church. This weakened the established church in Virginia even more. Perhaps Asbury dropped his opposition to separation as a result of speaking often in the Central Virginia Piedmont during the early 1780s where Methodist sentiment was strong for severing ties with the Anglican Church. In fact, his journal records that in the very year of the separation, 1784, he preached to seven hundred "people of feeling" at local preacher Tandy Key's meeting house at North Garden in Albemarle County.[130] In 1785 and 1786, another Methodist Superintendent, Thomas Coke, preached in a chapel near "Charleville," and his journal says he was "met by our valuable friend, Brother Henry Fry." [131]

In 1784, the Reverend John Blair Smith, the new Presbyterian president of Hampden-Sydney College (and brother of Samuel Stanhope Smith), joined Waddell in drafting a petition opposing incorporation of the Episcopal Church. Recognizing that the Episcopal Church was likely to retain some connection with the state, prominent Presbyterians decided to support a general assessment for the clergy of *all* denominations, instead of just favoring Episcopalians. They saw this as a more "*liberal plan*" to support the "institutions for inculcating the great fundamental principles of all religion, without which society could not easily exist."[132] Not all citizens in the Piedmont thought public support for religion wrong if done impartially. For example, "the citizens of Amherst County, Virginia, on November 27, 1783, . . . petitioned their representatives not to ignore the 'Important Business' of supporting religion or 'think it beneath your Dignity to become Nursing Fathers of the Church.'"[133] On the other side, John Leland, who, according to Ralph L. Ketcham, was "violently opposed to the assessment, was a lobbyist in Richmond [for the Virginia Baptist General Committee] where he no doubt worked with Madison" to defeat a general assessment for the support of religion.[134] Leland's view was supported by Zachariah Johnston, head of the Religion Committee in the House of Delegates and an elder of Tinkling Spring Presbyterian Church in Augusta County, and by James Madison who thought a general assessment was dangerous because it perpetuated the state's illegitimate role in religious taxation.[135] In short, both sides of the general assessment debate had evangelical proponents from the Piedmont, and the Committee for Religion itself was dominated by churchmen from the Piedmont. In addition to James Madison, the Committee included men such as French Strother, a vestryman of St. Mark's Parish in Culpeper (in present day Madison County), and Methodist preacher Henry Fry. Fry wrote in his autobiography that: "I was prevailed on to serve as a delegate to the Legislature to present their petition against the [general assessment]"; and his biographer said that it was Jefferson who recruited him.[136] Another member of the Committee was Wilson Cary Nicholas, an active Episcopalian layman in Albemarle County, who Gaillard Hunt said, along with his brother George Nicholas, deserved the "credit for planning the campaign against the [general assessment] bill."[137] George prevailed on Madison to write his "Memorial and Remonstrance" in the spring of 1785 against any state-enforced religious assessment whatsoever.

Madison's "Remonstrance" secured 1,552 signatures, mostly from the Piedmont, and it is credited, along with fifty-nine other religious petitions, with turning the political tide against the general assessment bill "Establishing a Provision for Teachers of the Christian Religion." When the legislature reconvened on 17 October 1785, it had received about sixty petitions opposed to a general assessment and only eight in favor. The petition with more signatures than any other had a strong Evangelical flavor. It prayed that the churches would be freed from state control so that "deism" could be "put to open shame and its dread Consequences removed" by the exertions of preachers who were "inwardly moved by the Holy Ghost."[138]

Madison thought the defeat of the general assessment measure was an opportune occasion to reintroduce Jefferson's "Bill for Establishing Religious Freedom," which was first presented to the legislature in 1779 by John Harvie of Charlottesville's Calvinistical Reformed Church. It was passed and signed into law on 19 January 1786. The Reverend Fry wrote: "What was called the Religious Bill, passed this Session, putting all Societies on an equal footing."[139] Since their goal was equality, not secularism, Madison and others in the Evangelical political alliance saw no contradiction in their concurrent support for the religious freedom bill and a law "which compelled Sunday as a day of rest" and punished Sabbath breakers.[140]

The Republican-Evangelical Coalition in the Piedmont, 1788-1813

Thomas E. Buckley tracks the "emergence of the evangelical leadership [of Virginia] in the 1790s as a self-conscious political element, aware of their ability to influence and shape the political process."[141] This awareness gave rise to a new political movement. The Republican Party was forged from an alliance of political liberals and Evangelical dissenters, especially the Baptists and Methodists, fighting ecclesiastical domination. In his book *Religion and the American Mind*, Harvard historian Alan Hiemert observes that in the "Republican Revival" "[t]here were many preachers—many more than historians allow—who avidly and vocally supported the Republican party, and did so in the conviction that Republicanism embodied the first principles of evangelical Christianity. . . . Evangelical Republicans were aroused against what they called 'Federal religion.'" Many clergymen "found their way into state legislatures . . . [and] mingled the two careers, generally with their people's understanding that Republican politics was an appropriate channel for the expression and achievement of evangelical goals."[142]

John Leland, having preached over 3,000 sermons and baptized seven hundred people in fourteen years, was instrumental in bringing the Baptists into the political alliance. He purportedly met with Madison in February 1788 and agreed to support him if Madison would back an amendment to the proposed U.S. Constitution guaranteeing religious freedom. Madison was joined in the Virginia ratification convention by the Reverend Charles Clay and the Nicholas brothers from Albemarle. Madison sent letters to Baptist pastors George Eve and Aaron Bledsoe of Albemarle and Orange counties in 1788 and 1789; and, having garnered Baptist support, Madison was elected to Congress in 1789.

Jefferson and Madison began to organize the Democratic-Republican Party by encouraging many of their friends and supporters to stand for public office. The Reverend Charles Clay had moved from Albemarle to Bedford County in 1785, and in 1790 he received a letter of endorsement from Jefferson saying: "I understand you are a candidate for . . . Congress. . . . I am sure I shall be contented with such a representative as you will make. . . . [Y]ou are too well informed a politician, too good a judge of men, not to know, that the ground of liberty is to be gained by inches, that we must be contented to secure what we can get from time to time, and eternally press forward for what is yet to get."[143] Clay failed to win his election but other Evangelical Republicans won.[144] In 1791, for example, the Baptist evangelist John Waller ran and won a seat representing Spotsylvania in the House of Delegates.[145]

Methodist Henry Fry continued to be active in local politics, although no longer as a member of the Virginia legislature after 1786. Another Methodist preacher was Tandy Key (1754-1838) who replaced Reverend Charles Wingfield as magistrate of Albemarle County in 1804, and later became Sheriff in 1809. Key's Meeting House near North Garden was host to Bishop Asbury in 1800, 1808, and 1809. James O'Kelly, the most prominent Methodist minister and revival leader in Virginia, first led the Methodist political agitation against slavery in 1789. He later led a split of at least 10,000 people away from the Methodist Church, and in 1793 he named the new denomination the "Republican Methodists."[146] This name indicates how much O'Kelly's independent churches identified with Jefferson's new Republican Party in Virginia. This name was soon changed, but the political allegiances remained the same.[147]

The second pastor of Albemarle Baptist Church, William Woods, preached at the Lewis Mountain Meeting House in Charlottesville in 1780 and thereafter. John Turpin writes that "at the urgent solicitation of Thos. Jefferson he surrendered his credentials as a minister and became a candidate for the Legislature, and was elected."[148] Woods "surrendered" his ministerial credentials (still a barrier to the Virginia legislature) in April 1798, and Jefferson rejoiced at Woods' election over Peter Carr in a letter to John W. Eppes in 1799.[149] In an 1805 letter to Woods, Jefferson "congratulat[ed] him on his reelection."[150] Woods served in the legislature until 1809.

Revivalism and Republicanism in the Virginia Piedmont went hand in hand throughout the presidential terms of Jefferson and Madison. Even the emotional itinerant camp meeting evangelist, Lorenzo Dow, who preached to four thousand people in Albemarle County in 1804, unabashedly promoted Jeffersonian ideas and politics. He returned to the Piedmont again in 1805, and then went to Washington where he was "invited to preach in Congress-Hall before the House."[151] Also, he apparently met with President Jefferson. In Jefferson's papers is a letter from Henry Fry dated 26 February 1805 in which Fry said Lorenzo Dow was the bearer of the letter. Fry told Jefferson that Dow had a "desire to visit Europe" and to preach there as he did in America, and therefore requested Jefferson to make "a personal interrogation" and give him "advice and direction of what may be needful."[152] Shortly thereafter, in November 1805, Dow sailed for England having received official "American protection under the seal of the United States, from [Secretary of State] Mr. Madison."[153] Jon Butler notes that "Dow regularly carried letters on his travels from political officials, especially Jeffersonian republicans like James Madison."[154] Although Dow usually kept moving from place to place, in 1812 and 1813 he lived temporarily in Buckingham County and filled the pulpit for Preddy's Creek Baptist Church in Albemarle County.[155] While in the Piedmont in 1812, he wrote a political pamphlet in support of Jefferson, Madison, and Republican principles.[156]

Even Presbyterian leaders in Virginia, who were not that supportive of camp meetings, also worked closely with the Republicans. Most prominent among them was John Holt Rice who was licensed for the ministry in 1803 at a meeting in Albemarle County and later said: "The more decidedly a man is a Presbyterian, the more decidedly is he a Republican."[157]

By the turn of the century, the Democratic-Republicans of the Central Virginia Piedmont were closely wed to the Evangelicals and increasingly influential in Virginia and national politics. The alliance of religious communities and the Republicans in the Piedmont is summed up best by Jefferson himself. It was noted earlier that Jefferson purportedly attended some meetings of the first Albemarle Baptist Church in 1774. Its second pastor, William Woods, had become a member of the legislature in 1798, and Jacob Watts became its third pastor. This congregation added the words "Buck Mountain" to its name when it moved in 1801 from the Lewis Mountain Meeting House to the town of Earlysville north of Charlottesville. In 1809, when Jefferson was preparing to retire from the presidency and return to his home county, he received a letter from the church saying that they were "well pleased" with his "Conduct."[158] Jefferson had received many appreciative letters from around the nation as his return to private life drew near, but his written response to this congregation on 13 April stated that their "approbation of my conduct is the more valued as *you have best known me.*" Jefferson expressed his "affectionate esteem and respect" for them and acknowledged their political partnership. He said, "[*w*]*e have acted together* from the origin to the end of a memorable Revolution."[159] The evidence shows that such coordinated action was common with many congregations.

Conclusion

The evidence presented in this chapter shows that in the lifetimes of Jefferson and Madison, religious communities exercised significant influence in the Central Virginia Piedmont. These communities were birthed or renewed by frequent spiritual awakenings led by prominent resident preachers, such as Deveraux Jarratt, Charles Clay, Elijah Craig, John Leland, James Waddell, and Henry Fry. They were strengthened by nationally-prominent Evangelicals who visited and preached in the region, such as Samuel Davies, Francis Asbury, James O'Kelly, and Lorenzo Dow (who also resided briefly in the area). Albemarle County was the strongest center in the entire state for camp meeting revivals in the first few years of the nineteenth century.

This study has shown that the Piedmont's Anglican Church was unusually tolerant of new religious communities, and also that it was more independent, self-governing, and Evangelical than most Anglican parishes. Newer communities, such as the Separate Baptists, Presbyterians, and Methodists, arose to lead the struggle for religious freedom, with the Central Virginia Piedmont producing more petitions for this cause than any other section of the state. Some of the most prominent patriot leaders in the Piedmont during the War of American Independence and early national period were active church laymen (such as Philip Mazzei, George Gilmer, John Harvie, and brothers Wilson Cary and George Nicholas), or were preachers (such as Alexander Balmaine, Charles Clay, James Waddell, and William Woods). Indeed, Jefferson, Madison, and the Evangelicals of Central Virginia were close friends and political partners in enacting the Virginia "Statute for Establishing Religious Freedom" and building the Democratic-Republican Party.

The discoverable facts suggest that Jefferson and Madison were not leaders of a secular group distinct from their religious culture; rather, they were part and parcel of it.[160] While it would be incorrect to argue that outside cultural, theological, and philosophical forces (including influences that were non-Christian or deistic) had no impact on men such as Jefferson and Madison, it would be equally, if not more, misleading to emphasize these influences while ignoring the impact of the religious communities of the Central Virginia Piedmont where they spent most of their lives. If Jefferson himself publicly and voluntarily identified with Evangelical ministers such as Charles Clay, or said that it was the Baptists of Albemarle County who understood him "best," then scholarly research and discussion must address this important source of influence and perspective.[161]

Notes

1. See Catherine Seaman, *Tuckahoes and Cohees: The Settlers and Cultures of Amherst and Nelson Counties, 1607-1807* (Sweet Briar, Va.: Sweet Briar College Press, 1992); John Hammond Moore, *Albemarle: Jefferson's County, 1727-1976* (Charlottesville: Albemarle County Historical Society; University Press of Virginia, 1976), 68-86. See also David Hackett Fischer, *Albion's Seed: Four British Folkways in America* (New York: Oxford University Press, 1989).

2. See William Meade, *Old Churches, Ministers and Families of Virginia*, 2 vols. (Philadelphia: Lippincott Co., 1857), 1:456-457. Gavin died in 1750.

3. Frances M. Walker, *The Early Episcopal Church in the Amherst-Nelson Area* (Lynchburg, Va.: J.P. Bell Co., 1964), 10-16. See also Ralph Fall, *The Diary of Robert Rose, 1746-1751* (Verona, Va.: McLure Press, 1977).

4. The first was called Ballenger Creek Church. Three were in southern Albemarle County (Ballenger Creek, Hardware River or Clear Mount, and Rockfish River) and two in Nelson County (Maple Run Church and Key's Church). None of these now exist. Ballenger Creek Church ceased having services in 1785 and was in ruins by 1814. The Hardware River Church was replaced in 1775 by a new church near an iron forge at the falls on the river. The Forge Church burned down in the early twentieth century but the site is near the present "Redlands." See Jo McCleskey, *St. Anne's Parish, Albemarle County, Virginia* (Albemarle County, Va.: self-published, 1996), 6-10. Dissenters were not legally allowed to build "churches" until after 1776.

5. Katharine L. Brown, *Hills of the Lord: Background of the Episcopal Church in Southwestern Virginia, 1738-1938* (Roanoke: Diocese of Southwestern Virginia, 1979), 12.

6. This statistic is based on Joan R. Gundersen's assertion that only four to ten of the 128 ordained ministers as of 1776 were Evangelical. Joan R. Gundersen, *The Anglican Ministry in Virginia, 1723-1776: A Study of a Social Class* (New York: Garland Publishing, 1989).

7. Gundersen, *Anglican Ministry in Virginia*, 196-197, 268. Marye was licensed in 1755 and served in Spotsylvania County's St. George's Parish from 1755 to 1761 and again from 1768 until his death in 1780.

8. Gundersen, *Anglican Ministry in Virginia*, 197.

9. Joan Rezner Gundersen, "The Myth of the Independent Virginia Vestry," *Historical Magazine of the Protestant Episcopal Church* 44 (1975): 137.

10. Oliver Perry Temple, *The Covenanter, the Cavalier, and the Puritan* (Cincinnati, Oh.: Robert Clarke Co., 1897), 17-35. See also Joseph A. Waddell, *Annals of Augusta County, Virginia, 1726-1871*, 2d ed. (Bridgewater, Va.: C. J. Carrier Co., 1958), 13-14; and Howard McKnight Wilson, *The Tinkling Spring: Headwater of Freedom* (Fishersville, Va.: Tinkling Spring and Hermitage Presbyterian Churches, 1954). This building still stands (although greatly remodeled) at Mechum's River but is now used by the Baptists. A second congregation built Rockfish Meeting House in 1746 in what is now Nelson County on Route 151.

11. Edgar Woods, *Albemarle County in Virginia* (Charlottesville, Va.: Michie Co., 1901), 130.

12. Gaillard Hunt, *The Life of James Madison* (New York: Doubleday, Page and Co., 1902), 13.

13. George M. Marsden, *The Soul of the American University: From Protestant Establishment to Established Nonbelief* (New York: Oxford University Press, 1994), 59-60.

14. In his "Autobiography," Jefferson acknowledged that Small "probably fixed the destinies of my life" since, besides being Jefferson's only regular professor, he became his "daily companion when not engaged in the school, and from his conversation I got my first views." *The Writings of Thomas Jefferson*, ed. Andrew A. Lipscomb and Albert Ellery Bergh, 20 vols. (Washington, D.C.: The Thomas Jefferson Memorial Association, 1904-05), 1:3 [hereinafter *Writings of Jefferson*]. Small, it should be noted, was not a clergyman.

15. The similarity in names of the Reverend James Maury of Fredericksville parish and the Reverend James Marye of St. Thomas parish in Orange County has given rise to some confusion as to whom was Madison's tutor. It seems more likely that Marye, who was minister in the Madisons' parish beginning in 1761, was his tutor. See generally Ralph Ketcham, *James Madison: A Biography* (New York: Macmillan, 1971), 9, 17-20.

16. For more information on Witherspoon's influence, see Mary-Elaine Swanson, *The Education of James Madison: A Model For Today* (Montgomery, Al.: The Hoffman Education Center for the Family, 1992), and Swanson's chapter in this book. Also see Ana Esther Rivera de Simpkins, "James Madison and Education 1751-1796" (Ph.D. diss., University of Virginia, 1998).

17. A. James Reichley, *Religion in American Public Life* (Washington, D.C.: The Brookings Institution, 1985), 90-91. These diverse philosophical influences in Jefferson's thought are discussed in Garrett Ward Sheldon's chapter in this book.

18. Meade, *Old Churches, Ministers and Families of Virginia*, 1:456-457.

19. James H. Hutson, *Religion and the Founding of the American Republic* (Washington, D.C.: Library of Congress, 1998), 101, 33.

20. Hutson, *Religion and the Founding of the American Republic*, 22.

21. The earlier Mountain Plains congregation was affiliated with the "Old Side" Presbyterians who were tradition-minded, insisted upon a university-educated clergy, and therefore did not favor the new revivalists associated with the Great Awakening. A "New Side" group of Presbyterians, being more evangelical and fervent, were trained in the Log Colleges of William Tennent north of Philadelphia. Beginning around 1741, the Old School Presbyterians refused to support the New Side revivalist-oriented Presbyterians. The D. S. Church was on the southwest face of a hill later known as Stillhouse Mountain, about two miles west of the University of Virginia. The building was erected shortly after 1747. The name "D. S." has an uncertain origin, but it probably corresponds to the initials of Daniel Stockton who owned a tavern near the meeting house and was one of the first families in the church. Others have suggested that "since these same initials appear as the designation for meetinghouses throughout Virginia, they probably can be translated as 'Dissenter.'" Moore, *Albemarle*, 78 n. 10; Woods, *Albemarle County in Virginia*, 129-131.

22. Robert E. Simpson, *History of First Presbyterian Church, Charlottesville, Virginia, 1839-1989* (Charlottesville, Va.: First Presbyterian Church, 1990), 10. See also *Minutes of the Presbytery of Hanover, 1755-1769*, Union Theological Seminary, Richmond, Virginia. The North Garden Meeting House was also used by other denominations up to 1892.

23. Devereux Jarratt, *The Life of the Reverend Devereux Jarratt* (Baltimore: Warner and Hanna, 1806), 50. See also Rhys Isaac, *The Transformation of Virginia, 1740-1790* (Chapel Hill, N.C.: Institute of Early American History and Culture; University of North

Carolina Press, 1982), 126-130. Fluvanna County, where Jarratt worked, was then part of "big Albemarle" County.

24. Samuel Davies spoke of the Blacks in his diary in 1756, saying that "sometimes, when I have awaked about two or three a-clock in the morning, a torrent of sacred harmony poured into my chamber, and carried my mind away to Heaven. In this seraphic exercise, some of them spend almost the whole night." John Todd started classes so that hundreds of slaves could learn to read the Bible. He said that on the Sabbath the slaves spent time "learning to read at home, or in praying together, and singing the praises of GOD and the Lamb." Mechal Sobel, *The World They Made Together: Black and White Values in Eighteenth-Century Virginia* (Princeton, N.J.: Princeton University Press, 1987), 184.

25. Woods, *Albemarle County in Virginia*, 131. In 1776, Irvin also took over the responsibilities of Samuel Black at the Rockfish and Mountain Plains meeting houses. The D. S. and North Garden churches got a new pastor named Samuel Leake.

26. Ketcham, *James Madison*, 54-59. Luckey (1750-1823) preached in Maryland from 1775 to 1799. Irwin (1756-1812) was a minister in Pennsylvania from 1774 to 1812 and was evidently "a special friend" of Madison. See letter from James Madison to William Bradford, 9 November 1772, *The Papers of James Madison*, ed. William T. Hutchinson et al., 17 vols. to date (Chicago: University of Chicago Press, 1962-), 1:76 n. 5 [hereinafter *Papers of Madison*].

27. Letter from James Madison to William Bradford, 5 September 1773, *Papers of Madison*, 1:93. Again, in 1775, Madison said that "[w]e had with us . . . the Reverend Moses Allen . . . a Dissenting Ecclesiastic. . . . I had his Company for several days during which time He preached two Sermons with great Approbation. His discourses were above the common run." Letter from James Madison to William Bradford, 20 January 1775, *Papers of Madison*, 1:136.

28. William B. Sprague, *Annals of the American Pulpit* (New York: Robert Carter & Brothers, 1858), III:337.

29. William Henry Foote, *Sketches of Virginia, Historical and Biographical* (Philadelphia: William S. Martien, 1850), 447. See also Woods, *Albemarle County in Virginia*, 131. Albemarle's D. S. Church was the host for the Presbyterian meetings in 1771, 1772, and 1775, and Rockfish Church in Nelson County was host in 1772, 1773, and 1775. It met in Amherst County in 1774.

30. See generally Joseph Martin Dawson, *Baptists and the American Republic* (Nashville, Tenn.: Broadman Press, 1956), 82-86; William L. Lumpkin, *Baptist Foundations in the South: Tracing through the Separates the Influence of the Great Awakening, 1754-1787* (Nashville, Tenn.: Broadman Press, 1961), 87-120.

31. John B. Boles, *A Bicentennial History of Chestnut Grove Baptist Church, 1773-1973* (Richmond, Va.: Lewis Printing Co., 1973), 5-7. See also John B. Turpin, *A Brief History of the Albemarle Baptist Association* (Richmond, Va.: Virginia Baptist Historical Society, [1891]); Woods, *Albemarle County in Virginia*, 132.

32. Woods, *Albemarle County in Virginia*, 133.

33. Woods, *Albemarle County in Virginia*, 176-177. Dawson later frequently served as the moderator of the Albemarle Baptist Association.

34. Isaac, *Transformation of Virginia*, 192-193. See also Robert B. Semple, *A History of the Rise and Progress of the Baptists in Virginia* (Richmond, Va.: Pitt and Dickinson Publishers, 1894), 489-492 (extract from the journal of Elder John Williams who was at this meeting).

35. Hutson, *Religion and the Founding of the American Republic*, 103.

36. Semple, *History of the Rise and Progress of the Baptists in Virginia*, 23-24; Carlos Allen, "The Great Revival in Virginia, 1783-1812" (master's thesis, University of Virginia, 1948), 44-45.

37. James B. Taylor, *Virginia Baptist Ministers* (Richmond, Va.: Yale and Wyatt, 1837), 83. See also Allen, "The Great Revival in Virginia," 45-46.

38. Dawson, 95-102. See also Lyman H. Butterfield, "Elder John Leland, Jeffersonian Itinerant," *Proceedings of the American Antiquarian Society* 62 (1952): 167-183.

39. Jarratt, *The Life of the Reverend Devereux Jarratt*, 35-36.

40. David L. Holmes, "Devereux Jarratt" (paper presented at a symposium on "Religious Culture in Jefferson's Virginia" at the University of Virginia, Charlottesville, Virginia, 19-20 January 1996), 3.

41. Gundersen, *Anglican Ministry in Virginia*, 75, 194-195.

42. Gundersen, *Anglican Ministry in Virginia*, 195. Clay is known to have visited and preached where Jarratt lived in Dinwiddie County, probably at Jarratt's invitation. See notation on sermon #47. Only between three and eight percent of Anglican clergy at the time were Evangelical. Gundersen says that "Jarratt, [Archibald] McRoberts, Clay and [Samuel] Shield were probably all evangelicals." Gundersen also lists six others that most probably were Evangelicals or at least supportive of Evangelicalism: James Marye, Jr. of Spotsylvania/Orange counties, Alexander Balmaine of Augusta County, Robert McLaurine of St. James Southam Parish, Thomas Lundie, Henry Skyring, and William Dunlap. Gundersen, *Anglican Ministry in Virginia*, 197.

43. Harry S. Stout, *The New England Soul: Preaching and Religious Culture in Colonial New England* (New York: Oxford University Press, 1986), 4-5. Stout notes that "[p]ublished sermons . . . are not necessarily representative of regular preaching, nor can we be certain they are . . . what the clergy offered the public on a weekly basis."

44. There are nine folders of sermons in the Clay Family Papers, plus Clay's *Account Book*, which covers the years 1773-1818, and a subscription list that includes the name of "Thomas Jefferson." The titles of Clay's sermon and sermon numbers are my own. I have supplied them in order to identify them easily. Clay's sermons usually had an opening text without a title.

45. Meade, *Old Churches, Ministers and Families of Virginia*, 2:49 (emphasis added). Meade, an Evangelical, emphasized in his historical work others who were of similar persuasion. Meade's praise of Clay confirms his uncommon ministry.

46. William H. B. Thomas, *"Faith of Our Fathers! . . .": Religion and the Churches in Colonial Orange County* (Orange, Va.: Orange County Bicentennial Commission, Bicentennial Series No. 2, 1975), 14. Jarratt described these meetings in *A Brief Narrative of the Revival of Religion in Virginia*. See H. Shelton Smith, Robert T. Handy, and Lefferts A. Loetscher, eds., *American Christianity: An Historical Interpretation With Representative Documents* (New York: Charles Scribner's Sons, 1960), 1:367-371.

47. In 1774, Fry began to attend Baptist meetings near him on Crooked Run. He prevailed on them to allow a Methodist itinerant named Robert Williams to preach to them at their Association meeting in 1774. When the Baptists reacted in opposition to Williams, Fry invited him home to preach and there Fry had his religious experience. It was two more years before another Methodist, Philip Gatch, came nearby.

48. Philip Slaughter, *Memoir of Col. Joshua Fry . . . with an Autobiography of his Son, Rev. Henry Fry* (Richmond, Va.: Randolph and English, 1880), 84 ff. Slaughter quotes from the Central Gazette, published many years later in Charlottesville, which said "[h]e [was] a minister of the Methodist Church which . . . he maintained . . . for 48 years

and was emphatically styled the 'Father of his Church.'" Fry records preaching at Maupin's in 1783. Daniel Maupin gave the land for the earliest Methodist meeting houses in the area. The church that met at Maupin's is known today as Mount Moriah Methodist Church.

49. Francis Asbury, *The Journal of the Rev. Francis Asbury*, 3 vols. (New York: N. Bangs and T. Mason, 1821), 1:312-313. For a Virginia Methodist history that includes material on Fry and Gatch, see Dorothy M. Lupold, "Methodism in Virginia From 1772-1784" (master's thesis, University of Virginia, 1949).

50. Hutson, *Religion and the Founding of the American Republic*, 32-33, quoting Stephen A. Marini, "Religion, Politics, and Ratification," in *Religion in a Revolutionary Age*, ed. Ronald Hoffman and Peter J. Albert (Charlottesville: United States Capitol Historical Society, University Press of Virginia, 1994), 188, 193.

51. See editorial notes, "Subscription to Support a Clergyman in Charlottesville," February 1777, and "Testimonial for Charles Clay," 15 August 1779, *The Papers of Thomas Jefferson*, ed. Julian P. Boyd, 27 vols. to date (Princeton, N.J.: Princeton University Press, 1950-), 2:6-9, 3:67 [hereinafter *Papers of Jefferson*]. Two subscriptions were used to raise the support of a clergyman. The first one called the church the "Protestant Episcopal Church." The name "Calvinistical Reformed Church" is used in this chapter.

52. "Subscription to Support a Clergyman in Charlottesville," February 1777, *Papers of Jefferson*, 2:6-9. The editor notes that "TJ not only pledged the largest sum among the subscribers but continued payments for others as well as himself over several years." *Papers of Jefferson*, 2:8. See also *Jefferson's Memorandum Books: Accounts, with Legal Records and Miscellany, 1767-1826,* ed. James A. Bear, Jr. and Lucia C. Stanton, 2 vols., *The Papers of Thomas Jefferson*, ed. Charles T. Cullen, second series (Princeton: Princeton University Press, 1997), 1:460 (9 March 1778), 470 (18 August 1778), 478 (28 April 1779), 483 (15 August 1779) [hereinafter *Memorandum Books*]. Gilbert Chinard is the only biographer to quote Jefferson's "Subscription" document to support the Reverend Clay, but then he misses its significance. Chinard, *Thomas Jefferson: The Apostle of Americanism*, 2d ed. (Ann Arbor, Mich.: University of Michigan Press, 1957), 103-105.

53. Elizabeth C. Langhorne, *A History of Christ Church, Glendower* (Albemarle County, Va.: Christ Church, 1957), 6. On page 19, the vestry book shows that Clay had quit as its minister as of 22 December 1780 because it speaks of him as "the late Rev'd Mr. Clay." Other historical sketches say he stopped preaching after 1777. See Walker, *The Early Episcopal Church in the Amherst-Nelson Area,* 51. Clay apparently had an ongoing salary dispute with the vestry prior to the establishment of this new church.

54. Thomas Jefferson, "Testimonial for Charles Clay," 15 August 1779, *Papers of Jefferson*, 3:67. On the exact same day, Jefferson sent financial support to Clay for parochial services. *Memorandum Books*, 15 August 1779, 1:483. It seems to apply to his ministry in the Calvinistical church.

55. *Memorandum Books*, 15 August 1779, 1:483.

56. Three times—3 April 1777, 17 June 1778, and 10 September 1778—Jefferson gave to *both* St. Anne's and Fredericksville parishes on the exact same day. *Memorandum Books*, 1:443 (3 April 1777), 466 (17 June 1778), 470 (10 September 1778). It was unusual for someone to give his tithes to two different parishes, but perhaps it was given because of their ministers' help in preaching in the "common temple" of the courthouse in Charlottesville. He paid the Fredericksville parish minister, Matthew "Maury to preach at Charlottesville" on 29 June 1782. *Memorandum Books*, 1:520. Perhaps this was for the Calvinistical Reformed Church as well.

57. John B. Boles, *The Great Revival, 1787-1805* (Lexington: University Press of Kentucky, 1972). Notice the dates given by Wesley M. Gewehr, *The Great Awakening in Virginia, 1740-1790* (Durham, N.C.: Duke University Press, 1930). Both John Boles and Carlos Allen date the start of the Second Great Awakening in the 1780s, which means that it overlapped with the ending of the First Awakening, according to Gewehr.

58. Maury performed the wedding of Thomas Mann Randolph and Martha Jefferson at Monticello in February 1790. He also taught school, and Meriwether Lewis was among his pupils. South of Albemarle County, Amherst Parish's ministers were John Buchanan in 1780 and John White Holt in 1787. See Brown, *Hills of the Lord*, 26-27.

59. Gundersen, *Anglican Ministry in Virginia*, 238; Brown, *Hills of the Lord*, 130.

60. Foote, *Sketches of Virginia*, 427-428. See also Boles, *The Great Revival*, 38.

61. Gewehr, *The Great Awakening in Virginia*, 167-168.

62. Foote, *Sketches of Virginia*, 428. Foote not only ignores the revival in areas north of the James River, but also implies that these churches were worldly because the Presbytery in 1791 heard accusations against them (the Reverend Irvin of Albemarle County was one of those charged with sin, but exonerated). See *ibid.*, 433-434.

63. Diary of Col. Francis Taylor, 1786-1799 (microfilm, University of Virginia Library). During the War of American Independence, Col. Taylor's Albemarle County Battalion (a.k.a. the Convention Army Guard Regiment) guarded British and Hessian prisoners of war at a camp west of Charlottesville.

64. Wilson, *Tinkling Spring*, 194.

65. William Wirt, *The Letters of the British Spy* (Chapel Hill, N.C.: University of North Carolina Press, 1970), 195-205. Wirt's popular story of Waddell's sermon is found in many collections of American literature. Unable to find an adequate replacement, the D.S. and Milton churches unfortunately declined sharply when Waddell died.

66. Semple, *History of the Rise and Progress of the Baptists in Virginia*, 59.

67. Taylor, *Virginia Baptist Ministers*, 83-85.

68. *The Writings of the Late Elder John Leland*, ed. L. F. Greene (New York: G. W. Wood, 1845), 105, 115.

69. Sobel, *The World They Made Together*, 180.

70. *Writings of the Late Elder John Leland*, 98. Leland also said that "they are remarkably fond of meeting together, to sing, pray, and exhort, and sometimes preach."

71. See Diary of Col. Francis Taylor.

72. Foote, *Sketches of Virginia*, 412.

73. Jesse Lee, *A Short History of the Methodists* (Baltimore, Md.: Magill and Clime, 1810), 134; Smith et al., *American Christianity*, 520.

74. Gewehr, *The Great Awakening in Virginia*, 167-168, 242-244.

75. Woods, *Albemarle County in Virginia*, 134-135. See also Mary Rawlings, *The Albemarle of Other Days* (Charlottesville, Va.: Michie Co., 1925), 101 ("The oldest Methodist church in the County was . . . erected prior to 1788.").

76. Robert P. Davis et al., *Virginia Presbyterians in American Life: Hanover Presbytery, 1755-1980* (Richmond, Va.: Hanover Presbytery, 1982), 61.

77. Hutson, *Religion and the Founding of the American Republic*, 105.

78. Allen, "The Great Revival in Virginia," 69-70, 103-104; and William W. Bennett, *Memorials of Methodism in Virginia* (Richmond, Va.: self-published, 1871), 489-490. Allen provides one of the few historical accounts of the Great Revival that adequately highlights events in Albemarle County and areas nearby, and gives due attention to

its leader Henry Fry. Bennett includes much local history which is, perhaps, due to the fact that he was the pastor of a Methodist church in Charlottesville for a while and had great access to local records and oral histories.

79. Bennett, *Memorials of Methodism in Virginia*, 490-491.

80. Peggy Dow, *The Dealings of God, Man, and the Devil; as Exemplified in the Life, Experience, and Travels of Lorenzo Dow* (New York: Cornish, Lamport and Co., 1852), 87. Dow's journal entry for this is number 653. Dow also participated in an 1802 camp-meeting in Albemarle.

81. Allen, "The Great Revival in Virginia," 78-79. See also Nathan O. Hatch, *The Democratization of American Christianity* (New Haven, Conn.: Yale University Press, 1989), 49.

82. This text is from an exhibit at the Monticello Visitors Center in Charlottesville, 1997.

83. See Charles L. Perdue, Jr., ed., *The Negro in Virginia* (New York: Hastings House, 1940), 111-112; Bennett, *Memorials of Methodism in Virginia*, 522.

84. Allen, "The Great Revival in Virginia," 56-58.

85. Allen, "The Great Revival in Virginia," 89-91, 96.

86. Hamilton James Eckenrode, *Separation of Church and State in Virginia: A Study in the Development of the Revolution* (Richmond, Va.: Davis Bottom, 1910), 66.

87. Joseph Martin Dawson, *Baptists and the American Republic* (Nashville, Tenn.: Broadman Press, 1956), 29.

88. *The Christian Watchman*, 14 July 1826, 13. See also *The Religious Herald*, 23 October 1829, 16; and Lewis Peyton Little, *Imprisoned Preachers and Religious Liberty in Virginia* (Lynchburg, Va.: J. P. Bell Co., 1938), 142. The source of the information in the *Christian Watchman* was the Reverend James Fishback of Lexington, Kentucky, who got his information directly from his neighbor the Reverend Andrew Tribble (d. 1822). It is certainly plausible that this discussion took place since Dolly and James Madison were still alive when this account was published, and they lived very close to the influential Blue Run Baptist Church. Records also exist of later meetings and correspondence between Jefferson and Baptists in the area. See letter from Thomas Jefferson to the Members of the Baptist Church of Buck Mountain in Albemarle, 13 April 1809, *Writings of Jefferson*, 16:363-364. Furthermore, Tribble's replacement at Goldmine Baptist in Louisa, John Leland, certainly became well known to Jefferson, even visiting him in the White House. See Butterfield, "Elder John Leland, Jeffersonian Itinerant," 224-227. Fishback also corresponded with Jefferson in 1809.

89. Davis et al., *Virginia Presbyterians in American Life*, 43.

90. Gundersen, *Anglican Ministry in Virginia*, 149, 244.

91. Hugh Blair Grigsby, *The History of the Virginia Federal Convention of 1788* (Richmond, Va.: Virginia Historical Society, 1891), 1:255-258.

92. "Testimonial for Charles Clay," 15 August 1779, *Papers of Jefferson*, 3:67.

93. "Subscription to Support a Clergyman in Charlottesville," February 1777, *Papers of Jefferson*, 2:6.

94. These are Jefferson's words that Daniel Webster recorded when discussing the 1774 Fast Day during a visit to Monticello in 1824. See *The Papers of Daniel Webster*, ed. Charles M. Wiltse (Hanover, N.H.: University Press of New England, 1974), 1:374.

95. Jefferson, "Autobiography," *Writings of Jefferson*, 1:11. See "Thomas Jefferson and John Walker to the Inhabitants of the Parish of St. Anne," 1774, *Papers of Jefferson*, 1:116-117.

96. "Subscription to Support a Clergyman in Charlottesville," February 1777, *Papers of Jefferson*, 2:6.

97. Jefferson, "Autobiography," *Writings of Jefferson*, 1:11.

98. Moore, *Albemarle*, 46-47.

99. Printed sermons from the northern states are more readily available to modern scholars; thus, there are more studies of political preaching in the North. Collections of political preaching in the South are far more rare and, therefore, of great value to historians of religion and culture. See Alice M. Baldwin, "Sowers of Sedition: The Political Theories of Some of the New Light Presbyterian Clergy of Virginia and North Carolina," *William and Mary Quarterly*, 3d ser., 5 (1948): 52-76.

100. The sermon has added the word "in" where it previously had read "on the eve of." This indicates that the sermon was, indeed, preached in both 1775 and 1780.

101. The Continental Congress was deliberating in both the summer and fall of 1775.

102. One detached fragment states: "June 5, 1776 in Old C. Courthouse," and another fragment reads: "to the minute Company Feb. 28, 1777 at Charlottesville." Grigsby confirms that it was "preached at Charlottesville before a company of Minute-men" in 1777. Grigsby, *The History of the Virginia Federal Convention of 1788*, 1:255. The sermon also has pages inserted to address the military. The 1776 delivery took place when Jefferson was in Philadelphia.

103. Grigsby, *The History of the Virginia Federal Convention of 1788*, 1:255. See also the Clay Family Papers.

104. The journal of a Hessian officer who was a prisoner at the Barracks, Schueler von Senden, has this interesting entry around the year 1780: "I keep a lot of company with Chaplain Kohli; either I visit with him, or he visits me." It is most likely that this "Kohli" was Clay, but the name was either poorly translated from the German manuscript or poorly remembered by the foreign author of the journal. "Excerpt from the Schueler von Senden Journal; 30 December 1778 through 21 November 1780," *Magazine of Albemarle County History* 41 (Charlottesville, Va.: Albemarle County Historical Society, 1983), 135, 130.

105. See George J. Cleaveland, "The Church of Virginia Established and Disestablished," in *Up From Independence: The Episcopal Church in Virginia* (Orange, Va.: Interdiocesan Bicentennial Committee of the Virginias, 1976), 38.

106. Waddell, *Annals of Augusta County, Virginia*, 235-236.

107. Foote, *Sketches of Virginia*, 375-377; Waddell, *Annals of Augusta County, Virginia*, 281, 298-299, 329-331; Wilson, *Tinkling Spring*, 198-203. When news reached them in 1781 that British troops led by Banastre Tarleton had chased Governor Jefferson and the legislature out of Charlottesville, Waddell preached to his congregation the next Sunday morning that it was their religious duty to obtain arms and march to Rockfish Gap (on the border of Albemarle County) to defend the Shenandoah Valley. He was among the men the next morning at the Gap ready to fight. Many of these men from Waddell's church, under the command of Elder Zachariah Johnston, marched into Albemarle County and joined up with Lafayette's division of the Continental Army located southeast of Charlottesville.

108. Moore, *Albemarle*, 50-51. See also "Papers, Military and Political, 1775-1778, of George Gilmer, M.D., of Pen Park, Albemarle County, VA," in *Miscellaneous Papers 1672-1865 . . . in the collections of the Virginia Historical Society* (Richmond: Virginia Historical Society, 1887), 71-139.

109. Howard Marraro, *Memoirs of the Life and Peregrinations of the Florentine Philip Mazzei, 1730-1816* (New York: Columbia University Press, 1942), 213-215.

110. Semple, *History of the Rise and Progress of the Baptists in Virginia*, 492-494.

111. Turpin, *Brief History of the Albemarle Baptist Association*, 26. He "enter[ed] wagon and horses into public service to work on the Sabbath Day" to collect provisions for the Continental Army. Elder Woods was censured (but not excommunicated) by his church for this violation of God's "moral law," but shortly thereafter he was ordained a minister in July 1780. Ibid.

112. James Madison, as early as 1 December 1773, expressed support for religious liberty. He disagreed with the idea that "an Ecclesiastical Establishment [was] absolutely necessary to support civil society." Letter from James Madison to William Bradford, 1 December 1773, *Papers of Madison*, 1:101. Less than two months later, he told his friend from Princeton, William Bradford, that a "diabolical Hell conceived principle of persecution rages among some and to their eternal Infamy the Clergy can furnish their Quota of Imps for such business. This vexes me most of any thing whatever. There are at this [time?] in the adjacent County [Culpeper] not less than 5 or 6 well meaning men in close Gaol for publishing their religious Sentiments which in the main are very orthodox. . . . So . . . pray for liberty of conscience [to revive among us]." Letter from James Madison to William Bradford, 24 January 1774, *Papers of Madison*, 1:106. Lewis Peyton Little writes that Madison became motivated to pursue a legal career (instead of the ministry) when he "repeatedly appeared in the court of his own county to defend the Baptist nonconformists." Little, *Imprisoned Preachers and Religious Liberty in Virginia*, 130, 131. Madison wrote later that "he spared no exertion to save them from imprisonment & to promote their release from it." Douglass Adair, "James Madison's Autobiography," *William and Mary Quarterly*, 3d ser., 2 (1945): 198.

113. Madison's amendments to Article XVI are discussed in detail in Daniel L. Dreisbach's chapter in this volume on church-state debate in the Virginia legislature.

114. One was received from Albemarle, Amherst, and Buckingham on 22 October, and another from Albemarle and Amherst on 1 November. Another petition came from Augusta on 9 November, and one arrived from Lutherans in what is present day Madison County (but then Culpeper County).

115. Davis et al., *Virginia Presbyterians in American Life*, 50.

116. Smith et al., *American Christianity*, 442-445; Davis et al., *Virginia Presbyterians in American Life*, 50.

117. "Petition of Dissenters in Albemarle and Amherst Counties," 1 November 1776, *Papers of Jefferson*, 1:586-589. Among the prominent signatories were Gilmer, Mazzei, Woods, and Maupin.

118. Letter from William Irvin to Thomas Jefferson, pre-November 1776, *Papers of Jefferson*, 1:585.

119. "Declaration of the Virginia Association of Baptists," 25 December 1776, *Papers of Jefferson*, 1:660-661.

120. Robert Boyle Howell, *The Early Baptists of Virginia* (Philadelphia: The Bible and Publication Society, 1857), 164-165, 167-168. See also Edward Frank Humphrey, *Nationalism and Religion in America, 1774-1789* (Boston: Chipman Law Publishing Co., 1924), 382.

121. Charles F. James, *Documentary History of the Struggle for Religious Liberty in Virginia* (Lynchburg, Va., J.P. Bell Co., 1900), 102-107. See also Dawson, *Baptists and the American Republic*, 101. Howell's and James' accounts are often ignored by historians because the initial Baptist draft is not specifically mentioned in Jefferson's writings, yet neither was Leland's "Declaration of the Virginia Association of Baptists" cited above, al-

though it (and petitions from other religious groups) is found among *Papers of Jefferson*, 1:660-661.

122. John E. Kleber et al., eds., *The Kentucky Encyclopedia* (Lexington: University Press of Kentucky, 1992), 238-239. Craig's leadership among the Baptists in the Piedmont ended in 1781 when he and his brother Lewis Craig led six hundred Baptists in "the traveling church" to Kentucky.

123. Letter from Samuel Stanhope Smith to Thomas Jefferson, 19 April 1779, *Papers of Jefferson*, 2:253. This letter was in reply to a letter from Jefferson that is now missing.

124. Letter from Samuel Stanhope Smith to James Madison, 15 September 1778, *Papers of Madison,* 1:257 (emphasis added).

125. See Fred J. Hood, *Reformed America: The Middle and Southern States, 1783-1837* (University: University of Alabama Press, 1980), 7-26.

126. Harvie was appointed by the legislature to a committee, along with George Mason and Jerman Baker, to prepare two bills: one for religious freedom and the other for saving the property of the formerly-established church. See Eckenrode, *Separation of Church and State in Virginia*, 56. For more on the struggle for religious freedom in Virginia, see Thomas E. Buckley, *Church and State in Revolutionary Virginia, 1776-1787* (Charlottesville, Va.: University Press of Virginia, 1977).

127. Letter from Rev. John Todd to Thomas Jefferson, 16 August 1779, *Papers of Jefferson*, 3:69.

128. Waddell, *Annals of Augusta County, Virginia*, 304.

129. Buckley, *Church and State in Revolutionary Virginia,* 29 n. 50.

130. *The Journal and Letters of Francis Asbury*, ed. Elmer Clark, 3 vols. (Nashville, Tenn.: Abingdon Press, 1958), 1:459 (April 1784). Asbury stayed at Tandy Key's home again in 1800, 1808, and 1809.

131. See 24 May 1786 entry from Coke's journal, cited in Slaughter, *Autobiography of Henry Fry*, 83.

132. The Presbytery of Hanover to the Assembly, October 1784, in James, *Documentary History of the Struggle for Religious Liberty in Virginia*, 234-235. Some commentators have not understood that the Presbyterian decision to support a general assessment at this point was a reaction to the Episcopal Incorporation bill and, therefore, in their view a more liberal step away from state support for one church.

133. Hutson, *Religion and the Founding of the American Republic*, 61.

134. Ralph L. Ketcham, "James Madison and Religion: A New Hypothesis," in *James Madison on Religious Liberty*, ed. Robert S. Alley (Buffalo, N.Y.: Prometheus Books, 1985), 185.

135. Wilson, *Tinkling Spring*, 223-231.

136. Slaughter, *Autobiography of Henry Fry,* 100, 107. See Eckenrode, *Separation of Church and State in Virginia*, 109. At this time, Jefferson was in France. For most clergy, such as Anglican Charles M. Thruston of Frederick County, a seat in the legislature meant giving up their official ordination, but Fry's ordination was probably one of those performed unofficially at Broken Back Church in 1779 and, therefore, did not pose a problem. Slaughter, *Autobiography of Henry Fry*, 82.

137. Hunt, *Life of Madison*, 84.

138. Hutson, *Religion and the Founding of the American Republic*, 70, 74. This was from Westmoreland County on 2 November 1785.

139. Slaughter, *Autobiography of Henry Fry*, 102.

140. Thomas E. Buckley, "Establishing an Evangelical Culture: Religion and Politics in Jeffersonian Virginia" (paper presented at a symposium on "Religious Culture in Jefferson's Virginia" at the University of Virginia, Charlottesville, Virginia, 19-20 January 1996), 15. In 1961, the U.S. Supreme Court upheld Sunday laws in *McGowan v. Maryland*, citing Madison's support for this statute. See generally Daniel L. Dreisbach, "A New Perspective on Jefferson's Views on Church-State Relations: The Virginia Statute for Establishing Religious Freedom in Its Legislative Context," *American Journal of Legal History* 35 (1991): 172-204.

141. Buckley, "Establishing an Evangelical Culture," 3.

142. Alan Heimert, *Religion and the American Mind: From the Great Awakening to the Revolution* (Cambridge, Mass.: Harvard University Press, 1966), 534-536, 538, 541.

143. Letter from Thomas Jefferson to the Rev. Charles Clay, 27 January 1790, *Papers of Jefferson*, 16:129.

144. Clay wrote to Jefferson: "I have to thank you for your very obliging letter when I last offered myself as a Candidate for . . . Congress, the letter did me great honor, and was of very essential Service in the upper Counties." Clay said that he planned to run again once the districts were redrawn and asked Jefferson if he could send letters directly "to Some particular Gentlemen in each County to be delivered just before the election." Letter from Charles Clay to Thomas Jefferson, 8 August 1792, *Papers of Jefferson,* 24:283-284. This required greater involvement in the race than Jefferson desired. He wrote back, saying that he was "determined never to intermeddle with elections" beyond his general endorsement. Letter from Thomas Jefferson to Charles Clay, 1 September 1792, *Papers of Jefferson*, 24:367.

145. Thomas Thompson, "The Failure of Jeffersonian Reform: Religious Groups and the Politics of Morality in Early National Virginia" (Ph.D. diss., University of California, Riverside, 1990), 284. By 1793, however, Waller decided to move to South Carolina to be near a daughter.

146. W. E. MacClenny, *The Life of Rev. James O'Kelly and the Early History of the Christian Church in the South* (Raleigh, N.C.: Edwards and Broughton Printing Co., 1910), 114. MacClenny writes that this name was chosen probably because "the Republican Party was strong politically in Virginia at that time."

147. See William Warren Sweet, *Virginia Methodism: A History* (Richmond, Va.: Whittet and Shepperson, 1955), 128-134.

148. Turpin, *Brief History of the Albemarle Baptist Association*, 31.

149. Letter from Thomas Jefferson to J.W. Eppes, 21 December 1799. This is letter number 642 in the University of Virginia's collection of Jefferson Papers.

150. Letter from Thomas Jefferson to William Woods, 9 March 1805. "Calendar of the Correspondence of Thomas Jefferson," *Bulletin of the Bureau of Rolls and Library of the Department of State* (Washington: Department of State, 1903), ser. 6, vol. 10, no. 73, 199. Woods also wrote to Jefferson in 1807 and asked him "to accept a miniature 'mammoth cheese'" (similar to what Leland gave Jefferson in 1802). Letter from William Woods to Thomas Jefferson, 14 January 1807. "Calendar of the Correspondence of Thomas Jefferson," *Bulletin of the Bureau of Rolls*, ser. 6, vol. 12, no. 28, 199. Most of the preaching at his church was done by Jacob Watts after 1798 when Woods gave up his official ministerial credentials; however, he gave a farewell sermon in 1810 before moving to Kentucky.

151. Lorenzo Dow, *The History of Cosmopolite, or the four volumes of Lorenzo Dow's Journa*l (Wheeling, Va.: Joshua Martin, 1848), 331. His journal records that he

"spoke from these words: 'Righteousness exalteth a nation; but sin is a shame to any people' [Proverbs 14:34]."

152. Letter from Henry Fry to Thomas Jefferson, 26 February 1805, Library of Congress.

153. Dow, *History of Cosmopolite*, 252.

154. Jon Butler, *Awash in a Sea of Faith: Christianizing the American People* (Cambridge, Mass.: Harvard University Press, 1990), 287.

155. W.L. Mundy, *A Brief Historical Sketch* (Charlottesville, Va., 1921). This sketch is cited in Preddy's Creek's records.

156. Dow's political essay was called *Analects Upon Natural, Social and Moral Philosophy*, and it grounded all human rights upon "the great and universal 'Law of nature.'" Dow wrote boldly in praise of Jefferson and Madison, especially their position on church and state. See Dow, *The History of Cosmopolite*, 419-470. It is doubtful that Jefferson or Madison identified religiously with the camp meetings that were popular during Jefferson's presidency; however, it is likely that, being supported by men such as Dow and Fry, they would have attended some meetings for at least political reasons.

157. Thompson, "The Failure of Jeffersonian Reform," 365. Rice (1777-1831) became one of the most significant leaders in American Presbyterianism. Converted during the Great Revival in Virginia, Rice was licensed for the ministry by the Hanover Presbytery after preaching a sermon in its 1803 meeting at the Cove Church in Albemarle County. Rice settled in Richmond and later became Jefferson's most significant religious ally in the founding of the University of Virginia. See William Maxwell, *Memoir of the Rev. John H. Rice* (Philadelphia: J. Whetham, 1835).

158. Letter from Albemarle Buckmountain Baptist Church to Thomas Jefferson, 19 March 1809, in Garnett Ryland, *The Baptists of Virginia, 1699-1926* (Richmond: Virginia Baptist Board of Missions and Education, 1955), 168.

159. Letter from Thomas Jefferson to the Members of the Baptist Church of Buck Mountain in Albemarle, 13 April 1809, *Writings of Jefferson*, 16:363-364 (emphasis added).

160. Sadly, most modern biographers ignore much of this history; thus, the modern images of Jefferson and Madison are shaped without the context of their religious community. The unfortunate consequence of overlooking this religious history is that historians often mislabel or misidentify an important source of the movements for religious freedom and republicanism in Virginia.

161. James H. Hutson, Chief of the Manuscript Division of the Library of Congress and curator of the Library's 1998 exhibition on "Religion and the Founding of the American Republic," wrote an excellent book to accompany the exhibit. It is perhaps the best short history of the role of religion in American public life. It challenges long held assumptions and brings out much material that has been ignored elsewhere. Hutson states that "[f]or a long time, scholars argued that [the leaders of America's Revolution were] . . . nominally Christian, but committed to the agenda of the Enlightenment." Hutson then provocatively asserts and persuasively argues that according to recent authorities, "[t]his view is wrong." Hutson, *Religion and the Founding of the American Republic*, 19. In another excellent study of American colonial society, Patricia U. Bonomi concludes that there was "a far more vital religious culture than that portrayed by conventional historiography." Bonomi, *Under the Cope of Heaven: Religion, Society, and Politics in Colonial America* (New York: Oxford University Press, 1986), viii. Rhys Isaac's prize-winning book, *The Transformation of Virginia*, also helps to correct some assumptions about the religious cul-

ture in Virginia. It reveals a rich religious culture in the Old Dominion—an important foundation for what transpired in the lives of those who participated in the War of American Independence and the movement for religious freedom.

Chapter 2

Perceptions of a "Deist Church" in Early National Virginia

Thomas C. Thompson

In the late eighteenth century, deism was not an organized church, yet to orthodox Christians it seemed to function as one. It had no institutional hierarchy, but there were men who acted as its leaders. There was no deist creed, yet most deists agreed on general principles. Only sectarians felt comfortable in grouping together this heterogeneous assembly, calling the vaguely-defined enemy "deists." In the view of many, the center of deism in the United States was in Virginia, and during this period, Virginia sectarians often interpreted Jeffersonian policy in the light of their own concerns in an age of evangelical competition. Not until Jefferson's electoral victory in 1800 did deism cease to be a religious and political issue in the state. By then, most sectarians were convinced that deists had failed in their attempt to subvert the hearts and minds of Virginians.

Prominent deists were easily identified. Under the nebulous requirements for inclusion in the "sect," almost any holder of liberal religious views qualified as a deist; a large number of the gentry found itself tarred with the deist brush at one time or another.[1] Religious liberals often rejected the concept of the Trinity, or the divinity of Jesus, or the revelatory origins of the Bible. Jefferson rejected all of these tenets, and in many ways his theological "pilgrimage" recapitulated the experiences of many of his fellow gentry.[2] Sectarians outnumbered the adherents of these beliefs, who represented not one coherent group but rather a wing of contemporary religious thought. In fact, most English and colonial deists continued to flourish within the friendly confines of the Church of England.

While there may have been no actual "deist church," Presbyterians, Baptists, and Methodists often acted as if there was such an institution. Their struggle for toleration forged for Virginia sectarians a self-image that included memories of persecution by the gentry.[3] Most deists in Virginia were members of the gentry; in some ways, Virginia's deists inherited the mantle of Virginia's Anglican establishment. Thus many sectarians felt squeezed between "Deist[s] on the one hand and christians of different sentiments on the other."[4] They saw deism as a competing religious philosophy, one with a respectable intellectual (if not spiritual) lineage that seemed to have been well-established for most of the eighteenth century.

By mid-century, many critics of the Church of England in Virginia already condemned creeping deism. In particular, they were concerned that God seemed to have disappeared from sermons except as a remote Creator. Anglicans tended to emphasize each person's obligations to his fellow man, not God's demands on the individual. Anglican theology fell by the wayside, disappearing as a subject of discussion even as communicants remained devoted to the Church. Baptists were aghast at the ignorance of gentlemen about the institution they defended. Planters seemed to be "unacquainted with the articles of the Church, of which they professed themselves members; and many when asked about their articles could give no account of them, or in what book they were contained."[5]

It is not surprising that some gentlemen in this environment began to conceive of morality apart from institutional religion. A growing group within the gentry saw moral lapses not as religious offenses but rather as disturbances of the common peace. Activities previously condemned by both Church and state could be tolerated if they did not threaten the social structure. At the College of William and Mary, the Reverend Samuel Henley proclaimed that

> Any crime committed in Society can be punished as a crime against Society, alone. . . . As Society cannot be injured but by actions which violate its property or peace, those who demean themselves honestly and orderly ought not to be molested, on account either of their sentiments or worship.[6]

An anonymous planter concurred with Henley, observing that "[m]any will scarcely believe that Society can subsist on any Foundation but a Sameness of Religion. . . . [Yet] a Man may soon be convinced that there are flourishing and happy Governments where the Subjects, though of every denomination, yet live in Harmony."[7]

Liberal religious thinkers had replaced mysticism with moralism, asserting that moral laws could be deduced from general behavior just as natural philosophers deduced laws governing the universe. Rational religion emphasized moral behavior because it contributed to a rational and therefore moral and godly society.[8] On the one hand, evangelical piety, which relied on personal contact with an unknowable God, disturbed the gentry. In their view such piety emphasized individual belief over the moral good of the community. On the other hand, Sir John Randolph complained that theologians had been unable to construct "a true, uniform, consistent system of their own." They had instead made Christianity a "Science of Mighty Difficulty and Mystery . . . having no Tendency to influence Men's Minds to amend their Lives, but weak'ning the eternal Obligations of Morality."[9] Inconsistency and priestly intrigue confused men about God's requirements of them, requirements that could be summed up in the need to live a moral life. The basis of virtue might be disguised under a number of euphemisms: "a conduct agreeable to nature or reason," "the common good," or "the will of our

Creator," but whatever rational principle an individual used, "it must necessarily be what God hath appointed."[10]

By the 1770s, many of the gentry made a closer link between morality and social behavior than they did between morality and religious belief. As Presbyterian James Reid complained, gentlemen "diligently search the Scriptures; but the Scriptures which they search are the Laws of Virginia: for though you may find innumerable families in which there is no Bible, yet you will not find one without a Law-book."[11] The law represented the very thing Sir John Randolph wanted: a system of moral governance that was practical and understandable, with few of the mysteries dominating religion.

Randolph's position undercut the Established Church to which he belonged, and studies of disestablishment have emphasized the cooperation between rationalist gentry and evangelical dissenters. This cooperation demonstrates that on one issue rationalists and sectarians could work together.[12] Yet the erstwhile partners went their own ways during these years, their chief accomplishment being disestablishment.

Going their own ways sometimes brought the allies into conflict and sometimes took them on wildly divergent paths. While liberals cooperated with dissenters to bring down the Anglican establishment, they pushed for other changes that would do little to aid Presbyterians and Baptists. From the sectarian point of view, many liberal reforms had little to do with disestablishment; liberals seemed to be gathering power to themselves instead. Chief among these questionable reforms was the creation of a system of education for Virginia. When Jefferson was elected governor in 1779, he became an ex officio member of the board of visitors at the College of William and Mary. His sympathizers on the board, among them Edmund Randolph and John Page, juggled the faculty and curriculum of the college. The result was an institution purged of Tory influences and of its two professorships of divinity. The new "republican" faculty at the institution was beyond reproach, including the Reverend James Madison and George Wythe.[13] William and Mary might no longer be an Anglican institution, but it had become a liberal-dominated school and, as Ronald L. Hatzenbuehler remarked, one that continued to operate primarily as a training ground for the gentry.[14] For many Virginians, the issue revolved not only around removing the Established Church from the body of the state but also around finding its replacement. Sectarians feared that William and Mary would become a deist seminary designed to propagate unorthodox religious ideas of the most dangerous kind throughout the land.

The reform of William and Mary marked the beginning of serious controversy between rational and orthodox religious thinkers in Virginia. In this period, warnings against deists tended to be general and vague. "A Social Christian" criticized Jefferson as "one who disregards . . . a future state of rewards and punishments" and accused him of reckoning "the eternal concerns of our immortal souls of no more consequence than physicks or geometry."[15] Echoing many sectarians, he rejected rationalism as creating chaos through its denial of recognized eternal truths. "Social Christian" was followed by "A Citizen," who was concerned with

Jefferson's claim that God appealed only to human reason in furthering His divine plan. "A Citizen" stressed "the mighty and singular advantage of revelation" in determining "the clearest manifestations of our creators perfections, and of his will with regard to the duties he requireth of his creat[i]ons."[16] "Citizen" did not believe that the study of nature provided insight into the desires or character of God. Only God Himself, through the tool of revelation, could teach man what He desired. Like "Social Christian," "Citizen" deemed rationalism not only insufficient to understand Creation, but even dangerous to it.

Presbyterians in particular felt threatened by liberal educational initiatives. Two Presbyterian colleges, Hampden-Sidney and Liberty Hall, survived the war, and the church reacted to Jefferson's reform of William and Mary by founding Transylvania Seminary in Kentucky in 1786. Sectarians and liberals who feared that the Presbyterian Church would control all education in Virginia attacked the institution. Supporters of the school, such as Caleb Wallace, attempted to rebut the attackers' arguments. Wallace rejected the idea that morality could be separated from theology and preferred to include religious instruction at Transylvania because omitting it would produce "a powerful tendency to eradicate any remains of the Christian religion." The religion Wallace supported did not include "the Religion of Nature," because it "means everything, but means nothing that has yet been defined."[17] Wallace fought against any non-Presbyterian religious group influencing the fledgling school, including deists.

For most Baptists the debate with deists revolved not around education but around belief and unbelief. In 1783, Baptist preacher Henry Toler mused that "Unbelief is the source of all Sin and Misery. For Lack of Faith we are rendered useless to Society and consequently miserable in our own Souls." By 1785 Toler's concern had become a widely circulated Baptist lamentation that "Deism with its banefull Influence is spreading itself over the state."[18]

These protests against the evil effects of deism did produce some immediate results. Jefferson's "Bill for Establishing Religious Freedom" underwent several changes before its passage. The opening phrase originally indicated that men possessed an innate moral sense. This was deleted, as was the clause limiting God's suasive powers to "influence on reason alone."[19] Ironically, even Jefferson's "Statute for Establishing Religious Freedom" bore witness to the strength of the religious forces arrayed against him.

Yet there seem to have been few direct attacks on Jefferson's liberal religious opinions in the 1780s. Nevertheless, many Americans had an inkling of his liberal theology, largely through his *Notes on the State of Virginia*, first published in the United States in Philadelphia in 1788. The impact of Jefferson's *Notes* was widespread. Sectarian leaders knew that in rational Christianity they were dealing with a movement that possessed both a leadership and a literature. About to enter the state on a preaching tour in the early 1790s, Methodist leader Francis Asbury prepared for the deism he knew he would encounter. On a previous trip he noted that "[t]here is a great work of God in the lower counties of Virginia; but the Antinomian doctrines, so liberally set forth by some, greatly hinder."[20] Then he was concerned with Calvinist Presbyterian and Baptist revivals; this time he armed himself with a copy of Jefferson's *Notes* bought in Maryland. He hurriedly read "the most essential parts," certain that it behooved him to gain some acquaintance with the most prominent liberal writers.[21] Asbury did not rely wholly on the power of his preaching; he knew that the competition would come armed with philosophical arguments as well as emotional appeals.

Meanwhile, the rift between sectarians and liberals continued to widen. In Kentucky, Baptist preacher William Bledsoe, probably aware of the battles over Transylvania Seminary, painted a bleak picture of religion in the west. He found his labors opposed by both "the world and professors of Christianity" as deists, Baptists, Presbyterians, and Methodists all fought for influence.[22] Bledsoe's concerns were echoed by the church representatives gathered at Cedar Creek Meeting House for the May 1791 session of the Baptist Middle District Association. They condemned the "many false doctrines and anti-christian principles [that] are industriously spread through our land."[23] Yet as Bledsoe and others lamented the growth of what they viewed as pernicious beliefs, orthodox Christian churches also grew at an unprecedented rate. After 1787 an intensification of religious spirit spread over Virginia.

The revivals of the late 1780s demonstrated that traditional piety was not dead in the state despite the jeremiads of its citizens. Leading the way was the new Methodist Church. Methodism originated as a lay society within the Church of England and only separated from the parent body in 1785. Beginning in 1773, Methodist preachers began to roam the countryside much as their Baptist and Presbyterian predecessors had done.[24] The first postwar revivals began among the Methodists in 1785, and by the early 1790s there were approximately fifteen thousand Methodists in the state.[25]

Baptists, too, enjoyed the fruits of their labors. Most of the various splinter groups of the sect came together in the late 1780s to form the United Baptists of Virginia. By 1790 there were over two hundred Baptist churches in Virginia with more than twenty thousand members, or roughly double the number before the Revolution.[26] The revivals also led to the expansion of the Presbyterian Church. The settlement of Kentucky and the accretions of the 1787 revival stimulated the formation of the Synod of Virginia in 1788.[27] By the 1790s, Hampden-Sidney and Liberty Hall were the twin centers of a network that stretched along the Appalachians from western Pennsylvania to South Carolina and from the Piedmont of Virginia to the Illinois territory.

As the revival spread, sectarian proselytizing efforts also sensitized evangelicals to the threat posed by liberals. Religious freedom meant not only the right to worship as one wished, but also the right to proselytize freely. As the controversies at Transylvania Seminary demonstrated, sectarians perceived Jefferson's educational reforms as attempts to convert Virginians to deism. Thus they reacted to liberal initiatives exactly as they had earlier responded to Anglican power. They feared that liberals wanted a new establishment in which deist schoolteachers would systematically attempt to extirpate orthodox Christianity. Baptists and

Presbyterians, already shocked by the sudden Methodist success, regarded the rationalist tendencies of Virginia's elite as a powerful challenge to their own hold on the religious allegiance of the population.

Continued liberal emphasis on education provided a convenient focus for sectarian concern. Following the passage of the "Statute for Establishing Religious Freedom," Madison attempted to enact Jefferson's plan for a statewide system of education, but the attempt foundered on the rock of higher taxes. Money was not the only reason to question the plan: Baptists often looked askance at education, aware that most schools in Virginia were run by Presbyterian or Episcopalian clergy. Baptist minister John Leland emphasized that traditional clerical education was unnecessary, pointing out that "there are not more than three or four Baptist ministers in Virginia, who have received the *diploma* of M.A., which is additional proof that the work has been of God, and not of man."[28] Many felt constrained to distance themselves from the potent combination of religion and education. One early Baptist historian stated that "[s]o cordially did the Baptists abhor all proselyting, that they refused to employ education as an auxiliary to denominational advancement. They . . . looked with loathing upon any man who would use his influence as a teacher to give a denominational bias to the minds of his pupils."[29]

The outbreak of the French Revolution in 1789 also heightened American awareness of deism, which came to be called "French infidelity." At first, pro-French sentiment in the United States contributed to the distribution of deist material. By 1791 provincial newspapers like the *Virginia Gazette and Petersburg Intelligencer* were serializing Thomas Paine's *Rights of Man*. Nonetheless, it took time for the orthodox opposition to coalesce. Until 1794 most of the clergy in the United States supported the changes in France. The Baptist General Committee, for example, lauded "the Glorious Flame of liberty spreading throughout Europe." At that point, however, domestic political events stimulated a conservative reaction to "French principles."[30]

In 1795 the Jay Treaty helped to polarize pro-French and pro-British factions in the nation at large, and deism became an issue involving more than religious beliefs. To be a supporter of Hamilton and Adams, a Federalist, meant espousing religious orthodoxy and extolling the political theory of the British constitution. The political opposition, coming to be known as Republicans, praised the transformation underway in France and declared that religion had no place in government.

Like other Virginians, Baptists supported Jefferson and Madison, the obvious leaders of the Republicans. Commentators noted that "the violent party heat . . . frequently made its way into the pulpit and religious assemblies."[31] At the same time, despite Jefferson's image as their political champion, many Virginians continued to deplore the deist philosophy he espoused. As early as 1789 Patrick Henry attacked the deism he saw spreading over the state. He printed at his own expense Soame Jennings's *On Internal Evidences of Christianity*, an anti-deist tract, which he then carried around his court circuit in the 1790s, handing out copies to judges.[32] His friends commended him on his stance. Archibald Blair assured him that "I know you too well ever to believe that you would sacrifice *virtue, mo-*

rality, and *religion* to the prevailing mad philosophy." Blair, however, sounded a cautionary note. Even without implementing Jefferson's school system, deists had managed to spread their irreligious doctrines. In Blair's words, "our youths have imbibed the poison."[33] In this atmosphere even Henry continued to struggle with deism in his own mind for several years after he began his anti-deist campaign. When Presbyterian minister William Hill visited him in 1791, he found the aging statesman "feeling that trial of his faith, which in the novel form of French infidelity, tested hearts of Christian men, the latter part of the eighteenth century."[34] Perhaps Henry's own doubts account for the strength of his denunciation of deism and its adherents.

The conflict between deism and orthodox Christianity continually spilled over into the political arena. In 1794, the readers of the *Virginia Gazette* were treated to an exchange of charges and insults involving William Boyce, one of Surry County's representative in the House of Delegates. Edwin Hart, an enemy of Boyce, launched a volley aimed at Boyce's hypocrisy, claiming that although Boyce "pretends to be a staunch Anabaptist (and I believe a great enthusiast) he is not possessed of a true spirit of divination." Boyce responded by charging that Hart was a deist and therefore perfectly capable of lying under oath: "Baptists being bound by the oath taken on the Holy Evangelists of Almighty God, while the ca[n]did Deist feels not bound by the oath he takes on a book, the contents of which he openly professes to believe to be nothing but priestcraft."[35] By 1794 it was not bad to be a Baptist unless one was a hypocrite, but it was bad to be any kind of deist.

Sectarian leaders seldom pointed fingers at specific targets, preferring to bemoan the general lack of religious feeling among the populace. William Hill recorded many instances of backsliding and indifference as well as outright hostility to orthodox Christianity.[36] In the public realm, protracted exchanges like those in the *Richmond Chronicle* in 1795 between "Deisticus" and the religiously orthodox author of a series entitled "Common Sense" were by no means uncommon. At the time of the revivals in the late 1780s liberal religious thought had seemed on the defensive as evangelism spread over central and western Virginia. The situation changed thereafter; against a background of the apparent decline of Christian orthodoxy, deism assumed the frightening specter of an organized sect competing for the devotion of Virginians.[37] Baptist George Smith even described Thomas Paine's *Age of Reason* as "the Bible of the wicked."[38] If deism was a sect, then Jefferson was its priest, his proposed schools its temples, and dominion over the souls of Virginians its final goal.

Virginia, especially the area close to the District of Columbia, proved fertile ground for the spread of liberal religious ideas. Orthodox reaction against those ideas was also strong, and newspapers provided convenient battlegrounds for the debate. In 1795, an inhabitant of Fairfax County set out what might be regarded as a classic deist statement on the historical connection between religion and society. In detailing the growth of established churches, he observed that the ambiguities inherent in organized religion "required the adoption of compulsive measures to insure obedience." This coercion led inevitably to "despotism of the most baneful, degrading, and tyrannical description." Reason was clearly the key to a virtuous society, and the writer sardonically observed that "these ancient mysteries will never again be well understood unless the people should be debarred the exercise of their reason."[39]

The presidential election of 1796 brought these tensions into the open and gave political sanction to public statements of previous insinuations. Advocates of John Adams painted Jefferson as a weak-willed man who would conduct a "feeble and timid administration" that would be "guided and directed by our brethren the French."[40] They blamed at least part of the opposition to Adams on the spread of deism. "A Friend to Government" recalled that "many countries at various times have fallen into abject vassalage, in consequence of abandoning the principles of virtue and common good, which has always been the dire and baneful effect of infidelity."[41]

As the campaign progressed, proponents and detractors of "natural religion" came forward to contribute to the political debate. In 1796 a James City County "Freeholder" sparked an intense argument over Jefferson's religious principles. "Freeholder" complained that "[n]o man ought to be President, who does not profess and practice the christian religion—Does Mr. Jefferson profess to be of the society of christians? If he does, pray inform the public of what sect he belongs."[42] Jefferson's supporters saw this accusation as an attempt to wrest sectarian votes from him. "A Dissenter" held up the "Statute for Establishing Religious Freedom" as proof of Jefferson's "most profound reverence for the great Majesty of Heaven" and invoked the gratitude of sectarians to the man who was "the instrument of your relief from this oppression."[43]

"A Freeholder" was incredulous: "Is it of no moment to you whether your Chief Magistrate be a follower of Mahomet, a Deist, or an Atheist?" He downplayed the importance of Jefferson's statute and evoked a horrible picture of the country under Jefferson's rule with illustrations drawn from the worst excesses of the French Revolution. Under Jefferson, he warned, Virginians' "worship of Christ, should be changed into that of the Goddess of Reason, their Sabbaths into Decades, their Liberty into Licentiousness, and their Courts of Justice into the madness of Revolutionary Tribunals."[44] The publication of the third printing of Jefferson's *Notes on the State of Virginia* on the eve of the election only served to confirm these fears about the future of the nation with a deist as president.[45] Despite Jefferson's clear victory in Virginia in 1796 and his narrow loss in the nation at large, many Virginians demonstrated their inability to separate their attitudes toward his political stance from their dislike of his religious opinions. Sectarians could not countenance the leader of a deistic "sect" as the president of the United States.

In the minds of many Virginians, deism was the ideology of a subversive religious group, and they described it as such. Episcopal Bishop William Meade later characterized the growth of liberal religion as if he were discussing yet another sectarian challenge.

> The grain of mustard-seed which was planted at Williamsburg, about the middle of the century, had taken root there and sprung up and spread its branches over the whole State,—the stock still enlarging and strengthening itself there, and the roots shooting deeper into the soil. At the end of the century the College of William and Mary was regarded as the hotbed of infidelity and of the wild politics of France.[46]

Meade, like many others, saw deism as an integrated movement with William and Mary as the institutional center and Jefferson and his friends as leaders. William and Mary was indeed the one institution that critics could identify as liberal in tone. Bishop James Madison still presided over the school that Jefferson and his colleagues had reformed in 1779, and most Virginians realized that the bishop's liberal Episcopalianism verged on deism.[47] But liberalism remained largely uninstitutionalized, completely dependent on its individual adherents rather than on the organizational momentum that helped to buoy other belief structures in Virginia.

Given that many leading liberals were not even in Virginia during most of the 1780s and 1790s, Meade's perceptions seem almost paradoxical. Jefferson only returned from France in 1789 and immediately plunged into his new duties as Washington's Secretary of State. Madison, Monroe, and Edmund Randolph also served in the national government.[48] George Wythe and St. George Tucker no longer sat in the legislature, being fully occupied by their duties on the bench. Yet for many sectarians the spread of liberal religious thought seemed to have a momentum of its own. It resembled a phenomenon familiar to all evangelicals: a religious revival. The national political prominence of Virginia's rationalists seemed to indicate that the entire country was in danger of being overcome by deist principles.

Yet these accusations had little apparent effect on Virginians' voting in the election of 1800. Sectarians seem to have willingly ignored the religious aspects of the political campaign. In 1798 Baptist minister David Barrow decided to move to Kentucky for economic reasons and wrote a letter to his congregation justifying his decision. His tract displays the ability of sectarians to accept Jeffersonian political principles while maintaining the truth of their own religious beliefs. Barrow expressed a desire that "all false doctrines and heretical principles, may clearly be discovered, and sink into darkness, where they belong," but he denied that statesmen must subscribe to any particular or even general religious creed, proclaiming that "all religious tests, and ecclesiastical establishments, are oppressive, and infring[e] the rights of conscience."[49]

Other sectarians drew a similar distinction between religious opinions and political policy. Jeremiah Moore, a prominent Baptist, wrote to Jefferson in 1800 asking him to provide a summary of his political principles. Moore recognized Jefferson's efforts during the disestablishment campaign but was troubled by recent charges that Jefferson was aristocratic in temperament.[50] Aristocracy, to the Baptists, connoted an established church; Moore simply wanted to make sure that Jefferson had not changed his sentiments on the subject since 1786. He was not concerned with Jefferson's rational theology as long as liberal leaders continued to espouse the separation of church and state.

This ability to differentiate between religious opinion and political policy marks the beginning of American "civil religion." The concept of a "desectarianized" civil authority emerged slowly after the Revolution, and the struggle for disestablishment and subsequent denominational battles strengthened support for a government that would not favor any sect. And if government possessed no power to assist or hurt the holders of one religious creed, then the particular religious opinions of politicians lost their importance. Before civil religion represented the religious ideals shared by most Americans, it sanctified differences between religious sects and politically active individuals. As long as government officers respected the general feelings, though not the specific theology, of the various denominations, they were free to act without fear of moral censure.[51] Thus in 1799, as Virginia Baptists prepared to vote overwhelmingly for a deist presidential candidate, the Baptist General Committee continued to "lament the spreading torrent of infidelity, which is overwhelming thousands of our countrymen, in its tremendous vortex of destruction."[52]

Why were Virginia sectarians unable to separate religion and politics in 1796 and four years later demonstrate such a nicety of distinction? The answer seems to be that in the last half of the 1790s, regardless of their inflammatory rhetoric, they became assured that liberal religious ideas posed no serious threat to their own position. The Presbyterians and Baptists went ahead with their own agendas during the decade and in the process realized that the "deist church" had some serious problems.

As always, Presbyterian leaders planned to consolidate gains made during the revivals by focusing their efforts on Virginia's schools. William Graham, the rector of Liberty Hall, sought every possible means of support for his school. Graham claimed that the school's connection with the Synod of Virginia, which now included teaching a divinity course, served to "enlarge the sphere of public usefulness" of Liberty Hall. He protested that "it is not the design of this institution to limit her protection and instruction to any particular description of youth" despite the "considerable pecuniary aids" and the "full share of their counsels and influence" given by the Presbyterian synod to the school. Nevertheless, Graham could not convince Virginians that Liberty Hall was anything but a Presbyterian institution.[53]

While Graham pursued his plans, the increasing disillusion of Jefferson and Madison with Federalist policies briefly stimulated them to turn their attention back to Virginia, and leading liberals talked among themselves in the early 1790s of making a concerted push for educational reform.[54] A collision between Jefferson and Graham was inevitable. Their confrontation pointed up the continuing competition between Presbyterians and liberals for Virginia's scarce educational resources. In 1796 George Washington offered his hundred shares in the stock of the James River Canal Company to fund a college in western Virginia.[55] Graham wrote to Washington promoting Liberty Hall in no uncertain terms. In recounting the school's history, Graham somehow omitted the information that it had been founded under Presbyterian auspices, that the trustees were all Presbyterians, and that the authorized divinity school of the Synod of Virginia operated in conjunction with the school.[56]

Graham's petition outraged Jefferson, who had his own plans for Washington's stock. He had proposed to Washington that his James River Company stock as well as his Potomac River Company stock go toward moving the College of Geneva to the District of Columbia.[57] Instead, the stock went to the Presbyterian school, Liberty Hall, whose director had always vociferously opposed liberal educational plans. Washington, however, wanted the Virginia school to prepare students to attend a university in the District of Columbia, the founding of which he encouraged with the gift of his Potomac River Company stock. He obviously knew of Liberty Hall's Presbyterian ties and gave the shares to the school in spite of the connection.

Graham's victory spurred Virginia liberals to renew their own campaign. This time, however, they struck at Liberty Hall itself. As it was introduced in the legislature, the liberal plan essentially proposed to reform Liberty Hall in much the same way that William and Mary had been transformed in 1779. To eradicate Presbyterian influence the theological school was abolished and a new Board of Visitors included no Presbyterian clergymen or laymen.[58] Thus, despite Jefferson's chagrin at Washington's decision, the Liberty Hall incident initially worked to the benefit of his education reforms. As earlier canvassing had proved, there was strong support for those reforms among legislators, including Wilson Cary Nicholas and Mann Page.[59] Members of the general public also threw their weight behind education reform. "Philanthropos" declared that if he was a member of the legislature he would immediately introduce a local school bill. He even suggested items upon which taxes could be levied in order to raise the sums necessary to create the system.[60]

In 1796 Jefferson and his friends came closer than ever before to realizing their educational plans for Virginia. Playing on the public reaction to Graham's sleight-of-hand in obtaining Washington's shares, they not only wrested Liberty Hall away from the Presbyterians but also introduced Jefferson's education bill again.[61] Yet the resulting legislation did not completely embody the desires of the liberal leadership. Each county was given the power to establish local schools as it saw fit, and most county leaders decided to provide only meager support for education. The cost of establishing such schools weighed as heavily in the decision as it had a decade before. By the 1790s Virginians were paying less in local taxes than they ever had before, thanks largely to the disestablishment of the Church.[62] Much of the opposition to implementing the optional education bill no doubt stemmed from financial concerns supplemented by class consciousness. Jefferson remarked that the legislation "would throw on wealth the education of the poor; and the justices, being generally of the more wealthy class, were unwilling to incur that burden." He was not surprised to find that "it was not suffered to commence in a single county."[63] Probably just as important as the perpetually troubling question of raising taxes was the fact that private academies had by now spread throughout the state. In the twenty years between the beginning of the Revolution and the passage of the 1796 act, the Assembly issued charters of incorporation for at least twenty schools. Virginians who valued education had committed themselves to supporting these institutions, may of which were associated with a particular religious group, usually either Episcopalian or Presbyterian. By implementing the provisions of the 1796 act, county justices would supplant the schools to which they sent their own sons.[64]

Shocked by the liberal success, Virginia Presbyterians concentrated their efforts on reclaiming Liberty Hall. Hampden-Sidney and Liberty Hall launched a campaign that presaged the Dartmouth College case of 1819, successfully arguing that the liberal-sponsored changes represented a violation of Liberty Hall's 1782 charter.[65] They eventually regained control of the school and the legislature repealed the act eliminating sectarian influence at Liberty Hall, but the ill-feeling aroused by the controversy proved too much for Graham, who resigned in September 1796.[66] At the end of 1796, Liberty Hall had Washington's shares, and liberals had a rather doubtful education act.

Baptists, unlike Presbyterians, did not usually take their suspicions of liberals into the legislature. They seemed largely unconcerned with education. After the passage of the "Statute for Establishing Religious Freedom," they agitated for the dissolution of the glebes, land set aside in each parish for the support of the Anglican minister.[67] As long as the glebes remained the property of the Episcopal Church, religious freedom had not been achieved in Virginia. Religious freedom was an absolute for Baptists, and until it had been achieved, the Episcopal Church was still established. The General Committee warned against concluding that "we are alarmed, when there is no danger near."[68] Yet the danger they apprehended arose from Episcopal, not deist, institutions.

After 1796, as Republican opposition to the Federalist administration began to coalesce, the glebe issue became more important because Baptist votes often determined the outcome of electoral contests. At the 1797 House of Delegates elections, candidates felt compelled to state their opinions on the subject. In Fairfax County, John Hunter tried to sidestep the issue, soliciting the voters' "indulgence for a suspension of my opinion until I hear the subject fully discussed." The fact that a rival candidate had already declared in favor of selling the glebes by act of Assembly ultimately impelled Hunter to opine that the judiciary rather than the legislature had jurisdiction over the issue.[69]

Hunter's opponent, Augustine Smith, immediately claimed that Hunter implicitly favored reserving the glebes to the Episcopal Church. He challenged Hunter's assertion that the Court of Appeals should decide the issue. Smith, like the Baptists, thought that the continued existence of the glebes probably contravened the Declaration of Right. He argued that they had been confirmed in Episcopal hands by the Assembly and therefore could be taken away by the same body.[70] The election of Jefferson in 1800 allowed the legislature to turn back to the glebes, and early in 1802 it passed an act directing the sale of all lands belonging to the former Established Church except those currently occupied by an incumbent.[71]

One last battle for the glebes ensued in 1804 when the Episcopal Church challenged the right of the overseers of the poor in Chesterfield County to sell the vacant glebe of Manchester Parish. George Wythe originally ruled in the case of *Turpin v. Lockett* that the law was constitutional, but the plaintiffs took the case to the Court of Appeals presided over by Edmund Pendleton. Pendleton, a staunch Episcopalian, thought the act unconstitutional, and two of the other four judges agreed. Of the remaining two, William Fleming disqualified himself because he was from Chesterfield County. Only Spencer Roane supported Wythe's decision. But in an event worthy of a melodrama, Pendleton died the night before the court was to render its judgment and the Assembly elected St. George Tucker to the bench. Tucker agreed with Roane and Wythe, and, as Fleming still determined to disqualify himself, the court was deadlocked. The decision of the lower court stood and the law was upheld.[72]

With the question of the glebes apparently settled once and for all, Virginia Baptists showed their gratitude to those liberals who had made the *Turpin v. Lockett* decision possible. In their arguments Baptists had continually referred to Jefferson's "Statute for Establishing Religious Freedom," and their attorneys were Philip Norborne Nicholas and George Hay, both intimately connected with Jefferson's intellectual circle. The Middle District Association approved funds to be used to "manifestly declare our respect" to Hay and Nicholas "for their signal and zealous services, rendered not only to us, but to every friend of liberty."[73] Once again, liberals and Baptists stood side-by-side in the fight for religious freedom.

The experiences by which Baptists and Presbyterians came to a realization of deist impotence were very different. Presbyterians met liberal educational initiatives head-on and defeated them. Baptists worked with liberals and discovered their usefulness as political allies and their limitations as religious proselytizers. During the 1790s, sectarian opinion of liberal religion and liberal politics changed. At the beginning of this process, the liberal political organization and the "deist church" seemed to be one and the same. Sectarians hearkened back to the pre-Revolutionary symbiosis between gentry and Church and found it difficult to believe that the religious liberals around Jefferson did not aim at a similar relationship with deism. Yet Jeffersonian deists remained a subgroup within the gentry, and the fame of the liberal leaders often eclipsed the lack of popular support for many of their policies.

Without Jefferson's "Temples of Reason," as opponents characterized his statewide system of education, the deist priesthood could not develop deist congregations, and the weakness of the deist movement in Virginia was underlined by the increasing involvement of many prominent rationalists in the new federal government. By 1800 Jefferson was clearly cast as a national political leader, not as a Virginia religious figure. Sectarians might ritually decry the growth of deism, but they were setting up a straw man. When the Great Revival burst upon the scene soon thereafter, the strength of Virginia sectarians and the weakness of her deists was exposed for all to see.

Notes

1. In this chapter I use the term "liberal" to denote holders of rational or deist religious beliefs, not in the more general sociopolitical sense of scholars such as Joyce Appleby.

2. See Paul K. Conkin, "The Religious Pilgrimage of Thomas Jefferson," in *Jeffersonian Legacies*, ed. Peter S. Onuf (Charlottesville: University Press of Virginia, 1993), 19-49.

3. See Rhys Isaac, *The Transformation of Virginia, 1740-1790* (Chapel Hill: Institute of Early American History and Culture; University of North Carolina Press, 1982).

4. Letter from William Bledsoe to Robert Carter, 19 May 1790, Robert Carter Papers, Virginia Baptist Historical Society.

5. William Fristoe, *A Concise History of the Ketocton Baptist Association* (Staunton, Va., 1808), 66.

6. Samuel Henley, *The Distinct Claims of Government and Religion, considered in a Sermon preached before the Honorable House of Burgesses, at Williamsburg, in Virginia, March 1, 1772* (London, 1772), 5-6, 16.

7. "Timoleon," *Virginia Gazette* (Purdie and Dixon), 22 August 1771.

8. James Turner, *Without God, Without Creed: The Origins of Unbelief in America* (Baltimore: Johns Hopkins University Press, 1985), 53-64.

9. "Part of Sir John Randolph's Will," *William and Mary Quarterly*, 2d ser., 4 (1924): 287.

10. Henley, *Distinct Claims of Government and Religion*, 11-12.

11. James Reid, "The Religion of the Bible and the Religion of K[ing] W[illiam] County Compared," in *The Colonial Virginia Satirist: Mid-Eighteenth Century Commentaries on Politics, Religion, and Society*, ed. Richard Beale Davis, *Transactions of the American Philosophical Society*, n.s., 57, pt. 1 (Philadelphia, 1967): 52.

12. See Thomas E. Buckley, *Church and State in Revolutionary Virginia, 1776-1787* (Charlottesville: University Press of Virginia, 1977).

13. James McClurg served as professor of medicine, Robert Andrews as professor of moral philosophy, and Charles Bellini as professor of modern languages. On Charles Bellini, see "Charles Bellini, First Professor of Modern Languages in an American College," *William and Mary Quarterly*, 2d ser., 5 (1925): 1-29. See also letter from John Page to St. George Tucker, 28 September 1776, Tucker-Coleman Papers, College of William and Mary.

14. Ronald L. Hatzenbuehler, "Growing Weary in Well-Doing: Thomas Jefferson's Life Among the Virginia Gentry," *Virginia Magazine of History and Biography* 101 (1993): 24-32.

15. *Virginia Gazette* (Dixon & Nicolson), 11, 18 September 1779. "Social Christian" was probably a conservative Anglican reacting to Jefferson's plan to disestablish the Church.

16. *Virginia Gazette* (Dixon & Nicolson), 27 November 1779. See also *Virginia Gazette or Weekly Advertiser*, 16 February 1782.

17. *Kentucky Gazette*, 1 September 1787.

18. *Henry Toler Journal*, 15 July 1783, typescript copy at the Virginia Baptist Historical Society, University of Richmond, Richmond, Virginia; *Religious Petitions*

(from Westmoreland County), 2 November 1785, Virginia State Library. A similar petition came from Amherst County, 10 December 1785.

19. *The Papers of Thomas Jefferson*, ed. Julian P. Boyd et al., 27 vols. to date (Princeton, N.J.: Princeton University Press, 1950-), 2:545-546. For a summary of Jefferson's opinions of moral philosophy and religion and the best method of studying them, see letter from Thomas Jefferson to Peter Carr, 10 August 1787, *Papers of Jefferson*, 12:14-17.

20. *The Journal and Letters of Francis Asbury*, ed. Elmer T. Clark, 3 vols. (Nashville: Abingdon Press, 1958), I:696 (15 October 1791).

21. Asbury, *Journal and Letters*, I:732 (October 1792).

22. Letter from William Bledsoe to Robert Carter, 19 May 1790, Robert Carter Papers, Virginia Baptist Historical Society.

23. *Minutes of the Middle District Association* . . . (Richmond, Va., 1791), 6.

24. Devereux Jarratt, *The Life of the Reverend Devereux Jarratt, Rector of Bath Parish, Dinwiddie County, Virginia* (Baltimore, Md., 1806), 107-109.

25. Wesley M. Gewehr, *The Great Awakening in Virginia, 1740-1790* (Durham, N.C.: Duke University Press, 1930), 168-173; *Minutes of the Methodist Conferences, Annually Held in America, from 1773 to 1794, Inclusive* (Philadelphia, 1795), 144-148.

26. Robert B. Semple, *A History of the Rise and Progress of the Baptists in Virginia* (Richmond, Va., 1810), 388-389, 408; Robert G. Gardner, "Virginia Baptist Statistics 1699-1790," *Virginia Baptist Register* 21 (1982): 1020-1035. On the revival among the Baptists, see Semple, *Rise and Progress*, 36-39.

27. Minutes of the Virginia Synod, 22 October 1788, 26 September 1794, Union Theological Seminary, Richmond, Virginia.

28. John Leland, "The Virginia Chronicle," in *The Writings of the Late Elder John Leland*, ed. L.F. Greene (1845; reprint, New York: Arno Press, 1969), 105n.

29. Robert Boyle C. Howell, *The Early Baptists of Virginia* (Philadelphia: Bible and Publication Society, 1857), 125.

30. *Minutes of the Baptist General Committee* . . . (Richmond, 1791), 7. See Gary B. Nash, "The American Clergy and the French Revolution," *William and Mary Quarterly*, 3d ser., 22 (1965): 392-412.

31. Semple, *Rise and Progress*, 143. On the development of the Republican Party in Virginia, see Harry Ammon, "The Formation of the Republican Party in Virginia, 1789-1796," *Journal of Southern History* 19 (1953): 283-310; Norman Risjord and Gordon DenBoer, "The Evolution of Political Parties in Virginia, 1782-1800," *Journal of American History* 60 (1974): 961-984. The Goshen District Association perceived the Jay Treaty as particularly dangerous to American liberty.

32. William Wirt Henry, *Patrick Henry: Life, Correspondence and Speeches*, 3 vols. (New York: Wm. S. Martien, 1891), II:490.

33. Letter from Archibald Blair to Patrick Henry, 13 January 1799, in *Henry: Life, Correspondence and Speeches*, III:427.

34. William Henry Foote, *Sketches of Virginia, Historical and Biographical*, second series (Philadelphia: J.B. Lippincott, 1857), 181.

35. *Virginia Gazette and General Advertiser*, 10, 24 December 1794.

36. William Hill, *Autobiographical Sketches of Dr. William Hill* (Richmond, Va.: Union Theological Seminary Library, 1968), 91.

37. See John B. Boles, *The Great Revival, 1787-1805* (Lexington: University Press of Kentucky, 1972), 12-21.

38. Letter from George Smith to Isaac Backus, 15 May 1797, original letter at Virginia Baptist Historical Society. See also *The Diaries of Isaac Backus*, ed. William G. McLoughlin, 3 vols. (Providence, R.I.: Brown University Press, 1979), III:1254 n. 3.

39. *Columbian Mirror and Alexandria Gazette*, 28 February 1795.

40. *Columbian Mirror and Alexandria Gazette*, 4 October 1796.

41. *Columbian Mirror and Alexandria Gazette*, 7 May 1795.

42. *Columbian Mirror and Alexandria Gazette*, 27 October 1796.

43. *Columbian Mirror and Alexandria Gazette*, 29 October 1796.

44. *Columbian Mirror and Alexandria Gazette*, 5 November 1796.

45. The volume was published in Baltimore, but its publishers advertised for subscribers throughout Virginia. See, for example, *Virginia Gazette and Petersburg Intelligencer*, 13 September 1796.

46. William Meade, *Old Churches, Ministers and Families of Virginia,* 2 vols. (Philadelphia, 1857), I:175.

47. Charles Crowe, "Bishop James Madison and the Republic of Virtue," *Journal of Southern History* 30 (1964): 58-61.

48. Madison sat in the House of Representatives, Monroe served as a senator from Virginia until 1794, when he became minister to France, and Randolph was Attorney General until 1793, when he replaced Jefferson as Secretary of State.

49. Carlos R. Allen, Jr., ed., "David Barrow's *Circular Letter* of 1798," *William and Mary Quarterly*, 3d ser., 20 (1963): 448-450.

50. Letter from Jeremiah Moore to Thomas Jefferson, 12 July 1800, typescript copy at Virginia Baptist Historical Society.

51. This is essentially the position taken by Sidney Mead. It should be noted, however, that this concept of separation can be seen as the first step in a continuing process. From this beginning it is possible to move, as other historians have pointed out, toward a cult of secular heroes or toward a deification of the nation as a whole. These positions may be found in *American Civil Religion*, ed. Russell E. Richey and Donald G. Jones (New York: Harper & Row, 1974). See also Sidney Mead, *The Nation With the Soul of a Church* (New York: Harper & Row, 1975).

52. "Circular Letter, on the Observance of a Christian Sabbath," *Minutes of the General Committee . . .* (Richmond, 1799), 5.

53. *Virginia Gazette or General Advertiser*, 18 December 1793. The synod decided to establish a theological seminary in 1791. It went into operation just before Graham felt compelled to issue his disclaimer. *Minutes of the Synod of Virginia*, 29-30 September 1791, 27 September 1793.

54. See letters from the Right Reverend James Madison to James Madison, Jr., 12 November, and 24 December 1794, in *The Papers of James Madison*, ed. William T. Hutchinson et al., 17 vols. to date (Chicago: University of Chicago Press, 1962-), 15:374, 422 [hereinafter *Papers of Madison*]; letter from Thomas Jefferson to Wilson Nicholas, 22 November 1794, in *The Writings of Thomas Jefferson*, ed. Andrew A. Lipscomb and Albert Ellery Bergh, 20 vols. (Washington, D.C.: Thomas Jefferson Memorial Association, 1904-05), 9:291-292 [hereinafter *Writings of Jefferson*].

55. Howard Miller, *The Revolutionary College: American Presbyterian Higher Education, 1707-1837* (New York: New York University Press, 1976), 154-156. For

Washington's letter about the shares, see letter from George Washington to Governor Robert Brooke, 16 March 1795, in *The Writings of George Washington*, ed. John E. Fitzpatrick, 39 vols. (Washington, D.C., 1931-44), 34:149-150.

56. The pertinent records of the board of trustees and Graham's letter to Washington are reprinted in Foote, *Sketches of Virginia*, first series, 479-482.

57. Jefferson sent the proposal to Washington by way of Madison. See letter from Thomas Jefferson to James Madison, 23 February 1795, *Papers of Madison*, 15:479-480; letter from Thomas Jefferson to George Washington, 23 February 1795, *Writings of Jefferson*, 19:108-114.

58. *Journal of the House of Delegates*, 21 December 1796. For the text of the act, see *The Statutes at Large of Virginia, from October session 1792, to December session 1806, inclusive, in three volumes, being a continuation of Hening*, ed. Samuel Shepherd, 3 vols. (Richmond, Va.: Samuel Shepherd, 1835-6), II:44-45 (1796).

59. Letter from Thomas Jefferson to Mann Page, 30 August 1795, *Writings of Jefferson*, 9:306.

60. *Virginia Gazette and General Advertiser*, 9 December 1795.

61. *Journal of the House of Delegates*, 15 November, 22 December 1796.

62. H. James Henderson, "Taxation and Political Culture: Massachusetts and Virginia, 1760-1800," *William and Mary Quarterly*, 3d ser., 47 (1990): 103, 110-112.

63. Jefferson, "Autobiography," *Writings of Jefferson*, 1:71-72.

64. Sadie Bell, *The Church, the State, and Education in Virginia* (1930; reprint, New York: Arno Press, 1969), 168-169. Another thirty schools were incorporated between 1796 and 1810.

65. *The College of Hampden Sidney: Calendar of Board Minutes 1776-1876*, ed. Alfred J. Morrison (Richmond, Va., 1912), 48 (27 November 1797).

66. Shepherd, *Statutes at Large*, II:108-109 (1798); Foote, *Sketches of Virginia*, first series, 477-478.

67. For a detailed account of the Baptist and the glebes, see Thomas E. Buckley, "Evangelicals Triumphant: The Baptists' Assault on the Virginia Glebes, 1786-1801," *William and Mary Quarterly*, 3d ser., 45 (1988): 33-69.

68. *Columbian Mirror and Alexandria Gazette*, 25 June 1795.

69. *Columbian Mirror and Alexandria Gazette*, 23 March 1797.

70. *Columbian Mirror and Alexandria Gazette*, 4 April 1797.

71. Shepherd, *Statutes at Large*, II:314-316 (1802).

72. David John Mays, *Edmund Pendleton, 1721-1803: A Biography*, 2 vols. (Cambridge, Mass.: Harvard University Press, 1952), II:337-345.

73. *Minutes of the Middle District Association* . . . (Richmond, 1804), 4.

Part II

Theological and Philosophical Influences on Jefferson and Madison

Chapter 3

The Religious Beliefs of Thomas Jefferson

Charles B. Sanford

Thomas Jefferson's life confronts student and scholar alike with several puzzling contradictions. He was an aristocrat who championed the rights of the common man; a slave owner who bitterly attacked the institution of slavery; and a classical scholar who was also a scientist, architect, and inventor. He was a foreign diplomat and an isolationist president. He was a scrupulously moral person who has been accused of keeping a slave mistress. He was a pious man and regular church attender who harshly criticized organized religion.[1]

When one considers Jefferson's religion, one encounters even more questions and controversies. Today, Jefferson is revered for championing human rights and establishing religious freedom, but in his own time he was attacked as an "atheist, deist, or devil."[2] During the presidential campaign of 1800 many political pamphlets and newspaper articles were circulated attacking Jefferson as an "infidel and atheist."[3] Alexander Hamilton called Jefferson "an *Atheist* in Religion and a *Fanatic* in politics."[4] Numerous sermons were preached warning that if Jefferson was elected president, he would discredit religion, overthrow the church, and destroy the Bible. Upon hearing of Jefferson's election to the presidency, people in New England actually hid their Bibles to save them.[5] Jefferson's reputation as an atheist dogged him all his life, and to this day many people believe he was an atheist. As late as 1830, the Philadelphia public library refused a place on its shelves for books about Jefferson for this reason.[6]

In actuality, none of these charges against Jefferson were true. He attended church regularly, using his own well-worn prayer book. He and his family were baptized, married, and buried by the Anglican church, as recorded in the family Bible.[7] He was elected vestryman of his local church, and he supported the church generously. He wrote in his account book, "I have subscribed to the building [of] an Episcopalian church, two hundred dollars; a Presbyterian church, sixty dollars; and a Baptist church, twenty-five dollars."[8] Jefferson probably drew the plans for the Episcopal church in question.[9]

While president, Jefferson attended divine services in the House of Representatives—a practice his enemies sourly dismissed as nothing more than political expediency.[10] After his retirement to Monticello, Jefferson continued to attend church services, riding into Charlottesville on horseback carrying a small folding chair of his own invention. He described these services in a letter to Thomas Cooper: "In our village of Charlottesville, there is a good degree of religion, with a small spice only of fanaticism. We have four sects, but without either church or meeting-house. The court-house is the common temple, one Sunday in the month to each. Here, Episcopalian and Presbyterian, Methodist and Baptist, meet together, join in hymning their Maker, listen with attention and devotion to each others' preachers, and all mix in society with perfect harmony."[11]

The "Jefferson Bible"

Far from seeking to destroy the Bible, as his enemies charged, Jefferson had a lifelong interest in reading and studying the Bible. One of his earliest childhood recollections was of being called upon to say the Lord's Prayer for company before dinner. He also remembered being taught his prayers by his mother and the sung psalms of the Anglican church by a beloved older sister, Jane. This early training gave him a lifelong appreciation of devotional religion.[12]

In his later years, Jefferson wrote to a friend: "I never go to bed without an hour or half hour's previous reading of something moral, whereon to ruminate in the intervals of sleep."[13] The book he chose most often for these devotions was a Bible he had made himself by cutting out favorite passages from the Bible and pasting them in a bound volume. In times of crisis, Jefferson turned to the Bible. When his daughter Polly died, leaving only his oldest daughter Martha surviving of all his six children, he was found with the Bible in his hands seeking consolation. When he was dying, Jefferson was heard by his family to pray, quoting from the Bible, "Lord, now lettest thou thy servant depart in peace."[14]

When he was president, Jefferson wrote of studying the Bible at night after working on state papers. He called his study "The Philosophy of Jesus of Nazareth" and said it was an "abstract from the Evangelists of whatever has the stamp of the eloquence and fine imagination of Jesus."[15] It was made, he wrote, "by cutting the texts out of the book, and arranging them on the pages of a blank book, in a certain order of time or subject. A more beautiful or precious morsel of ethics I have never seen."[16] This work has been lost to posterity except for the title page and a few sheets which turned up at a book auction in 1934. Fortunately, when Henry S. Randall was writing his early biography of Jefferson, he heard of "Jefferson's Bible" and published a description of it, along with a list of its contents, which was furnished by Jefferson's grandson, George Wythe Randolph.[17]

Jefferson was so reticent about his religion that even his family did not learn of his Biblical studies until after his death when a more elaborate version, bound in red morocco leather with gold lettering, was found by a grandson in his library.[18] It was entitled, "The Life and Morals of Jesus of Nazareth," and consisted of Jefferson's clippings from New Testament Greek, Latin, French, and English translations (all of which Jefferson read) arranged in four parallel columns.[19] This work might also have been lost to posterity had it not been for the bibliographic detective work of Smithsonian Institution librarian Cyrus Adler. Learning of the existence of a "Jefferson Bible" by finding the mutilated New Testaments used by Jefferson, he eventually located the work in the possession of Jefferson's great-granddaughter and arranged for its purchase by the United States National Museum. A limited edition exactly reproducing the work—red morocco binding, gold edges, and all—was printed. Numerous editions of "Jefferson's Bible" have since been printed.[20]

Actually, it is misleading to call Jefferson's work a "Bible" since he included passages only from the "Evangelists," that is, the Gospels of Matthew, Mark, Luke, and John. He purposely omitted the Epistles of Paul, which contain so much theology, and the Book of Revelation, with its mysticisms and dreams. He also omitted all of the Old Testament.[21] "Jefferson's Bible" is essentially a "Harmony of the Gospels" similar to those still used in seminaries today.

Jefferson's aim in editing his own New Testament was to discover the real teachings of Jesus and reveal the true person of Jesus Christ. He believed that the Gospels contained "mysticisms, fancies and falsehoods" and that ignorant biographers and corrupt followers "distorted and deformed" Jesus and his teachings.[22] Garrett Ward Sheldon comments that Jefferson extracted "those portions of the Gospels which presented the ethics in their purest, most simple form. Ironically, it was his abiding and reverent belief in these Christian ethical teachings that led Jefferson to criticize the institutionalized church, but which also led many to question his religious sincerity."[23]

Jefferson was influenced in this enterprise by his friends Charles Thompson and Joseph Priestley who also made and sent to him copies of their "Harmonies of the Gospels." In these early harmonies, Jefferson and his friends took small parts of the life or teachings of Christ from each of the Gospel accounts, weaving them together into one narrative in such a way, Jefferson said, as to avoid "long repetitions of the same transaction."[24] Later Biblical scholars arranged in parallel columns the same incidents and sayings found in the four Gospels. Jefferson used four columns to compare different translations of the same passage. By minutely comparing in parallel columns the "repetitious" four gospel accounts, passage by passage and word for word, later scholars labored to establish which were the earlier and more authentic parts of the New Testament and thus indicate the original person, Jesus, and His true words. Jefferson similarly sought to identify the authentic words of Christ.[25]

Because of his Enlightenment studies, Jefferson possessed many of the tools of Biblical criticism. He read and admired the Greek philosophers and dramatists in the original Greek, and read Roman historians such as Livy and Cicero in Latin. He also read and studied the church fathers and Greek mythology. He used his knowledge of the Greco-Roman world of New Testament times to study the Bible in the manner of Biblical scholars today. Descartes, Spinoza, Grotius, Ernesti, and Diderot were Enlightenment authors studied by Jefferson who called for a critical and historical study of the Bible.[26]

"Jefferson's Bible" has been regarded by most scholars as an interesting but unimportant curiosity. However, a close study of the passages Jefferson selected and rejected for inclusion in the document reveals many clues to his religious beliefs. From the titles he gave his studies ("Philosophy of Jesus" and "Life and Morals of Jesus"), it is immediately apparent that Jefferson thought of the Christian religion as a philosophy and a body of ethical teachings rather than a mystery known by faith. In the system Jefferson devised in 1815 for his extensive personal library (still used by the Library of Congress), Jefferson catalogued books on religion under the subject "moral philosophy."[27]

"Jefferson's Bible" reflects the same emphasis on morality, reason, and intellect over faith, dogma, and emotion that is found in many of his other writings. Throughout his "Bible," Jefferson chose passages that appealed to his interest in moral lessons and omitted the theological and miraculous sections. To Jefferson and his Enlightenment friends, miracles violated God's laws of nature, something they were sure God would never do. Such was the opinion of many of Jefferson's deistic friends in France who were seeking to reform the monarchy and the Catholic state church. To these rationalists, Jesus' virgin birth and other miracles reported in the New Testament did not prove him to be the Son of God, but revealed him to be an "illegitimate imposter."[28]

Rejecting both the idea that Jesus was divine and the opposite argument that he was an impostor, Jefferson believed that Christ was the "best preacher" of a religious truth that "contains no mystery [and] needs no explanation,"[29] the "first of human sages" whose teachings were greater than those of Socrates or other ancient philosophers,[30] and "the most eloquent and sublime character" ever seen by man.[31] In the writings of Jesus' biographers, Jefferson found "sublime ideas of the Supreme Being, aphorisms, and precepts of the purest morality and benevolence, sanctioned by a life of humility, innocence, and simplicity of manners, neglect of riches, absence of worldly ambition and honors, with an eloquence and persuasiveness which have not been surpassed."[32] The passages Jefferson selected for his "Bible" reflect these beliefs about Jesus Christ.

It is instructive to compare "Jefferson's Bible" with a "Harmony of the Gospels" used in modern seminaries. In one I used in seminary, William Stevens and Ernest Burton arranged all the passages from the Gospels into 151 sections.[33] Jefferson included all or parts of 81 of these sections in his "Bible." These passages are evenly divided between sections about incidents in the life of Christ (41) and sections dealing with the teachings of Christ (40). This fact alone indicates how much of Jesus' life, in Jefferson's estimation, was concerned with being a teacher.[34]

True to his liberal convictions, Jefferson rejected the atonement passages of the New Testament, which see Jesus as the means of redemption of sinful man from the wrath of God by the sacrifice of Christ on the cross. It was by design, not accident, that Jefferson omitted from his "Bible" all of the writings of St. Paul. He copied approvingly in his student "commonplace" notebook this explanation of Pauline theology by the eighteenth-century English deist philosopher, Henry Saint-John, Viscount Bolingbroke:

> God sent his only begotten son, who had not offended him, to be sacrificed by men, who had offended him, that he might expiate their sins, and satisfy his own anger. Surely . . . god would have been satisfied, more agreeably to his mercy and goodness, without any expiation, upon the repentance of the offenders, and more agreeably to his justice with any other expiation rather than this.[35]

Jefferson commented, "he [Jesus] preaches the efficacy of repentance towards forgiveness of sin; I require a counterpoise of good works to redeem it."[36]

Reflecting his conviction that among Jesus' chief purposes was to reform religion and society in his own times, Jefferson included in his "Bible" many of Jesus' conflicts with the Jewish Scribes and Pharisees. He also devoted one tenth of the whole narrative to the New Testament account of Jesus' betrayal, arrest, trial, and tragic death. Elsewhere, Jefferson summed up the life of Jesus in this way:

> His parentage was obscure; his condition poor; his education null; his natural endowments great; his life correct and innocent: he was meek, benevolent, patient, firm, disinterested, and of the sublimest eloquence. . . . According to the ordinary fate of those who attempt to enlighten and reform mankind, he fell an early victim to the jealousy and combination of the altar and the throne, at about thirty-three years of age, his reason having not yet attained the *maximum* of its energy, nor the course of his preaching, which was but of three years at most, presented occasions for developing a complete system of morals.[37]

It was sinful men, not God, who killed Jesus. Here, Jefferson's "Bible" ends. Jefferson was true to his belief that Jesus was not a divine being but the greatest man that ever lived, for he omits the New Testament accounts of Jesus' resurrection, subsequent appearances, and ascension.

Some critics have charged that Jefferson's view of Christ was one-sided,[38] but it supported his vision of building a free, democratic, and enlightened country on this continent where people might develop their own potential using the abundant resources of God's creation free from the exploitation of nobles and priests. Jefferson began what was to be a long tradition in liberal American churches of trying to promote a vision of Jesus' moral and ethical teachings in the nation's political and social order. (It is not surprising that Jefferson saw a similarity between Jesus' struggles against the religious and political authorities in Jerusalem during the first century and his own struggle for religious freedom and political reform in eighteenth-century America, especially since at the very time he was working on his "Bible" he was smarting under abuse from political and religious opponents to his presidency.)[39] Granted, the task that Jefferson attempted, of reforming a simple agrarian society facing problems (such as creating democracy, overcoming slavery, and pursuing peace during the Napoleonic wars) according to the moral teachings of Jesus Christ, was monumental. This task was even more complex and difficult in the industrial age of the "robber barons" that followed, to say nothing of present global involvements. It is significant, however, that, just as there arose later generations of politicians and statesmen who followed Jeffersonian ideals for political and social change, there also arose later religious leaders who tried to apply the ethical reforms of Jesus Christ to American society as Jefferson had done. Jefferson thought in terms of the Enlightenment; Walter Rauschenbusch, in 1900 New York sweatshops, proclaimed the "Social Gospel"; Protestant church leaders today advocate "Christian Social Action" for social justice, racial integration, and a world free from hunger; and Catholic theologians write about "Liberation Theology." While there are interesting differences, as well as similarities, among these later liberal religious movements, their goals, emphases, and points of view are essentially Jeffersonian, according to Arthur Schlesinger, Jr.[40]

In his "Bible," Jefferson stressed Jesus' ethical teachings in the Sermon on the Mount and the Golden Rule.[41] So did later theologians. The remarkable thing is that Jefferson adopted so early many of the same ideas about religion and social reform that later religious liberals and activists espoused. As Schlesinger observed, Jeffersonian liberalism can be traced in American religion as well as in politics, although few scholars have noted this fact. Although Jefferson was criticized during his own lifetime and later for his liberal ideas about Christ, the account of Jesus that inspired him—of a great and good man of the highest ideals and simple, yet profound, teachings who died bravely for his beliefs, thereby promoting their continuation—has had a strong appeal to Americans through the years. Jefferson was among the few great men in history who not only studied and wrote about the meaning of the words and example of Jesus Christ for the human condition, but also used his beliefs about Jesus as a guide to accomplish needed social reforms. He was both a thinker and a doer.

To sum up, Jefferson valued religion for its moral codes, perhaps because of his legal training. As a scholar, he admired religion as a philosophy. Jefferson was an intellectual, and he thought reason was most important in religion. When his nephew Peter Carr left home to attend college, Jefferson advised him to make good use of his reason in his studies and in religion. He urged Carr to examine fearlessly all ideas of Christianity before the "tribunal of reason." "Do not be frightened from this enquiry by any fear of it's [sic] consequences," he wrote.[42] Reason results in a stronger religion than simply faith and revelation.

Importance of Reason

Jefferson often wrote of reason as the guide to his own religious thought and believed it was the means by which all people could know religious truth.[43] "[E]very man's reason," he wrote, "[is] his own rightful umpire."[44] To give up thinking for oneself was "the last degradation of a free and moral agent."[45]

This high confidence in reason and intellect in all matters, including religion, reveals that Jefferson was a true disciple of the Enlightenment. Isaac Newton, Francis Bacon, and John Locke were the heroes of the age. While displaying a prized painting of his heroes to Alexander Hamilton, Jefferson expressed his belief that they were "the three greatest men the world had ever produced," having laid the foundation of the physical and moral sciences. Hamilton, after a long pause, rejoined in typical fashion that he regarded Julius Caesar as "the greatest man that ever lived."[46]

Bacon was honored because he championed the modern scientific method of detailed observation of facts and logical analysis instead of the medieval method of theological synthesis. Jefferson early developed a knack for observation, as Bacon recommended. All his life, for example, he kept methodical records of the weather and his plantation crops and plants. His first published book, *Notes on the State of Virginia*, is filled with observations of the flora and fauna of Virginia, as well as reports on its people and customs.[47]

Jefferson saw Newton as the great thinker who pioneered the laws of the physical sciences and unlocked the secrets of the movements of the stars. The law of gravity seems pretty mundane to us today; but the discovery that the force that caused the apple to fall from the tree and held humans and animals firmly in their places on this round earth was the same force that guided the sun and moon and heavenly bodies in their appointed courses and could be formulated as a mathematical law came as a thunderclap revelation to people of the Enlightenment. All through the ages, mankind was helpless before the cataclysmic forces of nature caused by the wrath of the gods. Now it was seen that people could learn the laws by which the forces of nature operated and could be forever freed from fear and superstition. Newton believed that understanding the laws of nature revealed "the greater glory of God." Others hoped or feared that God would be dispensed with altogether. This dispute between science and religion continues to this day.[48]

Jefferson valued Locke because he sought to apply to the social and political arena the same principles of thought and knowledge that Newton and Bacon had applied to the physical world. As a social philosopher and statesman, Jefferson wanted to identify moral and social laws similar to the laws of nature which would help overcome the social and moral problems that impeded progress in creating the new American democracy.[49]

The important element in the thinking of all three of his intellectual heroes—Bacon, Newton, and Locke—was reason. Reason banished ignorance and superstition and led to knowledge and the advancement of progress in both science and religion.[50] To a clergyman friend Jefferson wrote: "truth and reason are eternal. They have prevailed. And they will eternally prevail."[51] Reason also was important in matters of religion, Jefferson believed, because it protected people against fanaticism. Jefferson relied on the reason bestowed on each person by God as the final "umpire of truth" in an argument with Miles King, who wrote to him trying to save him from atheism.[52] The chief question of this conflict over religion, which pursued Jefferson all his life, concerned the basis of authority in religion. The medieval church and evangelical groups stressed faith and revelation; Jefferson's new world of Newton, Bacon, and Locke stressed reason. The argument persists to this day.

Another important function of reason in religion, Jefferson argued, was to protect against "an indulgence in speculations hyperphysical and antiphysical,

[that] so uselessly occupy and disquiet the mind . . . plunging into the fathomless abyss of dreams and phantasms" of "deluded imagination."[53] Jefferson blamed the "whimsies of Plato's own foggy brain" for influencing early Christianity away from the simple teachings of Christ.[54] As a true believer in the Enlightenment, Jefferson thus sought to reform the church and society by the light of reason and to clear away the accumulated rubbish of religious superstition.[55]

Thomas Jefferson, thus, early came to believe that the "God of nature" had given the inner "oracle of reason" to each person as the true guide to religious insight. He worshiped this God and followed that oracle all his life.

Jefferson and the Rights of Man

The philosophers of the American Revolution searched for an argument that would undercut the old theory of the "divine right" of kings and cardinals to rule over the common people, which had been the foundation of medieval society. At the very end of his life, in a letter written to be read on the fiftieth anniversary of the signing of the "Declaration of Independence," Jefferson put the argument against the divine right of kings in ringing terms: "All eyes are opened, or opening, to the rights of man. . . . [T]he mass of mankind has not been born with saddles on their backs, nor a favored few booted and spurred, ready to ride them legitimately, by the grace of God."[56] In opposing the idea that God had given certain royal families or religious leaders a divine right to rule over other people at a certain period in history, the defenders of the American Revolution, such as Jefferson and Thomas Paine, went back to the creation of all people, free and equal, by the hand of God. Their belief in human rights and democracy was rooted in a religious belief in the Creator and the nature of man created by God. They then went on to elaborate the rights all people possessed by their God-created human nature, their "natural rights." These were rights that government could not take away. This was the "self-evident truth" upon which all else depended. So said Jefferson in the first sentence of the second paragraph of the "Declaration of Independence" into which he "managed to compress a cosmology, a political philosophy, [and] a national creed," to use Merrill D. Peterson's felicitous phrase.[57] John Locke theorized that these were the rights to hold on to one's life, to individual liberty, and to property improved by one's labor. Interestingly, Jefferson revised Locke's list of rights from "life, liberty, and property" to "life, liberty, and the pursuit of happiness," a more inclusive and suggestive phrase which, for good or ill, has characterized the American dream ever since.[58]

According to the Whigs, men soon came to see the advantages of living in society in order to protect these natural rights. Government thus was the result of a "social contract" to protect the natural rights of men; but if the contract was broken by the king, then the people had the right to overthrow him, just as Parliament had removed James II. Jefferson used the same argument against King George III in the "Declaration of Independence."[59]

With Jefferson's humanitarian interest in people and his lawyerly interest in government and society, it is not surprising that he devoted his life to the social and political reforms he thought necessary to enhance man's free enjoyment of his natural rights. He favored the extension of the vote to more people. He reformed Virginia's laws of inheritance to discourage the establishment of a landed aristocracy patterned after the English gentry.[60] He favored universal education to encourage the true aristocracy of "virtue and talents" instead of "an artificial aristocracy, founded on wealth and birth." "The natural aristocracy [of virtue and talents]," he wrote, "I consider as the most precious gift of nature, for . . . [the] government of society. . . . The artificial aristocracy is a mischievous ingredient in government, and provision should be made to prevent its ascendency."[61]

Jefferson always believed in the fundamental goodness and rationality of mankind, in contrast to those who believed that the mass of men were foolish, evil, and not to be trusted with self-government. He wrote to John Adams that he thought all through history people could be divided into "Whigs" (or democrats) and "Tories" (or aristocrats) on this basis.[62] He explained to another friend:

> The doctrines of Europe were, that men in numerous associations cannot be restrained within the limits of order and justice, but by forces physical and moral, wielded over them by authorities independent of their will. Hence their organization of kings, hereditary nobles, and priests. . . . We believed . . . that man was a rational animal, endowed by nature with rights, and with an innate sense of justice; and that he could be restrained from wrong and protected in right, by moderate powers, confided to persons of his own choice, and held to their duties by dependence on his own will.[63]

Jefferson had no high opinion of the aristocracy. He once wryly commented that he had not observed that wealth increased a man's intelligence. After close observation at the courts of England and France, he concluded that kings are like barn animals—pampered, overfed, and taught never to think. "[I]n a few generations they become all body and no mind. . . . And so endeth the book of Kings, from all of whom the Lord deliver us."[64]

Is There a God?

The question naturally arises, how could Jefferson base his argument for independence and democracy on the God-created nature of man if he did not believe in God? Was he really the French atheist his opponents charged? The charge seemed plausible. He had spent several years in France. He spoke and read French fluently, and was a good friend to many of the French reformers who were considered atheists. Jefferson never consented to the vilification of the French atheists. He knew them to be honorable men. Those reacting against traditional religion in Protestant countries with a long history of reform, he observed, had generally turned to deism, but in Roman Catholic France, where there was much more oppression, the reformers turned to atheism.[65]

To most religious people, especially Jefferson's enemies, there was little difference among an atheist, deist, or infidel. All were suspected of being nonbelievers, opponents of Christianity, and dangerous to society. Jefferson vigorously defended himself against the charge of being an atheist or deist in the derogatory sense.[66] But in the intellectual sense of being one who believed in the Deity as opposed to an atheist who did not, Jefferson was a staunch deist. His religious thought was steeped in the ideas of the English deists, Baron Herbert of Cherbury, Charles Blount, Matthew Tindal, John Toland, and Conyers Middleton.[67] His religious writings indicated a special debt to Lord Bolingbroke and Joseph Priestley, whom he had "read . . . over and over again." They formed "the basis of my own faith," he wrote to Adams.[68] Jefferson further explained to Adams his distinction between atheists and deists. The atheists say:

> that it is more simple to believe at once in the eternal pre-existence of the world, as it is now going on, and may forever go on by the principle of reproduction which we see and witness, than to believe in the eternal pre-existence of an ulterior cause, or Creator of the world, a Being whom we see not and know not, of whose form, substance and mode, or place of existence, or of action, no sense informs us, no power of the mind enables us to delineate or comprehend.

Continuing, Jefferson gave his eloquent response as a deist:

> On the contrary, I hold, (without appeal to revelation) that when we take a view of the universe . . . [t]he movements of the heavenly bodies, so exactly held in their course by the balance of centrifugal and centripetal forces; the structure of our earth itself, with its distribution of lands, waters and atmosphere; animal and vegetable bodies, examined in all their minutest particles; insects, mere atoms of life, yet as perfectly organized as, man or mammoth; the mineral substances, their generation and uses; it is impossible, I say, for the human mind not to believe, that there is in all this, design, cause and effect, up to an ultimate cause, a Fabricator of all things from matter and motion, their Preserver and Regulator while permitted to exist in their present forms, and their regeneration into new and other forms.[69]

For Jefferson, there was so much intelligence and planning evident in creation that it was impossible not to believe in God.

Interestingly, Jefferson's speeches and writings are replete with references to God. He uses terms such as "God," "Deity," "Almighty," "Supreme Being," "Creator," "Fabricator," "Intelligent and Powerful Agent," "Infinite Power," "Superintending Power," and "Supreme Being." Robert M. Healey researched twenty-six different terms used for God by Jefferson.[70] Jefferson's public addresses are studded with references to "that overruling Providence which governs the destinies of men and nations" and watches "over your own and our country's freedom and welfare."[71] In his Second Inaugural Address, Jefferson expressed his belief in "that Being in whose hands we are, who led our forefathers, as Israel of old, from their native land, and planted them in a country flowing with all the necessaries and comforts of life; who has covered our infancy with his providence, and our riper years with his wisdom and power. . . ." He prayed that God "will so enlighten the minds" of America's leaders and "guide their councils."[72]

Despite his intellectualism, there was a surprising conservatism in Jefferson's religion. He had an Anglican reverence for God and appreciation of worship. He firmly believed in God and His guidance of people and nations. He revered Christ as the world's greatest moral teacher. His great-grandson was quite correct in calling Jefferson a "conservative Unitarian."[73]

It is evident that Jefferson's belief in God and his habit of private devotions strengthened his personal life and his belief in a moral purpose to life. Behind his political philosophy were his religious convictions about God and the characteristics that God had given to man and his world. Jefferson believed in freedom and equality, for example, because people had been "endowed by their Creator" with these traits, and he believed people could govern themselves successfully in society because such was God's purpose. It was Jefferson's faith in God and the moral purposes underlying human life that gave him courage and purpose as a leader, strengthened him in times of discouragement and attack, and gave his life enduring meaning.

Jefferson and Religious Freedom

It is clear from the preceding evidence that Jefferson's revolutionary idea of forming a new, democratic government run by the people as proclaimed in the "Declaration of Independence" was firmly based on his religious convictions, despite the fact that his references to God were sometimes veiled. These religious convictions were even more important in Jefferson's work for religious freedom.

In the first place, religious freedom involved more than the civil state or even the church. It involved God and the human conscience. Jefferson wrote that each man is accountable to "our God alone" for his "particular principles of religion."[74] God "is the only rightful and competent Judge" of one's creed.[75] In his "Bill for Establishing Religious Freedom," Jefferson wrote:

> Almighty God hath created the mind free, and manifested his supreme will that free it shall remain by making it altogether insusceptible of restraint; that all attempts to influence it by temporal punishments, or burthens, or by civil incapacitations, tend only to beget habits of hypocrisy and meanness, and are a departure from the plan of the holy author of our religion.[76]

Religious freedom was for Jefferson among the most important of all the rights of man.

Jefferson began his development of the belief in religious freedom by emphasizing the importance of toleration. He repeatedly stated that it was essential to practice religious toleration since people would inevitably differ in their religious beliefs, just as they differed in tastes, talents, and appearances. It was "absurd," he declared, for some people to tell the Almighty he should make all people think or look alike.[77] To illustrate the foolishness of intolerance, he pointed to the former laws of France prohibiting eating potatoes and teaching the discoveries of Galileo that the earth revolved around the sun. He concluded: "Subject opinion to coercion: whom will you make your inquisitors? Fallible men. . . . And why subject it to coercion? To produce uniformity. But is uniformity of opinion desirable? No more than of face and stature."[78] According to Jefferson the lawyer, it is an error to believe "that the operations of the mind, as well as the acts of the body, are subject to the coercion of the laws. . . . The rights of conscience we never submitted, we could not submit. We are answerable for them to our God."[79] Jefferson was indebted to his wide reading from English reformers such as Locke, Shaftesbury, and Milton for many of these ideas on toleration.[80]

Locke had argued that no one had a right to use the civil law to punish his neighbor for different religious views, even if they were in error, since the neighbor injured no one but himself by his error. Jefferson used the same argument in his *Notes on Virginia* when he wrote that it did no injury to him for his neighbor to believe in "twenty gods, or no God," a statement for which he was roundly attacked by his religious opponents.[81]

Jefferson copied approvingly Locke's writing in his notes, "I cannot be saved by a worship I disbelieve and abhor."[82] He then commented: "Millions of innocent men, women, and children, since the introduction of Christianity, have been burnt, tortured, fined, [and] imprisoned. . . . What has been the effect of coercion? To make one half the world fools, and the other half hypocrites."[83] To force a person to say he believes in a religion that inwardly he does not is more than a crime against his human rights because it also makes him sin against his God.

If there was need for greater religious toleration in Europe in the eighteenth century, there was also a need for it in America, as Jefferson was well aware. In Virginia, he pointed out, the Presbyterians and Quakers, seeking religious freedom, had been persecuted by "the reigning sect." They could be deported for assembling together for their services, and their children could be taken away from them if they did not have them baptized in the Anglican church.[84] Not only the Quakers but also the Jews excited Jefferson's sympathy because of the persecution they had endured, especially because they were the "parent and basis of all those of Christendom," he wrote to a Jewish man.[85]

All his life Jefferson argued eloquently for a wider toleration of religions and peoples. He wrote: "Let us not be uneasy then about the different roads we may pursue [to heaven] . . . but, following the guidance of a good conscience, let us be happy in the hope that by these different paths we shall all meet in the end."[86] He argued that the very differences emphasized by various religious sects meant that people must choose from among them the one to which they would conform. "[B]ut if we chuse for ourselves," wrote Jefferson, "we must allow others to chuse also. . . . [T]his establishes religious liberty."[87]

As Jefferson saw it, however, toleration is not enough. It was an advance over the religious wars of the preceding centuries, but there was an inherent arrogance when John Locke advocated toleration by the Anglican church of some Protestant sects, but not Catholics (who supported a foreign prince, the Pope) or the Jews and Quakers (who did not believe in the Trinity).[88]

Jefferson's first struggle for religious freedom was in his native Commonwealth of Virginia, and it involved him in "the severest contests" of his political career.[89] He vowed to Edward Dowse never to "bow to the shrine of intolerance" and always "to maintain the common right of freedom of conscience."[90] In his *Notes on Virginia* and *Autobiography*, he recounted the history of church-state relations in Virginia and offered his rationale for seeking to separate the Anglican church in Virginia from its legally favored position.[91] The first royal grant to Sir Walter Raleigh specified that the colony of Virginia was to favor "the true Christian faith, now professed in the church of England." The colony was early divided into parishes with an Anglican minister in each who received a yearly salary in tobacco, a glebe house, and land paid for by the taxes of all parish inhabitants. Despite much persecution, other sects, especially the Presbyterians, gradually gained a foothold, partly, Jefferson believed, because the established clergymen were too busy with their farms and the classical day schools they conducted to attend to their pastoral functions. He explained that the dissenters from the established church

> were still obliged to pay contributions to support the pastors of the minority. This unrighteous compulsion, to maintain teachers of what they deemed religious errors, was grievously felt during the regal government, and without a hope of relief. But the first republican legislature, which met in '76, was crowded with petitions to abolish this spiritual tyranny. These brought on the severest contests in which I have ever been engaged.[92]

As Jefferson summarized the struggle, opinion in the legislature was so evenly divided that a series of compromises were reached in this and succeeding legislatures. The laws enforcing religious opinion and church attendance were repealed, and taxes to support the established church were suspended from year to year. Jefferson wanted the people to be free to support voluntarily whichever religious teacher won their approbation.[93] As he wrote in his notes on Locke's essay on toleration, "where he stopped short, we may go on."[94] In his draft of a constitution for Virginia in 1776, for example, Jefferson proposed: "All persons shall have full & free liberty of religious opinion: nor shall any be compelled to frequent or maintain any religious institution."[95]

Jefferson was appointed to a committee charged with revising Virginia's colonial laws to a code suitable for a democratic state. One of Jefferson's aims in revising the laws was "[t]o establish religious freedom on the broadest bottom."[96] It was not until 1786, after an arduous campaign led by Madison, that the Virginia legislature adopted Jefferson's bill guaranteeing religious freedom. By this time Jefferson was in France serving as American minister. He was jubilant, not only for the political victory in Virginia, but also for the enhancement of Enlightenment ideals abroad among European intellectuals.[97] The Virginia "Statute for Establishing Religious Freedom," Bill Number 82 of the revised code of Virginia, was only one of several concerning religion written by Jefferson, but it was by far the most important.[98] It was a milestone in human progress because it went beyond Locke's policy of toleration and enacted complete religious freedom not only for all Christian groups but also for all religious adherents, including "the Jew and the Gentile, the Christian and Mahometan, the Hindoo, and Infidel of every denomination."[99] The law was purposely drafted in sweeping terms:

> no man shall be compelled to frequent or support any religious worship, place, or ministry whatsoever, nor shall be enforced, restrained, molested, or burthened in his body or goods, nor shall otherwise suffer, on account of his religious opinions or beliefs; but that all men shall be free to profess, and by argument to maintain, their opinions in matters of religion.[100]

Some of Jefferson's critics feared that disestablishment would hinder the growth of the church, religion, and public morality. Jefferson, to the contrary, believed that disestablishment would make the church stronger and its pastors more zealous. But even if the opposite should prove to be the case, disestablishment was still necessary because the danger of religious oppression and tyranny outweighed the danger of religious indifference and public immorality.

Separation of Church and State

When ratification of the U.S. Constitution was debated, the lack of "a bill of rights providing clearly and without aid of sophisms for freedom of religion" clearly disturbed Jefferson.[101] Although Madison did not think a bill of rights was necessary, he agreed to propose one in order to ensure the adoption of the Constitution. Accordingly, he introduced in Congress on 8 June 1789 a set of proposed amendments. Addressing concern for religious freedom, Madison proposed: "The civil rights of none shall be abridged on account of religious belief or worship, nor shall any national religion be established."[102] This proposal was eventually shaped into the First Amendment. As finally adopted, the First Amendment declared:

> Congress shall make no law respecting an establishment of religion, or prohibiting the free exercise thereof; or abridging the freedom of speech, or of the press, or the right of the people peaceably to assemble, and to petition the Government for a redress of grievances.[103]

So, through his influence on Madison, Jefferson is given some credit for the First Amendment in the Bill of Rights guaranteeing religious freedom.

While president, Jefferson frequently defended religious freedom in correspondence with various religious groups. It was in one such greeting to the Danbury Baptist Association that Jefferson first articulated what has become a basic doctrine of the United States: the First Amendment, he wrote, had wisely erected "a wall of separation between Church and State."[104] Many other religious groups that had felt the sting of persecution in America wrote to thank Jefferson for his efforts to protect religious freedom, and they received courteous replies from him reiterating his devotion to freedom of religion.[105]

Because he believed the federal government should not interfere with religion, he went so far as to refuse to proclaim a national Thanksgiving Day when he was president.[106] In his Second Inaugural Address, he wrote:

> In matters of religion, I have considered that its free exercise is placed by the constitution independent of the powers of the general [federal] government. I have therefore undertaken, on no occasion, to prescribe the religious exercises suited to it; but have left them, as the constitution found them, under the direction and discipline of State or Church authorities acknowledged by the several religious societies.[107]

Although Jefferson has been praised over the years for his ringing declarations favoring civil rights, religious freedom, and separation of church and state, some scholars have questioned whether he intended to raise the wall separating church and state as high as the Supreme Court has done in recent years. M. Stanton Evans points out in his book, *The Theme is Freedom*, that Congress shall not establish an official national church, but the states are not prohibited from doing so. At the time of the "Declaration of Independence," nine of the colonies did have established churches and by the time of the Constitutional Convention, three New England states still had Congregational establishments. The First Amendment did not explicitly prohibit all ecclesiastical establishments; it merely proscribed an establishment by the federal government. In fact, Evans argues that some delegates at the Constitutional Convention favored the First Amendment in order to protect their own state established churches.[108] Jefferson apparently agreed that he did not want the federal government to interfere with the states' right to regulate religion.[109] If there had been a desire to establish a national church, it would have been difficult to get agreement on which should be the favored, established church for the whole nation. Finally, defenders of a national separationist policy have countered that even if the First Amendment's separation of church and state applied only to Congress, the Fourteenth Amendment applied First Amendment principles to the states.

In summary, it seems clear that Jefferson opposed a state-supported national church or the regulation of religion by the federal government. As a matter of federalism, he acknowledged that the states had the authority to support or regulate religious institutions. As a private citizen, however, he strongly opposed any government—state or federal—supporting a particular church or enforcing a religious belief.

Duty and the Moral Sense

Many have praised Jefferson for championing the rights of man; few have noted how much he stressed the duties of man. Let us consider his ideas on man's duties. When Jefferson defined the most important rights of man in the "Declaration of Independence" as "life, liberty, and the pursuit of happiness," he did not mean the frantic search for wealth and self-gratification many Americans follow today. "Happiness," he wrote, "[is] the aim of life[, but] Virtue [is] the foundation of happiness."[110] We practice virtue, he argued, because it gives us, like the good Samaritan, personal satisfaction to help those in distress.[111] God, he wrote, "has formed us moral agents . . . that we may promote the happiness of those with whom He has placed us in society, by acting honestly towards all, benevolently to those who fall within our way."[112] In a letter to Thomas Law, he concluded that "nature hath implanted in our breasts a love of others, a sense of duty to them, a moral instinct, in short, which prompts us irresistibly to feel and to succor their distresses."[113]

In contrast to Tories who believed the common man was incapable of governing himself and religious conservatives who believed in the sinfulness of human nature, Jefferson believed in the fundamental goodness of man and his ability to govern himself. Mankind was the creation of an all-wise, benevolent God who had "destined [man] for society" and "endowed [him] with a sense of right and wrong."[114] Jefferson thus balanced the pursuit of individual happiness against the greater good of society, flavored an epicurean appreciation of the finer things of life with a dash of Christian morality, and advocated both the rights of man for free, individual self-development and the duties that responsible people owed to their society. Jefferson wrote a chiding letter to his friend Edward Rutledge on this very point: "There is a debt of service due from every man to his country, proportioned to the bounties which nature and fortune have measured to him. . . . There is no bankrupt law in heaven, by which you may get off . . . pay[ing] your own debts."[115]

So strong was Jefferson's sense of duty that he tended to reduce all religion to the study of morality. In his library he classified religion as a division of "moral philosophy."[116] He frequently wrote in both private letters and official addresses about the necessity for moral men to fulfill their duties to society. Jefferson was himself the best example of an aristocrat of talent devoting himself to the cause of the common man. When political abuse was beating upon him, he longed wistfully for the peaceful life of a gentleman farmer and scholar, but his duty held him to the task of a statesman for his country.

Jefferson believed that not only was man endowed with a moral sense, but also men and nations were subject to a moral law. The source of both was God. He believed that God, the Creator, intending man for the joys of social living, implanted in man both moral sense and reason, by which he could perceive the moral law and desire to follow it. It was particularly important that individuals acknowledge and nurture the faculty of moral sense. He urged this upon family and friends. He wrote to his young daughter Martha when she left home to be tutored: "If ever you are about to say any thing amiss or to do any thing wrong, consider . . . your conscience, and be sure to obey it. Our maker has given us all, this faithful internal Monitor."[117] Writing to his nephew away at college, he developed the idea further:

> The moral sense, or conscience, is as much a part of man as his leg or arm. It is given to all human beings in a stronger or weaker degree. . . . It may be strengthened by exercise, as may any particular limb of the body. This sense is

> submitted indeed in some degree to the guidance of reason; but it is a small stock which is required for this: even a less one than what we call Common sense. . . . [L]ose no occasion of exercising your dispositions to be grateful, to be generous, to be charitable, to be humane, to be true, just, firm, orderly, couragious [sic].[118]

Jefferson explained the "moral sense" in a letter to Pierre Samuel Dupont de Nemours: "I believe with you that morality, compassion, generosity, are innate elements of the human constitution; . . . that justice is the fundamental law of society."[119] This sense of right and wrong in every human being made possible social order. He wrote to Peter Carr: "Man was destined for society. His morality therefore was to be formed to this object. He was endowed with a sense of right and wrong . . . [which] is the true foundation of morality."[120] "The Creator," he told Thomas Law, "would indeed have been a bungling artist, had he intended man for a social animal, without planting in him social dispositions."[121]

Beginning, then, with admonitions for good behavior and a lawyer's belief in the importance of law and justice, Jefferson moved on to a belief in human conscience and man's sense of morality as entities in their own right established in humanity by God. This belief in a moral law reflected his Enlightenment studies. Newton had shown the marvelous place of law in nature's wondrous order; Bacon and Locke had laid the foundations of law and understanding the processes of man's thinking and social organization that Destutt de Tracy, Dugald Stewart, P.J.G. Cabanis, Claude Adrien Helvetius, and David Hume elaborated on in various ways. What was more natural to believe than that there was a moral law governing the behavior of people and society similar to the law of gravity? Perhaps if men could use their reason to discover and practice the moral law, human progress would be faster than during the medieval times when people were oppressed by laws of the kings and the church. So Jefferson and the Enlightenment rediscovered in a new form "the law of the Lord proclaimed by the heavens that revives the soul" (Ps. 19), which the Psalms and the Old Testament expounded.[122]

Both individuals and nations are subject to the Moral Law, Jefferson argued in a state paper (written as a member of George Washington's cabinet) discussing whether or not the United States was bound by its treaty with France after the French Revolution overthrew the previous government. Man, he argued, "has been subjected by his creator" to the Moral Law:

> I appeal to the true fountains of evidence, the head and heart of every rational and honest man. It is there Nature has written her Moral laws, and where every man may read them for himself. He will never read there the permission to annul his obligations for a time, or for ever, whenever they become 'dangerous, useless, or disagreeable' [as Alexander Hamilton had argued].[123]

So Jefferson's belief in the moral sense was at the foundation of all his work, whether as a parent raising his children, an elder advising friends, or a statesman leading the nation. Although he stressed the importance of admonitions and education, it should not be concluded that he thought the moral sense was just the sum of the codes and beliefs that an individual had learned. It was deeper than that. It was "a moral instinct" that "nature hath implanted in our breasts."[124] Evidence of the moral instinct was to be found everywhere, for both children and adults had it, as well as people of all different societies.[125]

Jefferson's ideas of government and society stood upon the firm foundation of his belief in the moral nature, which, in turn, was rooted in a belief in God, the Master Creator of both the world of nature and the world of man. His argument was short and simple: "Man was created for social intercourse; but social intercourse cannot be maintained without a sense of justice; then man must have been created with a sense of justice."[126]

Although Jefferson was too much of an intellectual to repudiate entirely the role of reason in guiding human conduct, he feared the easy rationalizations that many people employed to excuse wrong conduct; so he depended on the feelings of the heart rather than the reasonings of the head to motivate men for their own good and that of society. As proof he pointed out that "morality, compassion, generosity are innate elements of the human constitution"[127]; that there is "a moral sense in man, individually or associated, . . . which the laws of nature have established between his duties and his interests."[128]; that it is the plan of a "wise creator" "that every human mind feels pleasure in doing good to another"[129]; and that "[God] has formed us moral agents . . . that we may promote the happiness of those with whom He has placed us in society."[130] The trait that was most necessary to enable men to live peacefully together in society was the very one that gave them the deepest happiness. So the moral law showed the glory of God in human society as Newton's law showed the glory of God in the heavens.

Salvation through Education

Although Jefferson was basically optimistic about human nature and he objected to Calvin's theology that taught that man was totally depraved, even he had to admit that there were some exceptions to the basic goodness of people. He thought much misery had been caused by morally deformed leaders such as "Napoleon and the Caesars."[131] He recognized that the seeds of moral decay are within all people. Man is often distracted "from right by the seductions of self-love."[132] The moral instinct is "the brightest gem with which the human character is studded, and the want of it [is] more degrading than the most hideous of the bodily deformities."[133]

To overcome the seeds of moral decay and defects in society, Jefferson believed in the importance of education. He knew democracy could not be entrusted to ignorant citizens. Writing from Europe, Jefferson urged a friend to "Preach . . . a crusade against ignorance." A democracy must educate the common people, and taxes for education were a small price to pay compared with what kings and priests would exact from ignorant followers.[134] He often commented on the importance of books and libraries to train citizens for freedom and self-rule, and he made proposals for the establishment of public libraries as well as public schools.[135] He wrote: "The light which has been shed on mankind by the art of printing, has eminently changed the condition of the world. . . . [I]t continues to spread, and while printing is preserved, it can no more recede than the sun return on his course."[136] Because of his passion for reading and study, Jefferson's personal library was the largest private library in America, some 7,000 to 8,000 volumes, which he sold to Congress when the first Library of Congress was burned during the War of 1812. He also chose and established the library for his University of Virginia.[137]

To further education for democracy, Jefferson early devised a plan for public education which he advocated all his life. He hoped that Virginia would follow the good example of New England where an educated and influential citizenry had resulted from its early development of town schools. Geography, which caused New England people to live in towns, was against him in Virginia, where people lived on scattered plantations. Jefferson's plan for public schools was not adopted until the 1870s, long after his death.[138]

In the later years of his life, Jefferson succeeded in establishing the state University of Virginia at Charlottesville. He shepherded laws through the legislature and repeatedly wrung funds from the legislature for it. He was the architect and building superintendent for the grounds and buildings; he drew up the curriculum and hired the professors; he selected the books and set up the library. Jefferson wanted his university to be a beacon of enlightenment and liberalism in the New World. Accordingly, he emphasized science and government and de-emphasized theology. He chose as one of the professors his friend Dr. Thomas Cooper who was eminently qualified but was an outspoken proponent of Unitarianism and foe of Calvinism. The Cooper appointment aroused vehement opposition from the Calvinists and finally had to be rescinded. Further opposition developed because Jefferson made no provisions for teaching religion, insisting that the separation between church and state prohibited the teaching of any one sect in a state institution. He did compromise to the extent that he offered space on the confines of the University where different denominations could establish their own seminaries.[139] He thought such an association would give seminarians "ready and convenient access and attendance on the scientific lectures of the University . . . and would fill the chasm [in the curriculum] now existing, on principles which would leave inviolate the constitutional freedom of religion, the most inalienable and sacred of all human rights."[140]

Jefferson did provide for the teaching of morality and philosophy according to the Enlightenment ideals by which he had lived all his life:

> It was not . . . to be understood that instruction in religious opinion and duties was meant to be precluded by the public authorities, as indifferent to the interests of society. On the contrary, the relations which exist between man and his Maker, and the duties resulting from those relations, are the most interesting and important to every human being, and the most incumbent on his study and investigation.[141]

The rights and duties of men and the pure teachings of Jesus, upon which all people agreed, could and should be taught, but the dogmas of religion that divided friends, thwarted religious freedom, and led to tyrannical church-state unions should be avoided.[142]

Jefferson believed the state should teach public morality. Garrett Sheldon comments that Jefferson's struggle to disestablish the Anglican church did not shake his personal Christian faith or "his abiding conviction that religious ethics are a necessary component of the just polity."[143] Moreover, there is much evidence that he believed that a democratic government had an obligation to its citizens to provide public education, teach public morality, and encourage religion in general. Indeed, he believed that without the restraints of morality and education, men could not live together in social harmony.

Jefferson and Immortality

I can not close this discussion of Jefferson and his religious beliefs without a brief mention of his ideas about human immortality. For good reason, scholars have been perplexed by his contradictory writings on immortality, for Jefferson himself was perplexed. The problem for Jefferson, as it is for many people today, centered on the question, "What is soul?" In the Enlightenment, the emerging sciences were studying animals and plants, physics and geology, cultures and societies. Jefferson could understand body and matter, but what was soul? Where was it located in a human being? What happened to it when a person died?

The medieval church fathers had speculated that humans had a material body and a spiritual soul and that soul was made up of a special ethereal and diffuse matter. This philosophical idea of man and the universe was under siege during the Enlightenment as scientific thought spread. Jefferson maintained that he was a materialist and rejected metaphysical spiritualism. He was influenced by his studies of Locke, Destutt de Tracy, Stewart, and Cabanis.[144]

John Adams first raised the question in correspondence between the two retired friends. What was meant by the words "matter" and "spirit"? Adams wondered.[145] He thought neither "saint," who believed in spirit, nor scientist, who thought everything was matter, knew what either spirit or matter really were.[146] Jefferson replied: "let me turn to your puzzling letter . . . on matter, spirit, motion. . . . It's [sic] croud of scepticisms kept me from sleep. I read it, and laid it down; read it, and laid it down, again and again."[147] He was forced back to the basic elements of philosophy, he said, according to which he could only know what he sensed. He could sense matter, which he defined as "bodies which are not myself." He could also see "motion" or bodies "changing place." In between was "*void*, or *nothing,* or *immaterial space.*" With these concepts "we may erect the fabric of all the certainties we can have or need. . . . To talk of *immaterial* existences is to talk of *nothings*. To say that the human soul, angels, god, are immaterial, is to say they are *nothings,* or that there is no god, no angels, no soul."[148] He explained, "I confess I should, with Mr. Locke, prefer swallowing one incomprehensibility rather than two. It requires one effort only to admit the single incomprehensibility of matter endowed with thought: and two to believe, 1st. that of an existence called Spirit, of which we have neither evidence nor idea, and then

2dly. how that spirit which has neither extension nor solidity, can put material organs into motion."[149]

There was much that was puzzling about life after death. Jefferson explained to Adams: "When I meet with a proposition beyond finite comprehension, I abandon it as I do a weight which human strength cannot lift: and I think ignorance, in these cases, is truly the softest pillow on which I can lay my head."[150] Adams was delighted with the phrase and agreed that there were "limits to which the human understanding may hope to go in this Inferior World . . . [and that there was a need for an] abundance of your pillows of Ignorance—an expression that I very much admire—on which to repose our puzzled heads."[151] Indeed, one of the attractions of dying for the two old men was the opportunity to satisfy their curiosity about life and death. They assured each other that they would find out the desired answers and laugh at their perplexities when they met in the hereafter.[152]

If Jefferson's mind could not believe in a spiritual soul, his heart was a different matter, for he was a man of sorrows, well acquainted with grief. His father died when he was only fourteen and four of his eight brothers and sisters died in their youth. He particularly missed his older sister Jane, who used to sing to him the liturgy of the Anglican church which gave him his lifelong appreciation of the Psalms and worship. His close friend and brother-in-law, Dabney Carr, also died young.[153] Of Jefferson's family, only two daughters lived to maturity. In 1804 one of them died. Jefferson grieved, not only for his lost daughter, but also for fear he would lose all his family. He wrote to his college friend, John Page: "I, of my want, have lost even the half of all I had. My evening prospects [of a happy retirement] now hang on the slender thread of a single life."[154] Fortunately, he was spared and did retire to live out his days at Monticello with his daughter Martha and her children.

The worst blow of all came in 1782 when, after a long illness during which he was constantly at her side, Jefferson's wife died. Theirs had been a particularly close and happy marriage. He went nearly insane with grief. He refused to take his place in the Virginia legislature; indeed, he wrote later that he was "absolutely unable to attend to any thing like business." Although just a child, daughter Patsy remembered his grief well: "He walked almost incessantly night and day, only lying down occasionally, when nature was completely exhausted. . . . When at last he left his room, he rode out, and from that time he was incessantly on horseback, rambling about the mountain, in the least frequented roads, and just as often through the woods. In those melancholy rambles, I was his constant companion, a solitary witness to many a violent burst of grief."[155] At last his friends persuaded him to accept the post of America's minister to France and time healed his sorrow, a salve that Jefferson ever afterwards was wont to offer to friends with similar losses as the only real cure for grief.

So, though Jefferson's scientific mind could not believe in an immaterial soul, his grieving heart could not believe his dear ones were just bodies moldering in the grave. After his death, his family found small envelopes with locks of hair from his wife and each of his lost children in a secret drawer of his private cabinet with words of endearment written in his own hand. They showed signs of frequent handling.[156]

When John Adams' wife died, the one whom he called "the dear Partner of my Life for fifty four Years as a Wife and for many Years more as a Lover,"[157] Jefferson wrote to comfort his old friend:

> I know well, and feel what you have lost, what you have suffered, are suffering, and have yet to endure. The same trials have taught me that, for ills so immeasurable, time and silence are the only medicine. I will not therefore, by useless condolances, open afresh the sluices of your grief nor, altho' mingling sincerely my tears with yours, will I say a word more, where words are vain, but that it is of some comfort to us both that the term is not very distant at which we are to deposit, in the same cerement, our sorrows and suffering bodies, and to ascend in essence to an ecstatic meeting with the friends we have loved and lost and whom we shall still love and never lose again. God bless you and support you under your heavy affliction.[158]

In the Adams-Jefferson letters there is evidence that Adams deferred to Jefferson's greater reading and knowledge of authors, but Jefferson was stimulated by Adams' deeper New England faith. Under Adams' prompting, Jefferson could agree that even if there was no soul or spirit, matter had many mysterious properties, such as magnetism, gravity, and the power of the brain to think.[159] Why not immortality for human beings? With the mind satisfied, Jefferson's heart could have its way, and he could affirm to Adams that after the death of our bodies we shall meet again in essence.[160]

A great national celebration was planned for the fiftieth anniversary of the signing of the "Declaration of Independence" on 4 July 1826, in Washington, D.C. and around the country. The festive mood turned solemn and introspective, however, when the news spread that, by the inscrutable workings of Providence, John Adams and Thomas Jefferson both died on 4 July 1826, as if, in the words of John Quincy Adams, "Heaven directed a new seal" upon the beliefs of America. Sometime before he died, John Adams inquired after his old friend Thomas Jefferson. Being informed that Jefferson was still alive, he murmured contentedly, "Thomas Jefferson still survives," implying that the goals and ideals of the American "Declaration of Independence" and American democracy were safe as long as Jefferson lived.[161] Time has proved this belief correct, for the ideas and faith of Thomas Jefferson have survived beyond his own age and spread to nations unknown in the eighteenth century.

Notes

1. See discussion in Charles B. Sanford, *The Religious Life of Thomas Jefferson* (Charlottesville: University Press of Virginia, 1984), 1-6. Many themes, as well as references, in this chapter are elaborated on in Sanford, *Religious Life of Thomas Jefferson*.

2. Letter from Jefferson to Mrs. M. Harrison Smith, 6 August 1816, *The Writings of Thomas Jefferson,* ed. Andrew A. Lipscomb and Albert Ellery Bergh, 20 vols. (Washington, D.C.: The Thomas Jefferson Memorial Association, 1904-05), 15:60 [hereinafter *Writings of Jefferson*].

3. Dumas Malone, *Jefferson and His Time*, 6 vols. (Boston: Little, Brown and Co., 1948-1981), 3:479-483.

4. Letter from Alexander Hamilton to John Jay, 7 May 1800, *The Papers of Alexander Hamilton,* ed. Harold C. Syrett (New York: Columbia University Press, 1976), 24:465.

5. Henry S. Randall, *The Life of Thomas Jefferson*, 3 vols. (New York, 1857), 1:495, 2:567-568, 3:620-622; and Malone, *Jefferson and His Time*, 3:481.

6. William D. Gould, "The Religious Opinions of Thomas Jefferson," *Mississippi Valley Historical Review* 20 (1933): 191.

7. Randall, *Life of Jefferson*, 3:555.

8. *Jefferson's Memorandum Books: Accounts, with Legal Records and Miscellany, 1767-1826,* ed. James A. Bear, Jr. and Lucia C. Stanton, 2 vols., *The Papers of Thomas Jefferson,* ed. Charles T. Cullen, second series (Princeton, N.J.: Princeton University Press, 1997), II:1403 (8 March 1824). Jefferson's account books are replete with references to donations to churches and preachers.

9. Henry Wilder Foote, *Thomas Jefferson: Champion of Religious Freedom, Advocate of Christian Morals* (Boston: Beacon Press, 1947), 6-9. See also Jefferson, "Subscription to Support a Clergyman in Charlottesville," February 1777, *The Papers of Thomas Jefferson*, ed. Julian P. Boyd, 27 vols. to date (Princeton, N.J.: Princeton University Press, 1950-), 2:6 [hereinafter *Papers of Jefferson*].

10. See Malone, *Jefferson and His Time*, 4:199; James H. Hutson, *Religion and the Founding of the American Republic* (Washington, D.C.: Library of Congress, 1998), 84-93.

11. Letter from Jefferson to Doctor Thomas Cooper, 2 November 1822, *Writings of Jefferson,* 15:404. See also Foote, *Thomas Jefferson,* 7-8.

12. Randall, *Life of Jefferson*, 1:17, 41-42.

13. Letter from Jefferson to Doctor Vine Utley, 21 March 1819, *Writings of Jefferson,* 15:187.

14. Randall, *Life of Jefferson*, 3:451, 101-102, 543-547.

15. Letter from Jefferson to William Short, 31 October 1819, *Writings of Jefferson*, 15:221.

16. Letter from Jefferson to Charles Thompson, 9 January 1816, *Writings of Jefferson,* 14:385.

17. Henry Wilder Foote, introduction to *The Jefferson Bible, with the Annotated Commentaries on Religion of Thomas Jefferson*, ed. O.I.A. Roche (New York: Clarkson N. Potter, Inc., 1964), 20; Randall, *Life of Jefferson*, 3:452, 654; Merrill D. Peterson, *Thomas Jefferson and the New Nation: A Biography* (New York: Oxford University Press, 1970), 960.

18. Randall, *Life of Jefferson,* 3:671-672.

19. See letter from Jefferson to F. A. Van Der Kemp, 25 April 1816, *Writings of Jefferson*, 15:2; letter from Jefferson to William Short, 31 October 1819, *Writings of Jefferson,* 15:220-221; letter from Jefferson to Charles Thompson, 9 January 1816, *Writings of Jefferson,* 14:385-386.

20. Cyrus Adler, introduction to "The Jefferson Bible," *Writings of Jefferson*, 20:7-19. O.I.A. Roche reprints the work and includes a facsimile of the original in his *Jefferson Bible*. A recent edition of "Jefferson's Bible" is *Jefferson's Extract from the Gospels,* ed. Dickinson W. Adams (Princeton, N.J.: University of Princeton Press, 1983), second series, *Papers of Jefferson.*

21. See letter from Jefferson to William Short, 13 April 1820, *Writings of Jefferson*, 15:244-245; and Jefferson's quotations from Locke and Bolingbroke in Gilbert Chinard, ed., *The Commonplace Book of Thomas Jefferson* (Baltimore: Johns Hopkins University Press, 1926), 387; Gilbert Chinard, ed., *The Literary Bible of Thomas Jefferson: His Commonplace Book of Philosophers and Poets* (1928; reprint, New York: Greenwood Press, 1969), 50-51.

22. Letter from Jefferson to Timothy Pickering, 27 February 1821, *Writings of Jefferson,* 15:323. See also letter from Jefferson to William Short, 13 April 1820, *Writings of Jefferson*, 15:244-245; letter from Jefferson to William Short, 4 August 1820, *Writings of Jefferson*, 15:257-259; letter from Jefferson to John Davis, 18 January 1824, *The Works of Thomas Jefferson*, ed. Paul Leicester Ford, Federal Edition, 12 vols. (New York: G.P. Putnam's Sons, 1905), 12:331-332 [hereinafter *Works of Jefferson*]; letter from Jefferson to Doctor Benjamin Rush, 21 April 1803, *Writings of Jefferson*, 10:383-384; Chinard, *Literary Bible*, 50.

23. Garrett Ward Sheldon, *The Political Philosophy of Thomas Jefferson* (Baltimore: Johns Hopkins University Press, 1991), 106, 15.

24. Letter from Jefferson to Joseph Priestley, 29 January 1804, *Writings of Jefferson*, 10:446. See also letter from Jefferson to Charles Thompson, 9 January 1816, *Writings of Jefferson,* 14:385-386.

25. See discussion by Ernest F. Scott, "The New Testament and Criticism," in *The Abingdon Bible Commentary*, ed. Frederick Carl Eiselen, Edwin Lewis, and David G. Downey (New York: Abingdon Press, 1929), 888; E.W. Burch, "The Structure of the Synoptic Gospels," *ibid.*, 872-873; and Helmet Heinrich Koester, *Encyclopedia Britannica* (1973), s.v. "Gospels."

26. See discussion by Ernst Cassirer, *The Philosophy of the Enlightenment* (Princeton, N.J.: Princeton University Press, 1951), 182-187, and discussion by Carl Friedrich Georg Heinrici, *The New Schaff-Herzog Encyclopedia of Religious Knowledge*, ed. Samuel MacAuley Jackson, 12 vols. (New York: Funk and Wagnalls, 1908), 2:170-176, s.v. "Biblical Criticism." Jefferson studied the works from his library of such Enlightenment critics as Descartes, Malebranche, Spinoza, Erasmus, Grotius, Diderot, as well as Greek and Roman classical writers. He also had in his library works of "Ancient History," those by Greek and Roman historians and the early church fathers, and "histories of Christ," of Evangelists and "Pseudo-evangelists," of the Bible and Apocrypha collected by Johann Fabricius. For authors and works, see E. Millicent Sowerby, comp., *Catalogue of the Library of Thomas Jefferson*, 5 vols. (Washington, D.C.: Library of Congress, 1952-59).

27. See "moral philosophy classification" in Charles B. Sanford, *Thomas Jefferson and His Library* (Hamden, Conn.: Archon Books, 1977), 63-65, citing Sowerby, *Catalogue of the Library of Thomas Jefferson*, 1:xi.

28. See letter from Jefferson to John Adams, 11 April 1823, *Writings of Jefferson*, 15:430; letter from Jefferson to William Short, 31 October 1819, *Writings of Jefferson*, 15:220-221; letter from Jefferson to William Short, 4 August 1820, *Writings of Jefferson*, 15:257-262.

29. Letter from Jefferson to George Logan, 12 November 1816, *Works of Jefferson*, 12:42.

30. Letter from Jefferson to F.A. Van Der Kemp, 25 April 1816, *Writings of Jefferson*, 15:2-3.

31. Letter from Jefferson to Joseph Priestley, 9 April 1803, *Writings of Jefferson*, 10:375.

32. Letter from Jefferson to William Short, 4 August 1820, *Writings of Jefferson*, 15:259. See also letter from Jefferson to William Short, 13 April 1820, *Writings of Jefferson*, 15:244.

33. William Arnold Stevens and Ernest De Witt Burton, *A Harmony of the Gospels for Historical Study* (New York: Charles Scribner's Sons, 1932).

34. See discussion in Sanford, *Religious Life of Thomas Jefferson*, 110-119.

35. See Jefferson's quotations from Bolingbroke, Chinard, *Literary Bible*, 57.

36. Letter from Jefferson to William Short, 13 April 1820, *Writings of Jefferson*, 15:244.

37. Jefferson, "Syllabus," 21 April 1803, *Writings of Jefferson*, 10:383.

38. See Daniel J. Boorstin, *The Lost World of Thomas Jefferson* (New York: Henry Holt, 1948), 156-161.

39. See letter from Jefferson to F.A. Van Der Kemp, 25 April 1816, *Writings of Jefferson*, 15:2; letter from Jefferson to Charles Clay, 29 January 1815, *Writings of Jefferson*, 14:233-234.

40. Arthur Schlesinger, Jr., "Reinhold Niebuhr's Role in American Political Thought and Life," in *Reinhold Niebuhr: His Religious, Social, and Political Thought*, ed. Charles W. Kegley and Robert W. Bretall (New York: Macmillan, 1956), 126-130. See generally Sanford, *Religious Life of Thomas Jefferson*, 138-140, and Merrill D. Peterson, *The Jefferson Image in the American Mind* (New York: Oxford University Press, 1960), 360-363.

41. See citations and discussion of selections from the Gospels used by Jefferson in his "Bible," Sanford, *Religious Life of Thomas Jefferson*, 123-125.

42. Letter from Jefferson to Peter Carr, 10 August 1787, *Papers of Jefferson*, 12:15-16.

43. Letter from Jefferson to Peter Carr, 10 August 1787, *Papers of Jefferson*, 12:15-16. See also letter from Jefferson to William Carver, 4 December 1823, *Works of Jefferson*, 12:327.

44. Letter from Jefferson to John F. Watson, 17 May 1814, *Writings of Jefferson*, 14:136. See also letter from Jefferson to Miles King, 26 September 1814, *Writings of Jefferson*, 14:196-198.

45. Letter from Jefferson to Francis Hopkinson, 13 March 1789, *Papers of Jefferson*, 14:650.

46. Letter from Jefferson to Doctor Benjamin Rush, 16 January 1811, *Writings of Jefferson*, 13:4.

47. Stuart Gerry Brown, *Thomas Jefferson* (New York: Washington Square Press, 1963), 188-190; Peterson, *Thomas Jefferson and the New Nation*, 30-31, 531-532;

Adrienne Koch, *The Philosophy of Thomas Jefferson* (New York: Columbia University Press, 1943), 93-94.

48. Brown, *Thomas Jefferson*, 198-199.

49. See Peterson, *Thomas Jefferson and the New Nation*, 46-48; Koch, *Philosophy of Thomas Jefferson*, 90.

50. Jefferson, *Notes on Virginia, Writings of Jefferson,* 2:222-223.

51. Letter from Jefferson to Rev. Samuel Knox, 12 February 1810, *Writings of Jefferson,* 12:360-361.

52. Letter from Jefferson to Miles King, 26 September 1814, *Writings of Jefferson,* 14:197. See also letter from Jefferson to William Carver, 4 December 1823, *Works of Jefferson*, 12:327.

53. Letter from Jefferson to John Adams, 15 August 1820, *Writings of Jefferson,* 15:275-276; letter from Jefferson to Miles King, 26 September 1814, *Writings of Jefferson,* 14:197.

54. Letter from Jefferson to William Short, 4 August 1820, *Writings of Jefferson,* 15:258. See also letter from Jefferson to John Adams, 5 July 1814, *Writings of Jefferson,* 14:148-149.

55. See discussion by Peter Gay, *The Enlightenment: An Interpretation* (New York: Alfred A. Knopf, 1967), 150-153.

56. Letter from Jefferson to Roger C. Weightman, 24 June 1826, *Writings of Jefferson*, 16:182. Jefferson may have been quoting the words of Rumbold, a Rye House plotter executed by James II, according to Douglass Adair, "The New Thomas Jefferson," *William and Mary Quarterly*, 3d ser., 3 (1946): 133.

57. Peterson, *Thomas Jefferson and the New Nation*, 90.

58. See Malone, *Jefferson and His Time*, 1:227-228; Brown, *Thomas Jefferson,* 209-210.

59. See Koch, *Philosophy of Thomas Jefferson,* 143. Sheldon argues that the Social Contract protected not only individuals but free colonies and states against large and tyrannical government. Sheldon, *Political Philosophy of Thomas Jefferson*, 142.

60. Jefferson, "Autobiography," *Writings of Jefferson*, 1:53-55, 64. See also Peterson, *Thomas Jefferson and the New Nation,* 113-124.

61. Letter from Jefferson to John Adams, 28 October 1813, *Writings of Jefferson,* 13:396. See also Lester J. Cappon, ed., *The Adams-Jefferson Letters,* 2 vols. (Chapel Hill: Institute of Early American History and Culture; University of North Carolina Press, 1959), 2:477-480.

62. Letter from Jefferson to John Adams, 27 June 1813, *Writings of Jefferson*, 13:280.

63. Letter from Jefferson to Judge William Johnson, 12 June 1823, *Writings of Jefferson,* 15:440-441.

64. Letter from Jefferson to Governor John Langdon, 5 March 1810, *Writings of Jefferson*, 12:377-379.

65. See letter from John Adams to Thomas Jefferson, 2 March 1816, *Writings of Jefferson,* 14:438-439; letter from Jefferson to Thomas Law, 13 June 1814, *Writings of Jefferson*, 14:139-140; letter from Jefferson to John Adams, 8 April 1816, *Writings of Jefferson,* 14:468-469.

66. See, for example, letter from Jefferson to Mrs. M. Harrison Smith, 6 August 1816, *Writings of Jefferson,* 15:59-61.

67. See Ernst Peter Wilhelm Troeltsch, *New Schaff-Herzog Encyclopedia*, 3:391-397, s.v. "Deism"; Arnold Smithline, *Natural Religion in American Literature* (New Haven: College and University Press, 1966), 9-18; Gay, *The Enlightenment*, 274-280. Jefferson had works by the deist writers Blount, Tindal, and Middleton in his library. See also letter from Jefferson to John Adams, 11 April 1823, *Writings of Jefferson*, 15:425-430; letter from Jefferson to John Adams, 13 October 1813, *Writings of Jefferson*, 13:387-394; letter from Jefferson to John Adams, 22 August 1813, *Writings of Jefferson*, 13:349-353; letter from Jefferson to Doctor Benjamin Waterhouse, 26 June 1822, *Writings of Jefferson*, 15:383-385.

68. Letter from Jefferson to John Adams, 22 August 1813, *Writings of Jefferson*, 13:352. See *Joseph Priestley: Selections from his Writings*, ed. Ira V. Brown (University Park: Pennsylvania State University Press, 1962), 294-297.

69. Letter from Jefferson to John Adams, 11 April 1823, *Writings of Jefferson*, 15:426-427.

70. Robert M. Healey, *Jefferson on Religion in Public Education* (New Haven, Conn.: Yale University Press, 1962), 27-28.

71. Letter from Jefferson to Stephen Cross, Topsham, 28 March 1809, *Writings of Jefferson*, 16:352; letter from Jefferson to the Society of Tammany, or Columbian Order, No. 1, of the City of New York, 29 February 1808, *Writings of Jefferson*, 16:303.

72. Jefferson, Second Inaugural Address, 4 March 1805, *Writings of Jefferson*, 3:383.

73. Thomas Jefferson Coolidge, "Jefferson in His Family," in *Writings of Jefferson*, 15:iv.

74. Letter from Jefferson to Miles King, 26 September 1814, *Writings of Jefferson*, 14:198.

75. Letter from Jefferson to Timothy Pickering, 27 February 1821, *Writings of Jefferson*, 15:324.

76. Jefferson, "A Bill for Establishing Religious Freedom," *Papers of Jefferson*, 2:545.

77. Letter from Jefferson to Charles Thom[p]son, 29 January 1817, *Works of Jefferson*, 12:52.

78. Jefferson, *Notes on Virginia*, *Writings of Jefferson*, 2:222-223.

79. Jefferson, *Notes on Virginia*, *Writings of Jefferson*, 2:221.

80. See Jefferson's notes on religion in *Papers of Jefferson*, 1:544-555; Chinard, *Commonplace Book*, 377-393.

81. Jefferson, *Notes on Virginia*, *Writings of Jefferson*, 2:221; Randall, *Life of Jefferson*, 3:621.

82. Chinard, *Commonplace Book*, 381.

83. Jefferson, *Notes on Virginia*, *Writings of Jefferson*, 2:223. See also letter from Jefferson to Mathew Carey, 11 November 1816, *Works of Jefferson*, 12:42; letter from Jefferson to George Logan, 12 November 1816, *Works of Jefferson*, 12:43.

84. Jefferson, *Notes on Virginia*, *Writings of Jefferson*, 2:218.

85. Letter from Thomas Jefferson to Joseph Marx, 1820, in Thomas Jefferson, *Democracy*, ed. Saul K. Padover (New York: D. Appleton-Century Co., 1939), 178-179; Saul K. Padover, *Jefferson* (New York: Harcourt, Brace and Co., 1942), 395. See also letter from Jefferson to Jacob de la Motte, 1 September 1820, in *ibid*.

86. Letter from Jefferson to Miles King, 26 September 1814, *Writings of Jefferson*, 14:198.

87. Jefferson, "Notes on Locke and Shaftesbury," *Papers of Jefferson,* 1:546.

88. Jefferson, "Notes on Locke and Shaftesbury," *Papers of Jefferson,* 1:548.

89. Jefferson, "Autobiography," *Writings of Jefferson,* 1:57.

90. Letter from Jefferson to Edward Dowse, 19 April 1803, *Writings of Jefferson,* 10:378.

91. Jefferson, *Notes on Virginia, Writings of Jefferson,* 2:217-225.

92. Jefferson, "Autobiography," *Writings of Jefferson,* 1:56-57.

93. See Jefferson, "Autobiography," *Writings of Jefferson,* 1:56-59; Peterson, *Thomas Jefferson and the New Nation,* 133-145.

94. Jefferson, "Notes on Locke and Shaftesbury," *Papers of Jefferson,* 1:548.

95. Jefferson, Second Draft of Virginia Constitution of 1776, *Papers of Jefferson,* 1:353.

96. Jefferson, *Notes on Virginia, Writings of Jefferson,* 2:191.

97. Letter from James Madison to Jefferson, 9 January 1785, *Papers of Jefferson,* 7:594-595; letter from James Madison to Jefferson, 22 January 1786, *Papers of Jefferson,* 9:195-196; letter from Jefferson to James Madison, 16 December 1786, *Papers of Jefferson,* 10:603-604; letter from Jefferson to William Carmichael, 22 August 1786, *Papers of Jefferson,* 10:288; letter from Jefferson to George Wythe, 13 August 1786, *Papers of Jefferson,* 10:244; letter from Jefferson to Mirabeau, 21 August 1786, *Papers of Jefferson,* 10:283.

98. See Daniel L. Dreisbach, "A New Perspective on Jefferson's Views on Church-State Relations: The Virginia Statute for Establishing Religious Freedom in Its Legislative Context," *American Journal of Legal History* 35 (1991): 182-183.

99. Jefferson was proud that the Virginia legislature rejected an amendment that would have restricted the act only to "the plan of Jesus Christ." Jefferson, "Autobiography," *Writings of Jefferson,* 1:67.

100. Jefferson, "A Bill for Establishing Religious Freedom," *Papers of Jefferson,* 2:546.

101. Letter from Jefferson to James Madison, 20 December 1787, *Papers of Jefferson,* 12:440.

102. James Madison, "Amendments to the Constitution," 8 June 1789, *The Papers of James Madison,* ed. Charles F. Hobson, Robert A. Rutland et al. (Charlottesville: University Press of Virginia, 1979), 12:201.

103. U.S. Constitution, amend. I.

104. Letter from Thomas Jefferson to the Danbury Baptist Association in the State of Connecticut, 1 January 1802, reprinted in Daniel L. Dreisbach, "'Sowing Useful Truths and Principles': The Danbury Baptists, Thomas Jefferson, and the 'Wall of Separation,'" *Journal of Church and State* 39 (1997): 468-469.

105. See, for example, letter from Jefferson to a Committee of the Danbury Baptist Association, in the State of Connecticut, 1 January 1802, *Writings of Jefferson,* 16:281-282; letter from Jefferson to Captain John Thomas, 18 November 1807, *Writings of Jefferson,* 16:290-291; letter from Jefferson to the General Meeting of Six Baptist Associations at Chesterfield, Virginia, 21 November 1808, *Writings of Jefferson,* 16:320-321; letter from Jefferson to the Society of the Methodist Episcopal Church at New London, Connecticut, 4 February 1809, *Writings of Jefferson,* 16:331-332.

106. Letter from Jefferson to the Rev. Samuel Miller, 23 January 1808, *Writings of Jefferson,* 11:428-430.

107. Jefferson, Second Inaugural Address, 4 March 1805, *Writings of Jefferson*, 3:378.

108. M. Stanton Evans, *The Theme Is Freedom: Religion, Politics, and the American Tradition* (Washington, D.C.: Regnery Publishing, 1994), 281-284.

109. Letter from Jefferson to the Rev. Samuel Miller, 23 January 1808, *Writings of Jefferson*, 11:428.

110. Letter from Jefferson to William Short, 31 October 1819, *Writings of Jefferson*, 15:223 ("Syllabus of the doctrines of Epicurus").

111. Letter from Jefferson to Thomas Law, 13 June 1814, *Writings of Jefferson*, 14:141.

112. Letter from Jefferson to Miles King, 26 September 1814, *Writings of Jefferson*, 14:197-198.

113. Letter from Jefferson to Thomas Law, 13 June 1814, *Writings of Jefferson*, 14:141.

114. Letter from Jefferson to Peter Carr, 10 August 1787, *Papers of Jefferson*, 12:15.

115. Letter from Jefferson to Edward Rutledge, 27 December 1796, *Writings of Jefferson*, 9:354-355.

116. Sanford, *Thomas Jefferson and His Library*, 64.

117. Letter from Jefferson to Martha Jefferson, 11 December 1783, *Papers of Jefferson*, 6:380.

118. Letter from Jefferson to Peter Carr, 10 August 1787, *Papers of Jefferson*, 12:15.

119. Letter from Jefferson to Dupont de Nemours, 24 April 1816, *Writings of Jefferson*, 14:490-491.

120. Letter from Jefferson to Peter Carr, 10 August 1787, *Papers of Jefferson*, 12:14-15.

121. Letter from Jefferson to Thomas Law, 13 June 1814, *Writings of Jefferson*, 14:142.

122. See Koch, *Philosophy of Thomas Jefferson*, 15-22, 113-123.

123. Jefferson, "Opinion on the Treaties with France," 28 April 1793, *Papers of Jefferson*, 25:609.

124. Letter from Jefferson to Thomas Law, 13 June 1814, *Writings of Jefferson*, 14:141.

125. See Koch, *Philosophy of Thomas Jefferson*, 15-18.

126. Letter from Jefferson to Francis W. Gilmer, 7 June 1816, *Works of Jefferson*, 11:535. See also letter from Jefferson to Peter Carr, 10 August 1787, *Papers of Jefferson*, 12:15; letter from Jefferson to Thomas Law, 13 June 1814, *Writings of Jefferson*, 14:142.

127. Letter from Jefferson to Dupont de Nemours, 24 April 1816, *Writings of Jefferson*, 14:490.

128. Letter from Jefferson to Caesar A. Rodney, 10 February 1810, *Writings of Jefferson*, 12:358.

129. Letter from Jefferson to John Adams, 14 October 1816, *Writings of Jefferson*, 15:76.

130. Letter from Jefferson to Miles King, 26 September 1814, *Writings of Jefferson*, 14:197.

131. Jefferson, "Autobiography," *Writings of Jefferson*, 1:152.

132. Letter from Jefferson to Dupont de Nemours, 24 April 1816, *Writings of Jefferson,* 14:489. See also quotations from Cicero in Chinard, *Literary Bible,* 76-77.

133. Letter from Jefferson to Thomas Law, 13 June 1814, *Writings of Jefferson,* 14:143.

134. Letter from Jefferson to George Wythe, 13 August 1786, *Papers of Jefferson,* 10:245.

135. See, for example, "A Bill for the More General Diffusion of Knowledge" and "A Bill for Establishing a Public Library," *Papers of Jefferson*, 2:526-535, 544-545.

136. Letter from Jefferson to John Adams, 4 September 1823, *Writings of Jefferson*, 15:465.

137. See discussion in Sanford, *Religious Life of Thomas Jefferson*, 65-67; and Sanford, *Thomas Jefferson and His Library*, 144-148.

138. See Jefferson, "Autobiography," *Writings of Jefferson,* 1:70-72; Jefferson, *Notes on Virginia, Writings of Jefferson*, 2:203-204. See discussion by Cappon, "The Advantages of Education," *Adams-Jefferson Letters,* 2:478-480.

139. Peterson, *Thomas Jefferson and the New Nation*, 961-988.

140. "Freedom of Religion at the University of Virginia," 7 October 1822, in Saul K. Padover, ed., *The Complete Jefferson* (New York: Tudor Publishing Co., 1943), 957-958.

141. Padover, *The Complete Jefferson,* 957.

142. See Healey, *Jefferson on Religion in Public Education*, 205-209.

143. Sheldon, *Political Philosophy of Thomas Jefferson*, 125.

144. See letter from Jefferson to John Adams, 15 August 1820, *Adams-Jefferson Letters*, 2:568; letter from Jefferson to John Adams, 14 March 1820, *Adams-Jefferson Letters*, 2:561-562. See discussion in Koch, *Philosophy of Thomas Jefferson*, 34-35; Boorstin, *The Lost World of Thomas Jefferson*, 112-119.

145. Letter from John Adams to Jefferson, 22 July 1813, *Adams-Jefferson Letters,* 2:363.

146. Letter from John Adams to Jefferson, 12 May 1820, *Adams-Jefferson Letters*, 2:564.

147. Letter from Jefferson to John Adams, 15 August 1820, *Adams-Jefferson Letters*, 2:567.

148. Letter from Jefferson to John Adams, 15 August 1820, *Adams-Jefferson Letters*, 2:567-568.

149. Letter from Jefferson to John Adams, 14 March 1820, *Adams-Jefferson Letters,* 2:562. See also letter from Jefferson to Doctor Thomas Cooper, 14 August 1820, *Writings of Jefferson,* 15:266; letter from Jefferson to Judge Augustus B. Woodward, 24 March 1824, *Writings of Jefferson*, 16:18-19.

150. Letter from Jefferson to John Adams, 14 March 1820, *Adams-Jefferson Letters,* 2:562.

151. Letter from John Adams to Jefferson, 12 May 1820, *Adams-Jefferson Letters,* 2:563.

152. See letter from John Adams to Jefferson, 12 May 1820, *Adams-Jefferson Letters,* 2:565; letter from Jefferson to John Adams, 8 January 1825, *Adams-Jefferson Letters*, 2:606.

153. Randall, *Life of Jefferson*, 1:41.

154. Letter from Jefferson to Governor John Page, 25 June 1804, *Writings of Jefferson,* 11:31.

155. Peterson, *Thomas Jefferson and the New Nation,* 246. See also Randall, *Life of Jefferson,* 1:380-382.

156. Randall, *Life of Jefferson*, 1:384.

157. Letter from John Adams to Jefferson, 20 October 1818, *Adams-Jefferson Letters,* 2:529.

158. Letter from Jefferson to John Adams, 13 November 1818, *Adams-Jefferson Letters,* 2:529.

159. Letter from Jefferson to John Adams, 15 August 1820, *Adams-Jefferson Letters,* 2:567-568.

160. Letter from Jefferson to John Adams, 13 November 1818, *Adams-Jefferson Letters*, 2:529.

161. Peterson, *The Jefferson Image in the American Mind*, 3-6.

Chapter 4

Liberalism, Classicism, and Christianity in Jefferson's Political Thought

Garrett Ward Sheldon

The scholarship in early American historiography has reached a consensus that three dominant ideological strains existed in Revolutionary and early Republican America: Classical Republicanism, Lockean liberalism, and Christianity.[1]

Thomas Jefferson's political philosophy reflects Christian, liberal, and classical republican qualities.[2] Given their widely divergent conceptions of human nature, politics, and ethics, the presence of these schools of thought in Jefferson's philosophy has led to difficulties in understanding the nature of Jeffersonian democratic theory. Scholars have at times argued persuasively that Jefferson's political ideas were purely Lockean or purely Aristotelian, citing evidence from Jefferson's own writings. By distinguishing between classical and liberal conceptions of human nature, political society, and social ethics, and by showing how Jefferson's thought at different times reflected each, one can establish the basis for a detailed historical analysis of the development of Jefferson's political philosophy in which those differences dissolve into a consistent and comprehensive worldview. Similarly, an examination of his Christianity within his political philosophy will reveal how Jefferson's religious ethics affected how he used liberal and classical ideas.

Classical Greek political thought conceived of man as a naturally social and political being. Aristotle declared that "man is by nature a political animal. . . . Men have a natural desire for life in society."[3] Aristotle distinguished man, who is *political*, from merely *social* creatures (such as bees or ants) by mankind's capacity for "reasoned speech."[4] But he also insisted that "the real difference between man and other animals is that humans alone have perception of good and evil, right and wrong, just and unjust."[5] These unique faculties of reasoned speech and moral choice render humans naturally social and political, as neither can be either developed or exercised in isolation; they make political society at once possible and necessary. And, as classical political philosophy regards these distinctive human faculties as the highest qualities in man, the political deliberation that develops and refines those faculties becomes man's noblest pursuit—cultivating his distinctive *telos* and creating a virtuous polity. As J. G. A. Pocock has shown, such development, for Aristotle, involved both moral and material preconditions. Aristotle's citizen must possess the economic independence enabling him to enter freely the public realm on an equal basis with his fellow citizens and a requisite moral character.[6]

Modern, liberal political philosophy conceives of man as naturally individual and independent. John Locke declared that man in his natural state is "free, equal and independent."[7] This free and separate condition derives from liberalism's conception of man as essentially a material being, ruled by the private physical senses that he shares with no one, guided by the pleasures and pains of this world, motivated primarily by a desire for continued life, or "self-preservation." Such material existence gives the natural right to those things ("life, liberty, and property") which insure that continued existence. The power of reason is employed by man to best secure those individual rights and that self-preservation. Man's rational faculties do not form an inevitable social bond, as much as the means to create a government that secures his individual freedom and independence, or right to privacy.

Jefferson's conception of man's nature appears liberal in his most famous document, the Declaration of Independence. Jefferson wrote: "We hold these truths to be sacred and undeniable; that all men are created equal and independent, that from that equal creation they derive rights inherent and inalienable, among which are the preservation of life, and liberty, and the pursuit of happiness."[8] Elsewhere, however, Jefferson's view of humanity seems classical. He declared in various letters that man is "an animal destined to live in society," because the "Creator . . . intended man for a social animal."[9] He criticized Hobbes's psychology (calling it a "humiliation to human nature")[10] and offered an alternative syllogism echoing Aristotle's conception of a naturally social and ethical humanity: "Man was created for social intercourse; but social intercourse cannot be maintained without a sense of justice; then man must have been created with a sense of justice."[11] On several occasions Jefferson seemed more inclined to ascribe an error on God's part than to admit that man is not naturally a social and ethical being: "The Creator would indeed have been a bungling artist, had he intended man for a social animal, without planting in him social dispositions."[12] Whether from Classical Republican Greek and Roman philosophy (with which we know he was familiar) or Scottish Moral Sense philosophy, this tendency in Jefferson's thought is non-Lockean.

Corresponding to its vision of human nature as consisting of free, equal, and independent individuals possessing natural rights to life, liberty, and property, liberalism conceives of politics as a limited state of delegated authority charged with preserving individual rights. For Locke, if all men were rationally self-interested and capable of respecting others' rights, no state would be necessary at all. But because some men violate the rights of others by threatening their lives or property, a government is instituted, by the consent of the governed, to secure the natural rights of individuals from invasion by others:

> to avoid, and remedy those inconveniences of the State of Nature . . . Men . . . join and unite into a community, for their comfortable, safe, and peaceable living one amongst another, in a secure Enjoyment of their Properties, and a greater Security against any that are not of it. . . . The great and *chief end* of Mens uniting into Commonwealths, and putting themselves under Government, *is the Preservation of their Property*.[13]

Because this liberal government is established by free individuals and limited to preserving their natural rights, if it ever ceases to perform its function (or worse, invades the peoples' rights), then those individuals that formed it may dissolve the government and establish one that will properly serve their interests. Such dissolution of government constitutes Locke's famous "right to revolution": "When by the Arbitrary Power of the Prince, the Electors, or ways of Election are altered, without the Consent, and contrary to the common Interest of the People, there . . . the *Legislative is altered* . . . [and] the People are at liberty to provide for themselves, by erecting a new Legislative."[14] Ethics are received privately, through family discipline and training and freely chosen church experience.

In contrast to Locke's conception of the state as limited to preserving individual rights, the ancients conceived of politics as cultivating man's highest faculties and establishing a polity of virtue and purpose. Aristotle maintained that man is naturally a social being, born with the capacity for reasoned speech and moral choice, but he also insisted that those attributes be cultivated and refined: "virtues are implanted in us neither by nature nor contrary to nature: we are by nature equipped with the ability to receive them, and habit brings this ability to completion and fulfillment. . . . [W]e are provided with the capacity [*dynamis*: potential] first, and display the activity [*energia*: actuality] afterward."[15] And the best way in which to develop man's social faculties is through direct participation in the politics of a small democratic society: "the state cannot be defined merely as a community dwelling in the same place and preventing its members from wrong-doing and promoting the exchange of goods and services. . . . [Rather, politics should] engender a certain character in the citizens and to make them good and disposed to perform noble actions."[16]

So, Aristotle's notion of citizenship implies the direct participation in local politics, which cultivates man's social and ethical faculties: "A citizen is in general one who has a share both in ruling and in being ruled . . . with a view to a life that is in accordance with goodness."[17] Such direct citizen participation in political affairs necessitates a small democracy, like the Greek polis, where everyone knows his fellow citizens: "In order to give decisions on matters of justice and for the purpose of distributing offices in accordance with the work of the applicants, it is necessary that the citizens should know each other and know what kind of people they are."[18] A liberal state limited to protecting private rights may easily be a vast representative democracy; but a classical republic that seeks to cultivate man's social faculties, which conceives of a "public" realm apart from private interest, requires small participatory democracy, and an economically independent citizenry, such as Jefferson's "wards."[19]

Jefferson's conception of politics seems at times to reflect the liberal, social contract view of a limited government devoted to preserving private rights. Again, this perspective appears in the Declaration of Independence: "to secure these ends, governments are instituted among men, deriving their just powers from the consent of the governed; [and] whenever any form of government shall become destructive of these ends, it is the right of the people to alter or to abolish it, and to institute new government."[20] This liberal view is also found in Jefferson's writings respecting the federal government, as evidenced in his first inaugural address: "[America requires] a wise and frugal government, which shall restrain men from injuring one another, which shall leave them otherwise free to regulate their own pursuits of industry and improvement."[21]

Still, much of Jefferson's writing concerning American democracy seems to advocate small participatory republics, cultivating man's innate social faculties and establishing a virtuous republic. Jefferson's extensive efforts in dividing the Virginia counties into wards of five to six square miles and one hundred citizens for educational, economic, and political purposes reveal strongly classical sympathies: "Each ward would thus be a small republic within itself, and every man in the State would thus become an acting member of the common government, transacting in person a great portion of its rights and duties . . . and entirely within his competence. The wit of man cannot devise a more solid basis for a free, durable and well-administered republic."[22] Elsewhere, Jefferson indicated that without such citizen participation in the virtuous republic, leaders would turn into "wolves" and the people would be reduced to "mere automatons of misery, to have no sensibilities but for sinning and suffering."[23] Thus, with respect to his efforts to amend Virginia's constitution, dividing the counties into small ward republics, Jefferson wrote, after the prophet Simeon (who, after seeing the infant Jesus, declared he had seen the salvation of God), "Could I once see this I should consider it as the dawn of the salvation of the republic, and say with old Simeon, '*nunc dimittis Domine*.'"[24]

Lockean social ethics are essentially negative by virtue of their moral imperative to not harm others, to refrain from infringing upon others' rights and freedom, allowing citizens to pursue their own interests in ways that they see fit. Individuals, society, and the state are obliged to respect the rights of the individual, especially as they relate to the individual's pursuit of his own self-interest (or self-preservation) and to the life, liberty, and property necessary to that pursuit. Conservative, laissez-faire economics, with its emphasis on leaving the market forces free to regulate themselves, without political interference, corresponds nicely with these negative liberal ethics.[25] Their political ascension is usually marked by the formal separation of ethics and politics, or church and state, or individual liberty of conscience.

The origins of such ethics reside in the epistemology emerging from modern empiricism, which relies on individual sensory perception as the sole source of knowledge. For, if no unified truth can emerge from the diversity of perceptions, no one is justified in prescribing moral lessons to others; the autonomous perception and judgment of the individual must be respected. No objective standards can exist above subjective choice, given such epistemological relativism. The one area where liberal psychology can legislate is with regard to material harm and loss, or violations of individuals' rights and freedom. Therefore, liberal social ethics are confined to restraining and punishing violence and theft (the state *qua* police), but otherwise leaving individuals free to their own devices. Ethics are taught in the "private" realms of family and church.

Classical social ethics are positive in the sense that they insist that it is not enough to merely refrain from injuring others; moral action requires an effort to improve others, encouraging the perfection of their souls. As Aristotle maintains that happiness comes from possessing a virtuous character, individuals are obliged to cultivate the highest goodness in others.[26] Socrates's rebuttal of Meletus's charge of corrupting the Athenean youth (that one is made better or worse by the quality of one's associates, making deliberate corruption of others harmful to oneself) commends an ethics that ties one's own goodness and happiness to those around one, and obliges one to cultivate others' goodness.[27] But such ethics imply an objective standard—revealed by God or determined collectively—that transcends individual perception and interest. Perhaps the best statement of these classical social ethics (which re-emerge in Christian ethics) is that made by Socrates at his trial after receiving the sentence of death:

> When my sons grow up, gentlemen, if you think they are putting money or anything else before goodness, take your revenge by plaguing them as I plagued you; and if they fancy themselves for no reason, you must scold them just as I scolded you, for neglecting the important things and thinking that they are good for something when they are good for nothing. If you do this, I shall have had justice at your hands.[28]

Thomas Jefferson's social ethics reveal a liberal inclination in his attack on the established Church of England and in his advocacy of the separation of church and state and the corollary right to religious freedom.[29] Yet, Jefferson's advocacy of religious freedom did not derive so much from an epistemological skepticism as from the hope that through the free expression of all religious denominations, the people might distill those simple teachings of Jesus that Jefferson considered the one true religion. His preference for Christian ethics also derived from his belief that they were the most advanced social ethics or morals governing human relations, and so most suited to a naturally social being and the most social of regimes—participatory democracy.

Jefferson's personal ethics also reveal a liberal reluctance to force his moral views on others, as he expressed in a letter to his grandson: "I never saw an instance of one of two disputants convincing the other by argument. [But] I have seen many, on their getting warm, becoming rude, and shooting one another."[30] Instead of preaching to others, Jefferson encouraged "asking questions, as if for information, or by suggesting doubts."[31] This seems mild, indeed, but it was also the method of Socrates and Jesus.[32]

Jefferson's conception of a virtuous American republic presumed the existence of a social ethic appropriate to a naturally social being possessing a divinely ordained moral sense. This to him was the religion of Christian ethics, which conformed to man's natural sympathies and fostered a sense of duty to his fellow citizens. As Jefferson wrote to John Adams:

> If, by *religion*, we are to understand *Sectarian dogmas*, in which no two of them agree, then your exclamation . . . is just, 'that this would be the best of all possible worlds, if there were no religion in it.' But if the moral precepts, innate in man, and made a part of his physical condition, as necessary for a social being, if the sublime doctrines . . . taught us by Jesus of Nazareth in which all agree, constitute true religion, then, without it, this would be, as you again say, 'something not fit to be named, even indeed a Hell.'[33]

If man were merely a solitary creature capable only of refining his own self-control and personal serenity—the ancient moralists would be enough. But Jefferson regarded man as essentially a social and political being, requiring participation in the human community for his full development and happiness, and therefore in need of an ethical creed that enhances relations among individuals and promotes social harmony.[34] It was into the world of classical self-perfection, insisted Jefferson, that Jesus gave a moral philosophy suited to man's true, God-given nature: "His [Jesus'] moral doctrines, relating to kindred and friends, were more pure and perfect than those of the most correct of the philosophers, . . . and they went far beyond both in inculcating universal philanthropy not only to kindred and friends, to neighbors and countrymen, but to all mankind, gathering all into one family, under the bonds of love, charity, peace, common wants and common aids. . . . [Herein lies] the peculiar superiority of the system of Jesus over all others."[35]

Christ's ethical teachings of love, repentance, and forgiveness, of universal brotherhood and charity provided, for Jefferson, "the most sublime and benevolent code of morals which has ever been offered to man" for his life in society.[36] "Epictetus and Epicurus give laws for governing ourselves, Jesus a supplement of the duties and charities we owe to others."[37]

While extolling the ethical teachings of Christ, Jefferson distinguished between the "genuine" lessons of Jesus and the "spurious" dogmas of various disciples and sectarian orders. To separate the true teachings of Christ from their specious imitations (which Jefferson considered as easily distinguishable as "the gold from the dross," the "grain from the chaff," or "as diamonds in a dunghill"),[38] he composed a *Philosophy of Jesus* and a *Life and Morals of Jesus* by extracting those portions of the Gospels which presented the ethics in their purest, simplest form.[39] Ironically, it was his abiding and reverent belief in these Christian ethical teachings that led Jefferson to criticize the institutionalized church, but which also led many to question his religious sincerity. His specific attacks on the church and clergy (especially the worldly established Anglican church of Virginia in which he was baptized and served as vestryman) reveal his love of Christian principles. Jefferson chastised the church for not living up to its divine mission, for not upholding the purity of the Christian faith in a corrupt world. He attacked the church for neglecting its duties, for its venality and hypocrisy in serving worldly authorities rather than measuring them against the high standards of Christian faith and by preaching poverty, peace, charity, and humility while practicing extravagance, persecution, and self-righteous pride.[40] Indeed, Jefferson's principal complaint against the church was that its distortions of Christ's ethical teachings, essential to a virtuous republic, drove good people away:

> They are mere usurpers of the Christian name, teaching a counter-religion made up of the *deliria* of crazy imaginations, as foreign from Christianity as is that of Mahomet. Their blasphemies have driven thinking men into infidelity, who have too hastily rejected the supposed author himself, with the horrors so falsely imputed to him. Had the doctrines of Jesus been preached always as pure as they came from his lips, the whole civilized world would now have been Christian.[41]

Jefferson's remedy for this perversion of true Christian teaching was the establishment of absolute religious freedom in America. Religious freedom and toleration, for Jefferson, was to serve the higher purpose of encouraging debate and dialogue among the various denominations, from which the simple ethical teachings of Christ, vital to Jefferson's vision of a virtuous republic, might be distilled and disseminated. He hoped that through freedom of religious practice and discussion that those basic teachings of Christ common to all denominations would gain ascendancy, bringing all religious people together and promoting peace and justice in the American republic. In his first inaugural address, Jefferson expressed this hoped-for effect of religious freedom, describing the country as "enlightened by a benign religion, professed, indeed, and practiced in various forms, yet all of them including honesty, truth, temperance, gratitude, and the love of man; acknowledging and adoring an overruling Providence."[42]

Thus, quite the contrary of emanating from a hostility or indifference toward Christianity, Jefferson's advocacy of religious freedom was designed to preserve true Christian teachings from the corruption of worldly institutions: "Had not the Roman government permitted free inquiry, Christianity could never have been introduced. Had not free inquiry been indulged at the era of the reformation, the corruption's of Christianity could not have been purged away. If it be restrained now, the present corruptions will be protected, and new ones encouraged."[43]

Jefferson's "Bill for Establishing Religious Freedom" began this process of cleansing the church by denouncing the established Anglican church for "impiously" obstructing the Christian faith:

> Almighty God hath created the mind free, and . . . all attempts to influence it by temporal punishments, or burthens, or by civil incapacitations, tend only to beget habits of hypocrisy and meanness, and are a departure from the plan of the holy author of our religion. . . . [T]he impious presumption of legislature and ruler, civil as well as ecclesiastical, . . . [to] have assumed dominion over the faith of others . . . tends also to corrupt the principles of that very religion it is meant to encourage.[44]

The official church that imprisoned orthodox (Baptist) preachers of the Gospel actually persecuted Christians rather than preserved the Faith. But the disestablishment of the Anglican church did not, for Jefferson, automatically result in complete religious freedom (by which he understood the exposure to various denominational creeds, from which the true, simple teachings of Jesus might be distilled). So, for example, Jefferson opposed the establishment of a Chair of Divinity at the University of Virginia, not because he wished to exclude religion from the public institution, but because a *single* Chair of Divinity would imply representation of only one denomination (just as had the established church): "It was not, however, to be understood that instruction in religious opinion and duties was meant to be precluded by the public authorities, as indifferent to the interests of society. On the contrary, the relations which exist between man and his Maker, and the duties resulting from those relations, are the most interesting and important to every human being, and the most incumbent on his study and investigation."[45]

Jefferson's solution to the problem of one dominant religious sect in the public university was not to exclude all religion from the institution, but to invite the free expression of *all* denominations within the university's walls.

> A remedy . . . has been suggested of promising aspect, which, while it excludes the public authorities from the domain of religious freedom, will give to the sectarian schools of divinity the full benefit the public provisions made for instruction in the other branches of science. . . . It has, therefore, been in contemplation, and suggested by some pious individuals, who perceive the advantages of associating other studies with those of religion, to establish their religious schools on the confines of the University, so as to give to their students ready and convenient access and attendance on the scientific lectures of the University. . . . Such establishments would offer the further and greater advantage of enabling the students of the University to attend religious exercises with the professor of their particular sect, either in the rooms of the building still to be erected . . . or in the lecturing room of such professor. . . . Such an arrangement would complete the circle of the useful sciences embraced by this institution, and would fill the chasm now existing, on principles which would leave inviolate the constitutional freedom of religion.[46]

The presence of all religious denominations within the walls of the public university would give students the opportunity to be exposed to all dogmas, from which, Jefferson hoped, they might distill that which was common to them all—the basic ethical teachings of Jesus—to the benefit of the virtuous American republic, without imposing a single religious creed or violating their religious freedom.

This understanding of freedom of religion is also revealed in Jefferson's description of religious life in Charlottesville, where the absence of church buildings compelled the separate denominations to worship together, taking turns conduction services in the public courthouse:

> In our village of Charlottesville, there is a good degree of religion, with a small spice only of fanaticism. We have four sects, but without either church or meeting-house. The court-house is the common temple, one Sunday in the month to

> each. Here, Episcopalian and Presbyterian, Methodist and Baptist, meet together, join in hymning their Maker, listen with attention and devotion to each others' preachers, and all mix in society with perfect harmony.[47]

Jefferson's tastes were rich and eclectic. He was drawn to, and he drew from, diverse sources. That was true of his scientific, aesthetic, and intellectual interests. It was also true of his political thought. As has been illustrated, this most famous American founder, Thomas Jefferson, blended the three dominant ideological strains in early American political thought: Classical Republicanism, Lockean liberalism, and Christianity.

Notes

1. See Donald S. Lutz, *A Preface to American Political Theory* (Lawrence: University Press of Kansas, 1992); Michael P. Zuckert, *The Natural Rights Republic: Studies in the Foundation of the American Political Tradition* (Notre Dame, Ind.: Notre Dame University Press, 1996); and my *The Political Philosophy of Thomas Jefferson* (Baltimore: Johns Hopkins University Press, 1991), from which this essay is largely taken.

2. By British liberal I mean primarily the political philosophies of Thomas Hobbes and John Locke; by Classical Republican I mean the political philosophies of Aristotle, Cicero, Montesquieu, and James Harrington. Christianity for Jefferson meant, primarily, Protestantism.

3. Aristotle, *The Politics,* trans. T. A. Sinclair (Baltimore: Penguin, 1962), bk. 1, ch. 2; bk. 3, ch. 6.

4. *Ibid*., bk. 1, ch. 2.

5. *Ibid*. Aristotle included the human affections as another source of man's natural propensity for society: "for it is our love of others that causes us to prefer life in a society; and they all contribute towards that good life which is the purpose of the state." *Ibid*., bk. 3, ch. 9.

6. J.G.A. Pocock, *The Machiavellian Moment: Florentine Political Thought and the Atlantic Republican Tradition* (Princeton, N.J.: Princeton University Press, 1975), 66-68; Aristotle, *Politics*, bk. 3, ch. 9.

7. John Locke, *Two Treatises of Government*, ed. Peter Laslett (New York: New American Library, 1965), 374.

8. From Jefferson's "original Rough draught," prior to Committee revisions, *The Papers of Thomas Jefferson*, ed. Julian P. Boyd, 27 vols. to date (Princeton, N.J.: Princeton University Press, 1950-), 1:423 [hereinafter *Papers of Jefferson*]. Much has been made of Jefferson's substitution of "pursuit of happiness" for Locke's "property" or "estate." My argument is that Jefferson's use of "happiness" reflects his Aristotelian bent, as seen as the ultimate end of human life in book 1 of Aristotle's *Nicomachean Ethics*, trans. Martin Ostwald (Indianapolis: Bobbs-Merrill, 1962).

9. Letter from Thomas Jefferson to John Adams, 14 October 1816, *The Adams-Jefferson Letters*, ed. Lester J. Cappon, 2 vols. (Chapel Hill: Institute for Early American History and Culture; University of North Carolina Press, 1959), 2:492 [hereinafter *Adams-Jefferson Letters*]; letter from Jefferson to Thomas Law, 13 June 1814, *The Complete Jefferson*, ed. Saul K. Padover (New York: Tudor, 1943), 1033 [hereinafter *Complete Jefferson*]. See also letter from Jefferson to Peter Carr, 10 August 1787, *The Writings of Thomas Jefferson*, ed. Andrew A. Lipscomb and Albert Ellery Bergh, 20 vols. (Washington D.C.: Thomas Jefferson Memorial Association, 1904-05), 6:257 [hereinafter *Writings of Jefferson*].

10. Letter from Thomas Jefferson to Francis W. Gilmer, 7 June 1816, *Writings of Jefferson*, 15:24.

11. *Ibid*., 15:25.

12. Letter from Thomas Jefferson to Thomas Law, 13 June 1814, *Complete Jefferson*, 1033. See also letter from Jefferson to Peter Carr, 10 August 1787, *Writings of Jefferson*, 6:257 ("He who made us would have been a pitiful bungler . . ."); letter from Jefferson to John Adams, 14 October 1816, in *Adams-Jefferson Letters*, 2:492 ("as a wise creator must have seen to be necessary in an animal destined to live in society").

13. Locke, *Two Treatises*, 369, 375, 395.

14. *Ibid.*, 457, 459.

15. Aristotle, *Nicomachean Ethics*, bk. 2, sec. 1103a. See also bk. 2, secs. 1103a-1103b ("virtues . . . we acquire by first having put them into action . . . we learn by doing . . . we become just by the practice of just actions").

16. Aristotle, *Politics*, bk. 3, ch. 9; and Aristotle, *Nicomachean Ethics*, bk. 1, sec. 1099b.

17. Aristotle, *Politics*, bk. 3, ch. 13. See also *Politics*, bk. 3, ch. 1 ("what effectively distinguishes the citizen from all others is his participation in Judgement and Authority, that is, holding office, legal, political, administrative"); bk. 3, ch. 5 ("there are different kinds of citizen, but . . . a citizen in the fullest sense is one who has a share in the privileges of rule").

18. *Ibid.*, bk. 7, ch. 4

19. *Ibid.*, bk. 1, ch. 8; bk. 3, chs. 4, 9; Pocock, *The Machiavellian Moment*, 66-68.

20. "Jefferson's 'original Rough draught' of the Declaration of Independence," *Papers of Jefferson*, 1:423.

21. Thomas Jefferson, "First Inaugural Address," 4 March 1801, *Complete Jefferson*, 386.

22. Letter from Thomas Jefferson to Major John Cartwright, 5 June 1824, *Writings of Jefferson*, 16:46.

23. Letter from Thomas Jefferson to Colonel Edward Carrington, 16 January 1787, *Writings of Jefferson*, 6:58; and letter from Jefferson to Samuel Kercheval, 12 July 1816, *Writings of Jefferson*, 15:40.

24. Letter from Thomas Jefferson to Governor John Tyler, 26 May 1810, *Writings of Jefferson*, 12:394.

25. For this reason, along with Locke's justification for the unlimited accumulation of property, C. B. Macpherson considers them the ethics of bourgeois individualism and capitalist social relations, see *The Political Theory of Possessive Individualism: Hobbes to Locke* (Oxford: Oxford University Press, 1962); *Democratic Theory: Essays in Retrieval* (Oxford: Clarendon Press, 1973), 228-233; and *The Life and Times of Liberal Democracy* (Oxford: Oxford University Press, 1977), 2.

26. Aristotle. *Nicomachean Ethics*, bks. 9, 10.

27. Plato, *The Last Days of Socrates,* trans. Hugh Tredennick (Baltimore: Penguin, 1954), 70-74.

28. *Ibid.*, 76.

29. Thomas Jefferson, "A Bill for Establishing Religious Freedom (1779)," *Complete Jefferson*, 946-947.

30. Letter from Thomas Jefferson to Thomas Jefferson Randolph, 24 November 1808, *Writings of Jefferson*, 12:199.

31. Ibid.

32. See Plato's Socratic Dialogues, esp. *Crito, Euthyphro, Gorgias, Protagoras, Meno,* book 1 of *The Republic;* and *The Gospels,* esp. *Matthew* 22:41-45; *Mark* 7:1-24; *Luke* 20:1-9; and *John* 18:33-39.

33. Letter from Thomas Jefferson to John Adams, 5 May 1817, *Adams-Jefferson Letters*, 2:512. See also Eugene R. Sheridan, introduction to Dickinson W. Adams, ed., *Jefferson's Extracts from the Gospels* (Princeton, N.J.: Princeton University Press, 1983), 3-42; William D. Gould, "Religious Opinions of Thomas Jefferson," *Mississippi Valley*

Historical Review 20 (September 1933): 191-208; George M. Knoles, "Religious Ideas of Thomas Jefferson," *Mississippi Valley Historical Review* 30 (September 1943): 187-204; J. Leslie Hall, "The Religious Opinions of Thomas Jefferson," *Sewanee Review* 21 (April 1913): 164-176; Charles B. Sanford, *The Religious Life of Thomas Jefferson* (Charlottesville, Va.: University Press of Virginia, 1984); Henry Wilder Foote, *The Religion of Thomas Jefferson* (Boston: Beacon Press, 1960).

34. So, Jefferson's criticism of the ancient moral philosophers runs along these lines: "In developing our duties to others, they were short and defective. They embraced, indeed, the circles of kindred and friends, and inculcated patriotism, or the love of our country in the aggregate, as a primary obligation; towards our neighbors and countrymen they taught justice, but scarcely viewed them as within the circle of benevolence. Still less have they inculcated peace, charity, and love of our fellow-men, or embraced with benevolence the whole family of mankind." Letter from Jefferson to Dr. Benjamin Rush, 21 April 1803, *Complete Jefferson*, 948.

35. Letter from Thomas Jefferson to Dr. Benjamin Rush, 21 April 1803, *Complete Jefferson*, 949-950.

36. Letter from Thomas Jefferson to John Adams, 12 October 1813, *Adams-Jefferson Letters*, 2:384.

37. Letter from Thomas Jefferson to William Short, 31 October 1819, *Writings of Jefferson*, 15:220.

38. Jefferson, quoted in Adrienne Koch, *The Philosophy of Thomas Jefferson* (New York: Columbia University Press, 1943), 23.

39. See Adams, ed., *Jefferson's Extracts from the Gospels*.

40. See letter from Thomas Jefferson to John Adams, 5 May 1817, *Adams-Jefferson Letters,* 2:512; letter from Jefferson to Wendover, 13 March 1815, *Complete Jefferson*, 953-955; and letter from Jefferson to Dr. Benjamin Waterhouse, 26 June 1822, *Complete Jefferson*, 956.

41. Letter from Thomas Jefferson to Dr. Benjamin Waterhouse, 26 June 1822, *Complete Jefferson*, 956. See also letter from Jefferson to John Adams, 5 May 1817, *Adams-Jefferson Letters*, 2:512; and letter from Jefferson to Peter Carr, 10 August 1787, *Writings of Jefferson*, 6:258-259.

42. Jefferson, "First Inaugural Address," 4 March 1801, *Complete Jefferson*, 385.

43. Jefferson, *Notes on the State of Virginia*, in *Complete Jefferson*, 675.

44. Jefferson, "A Bill for Establishing Religious Freedom," *Complete Jefferson*, 946-947. It was in relation to an established state church that Jefferson made his famous reference to the "wall of separation" between church and state (though even there he wishes for religious freedom to encourage citizens' "social duties," i.e., knowledge of Christian ethics):

> I contemplate with sovereign reverence that act of the whole American people which declared that their legislature should "make no law respecting an establishment of religion, or prohibit the free exercise thereof," thus building a wall of separation between church and State. Adhering to this expression of the supreme will of the nation in behalf of the rights of conscience, I shall see with sincere satisfaction the progress of those sentiments which tend to restore to man all his natural rights, convinced he has no natural right in opposition to his social duties.

Letter from Thomas Jefferson to a Committee of the Danbury Baptist Association, 1 January 1802, *Complete Jefferson*, 518-519.

45. Jefferson, 7 October 1822, *Complete Jefferson*, 957.

46. *Ibid.*, 957-958.

47. Letter from Thomas Jefferson to Doctor Thomas Cooper, 2 November 1822, *Writings of Jefferson,* 15:404, as quoted in Foote, *The Religion of Thomas Jefferson*, 7-8. Despite this ecumenical sentiment, Jefferson, two years later, contributed to the building of separate houses of worship, showing a decided partiality to his own Episcopal church. His account book of 8 March 1824 reads: "I have subscribed to the building of an Episcopal church, two hundred dollars; a Presbyterian church, sixty dollars; and a Baptist, twenty-five dollars." Foote, *The Religion of Thomas Jefferson*, 8. Jefferson's general appreciation of the relation between ethics and politics is revealed in a letter from Jefferson to Judge Augustus B. Woodward (24 March 1824, *Writings of Jefferson*, 16:19), in which he stated that he regarded "ethics, as well as religion, as supplements to law in the government of man"; and letter from Jefferson to William Johnson (12 June 1823, *Complete Jefferson*, 322) that the state's "moral rule of their citizens" will be enhanced by its "enforcing moral duties and restraining vice."

Chapter 5

Jefferson and Bolingbroke: Some Notes on the Question of Influence

Douglas L. Wilson

Consider this statement: "The faculty of distinguishing between right and wrong, true and false, which we call reason or common sense, which is given to every man by our own bountiful Creator, and which most men lose by neglect, is the light of the mind, and ought to guide all the operations of it."[1] Everything we know about Thomas Jefferson suggests that, early and late, he would have agreed wholeheartedly with this statement. If we had proof that, as a young man questing after intellectual direction, he actually read it, would we be justified in considering it the source of his own settled conviction? Did reading it, in a word, *influence* him in his way of looking at things? What, indeed, is the measure and the meaning of influence? In the discussion that follows, I hope to shed light on these questions by examining the case for a particular text having been influential on the thinking of Thomas Jefferson.

In 1765, Jefferson was a twenty-two-year-old legal apprentice studying for the bar. Late in that year, possibly after passing his bar examination in October, he began copying out extracts from a five-volume collection of Lord Bolingbroke's *Philosophical Works.*[2] Just how extensive these extracts were is unclear, but he later included some fifty-four entries, amounting to more than ten thousand words, in his literary commonplace book, a selection that far exceeds the word count of any other author represented. And not only were the extracts copied from the controversial Lord Bolingbroke numerous, they were provocative as well, framing in bold language heterodox religious opinions that were widely considered impious, if not heretical or blasphemous.

For all but specialists in eighteenth-century British history, it is necessary to inquire, who was Lord Bolingbroke, and why did Jefferson read and commonplace him so assiduously? But even for specialists, these are the right questions, for the Bolingbroke that Jefferson was reading in 1765 was not the Bolingbroke with which today's specialists are familiar. Henry St. John, the first Viscount Bolingbroke, was one of the most brilliant politicians of the early years of the eighteenth century, an ambitious and successful Tory minister under Queen Anne, who lost favor, fled the country, and was attainted in exile for intriguing with the Pretender. Thereafter a political outsider, Bolingbroke subsequently fell back on his considerable literary skills to bedevil and harass his political antagonists and thereby created a body of political and historical writing that was influential for much of the century. A colorful conversationalist and wit, Bolingbroke was greatly admired by such men as Voltaire, Jonathan Swift, and Alexander Pope, who went so far as to predict that Bolingbroke would "be the greatest man in the world, either in his own time, or with posterity."[3] As Merrill Peterson observed, for these and many others, "Bolingbroke was one of the century's giants."[4]

I

Thomas Jefferson became one of this long train of notable eighteenth-century admirers. His own politics seem to owe something, possibly a great deal, to Bolingbroke's analysis of what went wrong with English constitutional government after the Glorious Revolution of 1688. Jefferson owned and presumably read all of Bolingbroke's major political works, though he says little about this directly.[5] To his grandson, Francis Eppes, a young college student writing to ask his grandfather's opinion of a controversial figure, Jefferson described him as an "honest" man who made "bitter enemies of the priests and Pharisees of [his] day." Bolingbroke, Jefferson wrote, "was called indeed a tory: but his writings prove him a stronger advocate for liberty than any of his countrymen, the whigs of the present day. Irritated by his exile, he committed one act unworthy of him, in connecting himself momentarily with a prince rejected by his country. But he redeemed that single act by his establishment of the principles which proved it to be wrong."[6]

Bolingbroke's *Philosophical Works,* the five-volume work commonplaced at such length by Jefferson, was not about politics. The author himself wrote: "The foregoing Essays, if they may deserve even that name, and the Fragments or minutes that follow were thrown upon paper in Mr. Pope's lifetime, and at his desire."[7] Alexander Pope, the greatest poet of his age and an intimate friend, was apparently greatly interested in Bolingbroke's ideas at the time he was composing his influential "An Essay on Man." The four principal parts of Pope's poem are framed as "Epistles" addressed to Bolingbroke, just as Bolingbroke's four principal essays in the *Philosophical Works* are addressed to Pope. That Bolingbroke and Pope had been engaged in a philosophical conversation is confirmed by the *Essay*'s opening lines:

> Awake, my St. John! leave all meaner things
> To low ambition, and the pride of Kings.
> Let us (since Life can little more supply
> Than just to look about us and to die)
> Expatiate free o'er all this scene of Man;
> A mighty maze! but not without a plan;
> . . . .
> Eye Nature's walks, shoot Folly as it flies,
> And catch the Manners living as they rise;

> Laugh where we must, be candid where we can;
> But vindicate the ways of God to Man.[8]

Pope's poem first appeared in 1733 and was widely acclaimed not only as a poem but also as a brilliant presentation of the great philosophical issues of the age. But when Bolingbroke's five-volume collection appeared posthumously in 1754, it enjoyed only a brief period of notoriety, perfectly characterized by Dr. Johnson's famous remark that the work proved Bolingbroke a scoundrel and a coward: "a scoundrel for charging a blunderbuss against religion and morality; a coward, because he had not resolution to fire it off himself, but left half a crown to a beggarly Scotchman [David Mallet], to draw the trigger after his death!"[9] Even this notoriety was short-lived, and the work was quickly forgotten. Except for its inclusion in a nineteenth-century edition of Bolingbroke's complete writings, *Philosophical Works* has never been reprinted and is scarcely known even to specialists.

If a book can be redeemed by making a deep impression on one consequential reader, Bolingbroke's *Philosophical Works* succeeded, for these essays seem to have made such an impression on the young Thomas Jefferson. This is manifest, as I have argued elsewhere, in at least two ways. The first is the extraordinary amount of material from this source that Jefferson copied and later retained in his commonplace book. These fifty-four entries represent six times as many words as he included from any other single author and constitute nearly forty percent of the entire contents of the literary commonplace book. The other telling circumstance is the remarkable extent to which major tenets of Bolingbroke's philosophical program were ultimately embraced by Jefferson: a thorough-going materialism; a rejection of metaphysics and all speculation that appears to venture beyond the reach of human apprehension; an uncompromising commitment to reason as the final arbiter of knowledge and validity; a disposition to regard churchmen and theologians as the corrupters of Christianity; a distaste for the doctrines of Plato and his influence on Christian teachings; and a strong skepticism regarding the historicity of biblical accounts.[10]

As readers of the literary commonplace book are aware, Jefferson makes no comment on the material he copies into it, so we can only guess at or infer his reasons for commonplacing Bolingbroke's writings at such length. That the passages greatly interested him seems beyond doubt. A further conclusion that is often drawn is that he found in them a source of new and compelling ideas. This would be influence indeed, but one is obliged to ask: what is the evidence for it? Superficially, there are sentiments and opinions of Bolingbroke's that Jefferson seems to echo in his own writing and practice, and these are well known. The most famous is perhaps the correspondence between what Bolingbroke says about judging the Bible on the same basis as classical historians and what Jefferson told his nephew Peter Carr: "Read the bible then, as you would read Livy or Tacitus."[11] Paul K. Conkin points to the circumstantial evidence that, at least in his early years, "Jefferson's religious views departed in no significant respect from those of Bolingbroke."[12] Merrill Peterson has scrutinized the intellectual connections between Jefferson and Bolingbroke and has deftly laid out the salient points of comparison.[13] His conclusion is that "there can be no doubt of his influence on Jefferson's moral and religious beliefs. All the passages in the commonplace book are from the later philosophical essays wherein Bolingbroke appears as the antagonist of priestly fraud and metaphysical delusion. These writings made the strongest impression on Jefferson's mind."[14]

While agreeing with this analysis, I propose here to narrow the focus and pursue the question of influence in a particular aspect, namely, Bolingbroke's qualities as a writer. In brief, I would like to present some reasons for thinking that whatever influence the *Philosophical Works* had on Jefferson may have owed less to *what* Bolingbroke said than to the *way* he said it. I want to suggest that Jefferson's interest in Bolingbroke's qualities as a writer, as opposed to a philosopher, is of paramount interest in the question of influence.

II

My first point is essentially chronological. The ability to date Jefferson's commonplacing of Bolingbroke provides leverage on the question of influence, for it enables us to determine that Jefferson copied these entries more than five and a half years after coming to Williamsburg. We know that for the first two of these years, he was a student of William Small at the College of William and Mary. Small's almost daily contact with his student apparently had an enormous impact on the young man's thinking, and the question of influence here is detailed by Jefferson himself in a well-known testimonial from his *Autobiography:*

> It was my great good fortune, and what probably fixed the destinies of my life that Dr. Wm. Small of Scotland was then professor of Mathematics, a man profound in most of the useful branches of science, with a happy talent of communication, correct and gentlemanly manners, & an enlarged & liberal mind. He, most happily for me, became soon attached to me & made me his daily companion when not engaged in the school; and from his conversation I got my first views of the expansion of science & of the system of things in which we are placed.[15]

Had Jefferson stopped there, one might be tempted to conclude that the reference to "the system of things in which we are placed" was intended as narrowly scientific, but what follows makes clear a much broader scope of influence:

> Fortunately the Philosophical chair became vacant soon after my arrival at college, and he was appointed to fill it per interim: and he was the first who ever gave in that college regular lectures in Ethics, Rhetoric & Belles lettres. He returned to Europe in 1762 [an error for 1764], having previously filled up the measure of his goodness to me, by procuring for me, from his most intimate friend G. Wythe, a reception as a student of law, under his direction, and introduced me to the acquaintance and familiar table of Governor Fauquier, the ablest man who had ever filled that office. With him, and at his table, Dr. Small & Mr. Wythe, his amici omnium horarum, & myself formed a partie quarree, & to the habitual conversations on these occasions I owed much instruction.[16]

What Jefferson is indicating here, of course, is that his college years afforded him an education that went far beyond the curriculum of the College, and that as a result he was constantly exposed to advanced and liberal ideas in his daily intercourse with Dr. Small and at Governor Fauquier's table. This is influence with a vengeance, but what I wish to suggest is that by late 1765, Jefferson's philosophical initiation into the discourse of the Enlightenment at the hands of this free-thinking "partie quarree," along with his prodigious reading, would in all likelihood have made him familiar with most of the basic ideas he found and commonplaced in Bolingbroke. As Merrill D. Peterson has pointed out, "[m]uch of what Jefferson found in Bolingbroke's religious writings he might have found, and did find, in the tracts and treatises of a host of English deists in the first half of the eighteenth century."[17] In these circumstances, Bolingbroke is unlikely to have been the actual source for most of the Enlightenment ideas Jefferson espoused later in life.

III

My next point focuses on one of those ideas. Because the documentary evidence of Jefferson's intellectual endeavors prior to 1765 is so scanty, the Bolingbroke entries in the literary commonplace book constitute virtually the first concrete indication one gets of things like his budding deism and his skeptical views of orthodox Christianity and the Bible. Thus, in charting the lines of force in Jefferson's intellectual career, the Bolingbroke entries often appear to be a starting point. But attention to the entries in Jefferson's commonplace books in the light of their dating, along with other evidence, makes it possible to question and qualify such assumptions and see that Jefferson's interest in some of the issues addressed in the Bolingbroke entries do indeed antedate his reading of the *Philosophical Works* in 1765.

Perhaps no aspect of Jefferson's philosophical stance was so staunch and implacable as his materialism. Of the widely held and respectable ideas that he could never accede to, none was more emphatically rejected than the notion of a purely spiritual reality. "To talk of *immaterial* existences," he insisted late in life, "is to talk of *nothings*."[18] There can be little doubt that this approximates Bolingbroke's position in the *Philosophical Works* or that this is an issue that attracted the young Jefferson's attention, as he commonplaced several passages pertaining to it. Something of Bolingbroke's characteristic method, as well as his distinctive style, is captured in the following entry on the existence of "spirit or immaterial substance":

> it will cost a reasonable mind much less to assume that a substance known by some of it's properties may have others that are unknown, and may be capable, in various systems, of operations quite inconceivable by us, according to the designs of infinite wisdom; than to assume that there is a substance, concerning which men do not pretend to know what it is, but merely what it is not.[19]

For evidence of Jefferson's interest in this issue, we are definitely able to go back further than 1765. Earlier entries in the literary commonplace book indicate that it may have first presented itself to Jefferson in the 1750s over the question of the materiality of the human soul. Certainly, the soul is referred to frequently in the portion of his literary commonplace book that reflects his reading between the ages of about fifteen and twenty.[20] Charles B. Sanford has offered an extended discussion of Jefferson's wrestle with the problem of the materiality or immateriality of the soul.[21] A provocative passage copied from Cicero's *Tusculan Disputations* asserts: "For if the soul is the heart or blood or brain, then assuredly, since it is material, it will perish with the rest of the body; if it is breath it will perhaps be dispersed in space; if fire it will be quenched."[22] This is followed shortly by two further entries from the same source pointing to the impossibility of bodily functions in the afterlife: "And such was the extent of deception . . . that though they knew that the bodies of the dead were consumed with fire, yet they imagined that events took place in the lower world which cannot take place and are not intelligible without bodies"; "Yet none the less they wish the phantoms to speak and this cannot take place without tongue and palate, or without a formed throat and chest and lungs in active working."[23] It seems clear that what absorbed the attention of the commonplacer here was the paradox of bodily functions without benefit of a body.

There has recently come to light another document that shows Jefferson's continuing concern with the issue of the materiality of the soul, and it also antedates the commonplacing of Bolingbroke in 1765. The collection of historical documents recently formed by Richard Gilder and Lewis Lehrman includes an early letter, hitherto unknown, from Jefferson's correspondence with his college friend, John Page, dated 26 July 1764.[24]

> I like your proposal of keeping up an epistolary correspondence on subjects of some importance. I do not at present recollect any difficult question in natural philosophy, but shall be glad to have your opinion on a subject much more interesting. What that is I will tell you. In perusing a magazine some time ago I met with an account of a person who had been drowned. He had continued under water 24 hours, and upon being properly treated when taken out he was restored to life. The fact is undoubted, and upon enquiry I have found that there have been many other instances of the same kind. Physicians say that when the parts of the body are restrained from performing their functions by any gentle cause which does not in any manner maim or injure any particular part, that to restore life in such a case nothing is requisite but to give the vital warmth to the whole body by gentle degrees, and to put the blood in motion by inflating the lungs. But the doubts which arose in my mind on reading the story were of another nature. We are generally taught that the soul leaves the body at the instant of death, that is, at the instant in which the organs of the body cease totally to perform their functions. But does not this story contradict this opinion? When then does the soul take it's departure? Let me have your opinion candidly and at length on this subject.[25]

It seems likely that Jefferson's barely submerged purpose here is to belittle the notion of the soul as something separate or detachable from the body. Reinforcing this suggestion is the highly revealing caveat that he adds at this point in the letter: "And as these are doubts which, were they to come to light, might do injustice to a man's moral principles in the eyes of persons of narrow and confined views it will be proper to take great care of our letters. I propose as one mean[s] of doing it to put no name or place to the top or bottom of the letter, and to inclose it in a false cover which may be burned as soon as opened."[26] The letter, one notes, is not signed. Jefferson's suggested precautions may strike us as both amusing and revealing, but they are only called for because heterodox views are in the offing.

We have here clear evidence that Jefferson had been giving thought to the materiality of the soul for several years by the time he came to read about it in Bolingbroke's *Philosophical Works* in 1765. Certain other of Bolingbroke's ideas, such as the primacy of reason and the law of nature, are in some measure anticipated in Jefferson's earlier commonplacing of Cicero.[27] In these circumstances, it seems clear that what he found in Bolingbroke was not something entirely new, but rather a deft and memorable way of treating an issue that already interested him.

IV

What did the young Jefferson admire in Bolingbroke's presentation? Because Jefferson himself makes no comment, we are obliged to speculate. The passage most frequently cited by commentators is this: "No hypothesis ought to be maintained if a single phaenomenon stands in direct opposition to it."[28] But this passage is uncharacteristically brief, and its presumed directness and pithiness are not present in the original, but are actually the result of Jefferson's plucking Bolingbroke's precept out of a more discursive sentence structure.

It seems inescapable that Jefferson admired Bolingbroke's way with an argument. In a representative extract, we find that Bolingbroke, rather than simply protesting that some parts of the Bible involve the godhead directly in bloodthirsty and unworthy acts, begins with a bold premise that he knows will be very difficult to resist and that he also knows can be used to make his point as a simple matter of deduction:

> I say that the law of nature is the law of god. of this I have the same demonstrative knowledge, that I have of the existence of god, the all-perfect being. I say that the all-perfect being cannot contradict himself; that he would contradict himself if the laws contained in the thirteenth chapter of Deuteronomy, to mention no others here, were his laws, since they contradict those of nature; and therefore that they are not his laws. [of] all this I have as certain, as intuitive, knowledge, as I have that two and two are equal to four, or that the whole is bigger than a part.[29]

Here it is possible to imagine that, apart from the obvious substantive appeal, it is the strategy of argumentation that attracts Jefferson, the calculated use of *a priori* reasoning by a skillful advocate who usually prefers to ground his argument in facts and experience.

In the matter of rhetorical tactics, consider the following extract. Having received a classical education from clergymen, Jefferson was familiar with the parallel often drawn between the classical and biblical writers. Bolingbroke's strategy is to grant all the claims of his adversaries except one, but insist upon that as a sticking point.

> We have the concurrent testimony of the sacred writers: and it has been asked, whether we have not as much knowledge of them as we have of several profane

> writers whose histories pass for authentic?—we read the histories of Arrian, and even of Q. Curtius, tho' we do not know who the latter was, and the commentaries of Caesar, as authentic histories. such they are too for all our purposes; and if passages which we deem genuine should be spurious, if others should be corrupted, or interpolated, and if the authors should have purposely, or through deception, disguised the truth, or advanced untruth, no great hurt would be done. But is this the case of the scriptures? in them, besides all the other circumstances necessary to constitute historical probability, it is not enough that the tenor of facts and doctrine[s] be true; the least error is of consequence.[30]

One thing that Jefferson surely admired in Bolingbroke, which Dr. Johnson just as surely deplored, was his ability to so deploy his argument that logic itself would appear responsible for statements that were shocking in the extreme to orthodox Christians. No better example could be cited than a passage arguing against the divine origin of the Ten Commandments.

> To shew, then, the more evidently how absurd, as well as impious, it is to ascribe these mosaical laws to god, let it be considered that neither the people of Israel, nor their legislator perhaps, knew anything of [a]nother life, wherein the crimes committed in this life are to be punished;—if Moses knew that crimes were to be punished in [a]nother life he deceived the people in the covenant they made by his intervention with god. if he did not know it, I say it with horror, the consequence, according to the hypothesis I oppose, must be that god deceived both him and them.[31]

"I say it with horror," of course, fools no one, nor, one presumes, was it intended to; its purpose was rather to call attention to the dexterous feat of argumentation that Bolingbroke has just performed. This underscores a salient feature of Bolingbroke's performance that probably had great appeal for Jefferson, a person who liked bold thinking but hated reproach, and that is the cool and guileless manner in which Bolingbroke manages to say such shocking things.

V

In offering advice to students, one effort that Jefferson frequently urged was the assiduous cultivation of one's literary taste and abilities, or "style." In a letter written not long after his own student years, he urged a prospective law student to devote some portion of his day

> to acquiring the art of writing & speaking correctly by the following exercises. Criticise the style of any books whatever, committing your criticisms to writing. Translate into the different styles, to wit, the elevated, the middling and the familiar. Orators and poets will furnish subjects of the first, historians of the second, & epistolary and Comic writers of the third—Undertake, at first, short compositions, as themes, letters &c., paying great attention to the correctness and elegance of your language. Read the Orations of Demosthenes & Cicero. Analyse these orations and examine the correctness of the disposition, language, figures, states of the cases, arguments &c.[32]

It is abundantly clear from this and many like references in his correspondence that Jefferson was himself—and believed that much depended on being—an ardent student of the stylistic qualities that distinguished effective writing. In his maturity, he allowed that "what is called style in writing or speaking is formed very early in life while the imagination is warm, and impressions are permanent."[33]

Another way to get at the importance for Jefferson of the writerly qualities of Lord Bolingbroke is to compare Jefferson's response with that of his equally bookish friend, John Adams. We know from Adams's incomparable diaries that he read Bolingbroke at about the same stage of life, just after his graduation from Harvard.[34] Where Jefferson extracted passages without comment, for the most part, Adams simply reports in his diary, as he does for 7 August 1756, "Wrote pretty industriously in Bolin[g]broke."[35] Whether he wrote in a notebook or, as he did later in life, in the books themselves, is unknown. Somewhat later in his diary, Adams stages an imaginary dialogue, in which the figure of Virtue admonishes him: "Labour to get distinct Ideas of Law, Right, Wrong, Justice, Equity. Search for them in your own mind, in Roman, grecian, french, English Treatises of natural, civil, common, Statute Law.... Study Seneca, Cicero, and all other good moral Writers. Study Montesque, Bolin[g]broke, [Vinnius?], &c. and all other good, civil Writers, &c."[36] A few years later, but in the same self-critical mood, Adams faults himself for "too much Rambling and Straggling from one Book to another, from the Corpus Juris Canonici, to Bolingbroke, from him to Pope, from him to Addison, from him to Yoricks sermons, &c."[37] All of this reading of Bolingbroke must have had its effect, for in conversation a short time later, he reports that someone says to him in astonishment: "You have Ld. Bolin[g]broke by heart!"[38]

In his *Autobiography,* written late in life, Adams offers a terse opinion of Bolingbroke's *Philosophical Works,* then follows with a verdict on his style: "His Religion is a pompous Folly: and his Abuse of the Christian Religion is as superficial as it is impious. His Style is original andinimitable: it resembles more the oratory of the Ancients, than any Writings or Speeches I ever read in English."[39]

By contrast, in the letter to his grandson, Jefferson positively expatiates on Bolingbroke's style and follows with a brief but telling verdict on the *Philosophical Works:*

> Ld. Bolingbroke's ... is a style of the highest order: the lofty, rythmical, full-flowing eloquence of Cicero. Periods of just measure, their members proportioned, their close full and round. His conceptions too are bold and strong, his diction copious, polished and commanding as his subject. His writings are certainly the finest samples in the English language of the eloquence proper for the senate. His political tracts are safe reading for the most timid religi[o]nist, his philosophical, for those who are not afraid to trust their reason with discussions of right and wrong.[40]

What is notable here is not that Adams and Jefferson disagree on the value of the *Philosophical Works,* an unsurprising circumstance that is indicative of their marked intellectual differences.[41] It is rather their utter agreement on something that *does* surprise modern readers—Bolingbroke's superiority as a stylist. And here the stress that Jefferson lays on the specific qualities of that style testifies to both a keen acquaintance and prodigious esteem.

VI

What then is the upshot of this discussion of influence? It is simply this: that reading Bolingbroke's *Philosophical Works* in 1765 was of special importance for Thomas Jefferson—was influential on him—not so much for the novelty or profundity of the ideas contained therein but for their relevance to the ferment that was going on within him. Bolingbroke's writing took on a special importance because it was replete with (for him) stimulating observations, shrewdarguments, and felicitous language that helped crystallize certain ideas in his mind. The key to its importance may be said to lie in the fact that Jefferson was a developing writer, a young man peculiarly sensitive to language, who would become one of the most deliberate, dedicated, and prolific writers in American letters. He was consciously struggling in 1765 to learn his craft, the art of finding in language and argumentation suitable forms for his emerging thoughts. What he admired in Bolingbroke was something our modem sensibility prevents us from seeing clearly, just as we shake our heads in bewilderment at his youthful fondness for Thomas Otway or his extravagant admiration of the poems of Ossian. But as the letter to his grandson makes clear, what Jefferson most admired in Bolingbroke was his style, his artful way with words and ideas. The qualities that he named in the letter were the ones that ultimately mattered: a strong advocate, a "style of the highest order," beautifully turned periods, conceptions that are "bold and strong," and diction that is "copious, polished and commanding." Advocacy, style, conceptions, diction: these were the very elements that Jefferson in 1765 was attempting to master.

Notes

1. Lord Bolingbroke, as quoted in H. T. Dickinson, *Bolingbroke* (London: Constable, 1970), 160.

2. Henry St. John, *The Philosophical Works of the Right Honorable Henry St. John, Lord Viscount Bolingbroke,* ed. David Mallet, 5 vols. (London, 1754). For Jefferson's extracts, see Douglas L. Wilson, ed., *Jefferson's Literary Commonplace Book,* Second Series, *The Papers of Thomas Jefferson* (Princeton: Princeton University Press, 1989), §§4-34, 36-58.

3. Alexander Pope, as quoted in Simon Varey, *Henry St. John, Viscount Bolingbroke* (Boston: Twayne Publishers, 1984), 14.

4. Merrill D. Peterson, "Thomas Jefferson and the Enlightenment: Reflections on Literary

5. See E. Millicent Sowerby, ed., *Catalogue of the Library of Thomas Jefferson*, 5 vols.

6. Letter from Thomas Jefferson to Francis Wayles Eppes, 19 January 1821, *The Family Letters of Thomas Jefferson*, ed. Edwin Morris Betts and James Adam Bear, Jr. (Columbia: University of Missouri Press, 1966), 438.

7. Bolingbroke, *Philosophical Works*, 3:334.

8. Alexander Pope, "An Essay on Man," epistle 1, lines 1-6, 13-16.

9. Dickinson, *Bolingbroke*, 298.

10. *Jefferson's Literary Commonplace Book*, 156.

11. Letter from Thomas Jefferson to Peter Carr, 10 August 1787, *The Papers of Thomas Jefferson* , ed. Julian P. Boyd et al., 27 vols. to date (Princeton, N.J.: Princeton University Press, 1950-), 12:15 [hereinafter *Papers of Jefferson*]. *Cf. Jefferson's Literary Commonplace Book*, §58.

12. Paul K. Conkin, "The Religious Pilgrimage of Thomas Jefferson," *Jeffersonian*

13. See Peterson, "Thomas Jefferson and the Enlightenment," 102-111.

14. Peterson, "Thomas Jefferson and the Enlightenment," 104.

15. Thomas Jefferson, "Autobiography 1743-1790," *Thomas Jefferson: Writings,* ed. Merrill D. Peterson (New York: Library of America, 1984), 4 [hereinafter *Writings*].

16. Jefferson, "Autobiography," *Writings*, 4.

17. Peterson, "Thomas Jefferson and the Enlightenment," 104.

18. Letter from Thomas Jefferson to John Adams, 15 August 1820, *Writings*, 1443.

19. *Jefferson's Literary Commonplace Book*, §10.

20. For the dating of the entries, see *Jefferson's Literary Commonplace Book,* Appendices A, B, and D.

21. Charles B. Sanford, *The Religious Life of Thomas Jefferson* (Charlottesville, Va.: University Press of Virginia, 1984), Chapter 9, "Jefferson's Religious Ideas of Life After Death," 147-152.

22. *Jefferson's Literary Commonplace Book*, §62.

23. *Jefferson's Literary Commonplace Book*, §§64, 65.

24. Page's identity is assumed from the confidential character of the letter and the reference to astronomy, an interest that Jefferson and Page were said to share. I am grateful to the curator of the Gilder Lehrman Collection, Paul Romaine, for making a copy and transcription of the letter available to me. Since this was written, the letter in question has been published in *Papers of Jefferson*, 27:665.

25. Letter from Thomas Jefferson, 26 July 1764, *Papers of Jefferson*, 27:665.

26. Letter from Thomas Jefferson, 26 July 1764, *Papers of Jefferson*, 27:665.

27. *Jefferson's Literary Commonplace Book*, §§73, 63.

28. *Jefferson's Literary Commonplace Book*, §7.

29. *Jefferson's Literary Commonplace Book*, §36.

30. *Jefferson's Literary Commonplace Book*, §24.

31. *Jefferson's Literary Commonplace Book*, §37.

32. Letter form Thomas Jefferson to Bernard Moore, [c. 1770s], revised in 1814 and included in a letter to John Minor, 30 August 1814, in *The Works of Thomas Jefferson*, ed. Paul Leicester Ford, Federal Edition, 12 vols. (New York: G. P. Putnam's Sons, 1904), 11:425n.

33. Letter from Thomas Jefferson to John Banister, Jr., 15 October 1785, *Papers of Jefferson*, 8:637.

34. See L. H. Butterfield, ed., *Diary and Autobiography of John Adams,* 4 vols. (Cambridge, Mass.: Harvard University Press, 1961). I am grateful to David McCullough for directing my attention to these materials.

35. *Diary and Autobiography of John Adams,* 7 August 1756, 1:40.

36. *Diary and Autobiography of John Adams,* [January 1759], 1:73.

37. *Diary and Autobiography of John Adams*, 9 February 1761, 1:200.

38. *Diary and Autobiography of John Adams,* April 1761, 1:210.

39. *Diary and Autobiography of John Adams,* 3:264.

40. Letter from Thomas Jefferson to Francis Wayles Eppes, 19 January 1821, *Family Letters*, 438.

41. Merrill D. Peterson notes that this disparity "is suggestive of the intellectual differences that would divide them." Peterson, "Thomas Jefferson and the Enlightenment," 104.

Chapter 6

James Madison and the Presbyterian Idea of Man and Government

Mary-Elaine Swanson

The student of James Madison's life cannot help being struck by the persistent Scottish Presbyterian influence on him beginning in his early boyhood under a Scottish schoolmaster and continuing through his years at the Presbyterian College of New Jersey (now Princeton). While Madison never forsook his own Anglican faith, the Presbyterian view of man and government played a prominent role in his intellectual development. This is particularly true in relation to his experience at Princeton where its new president, the Reverend Dr. John Witherspoon, lately arrived from Scotland, exercised a decisive influence in forming Madison's religious and political convictions. The religious ideals Madison absorbed at Princeton played an important role in all his contributions to America's political history—from his draft for the article on religion in the Virginia Declaration of Rights (1776) ensuring the free exercise of religion, to his contributions to the Constitutional Convention in 1787 which made him "the Father of the Constitution," and finally to his drawing up of the Bill of Rights in 1789 at the First Congress under the new Constitution.

Before discussing these Presbyterian influences on Madison it is necessary to pause and consider what is meant by the words in the title of this chapter, "the Presbyterian idea of man and government." Why, one may be tempted to ask, would the ideas of any particular religious group have a bearing on Madison's development as a political thinker? To answer this question, one must understand the intellectual climate in the colonies when Madison was growing up. We must exchange for a moment the mostly secular views of man and government that prevail today for the deeply religious outlook shared by the American colonists of Madison's day.

Whether Anglicans, Congregationalists, or Presbyterians, they were sons and daughters of the Reformation. That great religious movement, we should remember, was not only about questions of individual conscience. It was quite as much about how the church should be governed. Anglicans, in both Great Britain and her North American colonies, were content with Henry VIII's Reformation which abolished allegiance to the Pope, made the English monarch head of the Church, and retained the old authority of Archbishop and bishops. But Congregational and Presbyterian dissenters from the Church of England, particularly those who had come to America in search of liberty to worship in accord with their religious convictions, believed that Christ's church should not be governed by any earthly monarch or bishopric. Rather, the dissenters' view was that it should be governed directly by the whole Congregation (as in the Congregational Church) or by their representatives, the elders, or Presbyters (as in the Presbyterian Church).

It is surely no accident that the very names of these dissenting churches that were so prominent in colonial days still reflect their denominational forms of government, as does the American descendant of the Church of England, which became known after the American Revolution as the Protestant Episcopal Church. As one Presbyterian historian has remarked:

> The term "Presbyterian," it should be emphasized, refers not to a particular type of doctrine or worship, but to a particular form of church government—government by presbyters, or elders. There are four types of church government: Papal, corresponding to political absolute monarchy; Episcopal, corresponding to political aristocracy; Presbyterian, or government by elected representatives, corresponding to political republicanism; Congregational, or direct control of church affairs by the members of the congregation, corresponding to political democracy.[1]

The Presbyterian form of government begins at the local church level with the Session, moves outward to the Presbytery, the Synod, and finally the General Assembly at the national level. All these levels of government correspond to expanding geographical areas. Along the way, this system of government is full of checks and balances in regard to the exercise of power.

Here we come to the core of the Presbyterian idea of man which lies behind its form of government. The doctrine of the Presbyterians in the American colonies, whether Scottish, English, or Scotch-Irish, was that of John Calvin, the sixteenth-century Genevan reformer. This doctrine stressed the sovereignty of God who alone has absolute power over men and women. To the Calvinist, fallen man was utterly depraved until redeemed by God. This fostered the idea that, whether in Church or State, no man or group of men should be entrusted with unlimited power.

Keeping in mind this background of the Presbyterian idea of man and government, let us now return to the influence it exerted upon James Madison. It began in Virginia when Madison's father enrolled him in a small school run by the Reverend Donald Robertson, a Scottish Presbyterian schoolmaster who had been educated at the University of Edinburgh. The school was located some seventy miles away from the Madison home on the plantation of the Reverend Robert Innes, where the boys boarded. Young Jemmy, as James Madison was then called, remained under Robertson's care for the next five years and appears to have found his teacher inspiring, for he later described him as "a man of extensive learning, and a distinguished Teacher."[2]

How much Madison may have imbibed from Robertson of the distinctively Presbyterian idea of man and government is hard to say. It would not have been part of Robertson's duties to teach his Anglican charges Presbyterian theology or theories of government. But something of the Scot's love of learning must have communicated itself to young Madison, and also, perhaps, the typical Scot's concern for justice—a concern born of a long history of repeated attempts by Scotland's neighbor England to dominate its religion and its government. Madison's interest in law and government may well have begun here. While at Robertson's school, he is known to have studied Justinian's *Institutes*, the codification of Roman laws bearing the name of the last emperor of the Christianized Roman Empire. He is also believed to have studied Montesquieu's *Spirit of Laws* which was being widely read and studied throughout the colonies.

Madison returned home in 1767 at age sixteen and continued his studies under a young minister of Scotch-Irish background who had just come from New Jersey to be the rector of the Madison's parish church. He lived with the family and tutored Jemmy and his brothers and possibly his sister Nelly, too. The Reverend Thomas Martin was a graduate of the Presbyterian College of New Jersey and must have spoken highly of it to Madison's father. Irving Brant, Madison's biographer, explains that this college had been started twenty-three years earlier by evangelical Presbyterians to promote evangelism and religious liberty.[3] It was independent of the Presbyterian Church, however, and was open to students of all denominations. Hence, the young Martin, an Anglican, had studied there.

When Madison's father decided to send him to the College of New Jersey, rather than to Virginia's own College of William and Mary, it may have surprised family and friends. In his *Autobiography*, Madison spoke of the unhealthy climate of Williamsburg.[4] Some biographers have said that his father was concerned about lax moral standards at William and Mary at that time. But, another reason—perhaps the most compelling one—may have been the Reverend Martin's enthusiastic recommendation of the College of New Jersey.

It was a remarkably fortunate choice. Just the year before Madison enrolled, Dr. John Witherspoon came from Scotland to be its president. Because Witherspoon is so little known today, it is worth noting here an excellent summary of his career given by an early Madison biographer, William Cabell Rives.

> At the ripened age of forty-six years, he brought with him the learning and science of his native country in its meridian glory . . . ; a sympathy and attachment for popular rights, nurtured in the contests he had waged against the claims of privilege and patronage in his mother church; a practical wisdom and talent for affairs acquired by the experience of life; and a conscientious courage and energy, all his own. . . . In these peaceful but fruitful fields, he labored earnestly and faithfully for the intellectual and moral training of the youth of America, till he was called by the course of events and the confidence of the country to play a more conspicuous and responsible part on the stage of public affairs. Henceforward, as one of the *working men* and active patriots of the Revolution, his name stands in imperishable connection not only with the Declaration of American Independence and the Articles of Confederation and perpetual union, of both of which he was a signer, but with all the great acts of Congress, from the beginning to the close of its glorious struggle.[5]

As a Scotsman, Witherspoon early sympathized with the colonial demands for local self-government under the English Constitution and soon became an ardent advocate of the patriot cause. It was not long before American Tories complained that Princeton had become a seminary of sedition. It must have galled New Jersey's strongly royalist governor, William Franklin (estranged son of patriot Benjamin Franklin) to be seated on the platform during commencement exercises in September 1770 and to be obliged to hear a debate on whether or not subjects "were obliged by the law of nature to resist their king, if he treats them cruelly or ignores the law of the state, and to defend their liberty," and still another debate on the subject of non-importation of English goods as a protest against English policies and whether or not this "reflects a Glory on the American merchants, and was a noble exertion of self-denial and public spirit."[6]

Of great importance to the students at the college were certain changes Dr. Witherspoon made in the curriculum. He expanded the course on Moral Philosophy, which he also taught, to include "the general principles of public law and politics."[7] There is every reason to believe that when young Madison took this course, his interest in these subjects, which may have begun under Robertson, received a strong impetus from Witherspoon's teaching. Certainly, Madison's later writings echo many of the ideas on the nature of man and government expressed by Witherspoon in this course. Many young men were similarly stimulated by Witherspoon's teaching on law and government, as is witnessed to by the fact that so many of them later became active in American politics, including a president of the United States (Madison), a vice-president, ten cabinet officers, twenty-one senators, thirty-nine congressmen, a Supreme Court justice, an attorney general of the United States, and twelve state governors. It has also been estimated that nearly one-fifth of the signers of the Declaration of Independence, one-sixth of the delegates to the Constitutional Convention, and one-fifth of the first Congress under the Constitution were graduates of the College of New Jersey.[8]

Considering the grumbling among Tories about the college when Madison was there, it is not surprising that Horace Walpole quipped in 1775: "Cousin America has eloped with a Presbyterian pastor." Indeed, Walpole may have been thinking of Witherspoon![9] But as Ralph Ketcham has observed: "The College of New Jersey in Madison's day *was* the seedbed of sedition and nursery of rebels Tory critics charged it with being, but that is not all: it was as well a school for statesmen trained to seek freedom and ordered government through the pursuit of virtue."[10]

What specifically did Madison learn at Princeton that helped shape his views of man and government? There are three areas of Witherspoon's teaching that particularly influenced Madison's political thought. These relate to the nature of man, the nature of good government, and the nature of religious liberty. First, he gained a healthy respect for Witherspoon's Calvinist view of man as a sinner prone to do evil ever since the Fall. Second, he learned that, as a direct result of man's fallen nature, many checks and balances in civil government are needed to curb lawless power and so prevent tyranny. Third, he learned from Witherspoon that because

God is absolute Sovereign of the universe, man's first allegiance is to Him who alone is the Lord of the conscience.

Witherspoon's Calvinistic views on the depravity of man are well expressed in the following passage from one of his finest sermons, *The Dominion of Providence over the Passions of Men*:

> Men of lax and corrupt principles take great delight in speaking to the praise of human nature, and extolling its dignity, without distinguishing what it was at its first creation, from what it is in its present fallen state. But I appeal from these visionaries' reasonings to the history of all the ages, and the inflexible testimony of daily experience. . . . A Cool and Candid attention, either to the past history or present state of the world, but above all, to the ravages of lawless power, ought to humble us in the dust.[11]

In another passage from one of his lectures on divinity, Witherspoon also spoke of the human history of the world as the history of human guilt and declared in Biblical terms that "from the first dawn of reason [they] show that they are wise to do evil; but to do good they have no knowledge!"[12]

Lest one think, however, from these and other similar passages that Witherspoon took only a dark view of human nature, there are other passages from his writings and speeches that indicate that he saw possibilities for good in human nature, after "it is purified by the light of truth, and renewed by the Spirit of the living God."[13] The goodness that remains in fallen man is the result of the preserving Providence of God. Furthermore, it is the overruling hand of Divine Providence that prevents the evil in men from having unlimited power.

Witherspoon taught the providential view of history, that is, Divine Providence is at work throughout history to accomplish the divine purposes. In the Fast Day sermon he gave on 17 May 1776, on *The Dominion of Providence over the Passions of Men*, he cited instances from English history that he believed showed the intervening hand of God in human affairs. Witherspoon became a delegate to Congress from New Jersey in 1776, just in time to speak strongly in favor of Independence. He is believed to have suggested inserting into the Declaration of Independence the eloquent phrase: "With a firm reliance on the protection of Divine Providence."[14]

The doctrine of Divine Providence and the providential view of history were not, of course, confined to Calvinists like Witherspoon. They were the common property of all Christians of that time. But for Calvinists, believing that the depravity of fallen man prevented him from reformation without the aid of his Maker, the doctrine of Divine Providence was especially vital.

Madison absorbed these teachings while at Princeton and they are reflected in his later writings, such as this passage from *The Federalist* where he reflects on all the seemingly insuperable difficulties facing the delegates at the Constitutional Convention, difficulties that, however, had been surmounted, thus permitting a new Constitution to appear. He wrote: "It is impossible for the man of pious reflection not to perceive in it a finger of that Almighty hand which has been so frequently and signally extended to our relief in the critical stages of the revolution."[15] In view of such words as these, it is not surprising to find Madison scholar Robert Rutland referring to him as "the dispassionate Founding Father whose chief interest in life was to prove that Americans had been chosen by Providence for an experiment to test man's capacity for self-government."[16] Certainly, Madison gained from his Presbyterian preceptor a balanced view of human nature in which it was possible to see that man was fallen but, with the aid of Divine Providence, was capable of achieving virtue and self-government.

Later, when Madison, the statesman, labored for a system of government sufficient for the new nation, he knew that man's flawed human nature must be taken into consideration. He observed in *The Federalist* that if men were angels, no government would be necessary, or if angels were to govern them, "neither external nor internal controls on government would be necessary." Since men were not angels, however, it was clear to Madison that "in framing a government which is to be administered by men over men, the great difficulty lies in this: you must first enable the government to control the governed; and in the next place oblige it to control itself."[17]

Here Madison had only to cast his mind back to the teaching he had received from Dr. Witherspoon at Princeton on the importance of a separation of powers and checks and balances between them to see the answer. Witherspoon followed the teachings of the French philosopher, Montesquieu, who greatly admired the separation of powers he saw in the English system of government. But to Montesquieu's ideas, Witherspoon added his own particular emphasis.

James H. Smylie, in a most perceptive article entitled "Madison and Witherspoon, Theological Roots of American Political Thought," highlighted the element that Witherspoon saw as essential if the separation of powers was to work out in practical terms. This essential element was a sufficient connection between the branches of government for one branch to be able to check the other.[18]

Witherspoon's reasoning is subtle but penetrates to the heart of the matter. In discussing forms of government in one of his lectures on Moral Philosophy, he wrote that

> where there is a balance of different bodies, as in all mixed forms, there must always be some *nexus imperii*, something to make one of them necessary to the other. If this is not the case, they will not only draw different ways, but will often separate altogether from each other. In order to produce this *nexus* [or interlacing], some of the great essential rights of rulers must be divided and distributed among the different branches of the legislature. Example: in the British government, the king has the power of making war and peace—but the parliament have the levying and distribution of money, which is a sufficient restraint.[19]

Witherspoon also asserted that "every good government must be complex, so that the one principle may check the other. It is of consequence to have as much virtue among the particular members of a community as possible; but it is folly to expect that a state should be upheld by integrity in all who have a share in managing it." He concluded by prescribing the remedy: "They [the branches of government] must be so balanced, that when every one draws to his own interest or inclination, there may be an even poise upon the whole."[20]

These words appear to have made a deep impression on Madison for we find him asking (again in *The Federalist*, No. 51): "To what expedient, then, shall we finally resort, for maintaining in practice the necessary partition of power among the several departments, as laid down in the Constitution?"[21] He replied to this pressing question by asserting that this can only be done "by so contriving the interior structure of the government as that its several constituent parts may, by their mutual relations, be the means of keeping each other in their proper places." He went on to say that

> the great security against a gradual concentration of the several powers in the same department, consists in giving to those who administer each department the necessary constitutional means and personal motives to resist encroachments of the others. . . . Ambition must be made to counteract ambition. The interest of the man must be connected with the constitutional rights of the place. It may be a reflection on human nature, that such devices should be necessary to control the abuses of government. But what is government itself, but the greatest of all reflections on human nature?[22]

Then, after saying that if men were angels no government would be necessary, Madison pointed out:

> This policy of supplying, by opposite and rival interests, the defect of better motives, might be traced through the whole system of human affairs, private as well as public. We see it particularly displayed in all the subordinate distributions of power, where the constant aim is to divide and arrange the several offices in such a manner as that each may be a check on the other—that the private interest of every individual may be a sentinel over the public rights.[23]

The Constitution that emerged from the ninety-nine days of debate at the Constitutional Convention contained many ingenious checks and balances between the departments of the new national government: (1) Congress could make laws, but not execute them; (2) the president could veto laws, but Congress could override his veto by a two-thirds majority; (3) all bills to raise revenue had to originate in the House of Representatives, but the Senate could propose or concur with amendments; (4) the president was to be commander-in-chief of the armed forces, but only Congress could declare war; (5) the President was to have the power to make treaties, but only with the advice and consent of the Senate; (6) the Supreme Court was to interpret the laws in the light of the Constitution, but could not make laws. Furthermore, its jurisdiction was subject to whatever exceptions and regulations Congress cared to make.

These checks and balances often seem meaningless and irksome to our modern secular mindset which tends to think in terms of the perfectibility of man rather than of his basically imperfect nature. But they were not mysterious to Madison whose point of view was shaped by his religious convictions. Dr. Smylie goes so far as to say that "the Calvinism of the College of New Jersey was woven into the fabric of the American Constitution and continues to inform America's political experiment."[24]

Madison's old teacher certainly gave his hearty approval to the Constitution's many checks on human nature, all designed to prevent excessive power from becoming lodged in any one of the three branches of government. That one of his favorite students, James Madison, had played a prominent role in the creation of the new Constitution he well knew. According to his biographer, Ashbel Green, Witherspoon was well-pleased with the new Constitution for "embracing principles, and carrying into effect measures, which he had long advocated, as essential to the preservation of the liberties, and the promotion of the peace and prosperity of the country."[25]

In addition to noting the checks and balances within the new national government, as laid out in the Constitution, Witherspoon may have noted that this new compound republic also provided cheeks and balances between the federal and state governments. Madison, who had imbibed Witherspoon's Calvinistic view of human nature, had struggled with the governmental problems caused by the human tendency to divide into factions, each trying to obtain dominion over the whole. In seeking to frame a more perfect form of union, he pondered long on this problem. In one of his most-quoted papers in *The Federalist* (No. 10), he asked if there was a cure to "the mischiefs of faction"? Could one remove its causes or control its effects? He concluded that the causes of faction could not be removed but could be controlled in an extended or compound republic in which power was diffused between the states and the nation. By extending the sphere of government he was convinced that while "factious leaders may kindle a flame within their particular states," they would be unable to spread their influence through the other states. Thus, "a rage for paper money, for an abolition of debts, for an equal division of property, or for any other improper or wicked project, will be less apt to pervade the whole body of the Union than a particular member of it."[26] For Madison, the new federal arrangement went far toward controlling the causes of faction that was, as he saw, "sown in the nature of man."[27] Indeed, we might say that the new Federal system was the ultimate in the checks and balances that Witherspoon had taken such pains to teach his students.

The third area in which the Presbyterian idea of man and government played an important role in Madison's development was that of religious liberty. When he graduated from the College of New Jersey in 1771, he stayed on in Princeton for six months to study theology and Hebrew with Dr. Witherspoon. It has been inferred from this fact that Madison was considering entering the ministry. Bishop William Meade of the Anglican Church in Virginia, who knew Madison, once observed that when he was a student at the College of New Jersey "a great revival took place, and it was believed that he partook of its spirit. On his return home he conducted worship in his father's house."[28] That Madison did not pursue this profession may have been because he went through a period of poor health and depressed spirits brought on by self-imposed overwork during his college years. He may have thought that he lacked the strong voice and eloquent speaking ability so necessary to a minister. (It was said of him at the Constitutional Convention that he was so short in stature it was difficult to tell when he was standing and that his voice was so weak as to be inaudible unless one were near him.)

He continued Biblical studies, however, making lengthy notes on both Old and New Testament passages. The evangelical zeal of his college days is reflected in letters he wrote to William Bradford, a classmate from Princeton. He wrote to Billey of the importance of becoming "fervent Advocates in the cause of Christ, & I wish you may give in your Evidence in this way."[29]

Madison evidently found it difficult at first to adjust to life at home in Virginia, perhaps because he brought back with him from President Witherspoon and the College of New Jersey not only a keen appreciation of the fundamental principles of civil government he had learned there but also a zeal for religious liberty. He was incensed by instances of persecution of dissenters in a neighboring county and told Bradford that he had "squabbled and scolded abused and ridiculed so long about it, to so little purpose that I am without common patience. So I leave you to pity me and pray for Liberty of Conscience to revive among us."[30]

In another letter, he told Bradford that he longed to visit him in Pennsylvania and to breathe his "free air."[31] It was in the free air of neighboring New Jersey that Madison had begun to experience the ideal of religious liberty practiced there, an ideal that Witherspoon extolled at Princeton. When Witherspoon, an evangelical Presbyterian, became president of the College of New Jersey it was already an institution dedicated to the pursuit of religious liberty. The college Charter in 1746 expressed the "earnest desire" that at the college "those of every religious denomination may have free and equal liberty and advantage of education notwithstanding any different sentiments in religion."[32]

This was very different from the position of Presbyterians in the Old World. There they accepted the long-held belief that an established state church was necessary to a well-ordered Christian society. Once in America, however, Presbyterians who settled in the middle colonies learned to live in harmony with Lutherans, Quakers, German Pietists, and others who had chosen to live in these colonies where religious liberty was practiced.

President Witherspoon became a leading exponent of this new breed of Presbyterian who desired "free and equal liberty," both civil and religious, for all Christians. From Witherspoon Madison learned the close connection between religious and civil liberty. In his sermon, *The Dominion of Providence*, Witherspoon declared: "There is not a single instance in history in which civil liberty was lost, and religious liberty preserved entire. If therefore we yield up our temporal property, we at the same time deliver the conscience into bondage."[33]

After independence from Great Britain was finally won, Witherspoon turned his thoughts to uniting the Presbyterian Church and creating a national body. According to Ashbel Green, Witherspoon wrote the Preface to the Plan of Government of the Church—which has survived to this day as the statement, Historic Principles of Church Order, at the beginning of the *Book of Order of the Presbyte-*

rian Church (USA). After citing the Westminster Confession's declaration that God alone is Lord of the conscience, the statement that follows is most significant:

> Therefore we consider the rights of private judgment, in all matters that respect religion as universal and inalienable: We do not even wish to see any religious constitution aided by the civil power, further than may be necessary for protection and security, and at the same time, be equal and common to all others.[34]

This was a position long taken by Witherspoon and other Presbyterians of the time. Small wonder then that when Madison, who had absorbed these views while in college, returned to Anglican Virginia he began to grapple with this vexing issue. He wrote to Bradford for information on the extent of religious toleration in Pennsylvania. Significantly, he asked his friend if he thought an "ecclesiastical establishment" was absolutely necessary to support civil society.

When Madison made his debut in politics as a delegate from Orange County to the Virginia Convention in Williamsburg, in April 1776, he put into action his convictions regarding religious liberty. It was as a member of the Committee to draw up a Declaration of Rights for Virginia that he suggested the momentous change in wording in the article on religion drafted by George Mason. For Mason's proposal that "all men shou'd enjoy the fullest Toleration in the Exercise of Religion, according to the Dictates of Conscience," Madison suggested that the words be changed to "all men are equally entitled to the full and free exercise of it [religion] according to the dictates of conscience." He knew that toleration implied a superior earthly power that might, or might not, choose to permit dissenting religious views, whereas the full and free exercise of religion implied an absolute right, one that came from God and not men. But he did not stop there; he added the words: "and therefore that no man or class of men ought, on account of religion to be invested with peculiar emoluments or privileges nor subjected to any penalties or disabilities."[35] This was an idea whose time had not yet come, and it did not pass, but his statement on "the free exercise of religion" did. The article on religion, as revised by Madison, became a model for the other states as they claimed their independence from Great Britain and drew up their declarations of rights.

In Virginia the Declaration of Rights was only an opening salvo in a long battle for complete religious liberty. Madison stood in the forefront of this battle along with his brilliant friend and political colleague, Thomas Jefferson. From the beginning it was Madison's Presbyterian friends who aided him in his efforts to secure religious liberty for all Virginians. When the first General Assembly under the new Constitution convened on 7 October 1776, it was flooded with petitions from dissenters complaining about the restrictions on their religious liberty imposed on them by the Anglican Church. Both Madison and Jefferson were on the committee that considered these petitions along with others from Anglicans urging continuance of the Church of England as the established church of Virginia.

Caleb Wallace, Madison's good friend from his Princeton days, and now a Presbyterian minister, is believed to have drafted the eloquent Memorial of the Hanover Presbytery praising the Declaration of Rights and its assertion of the right to the free exercise of religion but complaining that the members of the churches in their presbytery were still being forced to support the Episcopal clergy and to build and maintain their churches. Among the arguments the Reverend Wallace used to show how injurious religious establishments are to a nation were several that Madison later used in his "Memorial and Remonstrance against Religious Assessments."

Madison and Jefferson succeeded in enacting legislation exempting dissenters from contributions to support the established church, but dissenters were still indignant that marriages were only legal when performed by Anglican pastors. Another Memorial from Hanover Presbytery in 1784 shows that this problem had not yet been resolved, and that many impediments were still being put in the way of marriages outside the Church of England. In short, much political power still remained in the hands of the established Church.

Two more memorials from the Hanover Presbytery, in October 1784 and August 1785, respectively, continued to outline eloquently the reasons for complete religious liberty and freedom from an established church.[36] All of these Memorials were useful to Madison when, in 1785, he wrote his eloquent "Memorial and Remonstrance against Religious Assessments" while serving again in the Virginia House of Delegates after service in Congress from 1780 to 1783. The occasion for Madison's "Remonstrance" was the proposal by Patrick Henry for a tax to support the Christian religion or some Christian church or denomination. Madison seemed alone in seeing the fundamental error in this proposal. His main concern was that this bill would give the state the power to define the Christian faith, thus opening the door to renewed state control over religion and the loss of the religious liberty that his Presbyterian friends had been contending for so vigorously.

In majestic words that could have flowed from his old teacher's pen, asserting the sovereignty of God, Madison declared in the "Remonstrance":

> It is the duty of every man to render to the Creator such homage and such only as he believes to be acceptable to him. *This duty is precedent*, both in order of time and in degree of obligation, to the claims of Civil Society. *Before any man can be considered as a member of Civil Society, he must be considered as a subject of the Governour of the Universe*: And if a member of Civil Society, who enters into any subordinate Association, must always do it with a reservation of his duty to the General Authority; much more must every man who becomes a member of any particular Civil Society, do it with a saving of *his allegiance to the Universal Sovereign*.[37]

This passage reflects the Presbyterian idea of man and government that Madison had learned at Princeton, that is, because God is sovereign, his rightful power cannot be usurped by the state, and that under God's sovereignty all men stand as equals for all are sinners, yet all may be redeemed through His sovereign power.

In words that are remarkably similar in sentiments to those expressed by his old mentor, Dr. Witherspoon, in the latter's preface to the Presbyterian Plan of Government, Madison also wrote in his "Remonstrance" that a just government "will be best supported by protecting every Citizen in the enjoyment of his Religion with the same equal hand which protects his person and his property; by neither invading the equal rights of any Sect, nor suffering any Sect to invade those of another."[38]

The idea that faith in God must be arrived at voluntarily had been ingrained in him from his days at Princeton, and he appealed to his fellow Christians in Virginia to support the individual's liberty to assent voluntarily to the claims of Christianity and not to be forced to do so by the state.

Madison's stirring words reflect the evangelical approach to religious liberty held by Witherspoon and Madison's other instructors at the College of New Jersey:

> Whilst we assert for ourselves a freedom to embrace, to profess and to observe the Religion which we believe to be of divine origin, we cannot deny an equal freedom to those whose minds have not yet yielded to the evidence which has convinced us. If this freedom be abused, it is an offence against God, not against men: To God, therefore, not to man, must an account of it be rendered.[39]

A close reading of the "Remonstrance" shows that in no way was Madison hostile to the religion that had nourished and inspired him. In no way was he seeking to diminish its moral influence on the state. As Ralph Ketcham writes in his biography of Madison:

> There is no evidence that Madison's defence of religious liberty reflected any hostility to religion itself or to its social effects. On the contrary, he argued repeatedly that freedom of religion enhanced *both* its intrinsic vitality and its contribution to the common weal. He believed that attitudes and habits nourished by the churches could and did help importantly to improve republican government.[40]

Madison went on to help get Thomas Jefferson's celebrated "Statute for Establishing Religious Freedom" passed by the Virginia legislature in 1786 while Jefferson was away in France. Then, in drafting the federal Bill of Rights as a member of the First Congress under the Constitution, he helped secure the free exercise of religion at the national level.

While there were undoubtedly other influences on Madison throughout his long life, the Presbyterian idea of man and government, which he absorbed while at Princeton, played a strong role in forming his character and informing his later work as a creative statesman. It gave him a realistic view of human nature, the ability to discern the need for checks and balances in civil government, and, above all, a peculiarly Calvinistic conviction that man's first duty was to the supreme Sovereign of the Universe.

It is extremely fortunate that the future "Father of the Constitution," when young and eager to learn, came under the influence of Dr. John Witherspoon who, as a typical Presbyterian, gave so much time and thought to teaching what he believed to be a truly Christian idea of man and government.

Notes

1. Lefferts A. Loetscher, *A Brief History of the Presbyterians* (Philadelphia: Westminster Press, 1958), 113.

2. Douglass Adair, ed., "James Madison's Autobiography," *William and Mary Quarterly*, 3d ser., 2 (1945): 197.

3. Irving Brant, *James Madison*, vol. 1, *The Virginia Revolutionist* (Indianapolis, New York: Bobbs-Merrill Company, 1941), 73.

4. Adair, ed., "James Madison's Autobiography," 197.

5. William C. Rives, *History of the Life and Times of James Madison*, 4 vols. (1868; reprint, Freeport, N.Y.: Books for Libraries Press, 1970), 1:17–18.

6. Brant, *James Madison, The Virginia Revolutionist*, 94.

7. Rives, *Life and Times*, 1:18.

8. Varnum Lansing Collins, *President Witherspoon*, 2 vols. (Princeton: Princeton University Press, 1925), II:229. See also Rives, *Life and Times*, 1:121.

9. Martha Lou Lemmon Stohlman, *John Witherspoon: Parson, Politician, Patriot* (Philadelphia: Westminster Press, 1976), 15.

10. Ralph Ketcham, *James Madison: A Biography* (Charlottesville: University Press of Virginia, 1990), 44. It has been suggested by some that Witherspoon was more of a disciple of the Enlightenment than a Presbyterian evangelical. To many Christians, this term "the Enlightenment" conjures up visions of Voltaire and his disciples working to undermine all religion and replace it with a veneration for autonomous human rationality. The Scottish Enlightenment, however, although it included skeptics like David Hume, was another matter. It flourished, as Henry May observed, "in an environment shaped by Calvinism." Henry F. May, *The Enlightenment in America* (New York: Oxford University Press, 1976), 342. The basis for the idea that Witherspoon embraced the Scottish version of the Enlightenment seems to be because he used the works of Thomas Reid and Francis Hutcheson in his Moral Philosophy courses. Both of these men are associated with what historians call the Scottish Enlightenment. It should be noted, however, that both of these authors were Presbyterian clergymen and that while they were intensely interested in the extent and proper province of human reason, they did not think of it as other than the gift of God. A close attention to their writings reveals that they did not attempt to reconcile opposites—Christianity and godless rationalism—but sought rather to understand human rationality within the framework of Christianity. For a fuller discussion of Reid and Hutcheson and their works, see my book, *The Education of James Madison: A Model for Today* (Montgomery, Al.: The Hoffman Center, 1994), 42–53.

11. John Witherspoon, *The Dominion of Providence over the Passions of Men* (Philadelphia: R. Aitken, Printer and Bookseller, 1776), 12.

12. John Witherspoon, "Lectures on Divinity," cited by James H. Smylie in "Madison and Witherspoon: Theological Roots of American Political Thought," *Princeton University Library Chronicle* 22 (spring 1961): 121.

13. John Witherspoon, from a speech in Congress on the Confederation. Witherspoon, *The Works of John Witherspoon*, 2d ed., 4 vols. (Philadelphia: William W. Woodward, 1802), IV:350. In this speech, Witherspoon asked: "Shall we establish nothing good, because we know it cannot be eternal?" and argued, rather, for the need to settle the government "upon the best principles, and in the wisest manner, that it may last as long as the nature of things will admit."

14. See William McCauley Hosmer's discussion on Witherspoon's contribution in his paper, "Of Divine Providence in Our Declaration of Independence," 2d ed. (Warrenton, Oregon: Hosmer Enterprises, 1980).

15. Madison, in Alexander Hamilton, James Madison, and John Jay, *The Federalist* (New York: Tudor Publishing Co., 1937), no. 37, 245.

16. Robert A. Rutland, introduction to *James Madison: A Biography in His Own Words*, ed. Merrill D. Peterson, 2 vols. (New York: Newsweek Book Division, 1974), 1:9.

17. Madison, *The Federalist*, no. 51, 354.

18. Smylie, "Madison and Witherspoon," 123.

19. Jack Alan Scott, "A Critical Edition of John Witherspoon's Lectures on Moral Philosophy" (Ph.D. Diss., Claremont Graduate School, 1970), 138.

20. Scott, "Witherspoon's Lectures," 137.

21. Madison, *The Federalist*, no. 51, 353.

22. Madison, *The Federalist*, 354.

23. Madison, *The Federalist*, 355.

24. Smylie, "Madison and Witherspoon," 131.

25. Ashbel Green, "The Life of The Revd John Witherspoon," Manuscript in New Jersey Historical Society; microfilm in Princeton University Library, cited by Smylie, "Madison and Witherspoon," 130.

26. Madison, *The Federalist*, no. 10, 70.

27. Madison, *The Federalist*, 64.

28. Bishop Meade, *Old Churches, Ministers and Families of Virginia* (1872), cited by Brant, *James Madison, The Virginia Revolutionist*, 113.

29. Letter from James Madison to William Bradford, 25 September 1773, *The Papers of James Madison*, ed. William T. Hutchinson and William M. E. Rachal, 17 vols. to date (Chicago: University of Chicago Press, 1962), 1:96 [hereinafter *Papers of Madison*].

30. Letter from James Madison to William Bradford, 24 January 1774, *Papers of Madison*, 1:106.

31. Letter from James Madison to William Bradford, 24 January 1774, *Papers of Madison*, 1:106.

32. Edwin Scott Gaustad, *A Religious History of America* (New York: Harper & Row, 1974), 89–90.

33. Witherspoon, *The Dominion of Providence*, 40–41.

34. *The Constitution of the Presbyterian Church (USA)*, part II. *Book of Order*, 1997–98 (Louisville, Ky.: The Office of the General Assembly, 1997), G-1.0300.

35. Helen Hill Miller, *George Mason, Gentleman Revolutionary* (Chapel Hill: University of North Carolina Press, 1975), 150.

36. The five Hanover Presbytery Memorials have been reprinted in James H. Smylie, ed., "Jefferson's Statute for Religious Freedom: The Hanover Presbytery Memorials, 1776–1786," *American Presbyterians* 63 (winter 1985): 355-373.

37. "Memorial and Remonstrance," *Papers of Madison*, 8:299 (emphasis added).

38. "Memorial and Remonstrance," *Papers of Madison*, 8:302.

39. "Memorial and Remonstrance," *Papers of Madison*, 8:300.

40. Ketcham, *James Madison*, 167.

Part III

Jefferson and Madison on Church and State

Chapter 7

Church-State Debate in the Virginia Legislature: From the Declaration of Rights to the Statute for Establishing Religious Freedom

Daniel L. Dreisbach

In 1776 and the tumultuous decade that followed, Virginia was the epicenter of the former British colonies that would become the United States of America. It was the largest and most populous, prosperous, and influential of the former colonies. And, as the most central geographically, it had the potential to unify or divide the southern and northern extremities of the fledgling American confederation. Virginia also produced a wealth of leaders respected throughout the former colonies who played decisive roles in the independence movement. Events in the Commonwealth inevitably impacted other states; thus, they were carefully scrutinized. As John Adams of Massachusetts wrote to Patrick Henry of Virginia in the anxious days of June 1776, "we all look up to Virginia for examples."[1]

In the decades that followed independence, virtually every state scrambled to redefine the church-state arrangements they inherited from colonial times. In none was this process more dramatic and, in the end, celebrated than in Virginia. "From the outbreak of the American Revolution to the adoption of the federal Constitution, no state surpassed Virginia in speed and extent of alterations in Church-State relations."[2] By 1786, Virginia had replaced *toleration* with the principle of religious *liberty,* eliminated state restrictions on religious exercise, terminated direct tax support for the formerly established church, and placed churches on a purely voluntary footing. Although none moved with the speed and decisiveness of Virginia, other states were wrestling with the same issues and some were adopting similar policies. In many respects, "Virginia was a microcosm of the ferment taking place throughout the new nation."[3]

The struggle to redefine the Commonwealth's church-state arrangement was important to the entire nation. Thomas E. Buckley observed:

> [The Old Dominion] provided the most critical experiment of the Revolutionary era, for Virginia served as a politicoreligious microcosm in which the whole nation could study the alternatives for a church-state relationship and then choose from among them. . . . From Chesapeake Bay across the mountains to the Shenandoah Valley there existed both a church established by law and a reli-

> giously diverse society. In this largest and most populous of the new states with a leadership noted for its intellectual and political talent, all sides of the church-state controversy were ably represented: the traditional religionists who clung to the establishment ideal and insisted upon civil support for religion; the rationalists who believed religion to be an entirely personal affair and fought for an absolute separation of church and state; and dissenters of every stripe who, despite their own differences in polity and theory, wanted equal religious rights and a church freed from state control. For over a decade these Virginians developed the full range of arguments over the various alternatives presented for consideration: the retention of a single establishment, its replacement by a multiple system with state aid for all churches, the removal of religion from any relationship with civil authority, and the equality of religious groups without governmental assistance but free to influence society's morals and values.[4]

In the last two centuries, the dramatic story of disestablishment in Virginia has been recounted countless times; perhaps never more passionately than by the principal actors in this epic contest.[5] It has become a celebrated chapter in Virginia mythology. Historians, not surprisingly, have been drawn to the saga of church and state in revolutionary Virginia "because the sources are uniquely ample, the struggle was important and dramatic, and the opinions of Madison . . . and of Jefferson were fully elicited."[6] Also, as Buckley noted, Virginians confronted the full range of options regarding church-state relations available to the newly independent Americans. The struggle in Virginia reverberated far beyond the Commonwealth's borders and, indeed, the solutions worked out in the Old Dominion had a profound impact over the next two centuries on national and state church-state policies.

Although fundamental questions concerning prudential church-state policies in Virginia pre-dated independence and continued to percolate well into the nineteenth century, these vexing issues were never more prominently debated than during the tumultuous decade between 1776 and 1786. The issues debated in the Virginia legislature were complex and legion. Only a handful are discussed in this brief account.[7] This chapter focuses, first, on the drafting of Article XVI of the Virginia Declaration of Rights in May and June of 1776. Article XVI framed much subsequent debate in the Old Dominion. Explosive church-state controversies unleashed by Article XVI—such as the legal rights of dissenters—are then discussed. Of particular interest are various legislative initiatives raised in late 1776 and 1779 to redefine church-state relations and religious liberty in Virginia. This is followed by a brief description of the Virginia Committee of Revisors, which was instrumental in proposing key legislation that shaped church-state relationships in post-colonial, republican Virginia. Finally, attention is turned to the dramatic disestablishment struggle of the mid-1780s, culminating in defeat of a general assessment for support of religion and passage of the "Virginia Statute for Establishing Religious Freedom."

The Virginia Declaration of Rights

The Virginia Convention, which convened in Williamsburg on 6 May 1776, was arguably the most noteworthy political body ever assembled in the Commonwealth's history.[8] Composed largely of veterans of the old House of Burgesses, the Convention, on 15 May, passed a resolution instructing the Commonwealth's delegates at the Continental Congress to press for a declaration of independence from England.[9] The assembly also appointed a committee to prepare a state declaration of rights and plan of civil government.[10] Among those appointed to the committee were George Mason and the young, untested delegate from Orange County, James Madison, Jr.

George Mason was the chief architect of the Declaration of Rights. Some time in late May, he prepared a list of ten proposals to which others were added by Thomas Ludwell Lee and the committee.[11] The Virginia Declaration was printed in draft form, thoroughly debated, and amended before it was passed unanimously on 12 June. The singular achievement, the genius of Mason's Declaration of Rights, as Jefferson said of his own Declaration of Independence, was not in its "originality of principle or sentiment . . . [but rather] it was intended to be an expression of the American mind" with its brilliant "harmonizing sentiments of the day."[12] William C. Rives characterized the Declaration as "a condensed, logical, and luminous summary of the great principles of freedom inherited by us from our British ancestors; the extracted essence of Magna Charta, the Petition of Right, the acts of the Long Parliament, and the doctrines of the Revolution of 1688 as expounded by Locke,—distilled and concentrated through the alembic of his [Mason's] own powerful and discriminating mind. There is nothing more remarkable in the political annals of America than this paper. It has stood the rude test of every vicissitude."[13]

Committee drafts of the Declaration were printed and circulated widely up and down the Atlantic seaboard in late May and June, and it had an immediate and "profound impact on other Americans [in nascent states] whose task it was to create new governments."[14] "[B]y the time the last cannonade of the Revolution sounded," Robert A. Rutland observed, "every state either had fashioned a separate bill of rights or had passed statutes with similar provisions. In a good many cases the work was done with scissors, pastepot, and a copy of the Virginia Declaration—a fact that did not escape Mason's notice."[15] It is, perhaps, not too much to acclaim the Declaration of Rights, which Mason boasted was the "first in America,"[16] as "an intellectual guidepost of the American Revolution."[17]

Mason included an article on religion in the "first draught" of the Virginia Declaration. His original proposal declared:

> That as Religion, or the Duty which we owe to our divine and omnipotent Creator, and the Manner of discharging it, can be governed only by Reason and Conviction, not by Force or Violence; and therefore that all Men shou'd enjoy the fullest Toleration in the Exercise of Religion, according to the Dictates of Conscience, unpunished and unrestrained by the Magistrate, unless, under Colour of

> Religion, any Man disturb the Peace, the Happiness, or Safety of Society, or of Individuals. And that it is the mutual Duty of all, to practice Christian Forbearance, Love and Charity towards Each other.[18]

The committee slightly amended Mason's initial version before it was laid before the Convention on 27 May. It is this text that was printed and distributed widely in the Commonwealth and in other colonies:

> That religion, or the duty which we owe to our CREATOR, and the manner of discharging it, can be directed only by reason and conviction, not by force or violence; and therefore, that all men should enjoy the fullest toleration in the exercise of religion, according to the dictates of conscience, unpunished and unrestrained by the magistrate, unless, under colour of religion, any man disturb the peace, the happiness, or safety of society. And that it is the mutual duty of all to practice Christian forbearance, love and charity, towards each other.[19]

Although James Madison was certainly interested in all portions of the Virginia Declaration, only the final article providing for religious toleration stirred him to action. In "his first important public act,"[20] Madison objected to Mason's use of the word "toleration" because of the dangerous implication that religious exercise was a mere privilege that could be granted or revoked at the pleasure of the civil state, and was not assumed to be an equal, indefeasible right wholly exempt from the cognizance of the civil state and subject only to the dictates of a free conscience. Madison wanted to replace "toleration" with the concept of absolute equality in religious belief and exercise. Mason's proposal went further than any previous declaration in force in Virginia; however, it did not go far enough to satisfy Madison. As early as 1774, Madison had come to think of religious toleration (the ultimate objective of most reformers of his day) as only the halfway point on the road to religious liberty.[21] Madison eventually concluded that religious toleration—granted either by the civil state or by a religious authority—was inconsistent with freedom of conscience and was a woefully inadequate objective, for as Thomas Paine declaimed in 1791: "Toleration is not the *opposite* of Intolerance, but is the *counterfeit* of it. Both are despotisms. The one assumes to itself the right of withholding Liberty of Conscience, and the other of granting it. The one is the Pope armed with fire and faggot, and the other is the Pope selling or granting indulgences."[22] Paine's point is an important one and should not be lost in the venom with which it was made. Historically speaking, religious *toleration* is to be contrasted with religious *liberty*. The former often assumes an established church and is always a revocable grant of the civil state rather than a natural, unalienable right.[23] In Madison's mind, the right of religious exercise was too important to be cast in the form of a mere privilege allowed by the ruling civil polity and enjoyed as a grant of governmental benevolence. Rather, he viewed religious liberty as a natural and unalienable right, possessed equally by all citizens, that must be placed beyond the reach of civil magistrates.[24]

Madison's proposed revisions punctuated his aversion to the concept of mere toleration with a natural rights argument that all men are equally entitled to the free exercise of religious belief. It is not certain when Madison offered his amendments; however, they followed the Committee revision of 27 May. He first suggested the following alternative:

> That Religion or the duty we owe to our Creator, and the manner of discharging it, being under the direction of reason and conviction only, not of violence or compulsion, all men are equally entitled to the full and free exercise of it accord[in]g to the dictates of Conscience; and therefore that no man or class of men ought, on account of religion to be invested with peculiar emoluments or privileges; nor subjected to any penalties or disabilities unless under &c.[25]

Significantly, Madison retained the clause: "That Religion or the duty we owe to our Creator, and the manner of discharging it. . . ." The retention of this line suggests that both Mason and Madison construed "religion" as belief in a Creator and *all* of the duties arising from that belief. This notion is consistent with definitions of religion commonly used at that time, and it included deists but excluded atheists.[26] Most importantly, Madison replaced Mason's tentative statement, "all Men should enjoy the fullest Toleration in the Exercise of Religion," with the phrase, "all men are equally entitled to the full and free exercise of [religion] according to the dictates of Conscience." Madison thus jettisoned the language of toleration and moved toward the concept of absolute religious liberty. Key to this restatement was the word "equally," which was retained in subsequent drafts. This language meant that the unlearned Separate Baptists of central Piedmont had religious rights equal to those of the well-heeled Anglican aristocrats of Tidewater.[27] Madison also dropped the word "enjoy" preceding the phrase "free exercise of religion." The word was reinserted in Madison's subsequent amendment, but it was stricken from the final version. The clause stating "that no man or class of men ought, on account of religion to be invested with peculiar emoluments or privileges" was another radical feature of Madison's revisions. It would have effectively terminated legal and financial support for the ecclesiastical establishment in Virginia. ("[M]an or class of men" is a reference to a clergyman or religious sect.) Religious assessments would arguably have been proscribed. Furthermore, by striking out "force" and replacing it with "compulsion," Madison was expanding the protection afforded religious citizens to include a prohibition on all pressure or interference by the civil state in matters of conscience. Madison's revisions would have arguably deprived the Commonwealth of legal and financial power to support any church or clergy or to control the religious beliefs of citizens in any way.

Clearly, this revision was unacceptable to most delegates and, perhaps, to most Virginians. Unable to muster sufficient support for passage of this amendment, Madison drafted a second alternative providing for the free exercise of religion but carefully avoiding disestablishing the Anglican Church:[28]

> That religion, or the duty which we owe to our CREATOR, and the manner of discharging it, can be directed only by reason and conviction, not by force or violence; and therefore, that all men are equally entitled to enjoy the free exercise of religion, according to the dictates of conscience, unpunished and unrestrained by the magistrate, Unless the preservation of equal liberty and the existence of the

> State are manifestly endangered; And that it is the mutual duty of all to practice Christian forbearance, love, and charity towards each other.[29]

While retaining a regime of equality and liberty in religious exercise, Madison's second revision abandoned the quixotic attempt to disestablish the church. He also dropped the word "compulsion," "thus giving up the specific prohibition of religious control through civil processes." Madison was successful, however, in cutting Mason's "clause on disturbance of the peace down to the Lockeian principle of no interference with religion except to preserve civil society."[30] (Mason had given the magistrate latitude to restrain religious exercise that disturbed the tranquillity not only of society but also of individuals.) The clause qualifying religious exercise that is deemed a danger to the civil state was totally eliminated in the final version.

Once again, delegates to the Virginia Convention declined to endorse Madison's amendment as a whole. They were apparently uncomfortable with any suggestion that Madison's proposals might "sever the special relationship which bound Virginians to the church of their fathers."[31] The version finally adopted, however, included his clause declaring that "all men are equally entitled to the free exercise of religion." This episode brought Madison to the attention of his fellow delegates and distinguished him, along with Mason and Jefferson, as an able spokesman for the cause of religious liberty. In its final form, Article XVI of the Virginia Declaration of Rights provided:

> That Religion, or the duty which we owe to our CREATOR, and the manner of discharging it, can be directed only by reason and conviction, not by force or violence; and, therefore, all men are equally entitled to the free exercise of religion, according to the dictates of conscience; and that it is the mutual duty of all to practise Christian forbearance, love, and charity, towards each other.[32]

The final version, observed L. John Van Til, linked "Creator," "religion," and "conscience." "Religion is the way that a man relates to his Creator, but this relationship can be cared for only through conscience. Conscience employs reason and conviction, not force and violence; hence, conscience as the only way to discharge the duties of man toward his Creator must be at liberty. Significantly, the [article] adds that it is necessary therefore, to practice 'Christian forbearance, love, and charity towards each other.'"[33] This language rests on two important assumptions: first, that the rights of conscience envisioned by the Virginia Convention were to be exercised in a theistic context, and, second, that it involves not only a relationship between one man and his God, but also the relationship of each man to his neighbor.

Article XVI was thus embedded in the organic law of the Commonwealth. Its impact on law and policy was immediate, reported Virginia historian Hamilton James Eckenrode. Notwithstanding the limited intentions of the legislature as manifested by its rejection of several of Madison's sweeping amendments, "[p]rosecution for religious causes ceased. Disabilities on account of religion were removed. . . . Anglicans, Roman Catholics, Evangelicals, Jews, and unbelievers were placed on the same civil footing. . . . Virginia," Eckenrode boasted, "was ahead of the world, making the first legal statement of the principle of religious liberty."[34] Mason is rightly revered as the principal author of the Virginia Declaration of Rights, and it is his version of the article on religion, not Madison's, that was widely circulated and influential in the former colonies. Madison, it is recalled, did not offer his amendments until after the committee draft of the Virginia Declaration had been published and broadcast throughout the colonies and beyond. Mason wrote the initial script that, in the short term, would be greatly imitated[35]; yet, in the final analysis, it was the young James Madison that delivered the memorable, felicitous lines that would change the way later generations of Americans regarded the rights of conscience.

Religious Establishment and the Rights of Dissenters in Revolutionary Virginia, 1776-1779

Although delegates to the Virginia Convention may not have meant Article XVI to imply an end to the established church, that did not stop many religious dissenters from interpreting it that way. Accordingly, passage of Article XVI unleashed a torrent of petitions from religious dissenters demanding full equality in the exercise of religious belief and discontinuation of tax support and other special privileges granted the Commonwealth's established church. The dissenters' grievances were legion. In addition to disestablishment and free exercise of religion, they were concerned with specific practices and policies such as licensure of the clergy, regulation of assemblies and meetinghouses, and the right of dissenting ministers to perform legal marriages. The first republican legislature in Virginia, which convened in Williamsburg in early October 1776, was deluged by the dissenters' petitions. The spirit of these petitions was captured in a poignant plea from the Presbyterian stronghold of Prince Edward County: "The last Article of the [Virginia] Bill of Rights we also esteem as the rising Sun of religious Liberty, to *relieve* us from a long night of ecclesiastical Bondage: and we do most earnestly request and expect that you would go on to complete what is so nobly begun; raise religious as well as civil Liberty to the zenith of Glory, and make Virginia an Asylum for free enquiry, knowledge, and the virtuous of every Denomination." They asked the legislature, without delay, to "pull down all Church Establishments; abolish every Tax upon Conscience and private judgment."[36] In the words of another appeal, the petitioners, "haveing [sic] long groaned under the Burden of an Ecclesiastical establishment beg leave to move your Honourable House that this as well as every other yoke may be Broken and that the oppressed may go free."[37] Other memorialists petitioned "to put every religious Denomination on an equal Footing, to be supported by themselves independent one of another."[38] This outpouring was an immediate consequence of Article XVI. Indeed, many, if not most, of these petitions made direct appeal to the free exercise language of the Virginia Declaration.

The ensuing battle over tax support for the established church was to prove long and rancorous, prompting Jefferson to recollect in his retirement that the legislative in-fighting occasioned by "these petitions to abolish this spiritual tyranny . . . brought on the severest contests in which I have ever been engaged."[39] The long established order was reluctant to relinquish its legal privileges without a bruising fight. The acrimony was only deepened by the fact that, as Jefferson noted, "although the majority of our citizens were dissenters, . . . a majority of the legislature were churchmen."[40]

The Committee for Religion, to which the legislature had assigned these petitions, deadlocked in its deliberations on how to deal with the dissenters' demands. Thus, on 9 November 1776, the Committee was relieved of the task of considering these petitions, and the matter was referred to the House sitting as a Committee of the Whole.[41] The religion question was warmly debated in the House, resulting in the adoption of a set of sweeping resolutions on 19 November.[42] These resolves called for the repeal of all acts of the British Parliament that criminalized religious opinion, refusal to attend religious services, or modes of worship. Other resolves exempted dissenters from all taxation or forced contributions to the established church, and even removed any requirement that citizens contribute towards the support of their own ministers except upon a strictly voluntary basis. The several legislative acts that provided for clerical salaries were repealed, although all arrears of salary were to be paid present incumbents. The established church was given in perpetuity use of glebes, churches, chapels, and other possessions received from either public or private sources. "The net effect of these resolutions was to place all religious groups on a purely voluntary basis with respect to financial support, while giving the established church all the property and goods it possessed at the time."[43]

A committee of seventeen members—including Robert Carter Nicholas, a leading conservative churchman, and Jefferson, Madison, and Mason—was appointed to craft a bill in conformity with these resolutions.[44] In the ensuing deliberations, temporarily outmaneuvered by conservatives on the Committee, the proponents of church-state separation lost ground on the disestablishment issue, and the liberal tide of 19 November seemed to ebb.[45] The Committee charged with drawing up a bill was instructed "to limit itself to those measures which pertained to tax exemption for dissenters and the reservation of the church property to the use of the establishment and to add provisions for the parish poor, the collection of the lists of tithables, and clerical salaries."[46] In short, authority was withdrawn from the Committee to address the more sweeping disestablishment aspects of the resolutions of 19 November. The bill reported on 30 November confirmed that the "delegates had moved back into a position which unmistakably affirmed the existence of an established church in Virginia."[47] Jefferson, who in late November had been granted a special leave for the remainder of the legislative session, hurried back on 4 December, possibly to salvage what he believed to be the most salient features of the 19 November resolutions.[48] In concert with Jefferson, Mason was instrumental in crafting compromise language that was passed by the House on 5

December.[49] Mason's revisions to the "Bill Exempting Dissenters from Contributing to the Established Church" deftly preserved some of the phraseology and much of the substance of the 19 November resolutions,[50] yet it stopped short of complete, unequivocal disestablishment as Jefferson had desired:

> WHEREAS several oppressive Acts of Parliament respecting Religion have been formerly enacted, and Doubts have arisen and may hereafter arise whether the same are in Force within this Common-Wealth or not, for Prevention whereof Be it enacted by the General Assembly of the Common-Wealth of Virginia, and it is hereby enacted by the Authority of the same, That all and every Act [or Statute either] of [the] Parliament [of England, or of Great Britain], by whatsoever Title known or distinguished, which renders criminal the maintaining of any Opinions in Matters of Religion, forbearing to repair to Church, or the exercising any Mode of worship whatsoever, or which prescribes punishments for the same, shall henceforth be of no Validity or Force within this Common-Wealth.[51]

The bill, which quickly passed in the House and Senate with minor amendments,[52] "repealed all laws requiring church attendance and exempted dissenters from direct tax support for the Anglican Church, but left untouched the Act of 1705 which maintained the symbolic established church."[53] The statute, Thomas E. Buckley reported, left

> the established church in an ambiguous situation. No longer were the dissenters taxed to support a state church; nor were they forced to contribute to their own religious groups. The laity of the established church were also freed, at least on a temporary basis, from any taxation to support their own ministry. Religion in Virginia had become voluntary, and a man could believe what he wished and contribute as much or as little as he thought fit to whichever church or minister pleased him. He could also worship when and as he chose, within certain limits; for the Assembly maintained a measure of control over the external operations of the churches. The legislators had not officially yielded their authorization to license meetinghouses and dissenting preachers. Local magistrates, if they wished, might still claim a legal basis for restricting freedom of worship. However, the Revolutionary situation and popular sentiment for the rights of conscience precluded any consistent or widespread enforcement of these laws, and they effectually lapsed.[54]

Passage of the statute repealing the "oppressive acts of Parliament," observed Julian P. Boyd, editor of Jefferson's papers, "was due in large measure to the author of the [Virginia] Declaration of Rights. Even Mason, however, did not restore Jefferson's Resolution calling for the repeal of the Virginia Act of 1705, and their combined power was not equal to the task of disestablishing the Church of England."[55] Nonetheless, this legislation was a significant milestone on the road to eventual termination of an ecclesiastical establishment in Virginia. Jefferson's draft resolutions and legislation of late 1776 exempting dissenters from contributing to the support of the established church, refined by Mason's pen, were necessary precursors to, direct forerunners of, the subsequent Virginia "Statute for Establishing Religious Freedom."[56]

Among the issues deliberately left unresolved by the 1776 exemption act was the propriety of a general assessment for the support of all churches. The law concluded by stating that "nothing in this act contained shall be construed to affect or influence the said question of a general assessment, or voluntary contribution, in any respect whatever."[57] A typical general assessment proposal would tax all citizens for the support of religion, permitting each taxpayer to choose the church to which their assessments would be allocated. This arrangement, proponents argued, encouraged citizens to fulfill the "duty which we owe to our Creator" and promoted the beneficent role of religion in public life, without forcing citizens to subsidize a specific church or form of worship that they disbelieved. Hence, they said it was compatible with the free exercise of religion. Opponents, on the other hand, viewed the assessment as simply another odious form of religious establishment. This issue would become the subject of bitter legislative battles in 1779 and again in the mid-1780s.

The December 1776 legislation permanently exempted dissenters from being taxed to support the established church, but only temporarily suspended the salaries of Anglican clergy. The suspension was continued from one session to the next over the next several years.[58] (The exemption created a loophole whereby Anglicans could escape paying their own minister merely by declaring themselves "dissenters." The suspension of collecting taxes for clerical salaries thus temporarily afforded all citizens—dissenters and Anglicans alike—tax relief.)[59] By 1779 disestablishmentarians in the legislature agitated to make the suspension permanent and thus reach a more definite settlement of the church-state question. Numerous church-state issues had been percolating since long before independence, and with every passing year it became increasingly difficult to defer resolution of these issues. Article XVI of the Declaration of Rights had been in force for nearly three years, raising questions concerning the precise nature of church-state arrangements in the Commonwealth and the expectations of dissenters. There was great uncertainty and turmoil among the clerical ranks due to the suspension of salaries. Vestries were in a growing state of disarray and, indeed, facing calls for their complete dissolution. Thus, the spring 1779 session of the Virginia legislature was an important one for church-state relations.

The General Assembly took up a variety of items of importance to organized religion. On 17 May, the House instructed the Committee for Religion to examine and report on various requests to dissolve and reconstitute the vestries.[60] On 4 June, the House appointed a committee, composed of John Harvie, George Mason, and Jerman Baker, to bring in a bill "for religious freedom."[61] The trio was also directed to prepare a bill "for saving the property of the church heretofore by law established."[62] In response, on 12 June the committee submitted to the House two bills from Virginia's revised code: Jefferson's celebrated bill for establishing religious freedom and a bill for saving the property of the church heretofore by law established.[63] The bills were briefly considered, but the House voted to defer further action on the measures.[64] The postponement afforded lawmakers ample time to canvass public sentiment on these matters. In early June disestablishment forces in the legislature were deprived of their most effective advocate, Thomas Jefferson, who was elected to succeed Patrick Henry as governor.[65] The removal of his forceful voice from legislative deliberations frustrated the liberal campaign for church-state separation. The Committee for Religion was ordered to prepare a bill "for farther [sic] suspending the payment of salaries heretofore given to the clergy of the Church of England,"[66] which was presented and promptly passed by the House on 17 June.[67] Further discussion on a bill dissolving the vestries was shelved until the October session.[68] Thus, "[t]he [spring] session came to an end with the religion question in exactly the same position as before."[69]

The same church-state issues were, once again, prominent on the October legislative agenda. Petitions favoring and opposing Jefferson's religious freedom bill joined the steady stream of petitions on religion that had confronted the legislature since independence. By the time the legislature reconvened, "[t]he reaction in the press and the religious petitions clearly showed that the weight of public opinion favored some form of governmental intervention in religious matters, and this sentiment found support in the House of Delegates."[70] Jefferson's controversial bill was not even considered. Not content merely to leave Jefferson's bill in legislative limbo, on 25 October the conservative defenders of state assistance for religion introduced a general assessment bill for the "encouragement of Religion and virtue" and for the "Support of Religious Teachers and places of Worship."[71] The bill affirmed "that all persons and Religious Societies who acknowledge that there is one *God*, and a future State of rewards and punishments, and that *God* ought to be publickly worshiped, shall be freely tolerated." The bill specifically provided civil and religious privileges, such as the fruits of a general assessment and the right to incorporate, for those Christian societies and denominations that subscribed to five articles of faith (modeled on Article XXXVIII of the South Carolina Constitution of 1778), including that "there is one Eternal God and a future State of Rewards and Punishments, . . . the Christian Religion is the true Religion, [and] . . . the Holy Scriptures of the old and new Testament are of divine inspiration, and are the only rule of Faith."[72] This initiative was welcomed by petitioners seeking robust legislative action to encourage Christianity and restore public virtue, which were said to be in decline since the state had begun dissolving its legal and financial bonds with the church. While eschewing the old exclusive establishment model, the bill declared that "the Christian Religion shall in all times coming be deemed, and held to be the established Religion of this Commonwealth; and all Denominations of Christians demeaning themselves peaceably and faithfully, shall enjoy equal privileges, civil and Religious."[73] The bill, which was difficult to reconcile with Article XVI of the Declaration of Rights, was warmly debated in the legislature and fora of public opinion. Clearly, the legislature and society were sharply divided on the merits of the general assessment proposal. In the end, neither Jefferson's bill nor the general assessment measure could muster sufficient momentum to gain passage this session. Both were set aside for reconsideration by future Assemblies.[74]

On 18 November, Mason presented a bill "to repeal so much of the act for the support of the clergy, and for the regular collecting and paying the parish levies."[75] The bill repealed that portion of the December 1776 exemption act that had been temporarily suspended since its enactment (i.e., provisions providing salaries for clergy and authorizing the collection and payment of parish levies). A brief preamble set forth the sweeping objectives of the proposal: "To remove from the good People of this Commonwealth the Fear of being compelled to contribute to the Support or Maintenance of the former established Church, And that the Members of the said Church may no longer relye upon the Expectation of any Re-establishment thereof, & be thereby prevented from adopting proper Measures, among themselves, for the Support and Maintenance of their own Religion and Ministers."[76] The measure was passed on 13 December, stripped of the preamble in the course of deliberations.[77] This bill, in effect, permanently ended direct tax support for the formerly established church in Virginia. The Anglican Church had languished during the temporary suspension of clerical salaries, and it was hoped that with the end of tax subsidies the church, once organized on a voluntary basis, would be energized by competition in the marketplace of ideas. The operative portion of the bill had been reclaimed from the now tabled general assessment bill. Mason and his liberal allies had affixed the unequivocal preamble to the repeal bill, perhaps to signal their repugnance for the assessment bill from which it had been extracted and to dampen any prospects of reviving a general assessment scheme.[78]

Mason, on 26 November, reintroduced a somewhat revised bill "for saving the property of the church heretofore by law established to the members of the said church for ever."[79] Since the property of the Anglican Church had been acquired with taxes collected from the entire community, yet not all citizens were members of the Church, there was great controversy concerning the equitable dissolution of the temporal assets of the formerly established church, which many dissenters regarded as community—not solely Anglican—property.[80] The measure, in essence, respected the property interests of the formerly established church and gave parishioners significant control over important church matters, such as the removal of clergy. The proposal sought to balance some of the competing financial and governance interests manifested in the transition from establishment to disestablishment. Although the bill received a second reading, it was in effect killed by a postponement of further consideration until the next session.[81]

By the end of the 1770s, important, if tentative, steps had been taken toward redefining church-state relations in Virginia. Religious dissenters, allied with liberal disestablishmentarians, embraced Article XVI as a vehicle for reform. Energized by passage of Article XVI, religious dissenters impatiently demanded the legislature to enact a host of measures that they believed were natural extensions of Article XVI and republican reforms in revolutionary Virginia. Swift action on these measures was resisted by staunch defenders of state support for religion, who feared withdrawal of legal and financial assistance for the established church would undermine social order and public morality. The stage was set for a rancorous showdown over some of the most fundamental, intractable church-state issues.

Revision of the Laws of Virginia

The adoption of the "Declaration of Independence" on 4 July 1776 not only signaled political separation from England but also severed the colonies' formal legal links with the mother country. Thus it seemed desirable, indeed necessary, to bring the laws of the respective states into conformity with republican principles and to strip the existing legal codes of remaining vestiges of monarchical rule.

For many in the colonies, political independence was the ultimate objective of the American "rebellion"; but for Jefferson and his more forward looking colleagues, it was only the beginning.[82] "When I left Congress, in '76," Jefferson wrote in his *Autobiography*, "it was in the persuasion that our whole code must be reviewed, adapted to our republican form of government; and . . . it should be corrected, in all its parts, with a single eye to reason, and the good of those for whose government it was framed."[83] Among the patriots' most urgent tasks was to place the newly independent, fledgling states upon republican legal foundations. Accordingly, on 12 October 1776, Jefferson introduced a proposal in the Virginia legislature to revise the Commonwealth's legal code,[84] which passed on 26 October.[85] The legislature appointed a committee of prominent Virginians, chaired by Jefferson, to "revise, alter, amend, repeal, or introduce all or any of the said laws" of the Commonwealth.[86] In addition to Jefferson, the Committee appointed on 5 November 1776 included Edmund Pendleton, George Wythe, George Mason, and Thomas Ludwell Lee.[87]

Despite this formidable brain trust, it was soon apparent that the thirty-three-year-old Jefferson would assume the lion's share of the work in framing the revised code.[88] Jefferson recounted in his *Autobiography* that when the Committee "proceeded to the distribution of the work, Mr. Mason excused himself, as, being no lawyer, he felt himself unqualified for the work, and he resigned soon after. Mr. Lee excused himself on the same ground, and died, indeed, in a short time. The other two gentlemen, therefore, and myself divided the work among us."[89] Much of the work initially assigned to Lee and Mason eventually fell to Jefferson, and Pendleton's contributions were relatively minor.[90] Clearly, no one took a more prominent role in the legal reforms than Jefferson, and, in the final analysis, no one had more influence on Virginia law.[91]

The Committee of Revisors convened in Fredericksburg on 13 January 1777, to outline their objectives and distribute the work among themselves. The Committee first considered "whether [it] should propose to abolish the whole existing system of laws, and prepare a new and complete Institute, or preserve the general system, and only modify it to the present state of things."[92] Ironically, Jefferson, who rarely shied away from momentous challenges such as composing a "new Institute, like those of Justinian and Bracton, or that of Blackstone,"[93] advocated alterations only, while the usually more conservative Pendleton pressed for sweeping changes.[94] Jefferson's view prevailed, largely because a radical restructuring of the laws undoubtedly would have proven to be an "arduous undertaking," requiring "vast research, . . . great consideration and judgment" and, in all probability, would have exceeded the Committee's legislative mandate.[95]

According to Jefferson's account, the revised code—especially the bills abolishing the laws of entail and primogeniture and promoting general education and *religious freedom*—was purposed to create "a system by which every fibre would be eradicated of ancient or future aristocracy; and a foundation laid for a government truly republican."[96] After agreeing to a general plan of action, the Committee members distributed the work among themselves.[97] Jefferson, according to his biographer Dumas Malone, specifically assumed responsibility for drafting the bills pertaining to crimes and punishment, descents, education, and *religion*.[98]

Two years later, in February 1779, Wythe and Jefferson reconvened in Williamsburg. Meeting on a daily basis, they examined drafts of the revised code "sentence by sentence, scrutinizing and amending, until [they] had agreed on the whole."[99] On 18 June 1779, the Speaker laid before the House of Delegates a report on the revisal submitted by Jefferson (who recently had been elevated to the governor's office) and Wythe.[100] The revisors had prepared 126 bills, the titles of which were included in an accompanying catalog.[101] Several bills thought to have immediate application were extracted from the revised code and promptly enacted. Most of the revisal, however, was shelved for the next half decade. The uncertainties and pressures of war during this period distracted the legislators from considering the revised code as a whole.

In the autumn of 1785, Jefferson was the American minister in France. Nevertheless, he remained influential in the legislative strategy to enact these bills, with Madison acting as the chief sponsor.[102] By the mid-1780s, Madison had emerged a respected and influential figure in the legislature, and so successful was his handling of the revised code that under his legislative guidance nearly half of the bills were eventually enacted without significant amendment. On 31 October 1785, Madison revived Jefferson's dream of seeing the revised code enacted as a whole when he introduced in the Virginia legislature 118 of the bills contained in the *Report of the Revisors* that had not yet been enacted into law.[103] Thirty-five bills were adopted at this session of the legislature and another twenty-three were eventually passed in the autumn 1786 session.[104] It became apparent, however, that despite Madison's commitment to the revised code and Jefferson's desire to see the code enacted as whole, the legislature had no intention of acting on it as a united body of law. Instead, select bills were considered and voted upon in a piecemeal fashion. The most celebrated measure in the revised code was Bill 82—Jefferson's "Bill for Establishing Religious Freedom."

The Struggle for Religious Liberty in Virginia, 1784-1786

The enactment of the "Statute for Establishing Religious Freedom" was the culmination of a tumultuous and divisive legislative struggle that had gripped the Virginia legislature for a decade. The battle began with the adoption of Article XVI of the Declaration of Rights and smoldered until passage in 1786 of the "Statute for Establishing Religious Freedom." Shortly after the revised code was presented to the legislature and Jefferson was elevated to the governorship in June 1779, the House declined to enact the religious freedom bill. Despite its eloquence and the growing stature of its author, it proved too radical for the times.[105] While Jefferson, Madison, and Mason agitated to disestablish the state church, there was another influential group in the legislature that championed an alternative approach to church-state relations—a general assessment for the support of all churches. (Interestingly, both groups professed a common objective, which was to increase the influence of religion in society as an instrument of social order and stability. On the one hand, disestablishmentarians believed true religion would flourish if freed from the control and monopoly of the civil state. Proponents of a general assessment, on the other hand, argued that since religion is indispensable to social order and stability, the civil state has a duty to facilitate sustaining aid for religion lest religion's influence in the community be allowed to atrophy for the want of resources.)

The general assessment scheme proposed to tax citizens, not for the support of a single, official church "by law established," but for the support and maintenance of ministers in the Commonwealth's diverse Christian denominations. By 1779, the Virginia legislature had been inundated by petitions specifically requesting an assessment plan designed to rescue the financially strapped ecclesiastical institutions, as well as to enhance public morality. Public virtue, it was argued, had been in decline since tax support for the Anglican Church and its clergy had been suspended by the 1776 act exempting dissenters from contributing to the established church. Despite substantial pro-assessment sentiment in the Commonwealth, neither a general assessment measure nor Jefferson's bill was enacted in 1779. An epic legislative battle between supporters of the two statutory schemes raged for the next six years. The acrimonious contest climaxed in the mid-1780s, culminating in the enactment of the "Statute for Establishing Religious Freedom."

In the autumn session of 1784, the Virginia legislature was again presented with numerous petitions requesting an assessment for the support of teachers of the Christian religion. These petitions told of nations that had fallen because of the demise of religion and portrayed the alarming decline of morals in the Commonwealth. Some requests for the assessment argued that since religion was a general benefit to society, every citizen should be required to contribute to it. Petitioners observed that financial support was needed to encourage good candidates to enter the ministry. Support for the declining ecclesiastical institutions, proponents argued, was essential to maintaining republican virtues and preserving social order and stability.

On 11 November 1784, the House went into a Committee of the Whole and held an in-depth debate on the assessment issue.[106] The debate, in many respects, was a replay of the legislative struggle in 1779 when both Jefferson's religious freedom bill and a different, more sectarian assessment proposal were debated in the chambers of the Virginia legislature.[107] The delegates in favor of an assessment rallied behind the dominant personality in the House, Patrick Henry. With Jefferson in Europe serving as the American minister to France, leadership of the opposition fell to James Madison. Many leading Virginians, including George Washington, John Marshall, and Richard Henry Lee, were allied with the pro-assessment movement.[108] Noting these influential statesmen's support for a general assessment, the eminent church-state scholar Anson Phelps Stokes wrote, "[i]t is clear that most Protestants in Virginia at the time favored the encouragement of religion by the state through financial aid to the Christian churches."[109]

Patrick Henry won the first test of strength on the assessment issue by persuading his colleagues to adopt by a vote of 47 to 32 a resolution that stated: "the people of this Commonwealth, according to their respectful [respective?] abilities, ought to pay a moderate tax or contribution, annually, for the support of the christian religion, or of some christian church, denomination or communion of christians, or of some form of christian worship."[110] Henry was promptly appointed the chair of a committee commissioned to draft a bill providing a plan for a general assessment. If a proposal had been prepared quickly, all indications are that it would have won swift passage in both chambers of the General Assembly. Apart from Madison's opposition in the House, little organized resistance to an assessment was evident, and Henry effectively marshaled behind his cause delegates representing the most populous and wealthy constituencies in the Commonwealth.[111]

Alarmed at the growing support for Henry's assessment campaign and the perceived threat to religious liberty, Jefferson uncharitably suggested to Madison: "What we have to do I think is *devo*[u]*tly* to *pray* for *his* [Henry's] death."[112] Madison, however, had a less final solution: remove Henry from the legislature by having him elected governor. Thus, with Madison's calculated support, on 17 November 1784, Henry was elected to the governor's seat in an uncontested election.[113] With Henry removed from the legislative arena, advocates of a religious assessment lost the man one Virginia clergyman described as "the great Pillar of our Cause."[114] The forces for an assessment never regained the momentum lost with Henry's departure from the House. Henry's able rival, Madison, grasped the opportunity to defeat the elder statesman's project. By late November and into December, petitions opposing an assessment began to surface,[115] and sensing a shift in sentiment, Madison jubilantly expressed doubt that the assessment bill would pass.[116]

Nevertheless, on 2 December, Francis Corbin, the English-educated planter, lawyer, and delegate from Middlesex County, laid before the House a bill "establishing a provision for teachers of the christian religion."[117] This bill, drafted under Henry's direction, provided for a moderate tax, with an unfixed rate, upon all taxable property for the support of ministers, or teachers of the Christian religion.[118] The bill afforded each taxpayer the opportunity to designate the religious denomination that would receive this subsidy. Another provision was eventually added that directed undesignated revenues to "seminaries of learning" or other pious uses. This measure was very different from the 1779 general assessment bill. It did not explicitly proclaim Christianity the Commonwealth's established religion and, more importantly, it was stripped of the five creedal articles to which participating religious societies were required to subscribe. "While the 1779 bill had been directly oriented toward the public worship of God, the 1784 proposal was concerned with the religious instruction of man."[119] The bill received a second reading the following day.[120] The House, sitting as a Committee of the Whole, debated the assessment bill once again on 22 and 23 December 1784. According to Madison's account, "it was determined by a Majority of 7 or 8 that the word 'christian' should be exchanged for the word 'Religious.' On the report to the House the *pathetic zeal of the late governor Harrison* gained a like majority for reinstating discrimination."[121] Thus, a short-lived attempt to de-Christianize the bill by extending its benefits to all "who profess the public worship of the Deity," be they Mohammedans or Jews, failed.[122] On 23 December, at the conclusion of the two-day debate, Henry's bill was ordered by the narrow vote of 44 to 42 to be engrossed and read the third time.[123] When the bill came up for a third reading the following day, opponents of an assessment moved to postpone the final reading until the next legislative session in November 1785. The motion passed by a vote of 45 to 38.[124] It was further moved that the measure "be published in hand-bills" and distributed throughout the Commonwealth, and "that the people thereof be requested to signify their opinion respecting the adoption of such a bill."[125] Madison's side had won a temporary victory that afforded them time to consolidate and mobilize the opposition to the assessment bill.

In the interval between legislative sessions, Madison was inclined to wait quietly for the growing popular opposition to an assessment to manifest itself.[126] But allies in the House, notably brothers Wilson Cary Nicholas and George Nicholas, did not share his optimism. Silence, warned George Nicholas, "would be construed into an assent."[127] Thus, Madison was persuaded to draft the "Memorial and Remonstrance Against Religious Assessments" in the summer of 1785 and to circulate it anonymously.[128] The brothers Nicholas and George Mason, who knew of Madison's authorship, distributed the "Remonstrance" across the Commonwealth and orchestrated the successful drive to have it signed by their fellow citizens. Mason arranged and paid to have the "Remonstrance" printed and circulated throughout the Northern Neck region. He also sent it to influential citizens for their endorsement. For example, in a letter to his neighbor, George Washington, Mason wrote:

> I take the Liberty of inclosing you a Memorial and Remonstrance to the General Assembly, confided to me by a particular Freind, whose Name I am not at Liberty to mention; and as the Principles it avows entirely accord with my Sentiments on the subject (which is a very important one) I have been at the Charge of Printing several Copys, to disperse in the different Parts of the Country. You will easily perceive that all Manner of Declamation, & Address to the Passions, have been avoided, as unfair in themselves, & improper for such a Subject, and altho' the Remonstrance is long, that Brevity has been aimed at; but the Field is extensive.
>
> If upon Consideration, you approve the Arguments, & the Principles upon which they are founded, your Signature will both give the Remonstrance weight, and do it Honour.[129]

Washington declined to endorse the "Remonstrance," responding: "Altho' no mans Sentiments are more opposed to *any kind* of restraint upon religeous principles than mine are; yet I must confess, that I am not amongst the number of those who are so much alarmed at the thoughts of making People pay towards the support of that which they profess, if of the denominations of Christians; or declare themselves Jews, Mahomitans or otherwise, & thereby obtain proper relief."[130] Washington's ambivalence notwithstanding, the "Remonstrance" proved effective in galvanizing anti-assessment sentiment. Specifically crediting Mason and George Nicholas, Madison reported that the "Remonstrance" was "so extensively signed by the people of every Religious denomination, that at the ensuing session, the projected [assessment] measure was entirely frustrated."[131] Interestingly, Madison was so successful in shielding his authorship of the "Remonstrance" and Mason was so zealous in his support of it that there was contemporaneous speculation attributing the document to Mason's pen.[132] In at least four sections, Madison quoted Article XVI of the Declaration of Rights Mason had written for Virginia (these references may explain why some attributed the "Remonstrance" to Mason). Madison's "Remonstrance" was not alone among the petitions in this respect. As Rhys Isaac observed, "Almost every petition against establishment appealed to the Virginia Declaration—usually styled the 'Bill'—of Rights. This tablet of fundamental law served as the legitimation for demands directed from the spiritual domain of the evangelical churches into the secular realm of the legislature."[133]

Madison's argument was presented in the form of a "memorial" and "remonstrance," that is, a formal petition or complaint addressed to the legislature with an attached declaration of reasons. Thus, each of the document's fifteen numbered paragraphs begins with the word "because."[134] Madison argued that religion, or the duty owed the Creator, is a matter for individual conscience and not within the cognizance of civil government. All citizens are entitled to the full, equal, and natural right to exercise religion according to the dictates of conscience. "[T]he same authority which can establish Christianity, in exclusion of all other Religions," Madison warned, "may establish with the same ease any particular sect of Christians, in exclusion of all other Sects." The establishment of a particular church "violates that equality which ought to be the basis of every law." Furthermore, it is "an arrogant pretension" to believe "that the Civil Magistrate is a competent Judge of Religious Truths; or that he may employ Religion as an engine of Civil policy." Experience confirms that "ecclesiastical establishments, instead of maintaining the purity and efficacy of Religion, have had a contrary operation." The fruits of ecclesiastical establishment, Madison reported, have been "pride and indolence in the Clergy, ignorance and servility in the laity, in both, superstition, bigotry and persecution." Religious establishment in Virginia would be an unfortunate "departure from that generous policy, which, offering an Asylum to the persecuted and oppressed of every Nation and Religion, promised a lustre to our country, and an accession to the number of its citizens." Madison also rejected the view that religion could not survive without the sustaining aid of civil government, nor the civil government preserve social order and stability without the support of an established church. He believed, to the contrary, that true religion prospered in the public marketplace of ideas unrestrained by the monopolistic control of the civil authority. He thought it a contradiction to argue that discontinuing state support for Christianity would precipitate its demise, since "this Religion both existed and flourished, not only without the support of human laws, but in spite of every opposition from them. . . . [A] Religion not invented by human policy, must have pre-existed and been supported, before it was established by human policy." If Christianity depends on the support of civil government, then the "pious confidence" of the faithful in its "innate excellence and the patronage of its Author" will be undermined. The best and purest religion, Madison thus concluded, relied on the voluntary support of those who profess it, without entanglements of any sort with civil government—including those fostered by financial support, regulation, or compulsion.[135]

The "Remonstrance" was only one in a torrent of signed petitions in opposition to the assessment plan that deluged the legislature. The people, indeed, as their legislature requested, had expressed their opinion on the matter.[136] After only brief consideration in the fall of 1785, Henry's bill died quietly in committee. Hamilton James Eckenrode wrote that the "weight of [anti-assessment] petitions settled the fate of the 'Bill for Establishing a Support for Teachers of the Christian Religion.'"[137] Madison's "Remonstrance," while only one—albeit the most eloquent and forceful[138]—of the many petitions addressing this issue drafted and circulated in the summer of 1785, may well have been decisive in this legislative battle.[139]

Enthused by the demise of the general assessment plan, Madison brushed the dust off Jefferson's "Bill for Establishing Religious Freedom" from the revised code and pushed it to passage by a comfortable margin.[140] Jefferson's bill, much to the author's dismay, had languished without legislative action since June 1779. The statute provided in its brief enabling clauses:

> that no man shall be compelled to frequent or support any religious worship, place, or ministry whatsoever, nor shall be enforced, restrained, molested, or burthened in his body or goods, nor shall otherwise suffer on account of his religious opinions or belief; but that all men shall be free to profess, and by argument to maintain, their opinions in matters of religion, and that the same shall in no wise diminish, enlarge, or affect their civil capacities.[141]

The Virginia "Statute for Establishing Religious Freedom" has been described by the eminent historian Bernard Bailyn as "the most important document in American history, bar none."[142] Jefferson thought it among his most significant contributions to the Commonwealth and the nation, selecting his authorship of the statute as one of three achievements he wanted memorialized on his tombstone.[143] The statute's eloquent, artfully crafted preamble is a celebrated manifesto for intellectual freedom.[144] Madison boasted that the bill's passage "extinguished for ever the ambitious hope of making laws for the human mind."[145] The arguments advanced in the bill have been woven into the fabric of American political thought, and in the course of time the conventional interpretation of the bill has been adopted as the orthodox principle of American church-state relations.[146]

The prevailing interpretation of the religious freedom bill is that in its "sweeping language Jefferson sought to create an unbreachable wall of separation between Church and State and make religious opinions forever private and sacrosanct from intrusion."[147] As Harvard legal historian Mark DeWolfe Howe emphasized, however, Jefferson's bill did not "in its enacting clauses explicitly prohibit establishment."[148] Rather, the specific legal point of the bill was to terminate compelled religious observance and remove civil disabilities against dissenters who publicly expressed their religious opinions. Also, it should be noted that the religious freedom bill was the first of five consecutive bills in the revised code specifically addressing religious concerns. This legislative package included, along with the religious freedom bill, "A Bill for Punishing Disturbers of Religious Worship and Sabbath Breakers" and "A Bill for Appointing Days of Public Fasting and Thanksgiving."[149] These bills were apparently framed by Jefferson and sponsored by Madison in the Virginia legislature. Taken as a whole, these five bills do not promote a strict separation between church and state. Rather, they advance a flexible church-state model that fosters cooperation between religious interests and the civil state and proscribes governmental interference with freedom of religious beliefs. In short, they illustrate that Jefferson's and Madison's ultimate objective was less an absolute church-state separation than the fullest possible expression of religious belief and opinion.[150]

Madison's leadership and eloquence not only brought about the demise of the general assessment bill, but also revived Jefferson's long endangered religious freedom bill.[151] Both the religious freedom bill and the "Remonstrance" grew from the fertile soil of Article XVI of the Virginia Declaration of Rights. Jefferson's celebrated statute, written in 1777, was also shaped by the rancorous debate of 1776 that gave life to the bill exempting dissenters from contributing to the established church. This decade-long debate in the Virginia legislature redefined a centuries-old approach to church-state relations.

Conclusion

Article XVI of the Virginia Declaration of Rights commenced a crucial conversation on religious liberty and the prudential relationship between religion and the civil state. It framed church-state discourse in the Old Dominion throughout the revolutionary era. It was the starting point for Madison's "Remonstrance" and Jefferson's "Bill for Establishing Religious Freedom." Indeed, it was the tentative "first draft" of a proposal that was eventually shaped into the First Amendment to the U.S. Constitution.

The dramatic disestablishment saga, starting with Article XVI and culminating in the "Statute for Establishing Religious Freedom," has, in the course of time, become a celebrated chapter in the mythology of not only Virginia but also the nation. Courts and commentators, especially in the late twentieth century, have frequently referenced this episode in Virginia history to explain, advocate, or justify a national policy of church-state separation.[152] It is not clear, however, that events in Virginia necessarily ordained an emerging national consensus. Virginia, after all, went further and faster down the path of church-state separation than other states in the revolutionary era. Other states monitored events in revolutionary Virginia, but not all followed her disestablishment path. "Most other states," observed Thomas J. Curry, "did not soon accept the same definitive solution [adopted in Virginia], . . . so Virginia cannot be said to have served as a model for them."[153] Leaving aside the question whether or not Virginia was *the* model followed by other states and the nation, there are insights to be gained and lessons to be learned from studying the Virginia experience. The battles in Virginia revealed much about the church-state and religious liberty concerns of the founding generation.

Were the solutions crafted in revolutionary Virginia the framework for a national church-state policy enshrined in the First Amendment? No doubt the lessons learned in Virginia were recollected in the First Congress, which drafted the First Amendment, but so too were the experiences of other communities. Constitutional historian Leonard W. Levy instructed that "to understand what was meant by 'an establishment of religion' at the time of the framing of the Bill of Rights, the histories of the other states are equally important, notwithstanding the stature and influence of Jefferson and Madison as individuals."[154] Most states in the founding era retained various forms of religious establishment, including state churches and religious test oaths for officeholders. Furthermore, to ascertain the original understanding of the First Amendment, as framed by the First Congress and ratified by the states, attention must be devoted to the views of all members of the First Congress, not just Madison, and to the views of delegates at state ratifying conventions. In short, the First Amendment was the product of experiences and aspirations beyond those of Virginia alone.

The church-state arrangement eventually adopted in Virginia represents an approach persistent in the American experience since independence. Virginia embraced religious liberty, as opposed to mere toleration, separated the institutions of church and state, and placed all religious societies on a purely voluntary footing. These were radical innovations for the time, and they remain vital principles in the late twentieth century. Thus, the story of church and state in Virginia in the decade between 1776 and 1786 continues to loom large in the life of the republic.

Notes

Portions of this chapter were extracted from "George Mason's Pursuit of Religious Liberty in Revolutionary Virginia," *Virginia Magazine of History and Biography* (forthcoming); and are included here by permission of the Virginia Historical Society.

1. Letter from John Adams to Patrick Henry, 3 June 1776, *The Works of John Adams, Second President of the United States,* 10 vols. (Boston: Little, Brown and Co., 1850-56), IX:387.

2. Thomas J. Curry, *The First Freedoms: Church and State in America to the Passage of the First Amendment* (New York: Oxford University Press, 1986), 134.

3. Curry, *The First Freedoms*, 134.

4. Thomas E. Buckley, *Church and State in Revolutionary Virginia, 1776-1787* (Charlottesville: University Press of Virginia, 1977), 6.

5. Many of these recollections are referenced in the pages below.

6. Leonard W. Levy, *The Establishment Clause: Religion and the First Amendment*, 2d ed. (Chapel Hill: University of North Carolina Press, 1994), 60.

7. For a more complete discussion of the church-state debate in revolutionary Virginia, see Buckley, *Church and State in Revolutionary Virginia*, and Hamilton James Eckenrode, *Separation of Church and State in Virginia: A Study in the Development of the Revolution* (Richmond, Va.: Davis Bottom, 1910).

8. Eckenrode, *Separation of Church and State in Virginia*, 42.

9. *The Papers of Thomas Jefferson*, ed. Julian P. Boyd, 27 vols. to date (Princeton: Princeton University Press, 1950-), 1:290-291 [hereinafter *Papers of Jefferson*].

10. The architects of the new, independent government of Virginia viewed "A Declaration of Rights . . . as the basis and foundation of government." Therefore, they drafted and adopted the Virginia Declaration *before* framing a "Constitution, or Form of Government." William Waller Hening, ed., *The Statutes at Large; Being a Collection of all the Laws of Virginia, From the First Session of the Legislature, in the Year 1619* (Richmond, Va.: J. & G. Cochran, 1821), IX:109, 112 [hereinafter *Statutes at Large*]. "It is significant," observed Virginia constitutional historian A.E. Dick Howard, "that provision for a bill of rights preceded mention of a plan of government. The members of the 1776 Convention, steeped in Lockean notions of the social contract, might well have considered themselves in a state of nature upon the dissolution of the bond with Great Britain." They thought a declaration of man's natural rights was a logical step towards framing a new social compact. Howard, *Commentaries on the Constitution of Virginia,* 2 vols. (Charlottesville: University Press of Virginia, 1974), 1:34-35.

11. *The Papers of George Mason, 1725-1792,* ed. Robert A. Rutland, 3 vols. (Chapel Hill: University of North Carolina Press, 1970), 1:275 [hereinafter *Papers of Mason*].

12. Letter from Thomas Jefferson to Henry Lee, 8 May 1825, in *The Life and Selected Writings of Thomas Jefferson,* ed. Adrienne Koch and William Peden, The Modern Library (New York: Random House, 1944), 719 [hereinafter *Life and Selected Writings of Jefferson*]; Editorial Note, *Papers of Mason*, 1:279.

13.William C. Rives, *History of the Life & Times of James Madison,* 2 vols. (Boston: Little, Brown & Co., 1859), 1:137. See also Irving Brant, *James Madison: The Virginia Revolutionist* (Indianapolis, Ind.: The Bobbs-Merrill Co., 1941), 241 ("The Virginia Bill of Rights . . . is an amalgam of human rights fused in the crucible of revolution. It comes from Magna Carta, from the British Bill of Rights, from the long struggle to establish parliamentary supremacy, from Locke and Montesquieu, from Wycliffe and St. Augustine.").

14. Editorial Note, *Papers of Mason*, 1:276. See Brent Tarter, "Virginians and the Bill of Rights," in *The Bill of Rights: A Lively Heritage*, ed. Jon Kukla (Richmond: Virginia State Library and Archives, 1987), 6-7 (noting that it was the Committee draft of the Virginia Declaration that was widely circulated); Helen Hill Miller, *George Mason: Gentleman Revolutionary* (Chapel Hill: University of North Carolina Press, 1975), 142, 149-150 ("This draft, rather than the form finally adopted, was treated as the official version for many years.").

15. Robert A. Rutland, *George Mason: Reluctant Statesman* (Baton Rouge: Louisiana State University Press, 1961), 67 (footnote omitted). Another student of the Virginia Declaration observed:

> The most influential constitutional document in American history is . . . the committee draft of the Virginia Declaration of Rights, written by George Mason, and reported and printed "for the perusal" of the members of the Virginia Assembly on May 27, 1776. It was published in the *Virginia Gazette* of June 1, 1776, and thereafter republished in newspapers and magazines all over America, in England, and in Europe. It, and not the amended draft officially adopted on June 12, 1776, was the document from which Jefferson, Franklin, and Adams copied to make a preamble for the Declaration of Independence. Franklin copied it into the Pennsylvania and Adams copied it into the Massachusetts declarations of rights of 1776 and 1780, respectively. France copied it into her celebrated Declaration of Rights of 1789. All of the original American states that adopted declarations of rights copied from the committee draft. None copied from the official draft for around a half century. . . .
>
> Words, phrases and sentences copied from the committee draft of May 27, 1776, may be found in every Declaration of Rights adopted in America since May 1776, and in most of the other such declarations adopted elsewhere in the world.
>
> Mason's original draft—not the official—was used as the basis not only for the proposals of the Pennsylvania minority, but by the Maryland minority and the Virginia, New York, North Carolina, and Rhode Island majorities, in their ratifying conventions of 1787-1790, which proposals later became the federal Bill of Rights.
>
> The committee draft of the Virginia Declaration of Rights of May 27, 1776, stands with Magna Charta and the English Bill of Rights of 1689, as one of the three most influential constitutional documents in all the history of liberty. . . . It is the most copied of the three.

R. Carter Pittman, Book Review, *Virginia Magazine of History and Biography* 68 (1960): 110-111.

16. Letter from George Mason, 2 October 1778, *Papers of Mason*, 1:437. See also *ibid.*, 1:434 ("this was the first thing of the kind upon the Continent, and has been closely imitated by all the other States.").

17. Editorial Note, *Papers of Mason,* 1:291.

18. *Papers of Mason*, 1:278; *The Papers of James Madison*, ed. William T. Hutchinson and William M. E. Rachal (Chicago: University of Chicago Press, 1962), 1:172-173 [hereinafter *Papers of Madison*].

19. *Papers of Mason*, 1:284; *Papers of Madison*, 1:173.

20. *Papers of Madison*, 1:171. See also Gaillard Hunt, "James Madison and Religious Liberty," *Annual Report of the American Historical Association for the Year 1901* (Washington, D.C.: GPO, 1902), 165; William Lee Miller, *The First Liberty: Religion and the American Republic* (New York: Alfred A. Knopf, 1986), 5 ("James Madison was first moved to revolutionary ardor by the issue of religious liberty.").

21. Irving Brant, "Madison: On the Separation of Church and State," *William and Mary Quarterly*, 3d ser., 8 (1951): 5.

22. Thomas Paine, *Rights of Man* (1791), in *The Writings of Thomas Paine,* ed. Moncure Daniel Conway (New York: G. P. Putnam's Sons, 1894), II:325.

23. See Charles Fenton James, *Documentary History of the Struggle for Religious Liberty in Virginia* (Lynchburg, Va.: J.P. Bell Co., 1900), 201 (Religious liberty "differs from religious toleration . . . in that toleration implies the right to withhold, or to refuse license, whereas religious liberty means that the civil power has nothing to do with a man's religion except to protect him in the enjoyment of his rights.").

24. In his so-called "Autobiography," Madison wrote: "Being young & in the midst of distinguished and experienced members of the Convention he [Madison referring to himself in the third person] did not enter into its debates; tho' he occasionally suggested amendments; the most material of which was a change of the terms in which the freedom of Conscience was expressed in the proposed Declaration of Rights. This important and meritorious instrument was drawn by Geo. Mason, who had inadvertently adopted the word *toleration* in the article on that subject. The change suggested and accepted, substituted a phraseology which—declared the freedom of conscience to be a *natural and absolute* right." Douglass Adair, ed., "James Madison's Autobiography," *William and Mary Quarterly,* 3d ser., 2 (1945): 199 (emphasis in the original).

25. *Papers of Madison*, 1:174. Madison evidently meant that after "under" should follow the words of the Committee version—"colour of religion, any man disturb the peace, the happiness, or safety of society. And that it is the mutual duty of all to practice Christian forbearance, love and charity, towards each other."

26. See Michael J. Malbin, *Religion and Politics: The Intentions of the Authors of the First Amendment* (Washington, D.C.: American Enterprise Institute for Public Policy Research, 1978), 21.

27. Miller, *The First Liberty,* 5.

28. *Papers of Madison*, 1:171.

29. *Papers of Madison,* 1:174-175.

30. Brant, *James Madison: The Virginia Revolutionist,* 246.

31. Buckley, *Church and State in Revolutionary Virginia*, 19.

32. Hening, *Statutes at Large*, IX:111-112; *Papers of Mason,* 1:289; *Papers of Madison,* 1:175.

33. L. John Van Til, *Liberty of Conscience: The History of a Puritan Idea* (Phillipsburg, N.J.: Presbyterian and Reformed Publishing Co., 1972), 163.

34. Eckenrode, *Separation of Church and State in Virginia*, 45. See also Brant, *James Madison: The Virginia Revolutionist,* 249 ("The clause on religion [Article XVI] asserted, for the first time in any body of fundamental law, a natural right which had not previously been recognized as such by political bodies in the Christian world.").

35. There is a tradition that attributes authorship of Article XVI to Patrick Henry. This minority view is based largely on Edmund Randolph's imperfect recollection of the Convention recorded long after it adjourned. See "Edmund Randolph's Essay on the

Revolutionary History of Virginia," *Virginia Magazine of History and Biography* XLIV (1936): 47; Moncure Daniel Conway, *Omitted Chapters of History Disclosed in the Life and Papers of Edmund Randolph* (New York: G.P. Putnam's Sons, 1888), 30; William Wirt Henry, *Patrick Henry: Life, Correspondence and Speeches*, 3 vols. (New York: Charles Scribner's Sons, 1891), 1:430-435; Kate Mason Rowland, *The Life of George Mason, 1725-1792,* 2 vols. (New York, 1892), 1:235-239, 241. Randolph's faulty memory may have been based on the fact that Madison, who by his own admission was uncertain and inexperienced in legislative affairs and diffident about public speaking, apparently prevailed upon Patrick Henry to present his amendment to the Convention.

36. "Petition of Sundry Inhabitants of Prince Edward County," 11 October 1776, reprinted in *Virginia Magazine of History and Biography* 18 (1910): 41; *Journal of the House of Delegates of Virginia. Anno Domini, 1776,* 11 October 1776 (Richmond, Va.: Samuel Shepherd, 1828), 7 [hereinafter *JHD*].

37. "The Petition of the Dissenters from the Ecclesiastical establishment in the Commonwealth of Virginia," reprinted in *Virginia Magazine of History and Biography* 18 (1910): 265-266; *JHD*, 16 October 1776, 15.

38. "Dissenters Petition, Albemarle, Amherst and Buckingham," 9 November 1776, reprinted in *Virginia Magazine of History and Biography* 18 (1910): 257; *JHD*, 9 November 1776, 48; *Papers of Jefferson*, 1:587; *Papers of Mason*, 1:318.

39. Jefferson, *Autobiography,* in *Life and Selected Writings of Jefferson*, 41.

40. Jefferson, *Autobiography*, in *Life and Selected Writings of Jefferson*, 41. See also Jefferson, *Notes on Virginia*, in *ibid.*, 273 ("two-thirds of the people had become dissenters at the commencement of the present revolution"). But see Brant, *James Madison: The Virginia Revolutionist*, 295 (challenging Jefferson's statement).

41. *JHD*, 9 November 1776, 48.

42. *JHD*, 19 November 1776, 62-63.

43. Buckley, *Church and State in Revolutionary Virginia,* 33.

44. *JHD*, 19 November 1776, 63.

45. *Papers of Mason,* 1:319.

46. Buckley, *Church and State in Revolutionary Virginia*, 34; see also *JHD,* 30 November 1776, 76; *Papers of Jefferson,* 1:527.

47. Buckley, *Church and State in Revolutionary Virginia*, 34.

48. *Papers of Jefferson*, 1:528; *Papers of Mason,* 1:319.

49. *JHD*, 5 December 1776, 83. See *Papers of Jefferson*, 1:528, 533-534; *Papers of Mason*, 1:319.

50. *Papers of Jefferson*, 1:534.

51. "Amendment to the Bill Exempting Dissenters from Contributing to the Established Church," 5 December 1776, *Papers of Mason*, 1:318. The bracketed material does not appear in Hening, *Statutes at Large,* IX:164.

52. *JHD*, 9 December 1776, 89-90; Hening, *Statutes at Large*, IX:164-167.

53. *Papers of Mason*, 1:319.

54. Buckley, *Church and State in Revolutionary Virginia*, 36.

55. *Papers of Jefferson*, 1:528.

56. Editorial Note, *Papers of Jefferson,* 1:525.

57. Hening, *Statutes at Large*, IX:165.

58. Rhys Isaac, *The Transformation of Virginia, 1740-1790* (Chapel Hill: Institute of Early American History and Culture; University of North Carolina Press, 1982), 281; Eckenrode, *Separation of Church and State in Virginia,* 53.

59. Curry, *The First Freedoms,* 136.

60. *JHD*, 17 May 1779, 11. A bill "for the dissolution of vestries" was introduced in late May. JHD, 28 May 1779, 26.

61. *JHD*, 4 June 1779, 34.

62. *JHD*, 4 June 1779, 34.

63. *JHD*, 12 June 1779, 44. See "Bill for Establishing Religious Freedom" (Bill 82) and "Bill for Saving the Property of the Church Heretofore by Law Established" (Bill 83), in *Report of the Committee of Revisors Appointed by the General Assembly of Virginia in MDCCLXXVI* (Richmond, Va.: Dixon & Holt, 1784), 58-59 [hereinafter *Report of the Revisors*].

64. *JHD*, 14 June 1779, 46.

65. *JHD*, 1 June 1779, 29.

66. *JHD*, 15 June 1779, 48.

67. *JHD*, 17 June 1779, 53; Hening, *Statutes at Large,* X:111.

68. *JHD*, 19 June 1779, 59.

69. Eckenrode, *Separation of Church and State in Virginia,* 56.

70. Buckley, *Church and State in Revolutionary Virginia,* 56.

71. *JHD*, 25 October 1779, 24. The bill is reprinted in Buckley, *Church and State in Revolutionary Virginia*, Appendix I, 185-188.

72. A bill "concerning religion," in Buckley, *Church and State in Revolutionary Virginia,* 185-188. See generally *ibid.*, 56-60; Miller, *The First Liberty*, 17-22.

73. A bill "concerning religion," in Buckley, *Church and State in Revolutionary Virginia,* 185.

74. Following its second reading, the general assessment bill was discussed on numerous occasions. Finally, on 15 November, the House voted to put off further discussion of the measure until the following March. *JHD*, 15 November 1779, 56.

75. *JHD*, 18 November 1779, 61.

76. "A Bill Repealing the Act to Support Ministers of the Established Church," in *Papers of Mason*, 2:553.

77. *JHD*, 13 December 1779, 87; Hening, *Statutes at Large*, X:197-198.

78. Buckley, *Church and State in Revolutionary Virginia*, 61.

79. *JHD*, 26 November 1779, 72; *Papers of Mason,* 2:590-592.

80. See, for example, the claim of Baptist minister John Leland as reported in Buckley, *Church and State in Revolutionary Virginia,* 66.

81. *JHD*, 11 December 1779, 85-86.

82. Merrill D. Peterson, *Thomas Jefferson and the New Nation: A Biography* (New York: Oxford University Press, 1970), 100.

83. Jefferson, *Autobiography*, in *Life and Selected Writings of Jefferson*, 44.

84. *JHD*, 12 October 1776, 10. The House passed the bill on 17 October and sent it to the Senate for their concurrence. *JHD,* 17 October 1776, 16.

85. *JHD*, 26 October 1776, 28.

86. Hening, *Statutes at Large,* IX:175-177; *Papers of Jefferson,* 1:562-563.

87. *JHD*, 5 November 1776, 41. See *Papers of Jefferson,* 1:562-564.

88. See Editorial Note, *Papers of Jefferson*, 2:313 ("There can be no doubt that Jefferson was nominally and actually the leading figure in the revisal").

89. Jefferson, *Autobiography*, in *Life and Selected Writings of Jefferson*, 45.

90. Editorial Note, *Papers of Jefferson*, 2:316, 320.

91. See Noble E. Cunningham, Jr., *In Pursuit of Reason: The Life of Thomas Jefferson* (Baton Rouge: Louisiana State University Press, 1987), 54; Editorial Note, *Papers of Jefferson*, 2:306 (in the years 1776 to 1779, Jefferson was "a veritable legislative drafting bureau").

92. Jefferson, *Autobiography*, in *Life and Selected Writings of Jefferson*, 44.

93. Jefferson, *Autobiography*, in *Life and Selected Writings of Jefferson*, 44.

94. See Henry S. Randall, *The Life of Thomas Jefferson*, 3 vols. (New York: Derby and Jackson, 1857), 1:208.

95. Jefferson, *Autobiography*, in *Life and Selected Writings of Jefferson*, 44-45. Although the Revisors resolved to make only alterations to existing laws, Julian P. Boyd noted that the "Committee of Revisors so drastically altered many existing laws as to amount to the proposal of wholly new legislation (for example, Bill 86 concerning marriages)." Editorial Note, *Papers of Jefferson*, 2:315.

96. Jefferson, *Autobiography*, in *Life and Selected Writings of Jefferson*, 51.

97. Jefferson was given the task of reforming the whole field of the common law and statutes of England down to the foundation of the Virginia colony in 1607. The British statutes from 1607 to the end of the colonial era were assigned to Wythe, and the laws of the Commonwealth during the same period were assigned to Pendleton.

98. Dumas Malone, *Jefferson the Virginian* (Boston: Little, Brown and Co., 1948), 262. See also Cunningham, *In Pursuit of Reason*, 54-55 (noting that Jefferson's papers indicate that legislative matters relating to religion concerned Jefferson greatly during this period).

99. Jefferson, *Autobiography*, in *Life and Selected Writings of Jefferson*, 46.

100. *JHD*, 18 June 1779, 56-57.

101. The revised code was eventually printed in 1784 by order of the House of Delegates. See *Report of the Revisors*. Julian P. Boyd's editorial notes in *Papers of Jefferson* are the most thorough documentary and legislative examination of the revised code conducted to date. *Papers of Jefferson*, 2:305-665.

102. For a general description of Jefferson and Madison's transatlantic coordination of efforts to enact portions of the revisal, see Adrienne Koch, *Jefferson and Madison: The Great Collaboration* (New York: Oxford University Press, 1950), 26-31.

103. *JHD*, 31 October 1785, 12-15.

104. See Edward Dumbauld, *Thomas Jefferson and the Law* (Norman: University of Oklahoma Press, 1978), 137; Editorial Note, *Papers of Madison*, 8:389-402; Editorial Note, *Papers of Jefferson*, 2:322.

105. Miller, *The First Liberty*, 18.

106. *JHD*, 11 November 1784, 19.

107. For an account of the 1779 legislative debate, see text accompanying notes 60-74 above.

108. See Hunt, "James Madison and Religious Liberty," 168; Miller, *The First Liberty*, 27; Rives, *History of the Life and Times of Madison*, 1:602; Marvin K. Singleton, "Colonial Virginia as First Amendment Matrix: Henry, Madison, and Assessment Establishment," *Journal of Church and State* 8 (1966): 351-352.

109. Anson Phelps Stokes, *Church and State in the United States*, 3 vols. (New York: Harper and Brothers, 1950), 1:390.

110. *JHD*, 11 November 1784, 19. See Eckenrode, *Separation of Church and State in Virginia,* 86; Buckley, *Church and State in Revolutionary Virginia*, 91-92.

111. See Eckenrode, *Separation of Church and State in Virginia*, 88.

112. Letter from Thomas Jefferson to James Madison, 8 December 1784, *Papers of Madison,* 8:178.

113. *JHD,* 17 November 1784, 26-27. See Buckley, *Church and State in Revolutionary Virginia*, 100-102; Irving Brant, *James Madison: The Nationalist, 1780-1787* (Indianapolis, Ind.: The Bobbs-Merrill Co., 1948), 345-346; Singleton, "Colonial Virginia as First Amendment Matrix," 355.

114. Letter from the Reverend Samuel Shield to the Reverend David Griffith, 20 December 1784, David Griffith Papers, Virginia Historical Society, Richmond, Virginia.

115. See Eckenrode, *Separation of Church and State in Virginia,* 95-98.

116. See letter from James Madison to James Madison, Sr., 27 November 1784, *Papers of Madison,* 8:155; letter from James Madison to James Monroe, 4 December 1784, in *ibid.*, 8:175 ("The bill for the Religious Asst. was reported yesterday and will be taken up in a Come. of the Whole next week. Its friends are much disheartened at the loss of Mr. Henry. Its fate is I think very uncertain.").

117. *JHD,* 2 December 1784, 51.

118. The term "teacher" in this context referred to the minister of a church. See Chester James Antieau, Arthur T. Downey, and Edward C. Roberts, *Freedom from Federal Establishment: Formation and Early History of the First Amendment Religion Clauses* (Milwaukee: Bruce, 1964), 33.

119. Buckley, *Church and State in Revolutionary Virginia*, 108.

120. *JHD,* 3 December 1784, 52. See Eckenrode, *Separation of Church and State in Virginia,* 99-100.

121. Letter from James Madison to Thomas Jefferson, 9 January 1785, *Papers of Madison,* 8:229.

122. *JHD,* 22-23 December 1784, 80-81. See generally Eckenrode, *Separation of Church and State in Virginia,* 102; Buckley, *Church and State in Revolutionary Virginia*, 108; Daniel L. Dreisbach, "Thomas Jefferson and Bills Number 82-86 of the Revision of the Laws of Virginia, 1776-1786: New Light on the Jeffersonian Model of Church-State Relations," *North Carolina Law Review* 69 (1990): 167 n. 45.

123. See Eckenrode, *Separation of Church and State in Virginia*, 102; Buckley, *Church and State in Revolutionary Virginia,* 108.

124. *JHD*, 24 December 1784, 82.

125. *JHD*, 24 December 1784, 82.

126. Brant, *James Madison: The Nationalist,* 348; Eva T. H. Brann, "Madison's 'Memorial and Remonstrance': A Model of American Eloquence," in *Rhetoric and American Statesmanship,* ed. Glen E. Thurow and Jeffrey D. Wallin (Durham, N.C.: Carolina Academic Press, 1984), 12.

127. Letter from George Nicholas to James Madison, 22 April 1785, *Papers of Madison,* 8:264.

128. In his "Detached Memoranda," written late in his life, Madison recalled that it was "[a]t the instance of Col: George Nicholas, Col: George Mason & others, the memorial & remonstrance agst it [the assessment bill] was drawn up . . . and printed Copies

of it circulated thro' the State, to be signed by the people at large." Elizabeth Fleet, ed., "Madison's 'Detached Memoranda,'" *William and Mary Quarterly*, 3d ser., 3 (1946): 555.

129. Letter from George Mason to George Washington, 2 October 1785, *Papers of Mason,* 2:830-831. See also letter from George Mason to Robert Carter, 5 October 1785, *Papers of Mason,* 2:832-833.

130. Letter from George Washington to George Mason, 3 October 1785, *Papers of Mason*, 2:832.

131. Letter from James Madison to George Mason, 14 July 1826, Virginia Historical Society, Richmond, Virginia. See also letter from James Madison to General Lafayette, 24 November 1826, in *James Madison on Religious Liberty*, ed. Robert S. Alley (Buffalo, N.Y.: Prometheus Books, 1985), 86; Fleet, ed., "Madison's 'Detached Memoranda,'" 556 (the number of signatures added to the "Remonstrance" "displayed such an overwhelming opposition of the people that the proposed plan of a genl assessmt was crushed under it"); letter from James Madison to Thomas Jefferson, 22 January 1786, *Papers of Madison*, 8:473-474; Rives, *History of the Life and Times of Madison,* 1:632 ("When the Assembly met in October, the table of the House of Delegates almost sunk under the weight of the accumulated copies of the memorial sent forward from the different counties, each with its long and dense column of subscribers. The fate of the assessment was sealed. The manifestation of the public judgment was too unequivocal and overwhelming to leave the faintest hope to the friends of the measure. It was abandoned without a struggle."); Hunt, "James Madison and Religious Liberty," 169 ("There are few instances recorded where the tide of public opinion has been so completely turned by a single document as it was in this instance by Madison's remonstrance.").

132. Rowland, *Life of Mason*, 2:87; *Papers of Mason*, 2:835; *Papers of Madison*, 8:296.

133. Isaac, *The Transformation of Virginia,* 292.

134. "This petition is presented in the form of a *remonstrance,* that is, a protest, suggestively, of the 'faithful,' but it is not a mere protest, as are most present-day petitions. It is also a *memorial*, a declaration of reasons—every paragraph begins with a 'because'—in the tradition of the Declaration of Independence." Brann, "Madison's 'Memorial and Remonstrance': A Model of American Eloquence," 16.

135. Madison, "Memorial and Remonstrance," *Papers of Madison,* 8:298-304.

136. See note 125 above.

137. Eckenrode, *Separation of Church and State in Virginia*, 113.

138. The "Memorial and Remonstrance" is at once the most eloquent and succinct summation of Madison's views on church-state relations. Madison's biographer, Irving Brant, wrote: "This remonstrance against religious assessments continues to stand, not merely through the years but through the centuries, as the most powerful defense of religious liberty ever written in America." Brant, *James Madison: The Nationalist,* 352.

139. For a canvassing of the petitions filed in this legislative contest, see Rhys Isaac, "'The Rage of Malice of the Old Serpent Devil': The Dissenters and the Making and Remaking of the Virginia Statute for Religious Freedom," in *The Virginia Statute for Religious Freedom: Its Evolution and Consequences in American History,* ed. Merrill D. Peterson and Robert C. Vaughan (New York: Cambridge University Press, 1988), 146-156.

140. On 31 October 1785, Madison reintroduced in the Virginia House of Delegates Bill 82 from the revised code—"A Bill for Establishing Religious Freedom." *JHD*, 31

October 1785, 12-15. The measure was specifically brought to the attention of the House on 14 December. *Ibid.*, 92-93. The committee of the whole debated the bill the following day. *Ibid.*, 94. On 16 December, it was moved that Jefferson's trenchant preamble be struck entirely and replaced by Article XVI of the Virginia Declaration of Rights. This motion was defeated by a vote of 38 to 66, and the bill was ordered to be engrossed and read the third, and final, time. *Ibid.*, 95. The engrossed bill was read on 17 December and passed by a convincing majority of 74 to 20. *Ibid.*, 96. Before passage, however, Bill 82 survived a motion to postpone further consideration of the bill until the next legislative session, which was the same tactic successfully used to defeat Henry's assessment proposal a year earlier. The bill was read in the Senate for the first time on Saturday, 17 December 1785. *Journal of the Senate of the Commonwealth of Virginia* (Richmond: Thomas W. White, 1827), 17 December 1785, 54. The Senate read the bill a second time on 19 December and sent it to a committee of the whole for further consideration. *Journal of the Senate*, 19 December 1785, 56. When the Senate took up the bill again on Friday, 23 December, it voted narrowly to replace the preamble with Article XVI of the Virginia Declaration of Rights. *Journal of the Senate,* 23 December 1785, 61. The bill was read for the third time, passed, and returned to the House of Delegates. The House, once again, rejected the amendment altering Jefferson's preamble. *JHD*, 29 December 1785, 117; *Journal of the Senate*, 30 December 1785, 67. Unable to reconcile differences between the House and Senate versions of the bill, a conference committee was formed early in the new year. *Journal of the Senate*, 9 January 1786, 81. On 16 January 1786, the House considered and, perhaps reluctantly, accepted relatively minor Senate amendments. *JHD*, 16 January 1786, 143-144; *Journal of the Senate*, 16 January 1786, 92. The speaker signed the Act on 19 January 1786. *JHD*, 19 January 1786, 148.

141. Hening, *Statutes at Large,* XII:86; *Virginia Code, Annotated* (repl. vol. 1986), § 57-1. Jefferson's bill is reprinted in *Papers of Jefferson,* 2:545-547.

142. James H. Smylie, "Jefferson's Statute for Religious Freedom: The Hanover Presbytery Memorials, 1776-1786," *American Presbyterians Journal of Presbyterian History* 63 (1985): 355 (quoting Bailyn).

143. See *The Works of Thomas Jefferson,* ed. Paul Leicester Ford, Federal Edition, 12 vols. (New York: G. P. Putnam's Sons, 1905), 12:483. Jefferson also wished to be remembered as the author of the Declaration of American Independence and the father of the University of Virginia.

144. For a general survey of the legacy of Jefferson's religious freedom bill in Virginia and the nation, see Cushing Strout, "Jeffersonian Religious Liberty and American Pluralism," in *Virginia Statute for Religious Freedom,* 201-235.

145. Letter from James Madison to Thomas Jefferson, 22 January 1786, *Papers of Madison,* 8:474.

146. C. Randolph Benson noted that Jefferson's church-state views "in the course of time became the official American position." Benson, *Thomas Jefferson as Social Scientist* (Rutherford, N.J.: Fairleigh Dickinson University Press, 1971), 190-191.

147. Nathan Schachner, *Thomas Jefferson: A Biography* (New York: Thomas Yoseloff, 1957), 160.

148. Mark DeWolfe Howe, *The Garden and the Wilderness: Religion and Government in American Constitutional History* (Chicago: University of Chicago Press, 1965), 44.

149. *Report of the Revisors*, 58-60. See Daniel L. Dreisbach, "A New Perspective on Jefferson's Views on Church-State Relations: The Virginia Statute for Establishing Religious Freedom in Its Legislative Context," *American Journal of Legal History* 35

(1991): 172-204; Dreisbach, "Thomas Jefferson and Bills Number 82-86 of the Revision of the Laws of Virginia, 1776-1786," 159-211.

150. See Robert M. Healey, *Jefferson on Religion in Public Education* (New Haven, Conn.: Yale University Press, 1962), 140; Comment, "Jefferson and the Church-State Wall: A Historical Examination of the Man and the Metaphor," *Brigham Young University Law Review* 1978 (1978): 666-667.

151. Most historians of the era have characterized Jefferson's "Bill for Establishing Religious Freedom" as incompatible with, if not directly opposed to, the various general assessment bills considered by the Virginia legislature. See, for example, Leonard W. Levy, *Constitutional Opinions: Aspects of the Bill of Rights* (New York: Oxford University Press, 1986), 160 ("Confronted by two diametrically opposed bills [Jefferson's bill for complete separation between religion and government and a 1779 general assessment bill], the Virginia legislature was deadlocked, and neither bill could muster a majority"). This characterization, however, may be an inaccurate depiction of the way many Virginians viewed these proposals at the time. Some Virginians, including religious dissenters, saw no contradiction between supporting Jefferson's bill and requesting the Virginia legislature to enact a general assessment. See *Papers of Jefferson,* 2:548 (presenting evidence that some dissenters supported both a general assessment and Jefferson's bill); Buckley, *Church and State in Revolutionary Virginia,* 74 (noting a petition calling for both religious toleration and a general assessment); Singleton, "Colonial Virginia as First Amendment Matrix," 361 ("[I]t should be noted that some dissenters had, during the late 1770s, petitioned simultaneously for Jefferson's bill and for a common assessment"). Therefore, it may be erroneous to characterize Jefferson's bill and the various general assessment bills as opposing pieces of legislation. Significantly, the 1779 general assessment plan was more extreme than the 1784 version in the sense that the 1779 scheme favored, if not established, Christianity and outlined specific requirements of doctrine and worship. See Buckley, *Church and State in Revolutionary Virginia*, 108; Miller, *The First Liberty*, 26.

152. See Daniel L. Dreisbach, "*Everson* and the Command of History: The Supreme Court, Lessons of History, and Church-State Debate in America," in *Everson Revisited: Religion, Education, and Law at the Crossroads,* ed. Jo Renée Formicola and Hubert Morken (Lanham, Md.: Rowman & Littlefield, 1997), 23-57.

153. Curry, *The First Freedoms,* 134.

154. Levy, *The Establishment Clause*, 60.

Chapter 8

Mr. Jefferson's "Nonabsolute" Wall of Separation Between Church and State

Robert L. Cord

When one searches through Thomas Jefferson's many careers as politician and lawmaker in Virginia, as U.S. minister to France, as president of the United States, as "father" of the University of Virginia, *there is no evidence that Jefferson ever sought an absolute barrier between religion and government*. Instead, the irrefutable historical evidence suggests the contrary. The purpose of this chapter is to focus on Jefferson's concept of church-state separation and to establish—with primary historical sources—that Jefferson did not subscribe to any concept of an absolute wall of separation between church and state. My thesis is that although Jefferson fervently advocated a separation between church and state, for him that separation required only that government not pursue sectarian goals, not establish a religion, and not prefer one religion or religious point of view over all others. It follows that if Jefferson, as president, chose religious means to achieve a constitutional secular goal, then he did not necessarily think this violated the First Amendment as long as the governmental end was indeed secular.

The "absolutist" interpretation of the First Amendment establishment of religion clause has, for the most part, prevailed in U.S. Supreme Court church-state jurisprudence. It should come as no surprise that respected constitutional jurists and scholars have argued, and continue to argue, that the separation between church and state was historically intended to be absolute. Such is the case in a discussion of "Establishment of Religion" in *Congressional Quarterly's Guide to the U.S. Supreme Court*. According to the *Guide*, which received excellent reviews by many distinguished lawyers and constitutional scholars, Jefferson and Madison construed the establishment clause absolutely.[1] "Thomas Jefferson and James Madison," the reader is informed, "thought that the prohibition of establishment meant that a presidential proclamation of Thanksgiving Day was just as improper as a tax exemption for churches."[2] Assuming no intentional deception on the part of the author, I must conclude that whoever wrote this paragraph was ignorant of significant primary historical documents. The indisputable fact is that as president Madison issued at least four Thanksgiving Day proclamations.[3] Furthermore, in 1802, President Jefferson signed into federal law a measure providing, among other things, tax exemption for churches in Alexandria County.[4]

The publication of this misinformation in a source considered authoritative raises at least two very significant questions. First, given President Madison's Thanksgiving Day proclamations and the 1802 "Church Tax Immunity" law signed by President Jefferson, how could any knowledgeable student of the Constitution represent either of these two men as believing the First Amendment created an absolute wall between church and state? Second, how could these errors innocently become a part of the constitutional interpretation of the establishment clause, as put forth in a highly praised scholarly reference work on the Supreme Court?[5] Unfortunately, I believe the church-state views and actions of the "Founding Fathers," especially those of Jefferson and Madison, were grossly exaggerated and consequently misrepresented when the establishment clause was first interpreted and applied by the Supreme Court in 1947.

The *Everson* Precedent

Although the First Amendment was added to the Constitution in 1791, more than a century and a half passed before the U.S. Supreme Court addressed the meaning of the Amendment's prohibition: "Congress shall make no law respecting an establishment of religion." In 1947 the Court was asked to rule that a New Jersey law violated the constitutional principle of church-state separation because it authorized the use of government funds to reimburse the costs incurred by parents for transporting their children on public buses to private religious schools. In *Everson v. Board of Education of Ewing Township, New Jersey*, Justice Hugo L. Black wrote the opinion of a divided Supreme Court (5-4 decision). Black was joined in the majority by Justices Stanley Reed, William O. Douglas, Frank Murphy, and Chief Justice Frederick M. Vinson. The majority opinion drew heavily on Madison's successful fight for religious liberty in the Virginia Assembly in the mid-1780s, culminating in the enactment in 1786 of Jefferson's "Bill for Establishing Religious Freedom." Justice Black, for the Court, wrote this defining paragraph:

> The "establishment of religion" clause of the First Amendment means at least this: Neither a state nor the Federal Government can set up a church. Neither can pass laws which aid one religion, aid all religions, or prefer one religion over another. Neither can force nor influence a person to go to or to remain away from church against his will or force him to profess a belief or disbelief in any religion. No person can be punished for entertaining or professing religious beliefs or disbeliefs, for church attendance or non-attendance. No tax in any amount, large or small, can be levied to support any religious activities or institutions, whatever they may be called, or whatever form they may adopt to teach or practice religion. Neither a state nor the Federal Government can, openly or secretly, participate in the affairs of any religious organizations or groups and *vice versa*. In the words of Jefferson, the clause against establishment of religion by law was intended to erect "a wall of separation between church and State."[6]

In the last paragraph of the opinion, Justice Black reaffirmed the "absolute separationist" argument running throughout the entire opinion, and then—without any justifying arguments—the Court ruled that reimbursements from the public treasury for the transportation of parochial school students did *not* violate the First Amendment. Black's opinion blithely concluded: "The First Amendment has erected a wall between church and state. That wall must be kept high and impregnable. We could not approve the slightest breach. New Jersey has not breached it here."[7]

The Court's oxymoronic final holding splintered the bench. Not surprisingly, four justices thought New Jersey had indeed breached the constitutional wall of separation and dissented from what seemed to them to be an inexplicable decision by the majority. Writing the most comprehensive dissenting opinion in *Everson,* Justice Wiley Rutledge—joined by Justices Felix Frankfurter, Robert Jackson, and Harold Burton—asserted that the First Amendment was intended by its authors to be a complete and absolute barrier that precluded every use of public funds to support any religious enterprise.

> The [First] Amendment's purpose was not to strike merely at the official establishment of a single sect, creed or religion, outlawing only a formal relation such as had prevailed in England and some of the colonies. Necessarily it was to uproot all such relationships. . . . It was to create a complete and permanent separation of the spheres of religious activity and civil authority by comprehensively forbidding every form of public aid or support for religion.[8]

For the dissenters, the First Amendment barrier rendered unconstitutional the contested state reimbursement to parents for the bus fares of parochial school children.

Although joining Rutledge's opinion, Justice Jackson, in a dissent of his own, took delight in chiding the majority for their inconsistency between the broad interpretation of the establishment clause prohibition and their narrow decision permitting bus fare refunds:

> the undertones of the [Court's] opinion, advocating complete and uncompromising separation of Church from State, seem utterly discordant with its conclusion yielding support to their commingling in educational matters. The case which irresistibly comes to mind as the most fitting is that of Julia who, according to Byron's reports, "whispering 'I will ne'er consent,'—consented."[9]

In assessing the significance of the *Everson* precedent for future church-state constitutional questions, the 5-4 split on the Court over the transportation reimbursement is truly inconsequential. Of great consequence for establishment clause jurisprudence, however, was the unanimous agreement of the Court that the First Amendment did indeed mandate a "high and impregnable" wall of separation between church and state. As already discussed, until the last sentence in the Court's opinion, Justice Black's rhetoric differed little from Justice Rutledge's dissent. In the many establishment clause cases since *Everson*, appeals to the historical understanding of the First Amendment and the alleged "absolute separationist" views of Madison and Jefferson have been a consistent bill of fare.

"Absolute Separation" and "Nonabsolute Separation" of Church and State

Since *Everson,* the ongoing constitutional dispute on the Supreme Court has had little to do with the legitimate ends of government. Under our amended Constitution, few constitutional scholars would contest that the goals of government must be secular. The dispute among establishment clause scholars basically concerns whether, and to what extent, government may use sectarian means and/or sectarian institutions to achieve constitutional secular goals.

As mentioned above, Justice Rutledge, an "absolute separationist," contended that those who wrote the First Amendment establishment clause intended that there be a "high," "impregnable," and "complete" wall of separation between church and state. For "absolutists," the establishment clause requires that not only must the *ends* of government be exclusively secular but also the *means* that government uses to attain these goals must be exclusively secular.

"Nonabsolutists" interpret the establishment clause much more narrowly. For them, the establishment clause does *not* constitutionally require that only secular means may be used to reach government's secular ends. Instead, "nonabsolutists" argue that the means government employs to realize legitimate constitutional responsibilities may, in some instances, be sectarian ones. This interpretation of the establishment clause can, but does not necessarily, lead to greater commingling of religion and government. For "nonabsolutists," such a commingling does not necessarily violate the First Amendment. However, should government choose to use sectarian institutions as a means to reach some of its valid constitutional goals, it must be careful not to employ consistently the same religion, religious sect, or religious tradition. "Nonabsolutists" agree with "absolutists" that if a government entity favors one particular sectarian tradition as the means to reach its legitimate ends, such favored religious status—a characteristic of European religious establishments—would be unconstitutional.[10]

The historical evidence that sustains the thesis that Jefferson was a "nonabsolute separationist" will be examined below. This evidence leads to the inescapable conclusion that while Jefferson thought the First Amendment erected "a wall of separation between church and state," he did *not* see that constitutional wall as "high and impregnable."

Jefferson as Revisor of the Laws of Virginia

After declaring independence in 1776, the Virginia General Assembly—comprised of the House of Delegates and Senate—established a "committee to revise the [colonial] laws." Six prominent Virginians, including Jefferson, were appointed to this "Committee for the Revision of the Laws," which was authorized to recommend revisions reflecting Virginia's new sovereign status.[11] Although the Committee was established in 1776 under Jefferson's chairmanship, its recommendations—known as the *Revisal of the Laws of Virginia*—were not considered as a whole by the General Assembly until almost a decade later when formally proposed for adoption in 1785. On 31 October 1785, Madison introduced in the Virginia legislature over one hundred bills from the *Revisal*. With Jefferson serving as the American Minister to France, "the sponsorship of the reform rested upon James Madison." Nevertheless, as Madison was to later indicate, Jefferson during the years after 1776 was the nominal and the actual "leading figure in the revisal."[12]

In all, the "Committee of Revisors" prepared 126 bills, many of which were written by Jefferson. The most famous recommendation in the *Revisal* was Bill 82, Jefferson's celebrated "Bill for Establishing Religious Freedom," which Madison successfully guided through the legislature; it became law in 1786. Jefferson's bill effectively disestablished Virginia's Episcopal Church, declaring that

> no man shall be compelled to frequent or support any religious worship, place, or ministry whatsoever, nor shall be enforced, restrained, molested, or burthened in his body or goods, nor shall otherwise suffer, on account of his religious opinions or belief; but that all men shall be free to profess, and by argument to maintain, their opinions in matters of religion, and that the same shall in no wise diminish, enlarge, or affect their civil capacities.[13]

Madison's role in the Virginia legislature was much more than that of a stand in for Jefferson. In 1785 Madison wrote his "Memorial and Remonstrance Against Religious Assessments"[14] in opposition to "A Bill Establishing a Provision for Teachers of the Christian Religion."[15] The latter was supported by, among others, then Governor Patrick Henry. Jefferson and Madison's successful campaign for church-state separation in Virginia led not only to the passage of the "Bill for Establishing Religious Freedom" and disestablishment of the Episcopal Church in Virginia, but also to the defeat of the "Bill for Establishing a Provision for Teachers of the Christian Religion." Thus, the Supreme Court justices in *Everson* had substantial justification for crediting Jefferson and Madison with having legally implanted the concept and degree of separation between church and state in Virginia's post-colonial laws. This development, one could argue, was reflected in the federal Constitution of 1789 and the First Amendment of 1791.[16]

While it is clear from Bill 82 of the *Revisal* that Jefferson wanted religious freedom written into fundamental law, and he was opposed to the establishment of a state church, the bill does not, in itself, support the inference that Jefferson opposed *all* government support of religious activity. Bill 82 was carefully tailored to serve its specific purpose—to insure that Virginia no longer elevated the Episcopal or any other church to a legally preferred position, nor coerced its citizens to support a particular religious faith. To support the conclusion that Jefferson favored *absolute* church-state separation in Virginia, evidence must be found elsewhere.

The *Revisal* contained other proposals involving the relationship between religion and government. Ignored by the *Everson* Court was Bill 84, "A Bill for Punishing Disturbers of Religious Worship and Sabbath Breakers," and Bill 85, "A Bill for Appointing Days of Public Fasting and Thanksgiving."[17] The most accepted view is that Jefferson authored some fifty-one bills among which were Bills 82 and 84. Additionally, he may have written Bill 85.[18]

Madison introduced in the Virginia legislature Jefferson's Bill 84 punishing "Sabbath breakers" on the same day he introduced the "Bill for Establishing Religious Freedom." Below are the most relevant sections of Jefferson's "Bill for Punishing Disturbers of Religious Worship and Sabbath Breakers":

> Be it enacted by the General Assembly, that no officer, for any civil cause, shall arrest any minister of the gospel, licensed according to the rules of his sect, and who shall have taken the oath of fidelity to the commonwealth, while such minister shall be publicly preaching or performing religious worship in any church, chapel, or meeting-house, on pain of imprisonment and amercement, at the discretion of a jury, and of making satisfaction to the party so arrested. . . .
>
> If any person on Sunday shall himself be found labouring at his own or any other trade or calling, or shall employ his apprentices, servants or slaves in labour, or other business, except it be in the ordinary houshold [sic] offices of daily necessity, or other work of necessity or charity, he shall forfeit the sum of ten shillings for every such offence, deeming every apprentice, servant, or slave so employed, and every day he shall be so employed as constituting a distinct offence.[19]

Although Bill 84 was slightly amended—the word "Sunday" in the third paragraph was changed to "Sabbath Day"—the same Virginia legislature that in 1786 enacted Jefferson's "Bill for Establishing Religious Freedom" also enacted into law, that same year, Jefferson's bill punishing "Sabbath breakers."[20]

The power of a state to issue Thanksgiving Day proclamations was addressed in Bill 85.[21] It apparently did *not* become law, but it was introduced by Madison; and one manuscript copy indicates "in [the] clerk's hand, [that it was] endorsed by TJ."[22] The failure of Bill 85 to become Virginia law does not lessen the significance that Bill 85 was endorsed and probably written by Jefferson, the *Revisal's* chief architect.

When viewed together, Bills 82, 84, and 85 of the *Revisal* and Madison's "Memorial and Remonstrance" give a clear picture of what Jefferson and Madison believed was the appropriate relationship between church and state in Virginia in 1785-1786. First, they opposed a state church. Second, they opposed financing with tax dollars the teachers of one religious tradition. Third, they subscribed to the use of state authority to punish "Sabbath breakers." Fourth, they recognized the state's authority to declare days of public fasting and thanksgiving.

Whether or not the *Everson* Court and/or "absolutist" scholars were aware of the entire *Revisal* in 1947 is not clear. There is no question, however, that the *Revisal* contained additional proposals—authored and/or authorized by Jefferson—that addressed the relationship between religion and state government and that are contrary to the notion that Jefferson supported an *absolute* separation between church and state in Virginia.

Jefferson as President

Jefferson and Thanksgiving Day Proclamations

Cited as proof that Jefferson was an "absolute separationist" is the fact that as president he opposed the issuance of "Presidential proclamations of thanksgiving to God" because he thought they violated the establishment clause.[23] While presidents Washington[24] and Adams[25] had issued proclamations of national prayer, Jefferson broke with this tradition, stating his reasons in an 1808 letter to the Reverend Samuel Miller, a Presbyterian clergyman.[26]

For Jefferson, national Thanksgiving Day proclamations violated the U.S. Constitution in two regards: first, they offended the establishment clause as being religious ends in themselves, without any constitutional secular purpose; and second, Jefferson believed national proclamations about religion violated federalism or the constitutional distribution of powers between the states and the federal government. It should be noted that Jefferson did *not* say that the federal Constitution in all instances prohibited the issuance of Thanksgiving and fast day proclamations. Under the constitutional division of power, Jefferson acknowledged that the power to issue such proclamations rested with the respective states "as far as it can be in any human authority."[27] In colonial and state government settings Jefferson demonstrated a willingness to issue religious proclamations. For example, as a member of the House of Burgesses, on 24 May 1774, he participated in drafting a resolution appointing a "Day of Fasting, Humiliation, and Prayer."[28] In 1779, when Jefferson was governor of Virginia, he issued a proclamation decreeing a day "of publick and solemn thanksgiving and prayer to Almighty God."[29] This accords with his endorsement of the *Revisal's* Bill 85, which assumed that the states had the authority to issue such proclamations.

Significantly, when Madison succeeded Jefferson as president, he broke with Jefferson's policy, reinstated the practice, and issued at least four Thanksgiving Day proclamations during his presidency.[30]

Jefferson's "Wall of Separation between Church and State"

Almost all separationists, including many on the current Supreme Court, embrace the Jeffersonian phrase, "wall of separation between church and state." This metaphor, they argue, describes the constitutional position mandated by the First Amendment.[31] Ignoring other interpretations of church-state separation, the "absolute separationists" claim that Jefferson's "wall" metaphor has but one meaning, their own. They recognize no deviation.

There has been some dispute concerning whether or not the term "wall of separation" should be used to determine the limitations that the establishment clause imposes upon government because the phrase does not appear either in the original Constitution or any of its subsequent amendments. I have no problem with using Jefferson's phrase ("a wall of separation between church and state") as shorthand for the constitutional barrier that the Founding Fathers intended between government and religion so long as Jefferson's term is understood in the context in which he used it. Unfortunately, this Jeffersonian phrase has been misused by the U.S. Supreme Court from the outset, starting with Justice Black's interpretation of the establishment clause in *Everson v. Board of Education*. The use of Jefferson's metaphor by the *Everson* dissenters is no better.

Jefferson used the "wall of separation" phrase as president in a letter sent to the Danbury (Connecticut) Baptist Association on 1 January 1802.

> Believing with you that religion is a matter which lies solely between Man & his God, that he owes account to none other for his faith or his worship, that the legitimate powers of government reach actions only, & not opinions, I contemplate with sovereign reverence that act of the whole American people which declared that *their* legislature should "make no law respecting an establishment of religion, or prohibiting the free exercise thereof," thus building a wall of separation between Church & State. [A]dhering to this expression of the supreme will of the nation in behalf of the rights of conscience, I shall see with sincere satisfaction the progress of those sentiments which tend to restore to man all his natural rights, convinced he has no natural right in opposition to his social duties.[32]

Certainly, when Jefferson referred to "that act of the whole American People" declaring that "their legislature should 'make no law respecting an establishment of religion, or prohibiting the free exercise thereof,' thus building a wall of separation between Church & State,"[33] he simply affirmed the accepted constitutional interpretation of his day—that the First Amendment restricted only congressional authority. In 1802, it was generally accepted that the power to regulate matters pertaining to religion rested with the states. Jefferson was clearly aware that some states in 1802 had laws that financially and/or nominally preferred some religious views over others.[34] Therefore, he could only have meant that the First Amendment "wall of separation" was erected between church and state in regard to possible *federal* action, such as laws establishing a national church or prohibiting religious worship.

Perhaps most important about the Danbury Baptist letter is that Jefferson did *not* indicate that the First Amendment "wall of separation" was to be either "high" or "impregnable." To attribute these descriptive words—"high," "impregnable," and "complete"—to Jefferson puts absolutist words into Jefferson's mouth, as did all the *Everson* opinions, without justification cited or given. These adjectives—which Jefferson did not use in his Danbury Baptist letter—not only turn Jefferson into an "absolute separationist," they show him as contradicting several policy decisions and actions taken by him during his presidency.

Jefferson and the Kaskaskia Indians

In 1803 President Jefferson (the alleged "absolute separationist" who, according to the *Everson* Court, intended to keep religion and government in completely different spheres) asked the Senate to consent to a treaty with the Kaskaskia Indians negotiated during his presidency.[35] In the treaty Jefferson clearly pursued the secular governmental goals of preserving a friendship with these Indians, who helped establish peace near border settlements, and of having the Kaskaskia Indians "relinquish" their lands to the United States. In pursuit of these ends, however, he clearly employed sectarian means.

In return for their land and friendship, the third article of the treaty pledged the United States to support a Catholic priest in his priestly duties and to provide money to build a Roman Catholic church. Article Three provided:

> *And whereas,* The greater part of the said tribe have been baptised and received into the Catholic church to which they are much attached, the United States will give annually for seven years one hundred dollars towards the support of a priest of that religion, who will engage to perform for the said tribe the duties of his office and also to instruct as many of their children as possible in the rudiments of literature. And the United States will further give the sum of three hundred dollars to assist the said tribe in the erection of a church. The stipulations made in this and the preceding article, together with the sum of five hundred and eighty dollars, which is now paid or assured to be paid for the said tribe for the purpose of procuring some necessary articles, and to relieve them from debts which they have heretofore contracted, is considered as a full and ample compensation for the relinquishment made to the United States in the first article.[36]

Jefferson signed the ratified treaty on 23 December 1803.

Unlike Thanksgiving Day proclamations, Jefferson apparently did not think the treaty violated the establishment clause because it accomplished secular goals. If Jefferson had had the slightest doubt about the constitutionality of the "church-building" or "priest-supporting" provisions of the Kaskaskia Treaty, he could have used other, less blatant religious means. For example, an unspecified lump sum of money could have been put into the Kaskaskia Treaty along with another provision for an annual unspecified stipend with which the Indians could have built their church and paid their priest. Such unspecified sums and annual stipends were not uncommon and were provided for in at least two other Indian treaties made during Jefferson's administration, one with the Wyandots and other tribes, proclaimed 24 April 1806,[37] and another with the Cherokee nation, proclaimed 23 May 1807.[38] That these alternatives were available but not chosen illustrates again that Jefferson did not believe the establishment clause was necessarily violated when sectarian means were used to reach secular goals. Further supporting this interpretation was Jefferson's awareness that under Article VI of the federal Constitution a treaty made "under the authority of the United States" in violation of the Constitution would be a nullity.[39] In my judgment, Jefferson would not have submitted to the Senate for their advice and consent a treaty he thought violated the First Amendment principles concerning church and state.

The conclusion seems inescapable. If Jefferson believed in an absolute separation between church and state, then he surely would not have used his discretionary constitutional executive prerogatives to negotiate, submit, and sign a treaty involving the expenditure of federal monies for purposes that do not reflect "the principle of complete independence of religion and government."[40] None of this primary documentation appears or is alluded to in the *Everson* opinions.

Jefferson, the United Brethren, and "Propagating the Gospel"

On 1 June 1796, five years after ratification of the establishment clause, President George Washington signed into federal law "An Act regulating the grants of land appropriated for Military services, and for the Society of the United Brethren for propagating the Gospel among the Heathen."[41] The Society of the United Brethren had been incorporated to insure that lands previously granted by the Continental Congress to the "Moravian Brethren at Bethlehem in Pennsylvania" were used for their intended purpose—to support those Indian tribes already converted to Christianity.[42] Additionally, the Society could and did use some of the resources acquired from these lands, and land leases to non-Indian tenant farmers, to proselytize "among the neighboring heathen."[43] Rather than providing for the sale of these lands to the Society, as undoubtedly would be required under a regime of absolute church-state separation, Section Two of this statute established that "the patents for all lands located under the authority of this act, shall be *granted . . . without requiring any fee therefor*."[44] Under the terms of the law, the U.S. government placed approximately 12,000 acres of federal land into a controlling trust administered solely by the Society of the United Brethren, essentially to enlist their services in spreading the Christian faith to the "heathen" Indians located in the western part of the country. Although the original Act provided for termination of the land grant provision on 1 January 1800,[45] the deadline for acquiring land for the services in the original law was subsequently extended four times: once by the Fifth Congress;[46] twice by the Seventh Congress;[47] and once by the Eighth Congress.[48] The land grants available to the "United Brethren for propagating the gospel among the heathen" were finally allowed to expire on 1 April 1805. Jefferson, president during the terms of the Seventh and Eighth Congresses, signed into federal law each of the last three extensions. How can Jefferson's approval of federal land grants to a society dedicated to spreading the Christian faith be reconciled with the view that Jefferson believed the establishment clause erected a "high and impregnable" wall of separation between religion and the federal government?

Jefferson—who broke with tradition and refused to issue presidential Thanksgiving Day proclamations because he thought they violated the establishment clause—was not inclined to compromise his strong views on church-state separation. Consequently, he must *not* have viewed federal public support for religious activity and/or institutions (when used for constitutional *secular* ends) repugnant to the First Amendment's prohibition on religious establishments. Knowing Jefferson's strong subscription to church-state separation, any alternative interpretation of his action in these matters simply does not square with the historical facts.

It is important to note here that Jefferson's administration was religiously non-partisan in using sectarian means to achieve secular constitutional goals. When the Catholic church was used to achieve the secular end of having the Kaskaskia Indians cede their lands to the United States by the 1803 treaty, Jefferson used that church as the means to achieve his secular goal because the Catholic church was important to the Kaskaskia Indians. Similarly, where the "Society of

United Brethren for Propagating the gospel among the heathen" was useful in achieving a constitutional secular goal, the Society was chosen not because Washington, Adams, Jefferson, and the respective Congresses were trying to establish a favored church or religion. The "United Brethren" organized missionaries to meet the requirements of the 1796 Statute and its successors. That is why they were used in the Ohio Territory. In neither instance did Jefferson or his presidential predecessors consider these policies as putting any one religion, religious sect, or religious tradition into a legally favored status. In both instances the goal of the federal government was to realize specified secular ends, not to advance religion.

Is Jefferson's approval of federal land grants to a society dedicated to spreading the Christian faith consistent with the contention that he believed the establishment clause erected a "complete," "high and impregnable" wall of separation between religion and the federal government? The only tenable conclusion in these matters is that Jefferson, like his presidential predecessors, viewed nondiscriminatory federal support of religious activity for the attainment of secular ends not repugnant to the constitutional ban on national religious establishments.

Jefferson and Tax Exemption for Churches

As mentioned above, there seems to be no justification for the claim that President Jefferson viewed tax exemptions for real estate owned by churches—including church buildings themselves—as improper pursuant to the establishment clause. To the contrary, in 1802 President Jefferson signed an act of the Seventh Congress that in effect authorized tax exemptions for churches in Alexandria (District of Columbia).[49] If one takes the position that tax exemptions for churches is "an establishment of religion" forbidden by the First Amendment, then one bears the burden of explaining why President Jefferson—one of the foremost advocates of church-state separation among the Founding Fathers—supported such an exemption and signed it into federal law.[50]

Jefferson as "Father" of the University of Virginia

If the 5-4 split decision in *Everson v. Board of Education* clouded the significance of the justices' unanimous subscription to the absolutist "high and impregnable" wall interpretation of the establishment clause, then all confusion and doubt was dispelled the following year when the Court decided *McCollum v. Board of Education of Champaign, Illinois* (1948).[51] There an 8-1 majority supported a broad reading of the establishment clause's prohibitions with the same carefully selected and sparse history that had allegedly made credible the original intent arguments in *Everson*.[52] Applying the *Everson* Court's distorted "high and impregnable" wall doctrine in *McCollum*, the Supreme Court for the first time held a governmental action unconstitutional for violating the separation between church and state intended by the Framers of the First Amendment.[53]

The practices ruled unconstitutional in *McCollum*, unlike those in the *Everson* "bus transportation" case, required no expenditure of taxpayers' money. In

McCollum, a voluntary association called the "Champaign Council on Religious Education" asked the Board of Education to allow "public school pupils in grades four to nine inclusive" to attend weekly classes in religious instruction on public school premises.[54] Granting the request, the Champaign Board of Education instituted a "released time" program whereby students, with parental permission, could voluntarily attend religious instruction classes—30 to 40 minutes a week—as a substitute for secular education. Students who did not attend the religious instruction classes were not released from their secular educational obligations required by an Illinois compulsory education statute. Religious teachers of the Protestant, Roman Catholic, and Jewish faiths—"at no expense to the [public] school authorities, but . . . subject to the approval and supervision of the superintendent of schools"—provided religious instruction weekly in assigned public school rooms.[55]

Surviving all constitutional challenges, the released time program was upheld by the Illinois courts. On appeal, however, the U.S. Supreme Court overturned the Illinois judiciary and held that the program was unconstitutional. Again, Justice Black spoke for the Court. Black held that the Illinois released time program violated the establishment clause on essentially two grounds: first, that "the State's tax-supported public school buildings [were] used for the dissemination of religious doctrines"; and second, that the "State also affords sectarian groups an invaluable aid in that it helps to provide pupils for their religious classes through use of the State's compulsory public school machinery. This," said the Court, "is not separation of Church and State."[56]

Although citing *Everson*, neither the opinion of the Court nor the two separate concurring opinions in *McCollum* provided any new historical or other justifications for why these two propositions, even if true, breached the First Amendment's wall of separation between church and state. However, they did provide interpretations of church-state separation that are difficult to square with Jefferson's views on education.

One of Jefferson's proudest achievements was his founding in 1819 of the University of Virginia—an educational institution that has always been supported by public funds. In establishing the University, Jefferson was confronted with the problem of creating a public university free of religious dogma that must, in some comprehensive way, address the ideas found in religious opinion. Commenting that the 1818 report of the Commission to govern the University of Virginia "had not proposed that any professorship of divinity should be established in the University," Jefferson made clear that that decision was dictated by the principles of the Virginia Constitution and that

> [i]t was not . . . to be understood that instruction in religious opinion and duties was meant to be precluded by the public authorities, as indifferent to the interests of society. On the contrary, the relations which exist between man and his Maker, and the duties resulting from those relations, are the most interesting and important to every human being, and the most incumbent on his study and investigation. The

want of instruction in the various creeds of religious faith existing among our citizens presents, therefore, a chasm in a general institution of the useful sciences.[57]

A remedy to breach this chasm soon presented itself. In 1822, Jefferson wrote that if religious schools were established on the confines of the University, "[s]uch establishments would offer the further and greater advantage of enabling the students of the University to attend religious exercises with the professor of their particular sect." Additionally, the students of these religious schools would have "ready and convenient access and attendance on the scientific lectures of the University." Jefferson further suggested that if this arrangement came about,

> the regulations of the University should be so modified and accommodated as to give every facility of access and attendance to their students, with such regulated use also as may be permitted to other students, of the library which may hereafter be acquired, either by public or private munificence. But always understanding that these schools shall be *independent of the University and of each other*. Such an arrangement . . . would fill the chasm now existing, on principles which would leave inviolate the constitutional freedom of religion, the most inalienable and sacred of all human rights, over which the people and authorities of this state, individually and publicly, have ever manifested the most watchful jealousy.[58]

Despite all these aids provided by a public university to dedicated religious schools and their students, Jefferson indicated that the principle of church-state separation would be satisfied because all the religious educational entities are discrete institutions independent of the University of Virginia. In other words, Jefferson's position appears to be that even though all the students of the various religious schools would have available to them all the educational benefits of the University of Virginia and the same status as the University's students, separation of church and state in Virginia was not violated because the sectarian schools and the University were separate legal entities.

Would the commingling of the mission and resources of a public university and adjacent religious institutions, contemplated by the above regulations, pass constitutional muster under modern establishment clause jurisprudence? The University of Virginia's regulations discussed here would fail at least two, if not all three, of the "Lemon test" criteria used by the Supreme Court since 1971 to determine establishment clause violations under the First and Fourteenth Amendments.[59] Under *Lemon,* the University's accommodations for the religious school students, recommended by Jefferson, would almost certainly be nullified as having a "principal or primary effect that advances religion" and creating "an excessive government entanglement with religion."[60]

Two years later, in October 1824, Jefferson added to the University's "Regulations":

> Should the religious sects of this State, or any of them, according to the invitation held out to them, establish within, or adjacent to, the precincts of the University, schools for instruction in the religion of their sect, the students of the University will be free, and *expected to attend religious worship* at the establishment of their

> respective sects, in the morning, and in time to meet their school in the University at its stated hour.
>
> The students of such religious school, if they attend any school of the University, *shall be considered as students of the University*, subject to the same regulations, and *entitled to the same rights and privileges.*[61]

Was not this expectation in the University "Regulations" in essence a requirement that students participate in religious worship and instruction? If Jefferson saw the separation between church and state as an absolute, how could he write these religious activities into the obligations of *public* university students? In *McCollum* there was no hint, much less expectation, that the public school students were *required* by their public school to attend the religious instruction classes. As a matter of fact, they were not.

It seems certain that modern establishment clause doctrine could tolerate neither the state aid to religious activity provided by the "invitation" to religious sects to locate schools "within . . . the precinct of the University," nor the expectation that University students attend the place of worship established by their particular religious sect. I conclude that Jefferson's approach to public provisions that involve the commingling of religion and education is significantly different from the justices on the *Everson-McCollum* Court. While Jefferson's "Regulations" for the University of Virginia are certainly concerned that the University not be religiously partisan, thereby violating the Virginia Constitution, they also indicate a belief that the state has a responsibility to provide a well-rounded education for its citizens. Jefferson extended offers of help to religious schools as a means of reaching this fundamental state objective. How else can one explain Jefferson's "Regulations" to govern the University of Virginia, which reveal an offer to allow the use of the University's library, classes, and other facilities by students attending religious schools adjacent to the University's premises? Further, even though the appointment of a professor of divinity was *not* constitutionally consistent in a public university, Jefferson expected that the students of the University would be taught the tenets of their religion by the sectarian institutions invited to locate contiguous to the University. It should be emphasized that Jefferson thought some inquiry into religion and transcendental "truths" was vital to a comprehensive education. For the mutual benefit of all of Virginia's students, Jefferson's "Regulations" show an emphasis on a broad based education irrespective of whether students attended the University of Virginia, some other public school, or a religious school.

Those who embrace the absolutist interpretation of the establishment clause, whether they be on or off the Supreme Court, find little support for their strict separationist views in the "Regulations" that Jefferson wrote to govern the use of the University of Virginia's physical facilities and the religious activities "expected" of University students.

Some Conclusions

At least two conclusions can be drawn from this evidence. First, Jefferson did not think the First Amendment erected a "high and impregnable" wall of separation between church and state. Second, Jefferson did not necessarily view the use of sectarian institutions to reach secular constitutional ends as unconstitutional. Taken together, all the revised bills concerning religion that Jefferson drafted indicate that, while Jefferson worked hard and long to disestablish one specific church (the Episcopal Church) in Virginia, he was not hostile to the notion that religion and government might at times, in the public interest, collaborate. Of course that collaboration would have to take place in such a way as not to create government favoritism toward any one religion, religious sect, or religious point of view, including, I would suggest, non-theism. How else does one explain Jefferson's "Sabbath breaking" bill and the bill authorizing Virginia officials to appoint days for fasting and thanksgiving?

No opinion of the U.S. Supreme Court, beginning with *Everson v. Board of Education,* has tried to reconcile Jefferson's "Bill for Establishing Religious Freedom" with his "Sabbath breaking" bill to determine what Jefferson reasonably and consistently believed and sought to do in Virginia. Should a U.S. Supreme Court ever do so, it certainly would not encounter Jefferson fervently recommending legislation that would create a complete, impregnable, and unyielding wall of separation between church and the Commonwealth of Virginia. I do not see in any of Jefferson's recommended legislation hostility to the use of religion as a generic means to achieve secular goals constitutionally committed to government.

The "Regulations" Jefferson wrote for the University of Virginia, which governed the University's students and the use of its facilities, suggest a similar theme and indicate how Jefferson's views on the prudential relationship between religion and the state have been misperceived. Additionally, I do not think that President Jefferson thought the "Catholic Priest and Church Building Treaty" with the Kaskaskia Indians, as well as the three federal land grant laws for the "Society of the United Brethren for propagating the gospel among the Heathen"—all of which he signed—violated the First Amendment. Is one to believe seriously that as president Jefferson abandoned one of the basic commitments of his life? If Jefferson believed in a "high and impregnable" wall of separation between church and state—as did Justices Black, Rutledge, and the other Supreme Court justices in *Everson*—then we are virtually compelled to conclude that President Jefferson violated his constitutional oath of office and departed from one of the most cherished principles of his lifetime. The apparent contradiction between Jefferson's public record and the *Everson* Court's description of his views is avoided if Jefferson is viewed as a "nonabsolute separationist." It is clear, based on the evidence above, that the traditional interpretation of Jefferson as an "absolute separationist" is historically faulty, despite the fact that it is supported, and to a great degree perpetuated, by prominent and respected jurists and constitutional scholars.

If one does not compromise Mr. Jefferson's record, the evidence leads to a compelling conclusion. Like his presidential predecessors and the early federal Congresses—those closest to the creation of the federal Constitution and the First Amendment—Jefferson used sectarian institutions to reach constitutional secular governmental ends. That is a matter of objective historical fact documented here. Did Jefferson violate his own understanding of the constitutional principle of church-state separation, or did Jefferson's construction of the wall of separation differ from the modern Court's interpretation of the wall?

If one discards the U.S. Supreme Court's inventive adjectives—high, impregnable, and complete—to characterize Mr. Jefferson's "wall," then the historical record makes more sense. Jefferson's writings and public actions dictate a different definition of church-state separation. If Jefferson interpreted the establishment clause as nonabsolute and its prohibitions less restrictive than suggested by the *Everson-McCollum* Court, then the historical Jefferson violated neither his principles nor the dictates of the First Amendment as he tried to reconcile the actions of what Justice Douglas once called "a religious people" with the constitutional secular responsibilities assigned to government.[62]

Notes

1. *Congressional Quarterly's Guide to the U.S. Supreme Court* (Washington, D.C.: Congressional Quarterly, Inc., 1979), 461 ("The two men [Jefferson and Madison] most responsible for its [the establishment clause] inclusion in the Bill of Rights construed the clause absolutely.").

2. *Ibid.*

3. The following is the text of President Madison's Thanksgiving Proclamation of 4 March 1815:

> By the President of the United States of America.
>
> A Proclamation.
>
> The Senate and House of Representatives of the United States have by a joint resolution signified their desire that a day may be recommended to be observed by the people of the United States with religious solemnity as a day of thanksgiving and of devout acknowledgments to Almighty God for His great goodness manifested in restoring to them the blessing of peace.
>
> No people ought to feel greater obligations to celebrate the goodness of the Great Disposer of Events and of the Destiny of Nations than the people of the United States. His kind providence originally conducted them to one of the best portions of the dwelling place allotted for the great family of the human race. He protected and cherished them under all the difficulties and trials to which they were exposed in their early days. Under His fostering care their habits, their sentiments, and their pursuits prepared them for a transition in due time to a state of independence and self-government. In the arduous struggle by which it was attained they were distinguished by multiplied tokens of His benign interposition. During the interval which succeeded He reared them into the strength and endowed them with the resources which have enabled them to assert their national rights and to enhance their national character in another arduous conflict, which is now so happily terminated by a peace and reconciliation with those who have been our enemies. And to the same Divine Author of Every Good and Perfect Gift we are indebted for all those privileges and advantages, religious as well as civil, which are so richly enjoyed in this favored land.
>
> It is for blessings such as these, and more especially for the restoration of the blessing of peace, that I now recommend that the second Thursday in April next be set apart as a day on which the people of every religious denomination may in their solemn assemblies unite their hearts and their voices in a freewill offering to their Heavenly Benefactor of their homage of thanksgiving and of their songs of praise.
>
> Given at the city of Washington on the 4th day of March, A.D. 1815, and of the Independence of the United States the thirty-ninth.
>
> JAMES MADISON.

James D. Richardson, ed., *A Compilation of the Messages and Papers of the Presidents,* 20 vols. (New York: Bureau of National Literature and Art, 1897), II:545-546. Madison's "Thanksgiving Proclamations" of 9 July 1812, 23 July 1813, and 16 November 1814 are also available in *A Compilation of the Messages and Papers of the Presidents* [hereinafter *Papers of the Presidents*].

4. "An Act additional to, and amendatory of, an act, intituled 'An act concerning the District of Columbia,'" in Richard Peters, ed., *The Public Statutes at Large of the United States of America* (Boston: Charles C. Little and James Brown, 1845), 2:194 [hereinafter *U.S. Statutes at Large*]. See *Walz v. Tax Commission of the City of New York,* 397 U.S. 664, 677 (1970).

5. After I brought this matter to the attention of the publisher, the editors of the second edition of the *Guide to the U.S. Supreme Court* (Washington, D.C.: Congressional Quarterly, 1990) acknowledged that there is "considerable disagreement" among scholars concerning Jefferson's and Madison's understanding of the establishment clause and that President Madison issued Thanksgiving Day proclamations. *Ibid.*, 458.

6. *Everson v. Board of Education*, 330 U.S. 1, 15-16 (1947).

7. *Ibid.* at 18.

8. *Ibid.* at 31-32 (Rutledge, J., dissenting).

9. *Ibid.* at 19 (Jackson, J., dissenting)

10. See Robert L. Cord, "Church-State Separation: Restoring the 'No Preference' Doctrine of the First Amendment," *Harvard Journal of Law & Public Policy* 9 (1986): 129; and Robert L. Cord, *Separation of Church and State: Historical Fact and Current Fiction* (Grand Rapids: Baker Book House, 1988), 3-82. *Separation of Church and State* was first published in 1982 by Lambeth Press.

11. The "Committee of Revisors" was appointed in October 1776 by resolution of the General Assembly and included, in addition to Jefferson, George Mason (who resigned from the Committee), Thomas Ludwell Lee (who died before the Committee began its work), Edmund Pendleton, and George Wythe. See *The Papers of Thomas Jefferson*, ed. Julian P. Boyd, 27 vols. to date (Princeton, N.J.: Princeton University Press, 1950-), 2:305-324 [hereinafter *Papers of Jefferson*]. Boyd reproduced the *Revisal of the Laws of Virginia, ibid.*, 2:336-657 [hereinafter *Revisal*]

12. *Ibid.*, 2:307, 313.

13. *Ibid.*, 2:546.

14. Saul K. Padover, ed., *The Complete Madison: His Basic Writings* (New York: Harper & Brothers, 1953), 299-306.

15. "A Bill Establishing a Provision for Teachers of the Christian Religion," Papers of George Washington, Library of Congress; reprinted in Cord, *Separation of Church and State,* 242-243. To his lengthy dissent in *Everson v. Board of Education*, Justice Rutledge appended the entire texts of Madison's "Memorial and Remonstrance Against Religious Assessments" and the proposed Virginia "Bill Establishing a Provision for Teachers of the Christian Religion." 330 U.S. at 63-74.

16. In 1787, the First Congress proposed twelve amendments to the new Constitution. The first two amendments were not ratified at that time and the third proposed amendment by ratification became the First Amendment to the Constitution in 1791. See the "Resolution of the First Congress Submitting Twelve Amendments to the Constitution," *Documents on the Formation of the Union of the American States* (Washington, D.C.: Government Printing Office, 1927), 1063-1065.

17. *Papers of Jefferson*, 2:555-556 (emphasis added). Although the *Papers of Jefferson* cited here did not appear until 1950, three years after the *Everson* opinions were written, the text of the statute "Punishing . . . Sabbath Breakers" was published earlier and available to the Court in William Waller Hening, *The Statutes at Large; Being a Collection of all the Laws of Virginia* (Richmond: Printed for the editor by George Cochran, 1823), 12:336-337. Bill 85 did not become law; thus, it does not appear in Hening, *Statutes at Large*. However, the text of the bill, reprinted below, was available to the U.S. Supreme Court in 1947 before the publication of *Papers of Jefferson* in *Report of the Committee of Revisors Appointed by the General Assembly of Virginia in MDCCLXXVI* (Richmond: Printed by Dixon and Holt, 1784), 59-60. The complete text of Bill 85, "A Bill for Appointing Days of Public Fasting and Thanksgiving," is as follows:

> Be it enacted by the General Assembly, that the power of appointing days of public fasting and humiliation, or thanksgiving, throughout this commonwealth, may in the recess of the General Assembly, be exercised by the Governor, or Chief Magistrate, with the advice of the Council; and such appointment shall be notified to the public, by a proclamation, in which the occasion of the fasting or thanksgiving shall be particularly set forth. Every minister of the gospel shall on each day so to be appointed, attend and perform divine service and preach a sermon, or discourse, suited to the occasion, in his church, on pain of forfeiting fifty pounds for every failure, not having a reasonable excuse.

18. "Editorial Note," *Papers of Jefferson*, 2:318-320. See also Daniel L. Dreisbach, "Thomas Jefferson and Bills Number 82-86 of the Revision of the Laws of Virginia, 1776-1786: New Light on the Jeffersonian Model of Church-State Relations," *North Carolina Law Review* 69 (1990): 159-211.

19. *Ibid.*, 2:555.

20. Although this amendment is not noted in *Papers of Jefferson,* 2:555-556, the statute as adopted and reported in Hening, *Statutes at Large,* 12:337, replaced the word "Sunday" with "Sabbath day."

21. See note 17 above for the text of Bill 85.

22. *Papers of Jefferson,* 2:556.

23. Leo Pfeffer, *Church, State, and Freedom,* rev. ed. (Boston: Beacon Press, 1967), 157. It should be noted here that the late Professor Leo Pfeffer wrote many books on American Constitutional Law, including *The Liberties of an American* (Boston: Beacon Press, 1956); *This Honorable Court* (Boston: Beacon Press, 1965); *God, Caesar, and the Constitution* (Boston: Beacon Press, 1975). Professor Pfeffer also participated in the litigation of many establishment clause cases decided by the U.S. Supreme Court since *Everson* in 1947.

24. *Papers of the Presidents,* I:56 (3 October 1789). Washington issued another Thanksgiving Day proclamation on 1 January 1795, in *ibid.*, I:171-172.

25. Two of John Adams's proclamations can be found in *Papers of the Presidents,* I:258-260 (23 March 1798), and I:274-276 (6 March 1799).

26. Letter from Thomas Jefferson to the Reverend Samuel Miller, 23 January 1808, in Paul Leicester Ford, ed., *The Works of Thomas Jefferson,* Federal edition, 12 vols. (New York: G.P. Putnam's Sons, 1905), 11:7-9.

27. *Ibid.* Jefferson set forth his views on presidential Thanksgiving and Fast Day proclamations in the 1808 letter to the Reverend Samuel Miller:

> I consider the government of the U.S. as interdicted by the Constitution from intermeddling with religious institutions, their doctrines, discipline, or exercises. This results not only from the provision that no law shall be made respecting the establishment, or free exercise, of religion, but from that also which reserves to the states the powers not delegated to the U.S. Certainly no power to prescribe any religious exercise, or to assume authority in religious discipline, has been delegated to the general government. It must then rest with the states, as far as it can be in any human authority. But it is only proposed that I should *recommend,* not prescribe a day of fasting & prayer. That is, that I should *indirectly* assume to the U.S. an authority over religious exercises which the Constitution has directly precluded them from. It must be meant too that this recommendation is to carry some authority, and to be sanctioned by some penalty on those who disregard it; not indeed of fine and imprisonment, but of some degree of proscription perhaps in public opinion. And does the change in the nature of the penalty make the recommendation

> the less *a law* of conduct for those to whom it is directed? I do not believe it is for the interest of religion to invite the civil magistrate to direct it's [sic] exercises, it's [sic] discipline, or it's [sic] doctrines; nor of the religious societies that the general government should be invested with the power of effecting any uniformity of time or matter among them. Fasting & prayer are religious exercises. The enjoining them an act of discipline. Every religious society has a right to determine for itself the times for these exercises, & the objects proper for them, according to their own particular tenets; and this right can never be safer than in their own hands, where the constitution has deposited it.
>
> I am aware that the practice of my predecessors may be quoted. But I have ever believed that the example of state executives led to the assumption of that authority by the general government, without due examination, which would have discovered that what might be a right in a state government, was a violation of that right when assumed by another. Be this as it may, every one must act according to the dictates of his own reason, & mine tells me that civil powers alone have been given to the President of the U.S. and no authority to direct the religious exercises of his constituents.

Letter from Jefferson to the Reverend Samuel Miller, 23 January 1808, in *ibid*. (emphasis in the original).

28. *Papers of Jefferson,* 1:105-106.

29. *Papers of Jefferson*, 3:177-179.

30. Madison's Thanksgiving Day proclamations were issued on 9 July 1812, *Papers of the Presidents*, II:498; 23 July 1813, *ibid.*, II:517-518; 16 November 1814, *ibid.*, II:543; and 4 March 1815, *ibid.*, II:545-546.

31. See *Wallace v. Jaffree*, 472 U.S. 38, 91-92 (1985) (Rehnquist, J., dissenting).

32. Daniel L. Dreisbach, "'Sowing Useful Truths and Principles': The Danbury Baptists, Thomas Jefferson, and the 'Wall of Separation,'" *Journal of Church and State* 39 (1997): 468-469.

33. *Ibid.*

34. See Cord, *Separation of Church and State*, 4. The Congregational Church was the last of the state churches to be disestablished: in Connecticut in 1818, in New Hampshire in 1819, and in Massachusetts in 1833.

35. *Papers of the Presidents*, I:351.

36. "A Treaty Between the United States of America and the Kaskaskia Tribe of Indians," *U.S. Statutes at Large*, 7:78-79.

37. "A Treaty Between the United States of America, and the Wyandot, Ottawa, Chipawa, Munsee and Delaware, Shawanee, and Pottawatima nations," *U.S. Statutes at Large,* 7:88.

38. "A Convention Between the United States and the Cherokee Nation of Indians," *U.S. Statutes at Large*, 7:102.

39. In *Reid v. Covert*, 354 U.S. 1 (1957), Justice Black indicated in a plurality opinion "that no agreement with a foreign nation can confer power on the Congress, or on any other branch of Government, which is free from the restraints of the Constitution." *Id.*, at 16. On this point it appears his view was not challenged by the other justices.

40. Pfeffer, *Church, State, and Freedom*, 105.

41. "An Act regulating the grants of land appropriated for Military services, and for the Society of the United Brethren for propagating the Gospel among the Heathen," *U.S. Statutes at Large,* 1:490-491.

42. On 27 July 1787, the Continental Congress—which had on 20 May 1785 ordained that the "Towns Gnadenhutten, Schoenbrun and Salem" and adjoining lands with improvements were "reserved for the sole use of the Christian Indians who were formerly settled there"—had resolved that, among other things, "a quantity of land around and adjoining each of the before mentioned Towns amounting in the whole to ten thousand acres, and that the property of said reserved land be vested" in trust for these Indians with "the Moravian Brethren at Bethlehem in Pennsylvania, or a society of the said Brethren for civilizing the Indians and promoting Christianity." *Journals of the Continental Congress, 1774-1789,* edited from the Original Records in the Library of Congress by Roscoe R. Hill (Washington, D.C.: Government Printing Office, 1936), 33:429-430.

Pursuant to the July 1787 resolution and "[o]n a report of a committee consisting of Mr. [Abraham] Clarke, Mr. [Hugh] Williamson and Mr. [James] Madison to whom was referred a memorial of John Etwein of Bethlehem, president of the brethrens society for propagating the Gospel among the Heathen," the Continental Congress, on 3 September 1788, ordered that three tracts of land, one adjoining each of the towns, Gnadenhutten, Schoenbrun, and Salem on the Muskingum, be conveyed to the Moravian Brethren at Bethlehem in Pennsylvania in trust for the Christian Indians. *Journals of the Continental Congress*, 34:485-487.

43. "Progress of the Society of United Brethren In Propagating the Gospel Among the Indians," *American State Papers*, Class II, Indian Affairs, II:376-377 (Document No. 189).

44. *U.S. Statutes at Large*, 1:491 (emphasis added).

45. *Ibid.*

46. "An Act to amend the act intituled 'An act regulating the grants of land appropriated for military services, and for the Society of the United Brethren, for propagating the Gospel among the Heathen,'" *U.S. Statutes at Large*, 1:724.

47. "An Act in addition to an act, intituled 'An act, in addition to an act regulating the grants of land appropriated for military services, and for the Society of the United Brethren, for propagating the gospel among the Heathen,'" *U.S. Statutes at Large*, 2:155-156; "An Act to revive and continue in force, an act in addition to an act intituled 'An act in addition to an act regulating the grants of land appropriated for Military Services and for the Society of the United Brethren for propagating the Gospel among the Heathen,' and for other purposes," *ibid.*, 2:236-237.

48. "An Act granting further time for locating military land warrants, and for other purposes," *U.S. Statutes at Large*, 2:271-272.

49. See text accompanying notes 1-5 above.

50. "An Act additional to, and amendatory of, an act, intituled 'An act concerning the District of Columbia,'" *U.S. Statutes at Large,* 2:194. The federal statute continued the policy of tax exemption for churches in Alexandria County, Virginia that was operative before it was ceded to the District of Columbia. See *Walz v. Tax Commission of the City of New York*, 397 U.S. 664, 677 (1970).

51. 333 U.S. 203 (1948).

52. While there was only one vote to sustain the constitutionality of the "released time" program, not all eight justices joined the opinion of the Court authored by Justice Black. Justices Frankfurter and Jackson wrote separate opinions as to the disposition of the case and did not join Chief Justice Vinson and Justices Douglas, Rutledge, Burton, and Murphy, who subscribed to the opinion of the Court. Justice Stanley Reed was the lone dissenter.

53. In *Everson*, the Supreme Court held that the religion clauses of the First Amendment are incorporated into the "Due Process" clause of the Fourteenth Amendment and thus

applicable to the states. 330 U.S. at 8, 14-15. The Court first mentioned that the fundamental concept of liberty protected by the Fourteenth Amendment embodied the religion clauses of the First Amendment in *Cantwell v. Connecticut*, 310 U.S. 296, 303-304 (1940). A detailed discussion of this process can be found in Cord, *Separation of Church and State*, 85-101.

54. 333 U.S. at 207.

55. *Id.* at 208.

56. *Id.* at 212.

57. "Freedom of Religion at the University of Virginia," 7 October 1822, in Saul K. Padover, *The Complete Jefferson* (New York: Tudor Publishing Co., 1943), 957.

58. *Ibid.*, 958 (emphasis added). Jefferson similarly remarked with favor on an arrangement in his own community of Charlottesville, Virginia, that gave four Christian denominations equal access to the courthouse for Sunday services: "In our village of Charlottesville, there is a good degree of religion, with a small spice only of fanaticism. We have four sects, but without either church or meeting-house. The court-house is the common temple, one Sunday in the month to each. Here, Episcopalian and Presbyterian, Methodist and Baptist, meet together, join in hymning their Maker, listen with attention and devotion to each others' preachers, and all mix in society with perfect harmony." Letter from Thomas Jefferson to Doctor Thomas Cooper, 2 November 1822, in Ford, ed., *The Works of Thomas Jefferson*, 12:271.

59. In *Lemon v. Kurtzman*, 403 U.S. 602, 612-613 (1971), Chief Justice Warren Burger, writing for the Court, described an establishment clause test based on the "cumulative criteria developed by the Court over many years." In order for a statute to pass constitutional muster under the establishment clause, the Court held (1) it must have a secular legislative purpose; (2) its principal or primary effect must be one that neither advances nor inhibits religion; and (3) it must not foster an excessive government entanglement with religion.

60. *Ibid.*

61. "Regulations," 4 October 1824, in Padover, *The Complete Jefferson,* 1110 (emphasis added). Anson Phelps Stokes and Leo Pfeffer, advocates of an absolute separation between church and state, have indicated, despite what seems to be a clear requirement in the University's rules, that "no compulsion" to attend existed. Not only do they fail to provide adequate documentation for that interpretation of Jefferson's rules, they also fail to explain why Jefferson—who in their view was an absolute separationist—would even include this admonition regarding religious worship in the regulations of a public university in the first place. See Stokes and Pfeffer, *Church and State in the United States*, rev. ed. (New York: Harper and Row, 1964), 54.

62. *Zorach v. Clauson,* 343 U.S. 306, 313 (1952).

Chapter 9

Religion and Legal Reforms in Revolutionary Virginia: A Reexamination of Jefferson's Views on Religious Freedom and Church-State Separation

Daniel L. Dreisbach

In 1777 Thomas Jefferson drafted "A Bill for Establishing Religious Freedom," one of the most venerated documents in American history. This proposal was part of an ambitious revision of the laws of Virginia commenced following the political separation from England. The statute provided in its brief enabling clauses:

> That no man shall be compelled to frequent or support any religious worship, place, or ministry whatsoever, nor shall be enforced, restrained, molested, or burthened in his body or goods, nor shall otherwise suffer on account of his religious opinions or belief; but that all men shall be free to profess, and by argument to maintain, their opinion in matters of religion, and that the same shall in no wise diminish, enlarge, or affect their civil capacities.[1]

The religious freedom bill is a passionate affirmation of intellectual and spiritual independence that, in many respects, resembles Jefferson's better-known "Declaration of Independence."[2] "More than a statute," wrote Merrill D. Peterson, "it was an eloquent manifesto of the sanctity of the human mind and spirit."[3] James Madison grandly proclaimed that the bill's passage "extinguished for ever the ambitious hope of making laws for the human mind."[4]

The bill was not passed when it was first introduced in the Virginia legislature in 1779. Despite its eloquence and the growing stature of its author, it proved too radical for the times.[5] By the mid-1780s, church-state issues had once again begun to agitate the public mind. In the autumn session of 1784, the Virginia legislature received numerous petitions requesting an assessment that would require all citizens to pay an annual tax for the support of teachers of the Christian religion. These petitions told of nations that had fallen because of the demise of religion and described the alarming decline of morals in the Commonwealth.

Proponents of a general assessment rallied behind the dominant personality in the legislature, Patrick Henry. He championed legislation that would have imposed a modest property tax for the support of Christian clergymen.[6] James Madison, who opposed the measure, successfully moved to postpone final action on Henry's bill until the next legislative session in 1785.[7] In the interval, Madison labored diligently to mobilize opposition to the assessment, writing his "Memorial and Remonstrance Against Religious Assessments." The ground swell of anti-assessment sentiment—orchestrated in part by Madison's "Remonstrance"—settled the fate of Henry's bill, which died quietly in committee after only brief consideration in the autumn of 1785.[8] Enthused by this victory, Madison brushed the dust off Jefferson's religious freedom bill and guided it to passage in January 1786.[9]

The dramatic disestablishment struggle in revolutionary Virginia that culminated in the enactment of Jefferson's bill had a profound impact on church-state developments across the fledgling nation and arguably influenced the formulation of the First Amendment religion provisions. The religious freedom bill is, indeed, an eloquent expression of the author's devotion to religious liberty. Detached from its legislative and political context, however, it fails to capture Jefferson's versatile vision for church-state relations. The thesis of this chapter is that the bill must be interpreted in the light of Jefferson's complete legislative strategy for redefining church-state arrangements in Virginia. The religious freedom bill was only the first of five consecutive bills in Virginia's revised code addressing issues of concern to organized religion. These bills, which were framed by Jefferson and sponsored by Madison in the Virginia legislature, provide critical qualifications of the conventional separationist interpretation of the meaning and scope of the religious freedom bill. Taken together, they do not indicate a strict separationist arrangement; rather, they suggest that Jefferson and Madison endorsed a model that accommodated limited church-state cooperation in support of uninhibited religious belief and expression.

Judicial Interpretations of the Religious Freedom Bill

Biographers of Jefferson and students of church-state relations in revolutionary Virginia have typically described the religious freedom bill as the culmination of Jefferson's efforts to erect "an unbreachable wall of separation between Church and State and make religious opinions forever private and sacrosanct from intrusion."[10] Virginia historian Hamilton James Eckenrode viewed passage of the statute even more broadly as the event that "marked the end of the conservative effort to check and control the growth of democracy and the spread of liberal ideas."[11] The concepts enshrined in Jefferson's bill, it is frequently argued, found eventual expression and ultimate influence in the subsequently enacted First Amendment religion clauses.[12]

The United States Supreme Court has long relied on American history, especially the dramatic disestablishment struggle in revolutionary Virginia, to inform its separationist interpretation of the First Amendment religion clauses.[13] Indeed, if there is one constant in the confused arena of church-state law, it is that judges—regardless of their legal opinion—consistently have appealed to history to buttress their respective interpretations of the religion clauses.[14] As Justice Wiley Rutledge observed:

> No provision of the Constitution is more closely tied to or given content by its generating history than the religious clause of the First Amendment. It is at once the refined product and the terse summation of that history. The history includes not only Madison's authorship and the proceedings before the First Congress, but also the long and intensive struggle for religious freedom in America, more especially in Virginia, of which the Amendment was the direct culmination. In the documents of the times, particularly of Madison, who was leader in the Virginia struggle before he became the Amendment's sponsor, but also in the writings of Jefferson and others and in the issues which engendered them is to be found irrefutable confirmation of the Amendment's sweeping content.[15]

In the landmark case of *Everson v. Board of Education* (1947), the Supreme Court offered its first comprehensive interpretation of the constitutional pronouncement on church-state relations.[16] *Everson* was the "beginning of an impressive and influential body of [church-state] case law."[17] A divided Court upheld the constitutionality of state reimbursements to parents for money expended in the transportation of their children to and from parochial schools, rejecting the dissenters' argument that the tax supported program constituted an "establishment of religion." Despite its holding, the Court declared that the "First Amendment has erected a wall between church and state . . . [that] must be kept high and impregnable."[18]

More important than the legal holding itself was the separationist rhetoric used lavishly in both the majority and minority opinions and the Court's extensive reliance on selected historical events and documents to buttress its broad construction of the First Amendment nonestablishment provision.[19] In defining the establishment clause, Justice Hugo L. Black, writing for a slender majority of five justices, declared: "Neither a state nor the Federal Government can set up a church. Neither can pass laws which aid one religion, aid all religions, or prefer one religion over another."[20] In even more sweeping terms, Justice Rutledge asserted in a minority opinion that the First Amendment's purpose was "to uproot" all religious establishments and "to create a complete and permanent separation of the spheres of religious activity and civil authority by comprehensively forbidding every form of public aid or support for religion."[21]

In their efforts to interpret the establishment clause, the *Everson* Court and virtually all subsequent courts have turned most frequently to the words and deeds of Jefferson and Madison, not only because they led the disestablishment struggle in their native Commonwealth but also because their idea of the proper church-state arrangement is thought to be expressive of the purposes of the establishment clause.[22] In particular, the Supreme Court, as well as lower federal and state courts, have invoked Jefferson's "Bill for Establishing Religious Freedom" and Madison's "Memorial and Remonstrance" to inform their church-state pronouncements.[23]

These documents and the disestablishment movement in Virginia that inspired them, the justices have instructed, confirm that the two Virginians advocated a sweeping separation between church and state. In *Committee for Public Education and Religious Liberty v. Nyquist* (1973),[24] for example, Justice Lewis Powell recounted how the "debate over the relationship between Church and State" in revolutionary Virginia—the controversy generated by Patrick Henry's general assessment plan in particular—inspired "Madison's Memorial and Remonstrance, recognized today as one of the cornerstones of the First Amendment[ ]" which, in turn, set the stage for "Thomas Jefferson's Bill for Establishing Religious Freedom . . . [and] Virginia's first acknowledgement of the principle of total separation of Church and State."[25] Powell merely echoed the historical assertions of Justices Black and Rutledge in *Everson*.[26]

Conventional rules of interpretation recommend an examination of the text and the legislative deliberations by the body that framed the text as the starting point for the interpretation of a constitutional provision. Significantly, both Justices Black and Rutledge in their respective *Everson* opinions devoted considerable space to recounting the dramatic church-state controversy in colonial and revolutionary Virginia, yet they virtually ignored the legislative history of the First Amendment religion provisions. The interpretation of the establishment clause was, after all, at issue in *Everson*. The legislative history of the First Amendment, not the disestablishment battles in revolutionary Virginia, should have been the focus of the Court's historical review. Indeed, a striking feature of the Supreme Court's church-state opinions is the absence of a serious examination of the recorded debates in the First Congress leading to the framing of the religion provisions. One speculates that the Court has disregarded the text and legislative history of the First Amendment because they fail to support the Court's separationist analysis. It is also appropriate to question the legitimacy of the Court's near exclusive focus on the church-state battles in revolutionary Virginia. As Leonard W. Levy has argued, if the "object is to understand what was meant by 'an establishment of religion' at the time of the framing of the Bill of Rights, the histories of the other states are equally important, notwithstanding the stature and influence of Jefferson and Madison as individuals."[27]

The modern Supreme Court, like most historians, has concluded that the struggle for religious liberty in revolutionary Virginia—Jefferson's religious freedom bill in particular—found equivalent expression in the subsequently enacted First Amendment religion clauses. However, an inordinate reliance on Jefferson's celebrated bill, detached from its legislative context, misrepresents the versatile church-state model Jefferson envisioned for his native Commonwealth and the nation. The religious freedom bill, it is recalled, was only the first of five consecutive bills in Virginia's revised code that addressed church-state concerns. Collectively, these five bills suggest that Jefferson embraced a more accommodating view of church-state relations than the strict separationist model attributed to him in conventional judicial interpretations of his famous bill. Insofar as the Supreme Court has relied on an erroneous conception of Jefferson's church-state views to inform its First Amendment analysis, its legal pronouncements may lack analytical merit and historical validity.[28]

The legislative initiative that produced the revised code of Virginia, including Jefferson's celebrated bill and the succeeding four proposals addressing religious concerns, thus merits further historical scrutiny. Of particular importance is the collective impact of the five consecutive bills on conventional interpretations of Jefferson's model for church-state relations.

Religion and the Revised Code of Virginia

Jefferson's vision for church-state relations is often mischaracterized by those who interpret his "Bill for Establishing Religious Freedom" without reference to its legislative context. The bill was one of 126 measures in a revision of the laws of Virginia prompted by the Commonwealth's political separation from England. In the wake of independence, the Virginia legislature appointed a committee of prominent Virginians, chaired by Jefferson, to "revise, alter, amend, repeal, or introduce all or any of the said laws" of the Commonwealth.[29] The Committee of Revisors' mandate was to bring the laws of Virginia into conformity with republican principles and to strip the existing legal code of remaining vestiges of monarchical rule. In addition to Jefferson, the Committee, appointed in late 1776, included Edmund Pendleton, George Wythe, George Mason, and Thomas Ludwell Lee.[30]

For the next several years, Jefferson was consumed by the monumental task of revising the laws of Virginia. In February 1779, Wythe and Jefferson convened in Williamsburg. Meeting on a daily basis, Jefferson recounted in his autobiography, they examined drafts of the revised code "sentence by sentence, scrutinizing and amending, until [they] had agreed on the whole."[31] On 18 June 1779, they submitted to the House of Delegates a report on the revised code.[32]

The most celebrated bill in the revised code, Jefferson's "Bill for Establishing Religious Freedom," was debated in the legislature in December 1785 and signed into law in January 1786. This was Bill 82 of the revised code and the first of five consecutive bills addressing religious concerns. According to Dumas Malone, Jefferson specifically assumed responsibility for drafting the bills pertaining to crimes and punishment, descents, education, and *religion*.[33]

Pursuant to conventional common law rules of statutory construction, Jefferson's religious freedom bill should be interpreted in the light of the revised code as a whole, especially in the context of the four companion bills pertaining to religion. (These five consecutive bills were introduced to the legislature by James Madison on the same day as part of a unified legislative package.) In construing a statute susceptible of more than one plausible construction, consideration may be given to its relation to other statutes; and, if reasonably practicable, a statute should be explained in conjunction with other statutes in the same legislative package or relating to the same subject matter. Furthermore, it is the duty of the interpreter to reconcile, so far as is practical and reasonable, various sections of a statute or legislative package so as to render them a consistent, harmonious, and sensible whole. Accordingly, if a statute or legislative package is susceptible of more than one reasonable construction, one that will render it internally consistent (and constitutional) and the other that will render it internally inconsistent (and unconstitutional), then the interpreter should adopt that construction of the statute or legislative package that, without doing violence to its language, will render the diverse sections consistent (and constitutional).[34] In short, presumptions are indulged against interpretations that render a bill or legislative package internally inconsistent.

Some commentators have rejected the contention that Jefferson's religious freedom bill should be interpreted in the context of the entire revised code, especially the companion bills addressing religious concerns. Jefferson, it is argued, did not support the four companion bills or, perhaps, was forced by political exigencies to include bills in the revised code that he thought imprudent, unconstitutional (contrary to the Virginia Constitution), and/or contrary to natural rights. In my view, this argument is not sustained by the historical evidence and is contrary to conventional rules of sound construction. Absent compelling evidence to the contrary, it is reasonable to presume that legislators endorse measures they draft and/or sponsor, and that legislators in writing and/or sponsoring a statute act advisedly and deliberately in good faith, from a proper motive, and with the intent to conform to constitutional requirements and to enact a valid and effective statute. This presumption, of course, is subject to rebuttal.

Jefferson was the chief architect, if not the actual draftsman, of the five consecutive bills in the revised code addressing religious concerns. Although, as is documented below, eminent scholars have identified Jefferson as the author of these bills, a couple of them were revisions of provisions that had long been on the statute books of Virginia. Nonetheless, even if it was proven that Jefferson was not the actual draftsman of these bills or that the language of any one of them was not entirely original to Jefferson, the central thesis of this chapter would remain intact. Clearly, Jefferson was the chief architect of the revised code and was intimately involved in its preparation and presentation. It is widely acknowledged that virtually all the bills were framed by Wythe and Jefferson, and when the two men met in Williamsburg in February 1779 for a final revision of the bills, they examined the drafts "sentence by sentence . . . *until* [both men] *had agreed on the whole.*"[35] There is little doubt that in this role Jefferson, at the very least, authorized and endorsed all five bills which, it is argued in this chapter, modify conventional interpretations of the religious freedom bill.

Jefferson himself assumed responsibility for drafting the bills dealing with religious issues. Taken as a whole, these five bills do not make a convincing argument for the modern Supreme Court's construction of a "high and impregnable" wall of separation between church and state.[36] Rather, they suggest a flexible church-state model that fosters cooperation between religious interests and the civil government. They illustrate that Jefferson's ultimate objective was less an absolute separation of church and state than the fullest possible expression of religious belief and opinion.[37] The five consecutive bills from the revised code are examined below. Of special interest is the question whether or not Jefferson thought these companion bills were part of a coherent, consistent approach to church-state relations.

Bill Number 82: Bill for Establishing Religious Freedom

Bill 82 of the revised code, the Virginia "Statute for Establishing Religious Freedom,"[38] is one of the most profound and influential documents in American political history.[39] Jefferson counted it supreme among his contributions to the Commonwealth and the nation, selecting his authorship of the statute as one of three achievements he wanted memorialized on his gravestone.[40] For more than two centuries, the bill has proven to be a manifesto for intellectual freedom, not only in Virginia but also across the nation and around the world.[41] The arguments advanced in the bill have been woven into the fabric of American political thought, and in the course of time the conventional interpretation of the bill has been adopted as the orthodox principle of American church-state relations.[42]

The prevailing interpretation of Bill 82, as previously indicated, is that in its "sweeping language Jefferson sought to create an unbreachable wall of separation between Church and State and make religious opinions forever private and sacrosanct from intrusion."[43] As Harvard legal historian Mark DeWolfe Howe emphasized, however, Bill 82 did not "in its enacting clauses explicitly prohibit establishment."[44] Rather, Jefferson's bill—drawing inspiration from Locke's *Letter Concerning Toleration*[45]—was narrowly drawn to terminate compelled religious observance and remove civil disabilities against dissenters who publicly expressed their religious opinions.

The Virginia "Statute for Establishing Religious Freedom" consists of three sections. The first is the eloquent preamble (four times the length of the act itself), which sets forth in passionate terms the following reasons for the measure: First, "Almighty God hath created the mind free" and willed "that free it shall remain."[46] Jefferson maintained that the mind of man was not intended to be coerced into intellectual conformity. "[T]he holy author of our religion, who being lord both of body and mind," he argued, chose that religion should be propagated by reason and not by coercion. Second, "legislators and rulers, civil as well as ecclesiastical," have impiously "assumed dominion over the faith of others," and because of their own fallibility and use of coercion have "established and maintained false religions over the greatest part of the world." Third, it is "sinful and tyrannical" to compel a man to support a religion "which he disbelieves and abhors."[47] It is also an infringement on his freedom of choice to force him to support a "teacher of his own religious persuasion," because this inhibits the free encouragement of the minister whose moral pattern and righteousness the citizen finds most persuasive and worthy of support. Fourth, "civil rights have no dependance on our religious opinions, any more than our opinions in physics or geometry"; and, therefore, imposing religious qualifications for civil office deprives the citizen of his "natural right" and tends to corrupt religion by bribery to obtain purely external conformity. Fifth, it is undesirable to use civil magistrates to suppress the propagation of opinions and principles, even of allegedly false tenets, because "truth is great and . . . has nothing to fear from the conflict" with error "unless by human interposition disarmed of her natural weapons, free argument and debate." Jefferson concluded that "it is time enough" for officers of civil government "to interfere when principles break out into overt acts against peace and good order."[48]

The statute's second section, the operative portion, enacted the following provisions: In the Commonwealth of Virginia no citizen shall be compelled by civil government to attend or support any religious worship, place, or ministry, nor shall any citizen be punished or restrained by the civil government on account of his religious beliefs; but, on the contrary, every citizen shall be free to profess and contend for his religious beliefs, and such activity shall in no way affect one's civil capacities.[49]

The statute's third, and final, section acknowledged that any subsequent legislature has the authority to repeal the statute, but declared that if it does so, such action will be an infringement of natural rights.[50] "In the corpus of Jefferson's work," one commentator observed, "there is no equal in terms of binding future generations."[51]

Significantly, Jefferson's statute was not neutral towards religion.[52] The existence of "Almighty God" who "hath created the mind free" and willed "that free it shall remain," he reasoned, provided the rationale for governmental recognition of religious freedom.[53] The statute, which presumed a "Creator" involved in human affairs,[54] fell short of advocating an absolute principle that civil government and religion may never interact in a cooperative manner. This statutory recognition of the deity and Jefferson's assertion that religious liberty is derived from the "plan of the holy author of our religion"[55] offends many strict separationists today and arguably renders the measure constitutionally suspect under prevailing establishment clause analysis. As one modern jurist opined, "[i]f all endorsement by the state of Christian beliefs is forbidden, then any state that today enacted Jefferson's Bill for Establishing Religious Freedom would be violating the Establishment Clause!"[56] Jefferson's bill did not advocate, in the modern sense at least, a strict separation between religion and civil government, nor was it a blueprint for a wholly secular state. It was a bold and eloquent affirmation of the individual's right to worship God, or not, according to the dictates of conscience, free from governmental interference or discrimination.

Bill Number 83: Bill for Saving the Property of the Church Heretofore by Law Established

The second consecutive revised bill of importance to the religious establishment, Bill 83, was entitled "A Bill for Saving the Property of the Church Heretofore by Law Established."[57] Although never enacted,[58] Bill 83, in the words of a nineteenth-century biographer of Jefferson, "somewhat mitigated" the radical perception of Bill 82 held by some conservative backers of the established church.[59]

The property of the formerly established Anglican Church was a matter of considerable controversy in revolutionary Virginia. Since Anglican Church property had been acquired with taxes collected from the entire community, and not all citizens were members of the Church, there was great debate concerning the equitable dissolution of the Church's temporal assets once the Church was disestablished. Many dissenters regarded these assets as community property, not solely Anglican property. Bill 83, in essential parts, reserved to members of the Anglican Church all property in its legal possession. Legal title and control of Church assets, however, were to be transferred from the formal vestries to resident parish members who would be obligated to use the resources to support the ministry, but would be the sole judges of the conditions of such application. "This bill," according to one nineteenth-century commentator, "seems to have aimed to steer between a violation of vested rights, and using property for other purposes voluntarily devoted to religious objects by its owners—and the arming of a hierarchical body with perpetual power to use a fund contributed by *all* denominations for the exclusive support of a particular *class of tenets*."[60]

The purpose of Bill 83 was to protect certain property interests of the Anglican Church, which had recently lost its tax subsidies,[61] and to ensure that the Church could use its resources to meet outstanding contractual obligations. Reflecting democratic reforms of the time, the bill, in effect, shifted control of Church assets from formal vestries to resident parish members, thus further weakening the established ecclesiastical hierarchy. In this sense, the measure may have encouraged resident parishioners to take a more active role in local church governance and attendant religious concerns. Nonetheless, the measure sought specifically to preserve the property interests of the "church heretofore by law established." Insofar as the bill benefitted one sect exclusively, it would arguably violate the *Everson* Court's prohibition on "laws which aid one religion, aid all religions, or prefer one religion over another."[62] Viewed in this light, Bill 83 is difficult to reconcile with a strict separationist interpretation of Bill 82 or the First Amendment.

Bill Number 84: Bill for Punishing Disturbers of Religious Worship and Sabbath Breakers

On 31 October 1785, Madison introduced the third consecutive revised bill dealing with religion, which was entitled "A Bill for Punishing Disturbers of Religious Worship and Sabbath Breakers."[63] The editor of the most complete collection of Jefferson's papers attributed authorship of this bill, which was enacted on 27 November 1786 in a slightly amended form,[64] to Jefferson.[65]

Bill 84, in essential parts, exempted clergymen from being arrested while conducting religious services in any place of worship.[66] The measure also authorized severe punishments, including imprisonment and amercement, for disturbers of public worship or citizens laboring on Sunday. The bill's third paragraph, which undoubtedly offends modern judicial sensibilities, stated:

> If any person on Sunday shall himself be found labouring at his own or any other trade or calling, or shall employ his apprentices, servants or slaves in labour, or other business, except it be in the ordinary houshold [sic] offices of daily necessity, or other work of necessity or charity, he shall forfeit the sum of ten shillings for every such offence, deeming every apprentice, servant, or slave so employed, and every day he shall be so employed as constituting a distinct offence.[67]

The bill benefited adherents of all denominations by preserving the sanctity of religious worship. It did not, however, expressly require church attendance in order to avoid punishment for Sabbath breaking.

Bill 84 was not merely a "blue law." Rather, it affirmed civil government's responsibility to use its authority to protect the formal act of worship.[68] It restrained civil authorities from arresting a "minister of the gospel" while conducting a religious meeting, and provided that services of divine worship shall not be disrupted by private citizens or interrupted by public officials. Jefferson, it seems, believed that a society's commitment to religious freedom was served when civil government took affirmative steps to protect citizens from external disruptions during the act of worship.

The title of Bill 84 unequivocally states that the measure was written to punish profanation of the "Sabbath" day.[69] The religious aspect of the bill is evident in the use of the word "Sabbath" as compared with a religiously neutral term like "Sunday." The word "Sabbath" reflects the Judeo-Christian tradition of commemorating the Lord's "day of rest"[70] and the fourth commandment requirement that the Sabbath be kept free from secular defilement.[71] Jefferson's choice of the word "Sabbath" suggests that the measure was inspired by religious concerns, as opposed to wholly neutral purposes such as promoting recreation and rest from secular employment.[72] In short, there is no indication that the sponsors of this legislation advanced the bill for the secular purpose of lessening the burdens on laborers, in the same way progressive social legislation in the early twentieth century limited the number of working hours in a day.[73]

Bill 84 and Sunday closing laws in general arguably discriminate against individuals who choose not to preserve the sanctity of the "day of rest" observed by most Christians.[74] Acknowledgment of the Christian "Sabbath" in the official calendar and its preservation by law conflicts with a strict separationist ban on state support for organized religion or its activities. Modern advocates of church-state separation have criticized Sunday legislation less restrictive than Bill 84 as a breach in the "wall of separation."

Bill 84, however, is consistent with Jefferson's lifelong commitment to protecting the right of citizens to express their religious beliefs and opinions peacefully. His principal objective was to preserve the sanctity of worship and freedom of religious expression by deterring the disruption of such activities by private citizens or agents of the civil state. Bill 84 also suggests that Jefferson's desire to separate the institutions of church and state—compelling though it may have been—was merely a means of achieving the fullest possible freedom of religious expression. If religious liberty was realized in its richest sense through cooperation between the state and the church, then Jefferson, it would seem, endorsed such a limited union.[75]

Bill Number 85: Bill for Appointing Days of Public Fasting and Thanksgiving

The fourth in the series of five bills addressing religious concerns was a proposal entitled "A Bill for Appointing Days of Public Fasting and Thanksgiving."[76] This legislation, like the preceding bills, apparently was framed by Jefferson and introduced in the Virginia legislature by Madison on 31 October 1785.[77]

Bill 85 authorized the governor or chief magistrate of the Commonwealth, with the advice of the Council, to designate days for thanksgiving and fasting and to notify the public by proclamation. Far from simply granting the governor power to appoint "days of public fasting and humiliation, or thanksgiving," the bill included the following punitive provision: "Every minister of the gospel shall on each day so to be appointed, attend and perform divine service and preach a sermon, or discourse, suited to the occasion, in his church, on pain of forfeiting fifty pounds for every failure, not having a reasonable excuse."[78]

Although Bill 85 was never enacted, it was sponsored by Madison, and a surviving manuscript copy of the bill bears a notation in the "clerk's hand" indicating that the bill was "endorsed" by Jefferson.[79] The final disposition of this proposal is unimportant to the present discussion. The relevant consideration here is that Jefferson and Madison jointly sponsored a bill that is difficult to reconcile with the strict separationist church-state model frequently attributed to them.[80] Bill 85 graphically illustrates how extensive judicial reliance on the Virginia statute for religious freedom—to the exclusion of Jefferson's and Madison's other legislative contributions to the revised code—has misrepresented the church-state views of the two Virginians.

Another one of Jefferson's declarations pertaining to thanksgiving day proclamations is often cited by strict separationists as confirmation of Jefferson's separationist predilection. This, too, has mistaken his views on such proclamations. As president of the United States, Jefferson refused to designate a national day for fasting and thanksgiving. In a celebrated letter to the Danbury Baptist Association of Connecticut, which he used to explain why he declined to issue such proclamations, Jefferson wrote:

> Believing with you that religion is a matter which lies solely between Man & his God, that he owes account to none other for his faith or his worship, that the legitimate powers of government reach actions only, & not opinions, I contemplate with sovereign reverence that act of the whole American people which declared that *their* legislature should "make no law respecting an establishment of religion, or prohibiting the free exercise thereof," thus building a wall of separation between Church & State.[81]

Jefferson thereby erected the famous "wall of separation" that has become a persistent theme of modern church-state analyses. Indeed, the *Everson* Court indicated that the "wall" metaphor informed its interpretation of the establishment clause.[82]

Although Jefferson's "wall" metaphor is frequently invoked by the modern judiciary, his "Bill for Appointing Days of Public Fasting and Thanksgiving" is largely ignored. The *Everson* Court either was unaware of or disregarded Jefferson and Madison's joint sponsorship of Bill 85—a significant omission given the Court's reliance on Bill 82 and the Danbury letter.[83] Reference to Bill 85, authorizing the official designation of days for religious observances, arguably tempers the rhetoric of Bill 82 and undermines the Court's contention that the public actions of Jefferson and Madison substantiate the strict separationist interpretation of the religion clauses.

Because Bill 85 was written more than a decade before the religion clauses were added to the federal Constitution, one could argue that Jefferson's sponsorship of the bill is less relevant to his understanding of the First Amendment than the Danbury letter, which was written long after the First Amendment and which purports to interpret the religion clauses. Although this argument has merit from a chronological perspective, one cannot ignore the fact that the Supreme Court has stated that the words and deeds of Jefferson and Madison in their native Virginia, *prior* to the drafting of the First Amendment, are expressive of the purposes of the religion clauses and give content and meaning to the First Amendment. If the religious freedom bill, written long before the First Amendment, is thought to have influenced the original understanding of the religion clauses, then it seems plausible that Bill 85, proposed contemporaneously with Bill 82, also may have modestly informed the understanding of church-state relations in the founding era. In any case, Bill 85 illustrates that Jefferson and Madison, contrary to many strict separationists, did not consistently advocate absolute separation throughout their public careers.[84]

In marked contrast to the separationist imagery of the Danbury letter, in colonial and state government settings Jefferson demonstrated an accommodationist inclination on the religious proclamation issue. For example, as a member of the House of Burgesses, on 24 May 1774, he participated in drafting and enacting a resolution designating a "Day of Fasting, Humiliation, and Prayer."[85] Jefferson recounted in his *Autobiography:*

> We were under conviction of the necessity of arousing our people from the lethargy into which they had fallen, as to passing events [the Boston port bill]; and thought that the appointment of a day of general fasting and prayer would be most likely to call up and alarm their attention. . . . [W]e cooked up a resolution . . . for appointing the 1st day of June, on which the portbill was to commence, for a day of fasting, humiliation, and prayer, to implore Heaven to avert from us the evils of civil war, to inspire us with firmness in support of our rights, and to turn the hearts of the King and Parliament to moderation and justice.[86]

Jefferson seemed pleased with this accommodation between religion and the state in May 1774 through a "cooked up" religious proclamation issued to excite a public reaction against England.[87] In 1779, when Jefferson was governor of Virginia, he issued a proclamation decreeing "a day of publick and solemn thanksgiving and prayer to Almighty God."[88] This proclamation was issued after Jefferson had written Bill 82. The 1774 and 1779 religious proclamations, as well as Bill 85, did not figure in the *Everson* Court's examination of Jefferson's church-state views.

How is Jefferson's record on religious proclamations in Virginia reconciled with the position taken in the Danbury letter? A careful review of Jefferson's actions throughout his public career suggests that he believed, as a matter of federalism, the national government had no jurisdiction in religious matters, whereas state governments were free to accommodate and even prescribe religious exercises as they saw fit. A perusal of the Danbury letter reveals that Jefferson was not addressing the broad issue of separation between religion and *all* civil government (both federal and state); rather, he was examining the narrow issue of whether or not a separation between the entire *federal* government and religion was required by the First Amendment. The question presented, in other words, concerned whether the First Amendment restricted only the Congress in matters respecting an establishment of religion, or whether the prohibition extended to the co-equal branches of the federal government, thereby denying the executive branch the prerogative to issue religious proclamations.

The Danbury letter was not primarily a general pronouncement on the prudential relationship between church and state; rather, it was, more specifically, a statement delineating the legitimate constitutional jurisdictions of the federal and state governments on matters pertaining to religion. Jefferson placed the "wall of separation" between the federal regime and ecclesiastical establishments, not between religion and all civil government.[89] This interpretation is buttressed by Jefferson's second inaugural address:

> In matters of religion, I have considered that its free exercise is placed by the constitution independent of the powers of the general [federal] government. I have therefore undertaken, on no occasion, to prescribe the religious exercises suited to it; but have left them, as the constitution found them, under the direction and discipline of State or Church authorities acknowledged by the several religious societies.[90]

In a January 1808 letter to the Reverend Samuel Miller, Jefferson restated his reasons, rooted in federalism, for refusing to issue religious proclamations:

> I consider the government of the United States as interdicted by the Constitution from intermeddling with religious institutions, their doctrines, discipline, or exercises. This results not only from the provision that no law shall be made respecting the establishment or free exercise of religion [First Amendment], but from that also which reserves to the States the powers not delegated to the United States [Tenth Amendment]. Certainly, no power to prescribe any religious exercise, or to assume authority in religious discipline, has been delegated to the General [i.e., federal] Government. It must then rest with the States, as far as it can be in any human authority. . . .

> I am aware that the practice of my predecessors may be quoted. But I have ever believed, that the example of State executives led to the assumption of that authority by the General Government, without due examination, which would have discovered that what might be a right in a State government, was a violation of that right when assumed by another [i.e., the General or federal government]. Be this as it may, every one must act according to the dictates of his own reason, and mine tells me that civil powers alone have been given to the President of the United States, and no authority to direct the religious exercises of his constituents.[91]

Jefferson concluded that although state governments had the authority to act on matters pertaining to religion, such power was denied the entire federal regime, including the executive branch. Accordingly, Jefferson saw no contradiction between authoring a religious proclamation to be issued by *state* authorities and refusing to issue a similar proclamation as the *federal* chief executive.

Jefferson's commitment to protecting the public's recognition and expression of religious beliefs apparently encompassed statutory authorization for state representatives to designate days for religious observances and to sanction such observances in the official calendar. Bills 84 and 85, taken together, illustrate a church-state model whereby the church, although separated institutionally from civil government, could unite its mission with the state to encourage "religious morality" in society and the free and public expression of religious beliefs.[92] Indeed, insofar as social order and stability were fostered by religious and moral reflection, the civil state had legitimate reasons for designating days in the public calendar for fasting and thanksgiving to God and for creating incentives for public observance of days so designated. Jefferson did not advocate absolute church-state separation. To the contrary, as illustrated by these bills, he occasionally endorsed a friendly cooperation between church and state that fostered uninhibited religious expression, including public expression through official religious proclamations. These two bills were no less consistent with Jefferson's church-state model than the principles outlined in his celebrated statute for religious freedom.

Bill Number 86: Bill Annulling Marriages Prohibited by the Levitical Law, and Appointing the Mode of Solemnizing Lawful Marriage

The last of the five consecutive bills touching upon a religious concern was entitled "A Bill Annulling Marriages Prohibited by the Levitical Law, and Appointing the Mode of Solemnizing Lawful Marriage."[93] As the title indicates, the bill is pertinent to the present discussion in that it ostensibly enacted Biblical law by reference: "Be it enacted by the General Assembly, that marriages prohibited by the Levitical law shall be null; and persons marrying contrary to that prohibition, and cohabiting as man and wife, convicted thereof in the General Court, shall be amerced, from time to time, until they separate."[94] This bill was presented to the legislature by Madison on 31 October 1785, along with the preceding four bills.[95] According to Julian Boyd's editorial notes, Bill 86 passed the second reading in the legislature, but no final action was taken on it.[96]

The bill required couples that wished to live together as man and wife to obtain a marriage license and declare marriage vows in the presence of witnesses. Despite its reference to the Pentateuch, the bill significantly omitted any requirement that marriage ceremonies be performed under ecclesiastical authority. The exclusive authority of clergy in the established church to perform legally sanctioned marriages had been a source of bitter criticism in colonial and revolutionary Virginia from the rapidly growing nonconformist (and unlicensed) religious sects. In this sense, the bill may have further weakened the disintegrating monopoly formerly held by the officially established church.

The union of Biblical authority with the reformed legal code of Virginia is significant in the light of modern establishment clause jurisprudence. The judiciary, in recent years, has warned of the dangers of a close identification or "symbolic union" of the powers of civil government with religious institutions. The Supreme Court has counseled that if such an identification conveys a message of government endorsement or disapproval of religion, a core purpose of the nonestablishment provision has been violated.[97] The adoption of Biblical law by reference in the revised code represents at least a "symbolic union" of religion and the state that the Supreme Court today arguably would find unconstitutional.[98]

A New Perspective on Jefferson's Church-State Views

A perusal of the scholarship confirms that most historians of revolutionary Virginia and the First Amendment, as well as biographers of Jefferson, have neglected Jefferson's role in drafting Bills 83 to 86 of the revised code. They have, instead, focused on Bill 82 and the "wall of separation" Jefferson constructed in the Danbury letter. Similarly, although commentators have devoted considerable attention to Madison's legislative sponsorship of Bill 82, they have overlooked the fact that Madison, acting in concert with Jefferson, introduced in the Virginia legislature Jefferson's bills for punishing "disturbers of religious worship and Sabbath breakers" and for "appointing days of public fasting and thanksgiving."

One is struck by the lack of attention given Bills 83 to 86 by students of Jefferson and his times. Justice Rutledge's *Everson* opinion reveals that the Court knew the legislative history of the revised code and Jefferson's contribution to it as "chairman of the revising committee and chief draftsman."[99] Nonetheless, the Court declined to examine Bill 82 in its full legislative context. At least two general questions are raised by this pattern of omission. First, why have so many commentaries on Bill 82 examined the measure without reference to Bills 83 to 86? Second, are there unifying principles or themes of Jefferson's church-state views that offer a coherent framework for interpreting the five revised bills addressing religious concerns?

There is no dispute that Bill 82 is the preeminent of the five bills discussed in this chapter and deserves the attention it has received. Jefferson clearly considered the measure the most important of the proposals in the revised code.[100] Moreover, Jefferson counted the struggle for religious freedom in Virginia—which inspired Bill 82—among the severest contests of his public life.[101] These facts alone may account for the attention afforded Bill 82, to the near exclusion of the four succeeding measures.

Another, more uncomfortable, explanation concerns the inclination of modern commentators to revise the Jefferson image to serve contemporary political objectives or conform to modern ideals. As architect of the "wall of separation" and author of Bill 82, Jefferson "appears most congenial to modern eyes. It is here," an admiring biographer proclaimed, "that he takes his rightful position with the great liberating influences of all time."[102] This flattering perception of Jefferson may explain, in part, why many commentators have been unwilling to challenge the conventional view of Jefferson and Madison as libertarian champions of strict separation between church and state. Traditional portrayals of the two Virginians are inconsistent with their sponsorship of bills that imposed penalties on "disturbers of religious worship," "Sabbath breakers," and "ministers of the gospel" who failed to perform services on days appointed for fasting and thanksgiving. Accordingly, there is a tendency to disregard facts that conflict with, or at least complicate, modern idealizations of Jefferson.

Another explanation for the failure of virtually all biographers of Jefferson and students of church-state relations in revolutionary Virginia to recognize Jefferson's contributions to Bills 83 to 86 stems from an inordinate reliance on secondary sources. Most students of Jefferson have examined the religious freedom bill isolated from its legislative context or as interpreted by commentators. Few scholars, sadly, have returned to primary sources, such as the *Report of the Revisors*, to evaluate Bill 82 in its full legislative context. Extensive reliance on secondary source material has detached the religious freedom bill from the historical, political, and ideological milieu in which it was written and promulgated the misunderstandings of Jefferson's church-state views examined in this chapter.

A few historians have acknowledged that, taken together, the revised bills addressing religious concerns present a more relaxed model of church-state relations than that proposed by separationist proponents of the Jeffersonian "wall." Robert M. Healey, for example, argued that Bills 84 and 85 expose the myth that after Jefferson wrote the "Bill for Establishing Religious Freedom" he disavowed all wedding of church and state and espoused the "most rigid separation" between civil and ecclesiastical institutions.[103] Similarly, James Lafayette Gurley concluded that "Jefferson, as proved by his actions, did not hold to such a rigid view of complete separation of Church and State as some modern secularists have read into his famous 'wall of separation' metaphor."[104]

Many modern commentators, however, have disregarded Jefferson's complete work on the revised code, despite the fact that many studies afford considerable ink to Bill 82. For example, in his acclaimed book *The First Liberty: Religion and the American Republic* (1986), William Lee Miller devoted nearly seventy-five pages to a detailed examination of "A Bill for Establishing Religious

Freedom." Professor Miller wrote eloquently of the bill as the embodiment of truth, reason, and civilization. He acknowledged that the "same Assembly that passed Jefferson's religious liberty bill also passed a statute requiring the observance of Sunday as a day of rest" (Bill 84).[105] However, Miller reflected briefly on Bill 84, not to place Jefferson's church-state views in a context broader than that suggested by reference to Bill 82 alone, but to illustrate that despite passage of Jefferson's religious freedom bill in 1786, enlightened views on church-state separation did not yet prevail in the Virginia legislature. In other words, Bill 84 was the work of a reactionary remnant in the legislature. Professor Miller was apparently unaware that the bill punishing "Sabbath breakers" was *not* merely the product of reactionary forces, but emanated from Jefferson himself.

The most significant question raised by Bills 83 to 86 concerns their relation to Jefferson's overall vision for religious freedom and church-state relations. The bills reflect a church-state arrangement seemingly inconsistent with the strict separationist model frequently attributed to Jefferson. What are the unifying principles or themes of Jefferson's church-state views that may provide a coherent framework in which to interpret these revised bills?

As a preliminary consideration, one could argue that Bills 83 to 86 are merely aberrations in Jefferson's otherwise consistent devotion to the principle of complete independence of religion and civil government and do not reflect Jefferson's mature thinking on church-state relations as set forth in Bill 82 and the Danbury letter. Some commentators have suggested that Jefferson and Madison reluctantly sponsored accommodationist bills in the revisal they did not wholly endorse, perhaps to garner legislative backing for the separationist agenda they enthusiastically supported.[106] True, both Jefferson and Madison were consummate politicians skilled in the gentle art of compromise and coalition building, which often necessitated sacrificing stated positions to secure greater objectives, bolster coalitions, or advance future political objectives.[107] It is difficult to accept, however, that a principled Jefferson or Madison would have acceded to a statutory regime antithetical to the sweeping separation between church and state they purportedly embraced.[108] Political compromises on such vital issues concerning church-state arrangements in the Commonwealth would have been out of character for both Jefferson and Madison whose passionate devotion and adherence to principle on church-state matters were well known.[109]

There are recurring principles and themes in Jefferson's political thought that offer explanations for some apparent inconsistencies in his church-state policies. For example, a persistent theme of Jefferson's pronouncements on church-state relations is a commitment to the principle of federalism. Jefferson believed that while the First Amendment prohibited the federal government from making laws respecting an establishment of religion or abridging civil and religious liberties, the states reserved competent jurisdiction in such matters. Accordingly, although Jefferson thought government-sponsored activities and laws accommodating religion at the federal level (such as designating days for public fasting and thanksgiving) were unconstitutional, he saw no contradiction in permitting or even encouraging such practices at the state level.[110] Limited state cooperation with religious institutions, Jefferson believed, was acceptable if it advanced freedom of religious belief and expression. He also allowed the use of religious means to advance the legitimate secular goals of the civil state. Jefferson's church-state views have been frequently misunderstood by commentators who fail to comprehend that his "wall of separation" was less an instrument for a general separation of religious influences from all civil institutions than an affirmation of the principle of federalism.

The central pillar of Jefferson's church-state model and the unifying theme of Bills 82 to 86 is an unflagging devotion to freedom of religious belief and expression. Separation between church and state was not an end in itself; rather, it was a means toward achieving religious freedom. If free and uninhibited religious exercise was fostered through a limited interaction between church and state, Jefferson endorsed such a cooperative arrangement.

Jefferson's "wall" was intended to promote an environment in which freedom of religious belief and expression could flourish. His driving motivation was to place the rights of conscience beyond the control of magistrates and statist institutions. Jefferson believed republican government was improved by sentiments and habits nourished by religion; however, state churches inhibited the beneficent role of religion in society. Whenever the state enforced belief in doctrine, it burdened true religion, Jefferson thought. And whenever the church relied on civil government for financial support, it lost its purity and vitality. Thus, Jefferson believed that state churches, as a rule, corrupted civil government and religion, inhibited the emergence of truth by discouraging competition in the marketplace of ideas, and, as far as he could tell, brought no improvement in the morals of society. No concept, therefore, better communicated his personal idea of what was best for religion and best for society than the graphic "wall" metaphor. But the "wall" was only useful insofar as it advanced the end of religious freedom. If that end was best served by limited, strategic cooperation between church and state, Jefferson, it seems, was willing to breach the "wall of separation."

Conclusion

Jefferson has cast a long shadow across the nation's political landscape. Indeed, few figures have had a greater impact on American political thought.[111] The First Amendment pronouncements on church and state are, perhaps, the most innovative features of the American political experiment,[112] and few dispute they reflect Jefferson's genius. His "wall" metaphor is an enduring theme of modern church-state law, and the ideas expounded in the "Bill for Establishing Religious Freedom" have been woven into the fabric of American thought.

I do not suggest that the religious freedom bill inaccurately represents Jefferson's church-state views, nor do I argue that Bill 82 is undeserving of its honored reputation in American political thought. Rather, I argue that Jefferson's imprint on Bills 83 to 86 modifies conventional interpretations of Bill 82 and qualifies the strict separationist model the *Everson* opinions attributed to Jefferson. A distorted, historically inaccurate portrayal of the Jeffersonian model for church-state relations has been perpetuated by the near exclusive reliance on Bill 82 (detached from its legislative context) to illustrate Jefferson's church-state vision.

For two centuries, the Jefferson image has been shaped and reshaped to serve contemporary political objectives or to conform to modern ideals.[113] The record of church-state relations in revolutionary Virginia, given the Supreme Court's continuing reliance on this history to inform First Amendment doctrine, is similarly susceptible to manipulation by "law office historians" and ideologues with partisan goals.[114] The gloss, unfortunately, often obscures the true historical Jefferson and his contribution to church-state developments in the Commonwealth and the nation. The Supreme Court's failure to reference Bills 83 to 86, despite its extensive reliance on Bill 82, calls into question the legitimacy of its selective use of history to inform legal doctrine. "By superficial and purposive interpretations of the past," Mark DeWolfe Howe lamented, "the Court has dishonored the arts of the historian and degraded the talents of the lawyer."[115]

Jefferson's public declarations and private ruminations on church-state relations over the course of a long career are not entirely free of contradiction. Yet, a theme of devotion to freedom of conscience in religious belief emerges from Jefferson's public life. The "wall of separation" Jefferson espoused was not so much an end in itself as it was a *means* toward achieving the *end* of religious freedom, broadly defined. That is to say, nonestablishment or disestablishment was not an independent goal (something promoted for its own sake); it was a tool (or means) to advance the positive good (or end) of religious liberty. Too often students of Jefferson have viewed the "wall" in isolation, separated from the liberty it was intended to engender. Jefferson and Madison jointly sponsored five bills in Virginia's revised code that collectively demonstrate that neither man believed, in practice, in a high and impregnable wall of separation between religion and the civil government. These bills suggest that both men endeavored to protect and encourage public and private expressions of religious belief. True, they objected to the establishment of an official church and to state practices infringing on religious freedom, such as compelled tax support for teachers of an officially preferred religion. The "wall," however, was never meant to effect a complete and absolute separation between church and state prohibiting all religious influence in state-sponsored activities and laws.

Jefferson's chief aim was to foster freedom of religious expression, and if that objective was best served through statutory cooperation between church and state, he appeared willing to endorse it. To Jefferson, religious liberty meant that the civil authority must refrain from interfering with an individual's religion except to protect the individual in the enjoyment of the right to worship God, or not, according to the dictates of one's conscience.

Notes

Earlier versions of this chapter appeared in *American Journal of Legal History* 35 (1991): 172-204; and in *Religion, Public Life, and the American Polity*, ed. Luis E. Lugo (Knoxville: University of Tennessee Press, 1994). It is included here by permission of the *American Journal of Legal History* and University of Tennessee Press.

1. William Waller Hening, ed., *The Statutes at Large; Being a Collection of all the Laws of Virginia, From the First Session of the Legislature, in the Year 1619* (Richmond, Va.: J. & G. Cochran, 1823), 12:86 [hereinafter *Statutes at Large*]; *Virginia Code, Annotated* (repl. vol. 1986), § 57-1. Jefferson's bill is reprinted in *The Papers of Thomas Jefferson*, ed. Julian P. Boyd, 27 vols. to date (Princeton, N.J.: Princeton University Press, 1950-), 2:545-547 [hereinafter *Papers of Jefferson*].

2. See William B. Huntley, "Jefferson's Public and Private Religion," *South Atlantic Quarterly* 79 (1980): 299 (the "language of [Jefferson's bill] resembles that of the Declaration of Independence"); Willibald M. Plöchl, "Thomas Jefferson, Author of the Statute of Virginia for Religious Freedom," *Jurist* 3 (1943): 219 ("If the Declaration of Independence was a declaration against political tyranny, his Statute of Religious Freedom may be called the correlative Declaration against the suppression of free mind and conscience.").

3. Merrill D. Peterson, *Thomas Jefferson and the New Nation: A Biography* (New York: Oxford University Press, 1970), 134. See also Merrill D. Peterson, "Jefferson and Religious Freedom," *Atlantic Monthly* (December 1994): 113 ("the Virginia Statute for Religious Freedom . . . is, in fact, one of the main pillars of American democracy and a beacon of light and liberty to the world.").

4. Letter from James Madison to Thomas Jefferson, 22 January 1786, *The Papers of James Madison*, ed. Robert A. Rutland and William M. E. Rachal (Chicago: University of Chicago Press, 1973), 8:474 [hereinafter *Papers of Madison*].

5. William Lee Miller, *The First Liberty: Religion and the American Republic* (New York: Alfred A. Knopf, 1986), 18.

6. The general assessment proposal Henry supported, "A Bill Establishing a Provision for Teachers of the Christian Religion," is reprinted in Thomas E. Buckley, *Church and State in Revolutionary Virginia, 1776-1787* (Charlottesville: University Press of Virginia, 1977), 188-189.

7. *Journal of the House of Delegates of the Commonwealth of Virginia* (Richmond, Va.: Thomas W. White, 1828), 24 December 1784, 82 [hereinafter *JHD*].

8. William Henry Foote, *Sketches of Virginia, Historical and Biographical* (Philadelphia: William S. Martien, 1850), 1:431. Katherine L. Brown disputes Foote's account of the demise of Henry's bill in the autumn 1785 session of the legislature. Brown, "The Role of Presbyterian Dissent in Colonial and Revolutionary Virginia, 1740-1785" (Ph.D. diss., Johns Hopkins University, 1969), 392; Buckley, *Church and State in Revolutionary Virginia,* 158 n. 45 (same).

9. For a complete legislative history of the enactment of the religious freedom bill, see Hamilton James Eckenrode, *Separation of Church and State in Virginia: A Study in the Development of the Revolution* (Richmond, Va.: Davis Bottom, 1910), 113-115; Buckley, *Church and State in Revolutionary Virginia,* 155-165; Daniel L. Dreisbach, "Thomas

Jefferson and Bills Number 82-86 of the Revision of the Laws of Virginia, 1776-1786: New Light on the Jeffersonian Model of Church-State Relations," *North Carolina Law Review* 69 (1990): 163-170; Marvin K. Singleton, "Colonial Virginia as First Amendment Matrix: Henry, Madison, and Assessment Establishment," *Journal of Church and State* 8 (1966): 344-364.

10. Nathan Schachner, *Thomas Jefferson: A Biography* (New York: Thomas Yoseloff, 1951), 1:160. See also Edward Frank Humphrey, *Nationalism and Religion in America, 1774-1789* (Boston: Chipman Law Publishing Co., 1924), 404 (with passage of Jefferson's statute, "Virginia became the first government in the world to establish the absolute divorce of Church and State."); Editors' preface to *The Virginia Statute for Religious Freedom: Its Evolution and Consequences in American History*, ed. Merrill D. Peterson and Robert C. Vaughan (New York: Cambridge University Press, 1988), ix ("The Virginia Statute for Religious Freedom became the cornerstone of the unique American tradition of religious freedom and separation of church and state.") [hereinafter *Virginia Statute*].

11. Eckenrode, *Separation of Church and State in Virginia,* 116.

12. Merrill D. Peterson, for example, asserted that "[t]he principles of the [Virginia Statute for Religious Freedom] entered into the United States Constitution by way of the First Amendment. . . ." Editors' preface to *Virginia Statute,* ix. See also Humphrey, *Nationalism and Religion in America,* 406 (the principles of the religious freedom bill "were to be made a part also of the national Bill of Rights by the First Amendment to the Constitution"); A.E. Dick Howard, *Commentaries on the Constitution of Virginia*, 2 vols. (Charlottesville: University Press of Virginia, 1974), 1:293 ("The United States Supreme Court has taken the Virginia Bill [for Religious Freedom] and the First Amendment to be coextensive and has acknowledged the intended wall of separation implicit in both."); Singleton, "Colonial Virginia as First Amendment Matrix," 344-346 (noting that the U.S. Supreme Court has long maintained that the religion clauses have the same objective as Jefferson's bill).

13. See, for example, *Reynolds v. United States*, 98 U.S. 145, 162-164 (1878).

14. Book Note, *Harvard Law Review* 97 (1984): 1509.

15. *Everson v. Board of Education*, 330 U.S. 1, 33-34 (Rutledge, J., dissenting) (citations omitted).

16. 330 U.S. 1 (1947).

17. Paul G. Kauper, "*Everson v. Board of Education*: A Product of the Judicial Will," *Arizona Law Review* 15 (1973): 307. Arthur E. Sutherland similarly noted that *Everson* "has become the most influential single announcement of the American law of church and state." Sutherland, "Establishment According to *Engel,*" *Harvard Law Review* 76 (1962): 31.

18. *Everson,* 330 U.S. at 18.

19. A significant feature of the *Everson* opinions was the total lack of confrontation between the basic historical assumptions underlying the majority and minority opinions. Justice Black, for the Court, and Justices Jackson, Rutledge, Frankfurter, and Burton, in dissent, were unanimous in their description of the disestablishment movement in revolutionary Virginia and separationist interpretation of the establishment clause. See Daniel L. Dreisbach, "*Everson* and the Command of History: The Supreme Court, Lessons of History, and Church-State Debate in America," in *Everson Revisited: Religion, Education, and Law at the Crossroads*, ed. Jo Renée Formicola and Hubert Morken (Lanham, Md.: Rowman & Littlefield, 1997), 24-26.

20. *Everson*, 330 U.S. at 15.

21. *Id.* at 31-32 (Rutledge, J., dissenting).

22. Comment, "The Supreme Court, the First Amendment, and Religion in the Public Schools," *Columbia Law Review* 63 (1963): 79. See also Editors' preface to *Virginia Statute*, x ("The [Supreme Court] justices were much influenced in their understanding of the First Amendment by their understanding of the Virginia Statute for Religious Freedom and the circumstances that had produced it."); A. E. Dick Howard, "The Supreme Court and the Serpentine Wall," in *Virginia Statute*, 315 ("Tracing the events in Virginia that led to Madison's drafting of the 'Memorial and Remonstrance' and to the enactment of Jefferson's Bill for Establishing Religious Liberty, [Justice] Black concluded [in *Everson*] that the First Amendment was meant to provide 'the same protection against governmental intrusion on religious liberty as the Virginia statute.'") (quoting *Everson,* 330 U.S. at 13); Arlin M. Adams and Charles J. Emmerich, "A Heritage of Religious Liberty," *University of Pennsylvania Law Review* 137 (1989): 1572 n. 54 ("No other historical episode has influenced the Supreme Court's interpretation of the religion clauses more than the Virginia struggle. References to it abound in the Justices' opinions in religious liberty cases."); Gerard V. Bradley, "Imagining the Past and Remembering the Future: The Supreme Court's History of the Establishment Clause," *Connecticut Law Review* 18 (1986): 832 ("Justice Black essentially reduced the religion clauses to a federal codification of Thomas Jefferson's 'Bill for Establishing Religious Freedom,' the denouement of the 1784-85 Virginia controversy over public stipends for Protestant clergymen.").

23. For a list of state and federal judicial opinions that cite these documents, see Dreisbach, "Thomas Jefferson and Bills Number 82-86 of the Revision of the Laws of Virginia," 173-175 nn. 77-83. Justice Rutledge thought the "Remonstrance" was sufficiently important that he appended it to his *Everson* opinion. 330 U.S. at 63-72 (appendix to opinion of Rutledge, J., dissenting). See also *American Jewish Congress v. City of Chicago*, 827 F.2d 120, 136 (7th Cir. 1987) (Easterbrook, C.J., dissenting) (noting that the Supreme Court has relied on the "Memorial and Remonstrance" "too many times to count").

24. *Committee for Public Education and Religious Liberty v. Nyquist*, 413 U.S. 756 (1973).

25. *Id.* at 770-771 n. 28.

26. *Everson,* 330 U.S. at 13 ("This Court has previously recognized that the provisions of the First Amendment . . . had the same objective and were intended to provide the same protection against governmental intrusion on religious liberty as the Virginia statute [for religious liberty]."). See also *id.* at 39-40 (Rutledge, J., dissenting) (the great documents of the "Virginia struggle for religious liberty . . . became the warp and woof of our constitutional tradition" of church-state separation).

27. Leonard W. Levy, *The Establishment Clause: Religion and the First Amendment* (New York: Macmillan, 1986), 60.

28. Justice William Rehnquist similarly observed: "It is impossible to build sound constitutional doctrine upon a mistaken understanding of constitutional history." *Wallace v. Jaffree*, 472 U.S. 38, 92 (1985) (Rehnquist, J., dissenting).

29. Hening, *Statutes at Large* (1821), 9:175-177; *Papers of Jefferson* 1:562-563.

30. *JHD,* 5 November 1776, 41.

31. Thomas Jefferson, *Autobiography,* in *The Life and Selected Writings of Thomas Jefferson,* ed. Adrienne Koch and William Peden, The Modern Library (New York: Random House, 1944), 46 [hereinafter *Life and Selected Writings of Jefferson*].

32. *JHD,* 18 June 1779, 56-57. The revisors prepared 126 bills, the titles of which were included in an accompanying catalog. The revised code was printed in 1784 by order of the House of Delegates as a prelude to legislative action. See *Report of the Committee of Revisors Appointed by the General Assembly of Virginia in MDCCLXXVI* (Richmond: Dixon & Holt, 1784) [hereinafter *Report of the Revisors*]. The most complete legislative and documentary history of the revised code is found in *Papers of Jefferson,* 2:305-665. The editor, Julian P. Boyd, examined the legislative documents in laborious detail, attributing authorship of the revised bills to various members of the Committee of Revisors.

33. Dumas Malone, *Jefferson the Virginian* (Boston: Little, Brown & Co., 1948), 262. See also Noble E. Cunningham, Jr., *In Pursuit of Reason: The Life of Thomas Jefferson* (Baton Rouge: Louisiana State University Press, 1987), 54-55 (noting that Jefferson's papers indicate that legislative matters relating to religion concerned Jefferson greatly during this period).

34. It is a well-settled rule of the common law that in construing a statute capable of two or more plausible interpretations (so that the statute's meaning is doubtful), all acts *pari materia* (that is, all acts on the same subject matter) are to be taken together and to be construed so that all provisions may be harmonized (that is, avoid any contradiction or inconsistency), if possible. Theodore Sedgwick, *A Treatise on the Rules Which Govern the Interpretation and Construction of Statutory and Constitutional Law,* 2d ed. (New York: Baker, Voorhis and Co., 1874), 199-201, 209-212. See also Fortunatus Dwarris, *A General Treatise on Statutes: Their Rules of Construction, and the Proper Boundaries of Legislation and of Judicial Interpretation* (Albany, N.Y.: William Gould and Son, 1878), 144 ("Where there is a discrepancy or disagreement between two statutes, such interpretation should be given, that both may, if possible, stand together."), 145 ("All statutes in *pari materia* are to be read and construed together, as if they formed parts of the same statute, and were enacted at the same time."), 189 ("As one part of a statute is properly called in, to help the construction of another part, and is fitly so expounded, as to support and give effect, if possible, to the whole; so is the comparison of one law with other laws made by the same legislature, or upon the same subject, or relating expressly to the same point, enjoined for the same reason, and attended with a like advantage. . . . It is to be inferred, that a code of statutes relating to one subject, was governed by one spirit and policy, and was intended to be consistent and harmonious in its several parts and provisions. It is therefore an established rule of law, that all acts *in pari materie* [sic] are to be taken together, as if they were one law; and they are directed to be compared in the construction of statutes, because they are considered as framed upon one system, and having one object in view.").

35. Jefferson, *Autobiography*, 46 (emphasis added).

36. *Everson,* 330 U.S. at 18.

37. See Robert M. Healey, *Jefferson on Religion in Public Education* (New Haven, Conn.: Yale University Press, 1962), 140; Comment, "Jefferson and the Church-State Wall: A Historical Examination of the Man and the Metaphor," *Brigham Young University Law Review* 1978 (1978): 666-667.

38. *Report of the Revisors,* 58-59. The bill is reprinted in *Papers of Jefferson,* 2:545-547; Hening, *Statutes at Large,* 12:84-86.

39. Harvard historian Bernard Bailyn described the bill as "the most important document in American history, bar none." James H. Smylie, "Jefferson's Statute for Religious Freedom: The Hanover Presbytery Memorials, 1776-1786," *American Presbyterians Journal of Presbyterian History* 63 (1985): 355 (quoting Bailyn).

40. See Paul Leicester Ford, ed., *The Works of Thomas Jefferson*, Federal Edition, 12 vols. (New York: G. P. Putnam's Sons, 1905), 12:483. Jefferson also wished to be remembered as the author of the Declaration of American Independence and the father of the University of Virginia.

41. See *Bond v. Bond*, 144 W.Va. 478, 492, 109 S.E.2d 16, 23 (1959) ("[T]he Virginia Statute of Religious Freedom . . . is said to have formed a model for statutes and constitutional provisions throughout the land."). In a letter to Madison, written shortly after the bill was enacted, Jefferson proudly reported that

> The Virginia act for religious freedom has been received with infinite approbation in Europe, and propagated with enthusiasm. . . . It has been translated into French and Italian, has been sent to most of the courts of Europe, and has been the best evidence of the falsehood of those reports which stated us to be in anarchy. It is inserted in the new "Encyclopédie," and is appearing in most of the publications respecting America.

Letter from Thomas Jefferson to James Madison, 16 December 1786, *Life and Selected Writings of Jefferson,* 408-409.

42. C. Randolph Benson noted that Jefferson's church-state views "in the course of time became the official American position." Benson, *Thomas Jefferson as Social Scientist* (Rutherford, N.J.: Fairleigh Dickinson University Press, 1971), 190-191. See also Rhys Isaac, *The Transformation of Virginia, 1740-1790* (Chapel Hill: Institute of Early American History and Culture; University of North Carolina Press, 1982), 275 ("Since the 1780s, the principles proclaimed in the statute have become part of the idealized American way of life, and the passage of the bill through the legislature has been seen as a predestined triumph of progress.").

43. Schachner, *Thomas Jefferson,* 1:160.

44. Mark DeWolfe Howe, *The Garden and the Wilderness: Religion and Government in American Constitutional History* (Chicago: University of Chicago Press, 1965), 44.

45. For an examination of Locke's influence on Bill 82, see Sanford Kessler, "Locke's Influence on Jefferson's 'Bill for Establishing Religious Freedom,'" *Journal of Church and State* 25 (1983): 231-252; S. Gerald Sandler, "Lockean Ideas in Thomas Jefferson's Bill for Establishing Religious Freedom," *Journal of the History of Ideas* 21 (1960): 110-116.

46. Jefferson's words "that free it shall remain" were deleted from the preamble by Senate amendment on 16 January 1786.

47. Jefferson's words "and abhors" were deleted from the preamble by Senate amendment on 16 January 1786.

48. *Report of the Revisors,* 58; *Papers of Jefferson*, 2:545-546; Hening, *Statutes at Large*, 12:84-85.

49. *Report of the Revisors*, 58; *Papers of Jefferson*, 2:546; Hening, *Statutes at Large*, 12:86.

50. *Report of the Revisors*, 59; *Papers of Jefferson*, 2:546-547; Hening, *Statutes at Large*, 12:86.

51. Thomas E. Buckley, "The Political Theology of Thomas Jefferson," in *Virginia Statute,* 92. William Lee Miller similarly observed that "one can discover in this last paragraph the un-Jeffersonian desire, suppressed but real, to bind the future." Miller, *The First Liberty,* 63. See Peterson, "Jefferson and Religious Freedom," 122 (same).

52. See Benjamin Hart, *Faith & Freedom* (Dallas: Lewis and Stanley, 1988), 341-342 (Jefferson's "bill justifies itself on Protestant theological principles"); Buckley, "The

Political Theology of Thomas Jefferson," in *Virginia Statute*, 93 ("the statute is not neutral toward religion. . . . [It] presupposes a belief in God."); *American Jewish Congress v. City of Chicago,* 827 F.2d 120, 135 (7th Cir. 1987) (Easterbrook, C.J., dissenting) ("The preamble to the bill is itself an exercise in religious persuasion."); Steven D. Smith, "Separation and the 'Secular': Reconstructing the Disestablishment Decision," *Texas Law Review* 67 (1989): 968 (Jefferson's bill "rested on explicitly religious premises").

53. John Remington Graham argued that "[f]ar from ordaining a separation of church and state, the Virginia Statute of Religious Freedom proclaimed a cooperative friendship between the two: the existence of God who made the mind free was the statutory reason for governmental recognition of religious freedom." Graham, "A Restatement of the Intended Meaning of the Establishment Clause in Relation to Education and Religion," *Brigham Young University Law Review* 1981 (1981): 348.

54. Thomas E. Buckley contended that "[t]he God described here is not deistical, remote from human beings or unconcerned with their affairs. Rather, Jefferson posited a creator who is personally involved and expects an individual response expressed in sincere belief." Buckley, "The Political Theology of Thomas Jefferson," in *Virginia Statute*, 87.

55. *Report of the Revisors*, 58; *Papers of Jefferson*, 2:545; Hening, *Statutes at Large*, 12:84.

56. *American Jewish Congress v. City of Chicago*, 827 F.2d 120, 136 (7th Cir. 1987) (Easterbrook, C.J., dissenting). See also Smith, "Separation and the 'Secular,'" 969 n. 77 (arguing that under Justice O'Connor's "no endorsement" test Bill 82 "is presumably unconstitutional because of its religious references and overt reliance on religious premises."); Steven D. Smith, "The Rise and Fall of Religious Freedom in Constitutional Discourse," *University of Pennsylvania Law Review* 140 (1991): 193-196 (Jefferson's statute would be unconstitutional under current establishment clause doctrine because it sends a message endorsing religion and because the preamble expresses religious reasons for Virginia's adoption of the statute).

57. *Report of the Revisors*, 59. The bill is reprinted in *Papers of Jefferson*, 2:553-554.

58. For a legislative history and analysis of a 1779 version of the bill, see Daniel Durham Rhodes, "The Struggle for Religious Liberty in Virginia, 1740-1802" (Ph.D. diss., Duke University, 1951), 129-132. Rhodes attributed authorship of this bill to George Mason. See Robert A. Rutland, ed., *The Papers of George Mason,* 3 vols. (Chapel Hill: University of North Carolina Press, 1970), 2:590-592. Regardless of who actually drafted the bill, Jefferson clearly endorsed it.

59. Henry S. Randall, *The Life of Thomas Jefferson*, 3 vols. (New York: Derby and Jackson, 1857), 1:221. Randall implied that Bill 83 was the product of Jefferson's pen. *Ibid.*, 1:219-221. The editor of the Jefferson papers attributed authorship of the bill to Jefferson. *Papers of Jefferson*, 2:320.

60. Randall, *Life of Jefferson,* 1:221 (emphasis in original).

61. See "An act for exempting the different societies of Dissenters from contributing to the support and maintenance of the church as by law established, and its ministers, and for other purposes therein mentioned." Hening, *Statutes at Large*, 9:164-167.

62. *Everson*, 330 U.S. at 15.

63. *Report of the Revisors*, 59. The bill is reprinted in *Papers of Jefferson*, 2:555; Hening, *Statutes at Large*, 12:336-337.

64. The amendments are set forth in *Papers of Jefferson*, 2:556 nn. 1-5.

65. *Papers of Jefferson*, 2:318-320.

66. The Virginia code still contains a provision that exempts "[m]inisters of the gospel" from arrest "while engaged in performing religious services . . . and while going to and returning from such" services. *Virginia Code, Annotated* (1984), § 8.01-327.2.

67. *Report of the Revisors*, 59; *Papers of Jefferson*, 2:555; Hening, *Statutes at Large*, 12:337. This language from Bill 84 remained the law in Virginia without substantial amendment until 1960. See generally *Mandell v. Haddon*, 202 Va. 979, 121 S.E.2d 516 (1961) (legislative history of Sunday labor laws in Virginia). It is noteworthy that when the Virginia legislature enacted Bill 84 it apparently changed the fifth word of this paragraph from "Sunday" to "sabbath day." Hening, *Statutes at Large*, 12:337. Julian Boyd, editor of the *Papers of Jefferson*, did not note this change.

68. Healey, *Jefferson on Religion in Public Education*, 140.

69. *Report of the Revisors*, 59; *Papers of Jefferson*, 2:555; Hening, *Statutes at Large*, 12:336-337.

70. Genesis 2:2-3.

71. Exodus 20:8-11; Exodus 31:12-18.

72. Cf. *McGowan v. Maryland*, 366 U.S. 420 (1961) (Supreme Court upheld state Sunday closing law because the statute's present purpose and effect were not to aid religion by facilitating church attendance but to set aside a day for recreation and rest from secular employment).

73. Robert L. Cord, *Separation of Church and State: Historical Fact and Current Fiction* (New York: Lambeth Press, 1982), 219.

74. See William Gangi, review of *Separation of Church and State*, by Robert L. Cord, in *Harvard Journal of Law & Public Policy* 7 (1984): 600; Leo Pfeffer, *Church, State, and Freedom*, rev. ed. (Boston: Beacon Press, 1967), 278-279. One could argue that the word "Sabbath" was deliberately selected as an inclusive term that would enable various religious sects to observe the Sabbath on any day of the week designated by the sect. There is little, if any, historical evidence to support this interpretation.

75. See James Lafayette Gurley, "Thomas Jefferson's Philosophy and Theology: As Related to His Political Principles, Including Separation of Church and State" (Ph.D. diss., University of Michigan, 1975), 234.

76. *Report of the Revisors*, 59-60. The bill is reprinted in *Papers of Jefferson*, 2:556.

77. Julian P. Boyd, editor of the *Papers of Jefferson*, did not explicitly attribute authorship of this bill to Jefferson. He did not, however, reject the possibility that Jefferson drafted Bill 85. Boyd noted that Jefferson apparently endorsed Bill 85. *Papers of Jefferson*, 2:556. Other scholars have described Jefferson as the author of this bill. See, for example, Cord, *Separation of Church and State*, 220-221; Healey, *Jefferson on Religion in Public Education*, 135; Donald L. Drakeman, "Religion and the Republic: James Madison and the First Amendment," *Journal of Church and State* 25 (1983): 441; Comment, "Jefferson and the Church-State Wall," 657, 666.

78. *Report of the Revisors*, 60; *Papers of Jefferson*, 2:556.

79. *Papers of Jefferson*, 2:556.

80. Indeed, the punitive provisions of Bill 85 are difficult to reconcile with that portion of Bill 82 declaring "that no man shall be compelled to frequent or support any religious worship, place, or ministry whatsoever." *Report of the Revisors*, 58; *Papers of Jefferson*, 2:546; Hening, *Statutes at Large*, 12:86. One speculates that Jefferson simply assumed that all clergymen would welcome religious day proclamations and holding services on days so appointed. Thus, Jefferson may have been blind to the potentially coercive feature

of the bill for some ministers. It is similarly difficult to reconcile this bill with Justice Black's interpretation of the religion clauses in *Everson:* "The 'establishment of religion' clause of the First Amendment means at least this: Neither a state nor the Federal Government . . . can force nor influence a person to go to or to remain away from church against his will. . . . No person can be punished . . . for church attendance or non-attendance." *Everson,* 330 U.S. at 15-16. See also *Zorach v. Clauson,* 343 U.S. 306, 314 (1952) ("government . . . may not coerce anyone to attend church, to observe a religious holiday, or to take religious instruction.").

81. Letter from Thomas Jefferson to Messrs. Nehemiah Dodge, Ephraim Robbins, and Stephen S. Nelson, A Committee of the Danbury Baptist Association in the State of Connecticut, 1 January 1802, reprinted in Dreisbach, "'Sowing Useful Truths and Principles': The Danbury Baptists, Thomas Jefferson, and the 'Wall of Separation,'" *Journal of Church and State* 39 (1997): 468-469.

82. *Everson,* 330 U.S. at 16 ("In the words of Jefferson, the clause against establishment of religion by law was intended to erect 'a wall of separation between church and State.'").

83. Justice Rutledge, in dissent, offered a legislative history of the revised code. He acknowledged the contributions of Jefferson in drafting and Madison in sponsoring the revised code. *Everson,* 330 U.S. at 35 n.15 (Rutledge, J., dissenting). Thus, the *Everson* Court knew the legislative history of Bill 82 and should have known of companion Bills 83 to 86.

84. Many separationist commentators contend that throughout their public careers Jefferson and Madison were consistent advocates of absolute church-state separation. See, for example, Pfeffer, *Church, State, and Freedom,* 105 ("Throughout his adult life Jefferson never swerved from his devotion to the principle of complete independence of religion and government."); Leonard W. Levy, *Jefferson and Civil Liberties: The Darker Side* (Cambridge, Mass.: Harvard University Press, Belknap Press, 1963), 21 ("Jefferson's record on religious liberty was really quite exceptional—an almost consistent demonstration of devotion to principle."); *Everson,* 330 U.S. at 41 (Rutledge, J., dissenting) ("Madison and his coworkers made no exceptions or abridgments to the complete separation they created."); R. Freeman Butts, *The American Tradition in Religion and Education* (Boston: Beacon Press, 1950), 49 (Madison "never swerved from that principle [of separation of church and state], and it was paramount in his mind when he took part in framing the First Amendment."); Ralph Ketcham, *James Madison: A Biography* (New York: Macmillan, 1971), 165 ("In fact, religious liberty stands out as the one subject upon which Madison took an extreme, absolute, undeviating position throughout his life."); Lance Banning, "James Madison, the Statute for Religious Freedom, and the Crisis of Republican Convictions," in *Virginia Statute,* 113 (Madison "seems from that point forward [June 1776], with unwavering consistency, to have envisioned total freedom of opinion, absolute equality for various denominations, and an end to the prevailing intermixture of the logically distinctive spheres of politics and religion."); Irving Brant, "Madison: On the Separation of Church and State," *William and Mary Quarterly,* 3d ser., 8 (1951): 24 ("Whatever inconsistencies there may be in Madison's position on other public questions, none can be found in his record upon freedom of religion.").

85. *Papers of Jefferson,* 1:105-107.

86. Jefferson, *Autobiography,* 8-9.

87. Martin E. Marty observed that this resolution "is hardly a noble charter, but it does show that Jefferson did, on occasion, allow for acts that clearly contradicted the [religious freedom] bill of 1779 and the statute of 1786." Marty, "The Virginia Statute Two Hundred Years Later," in *Virginia Statute*, 9.

88. "Proclamation Appointing a Day of Thanksgiving and Prayer," 11 November 1779, *Papers of Jefferson,* 3:177-179.

89. See Cord, *Separation of Church and State*, 115 ("By this phrase Jefferson could only have meant that the 'wall of separation' was erected 'between church and State' in regard to possible federal action. . . . Therefore, to leave the impression that Jefferson's 'separation' statement was a universal one concerning the whole of the federal and state political system is extremely misleading."); M. Stanton Evans, *The Theme Is Freedom: Religion, Politics, and the American Tradition* (Washington, D.C.: Regnery Publishing Inc., 1994), 288 ("The wall of separation, instead, was *between the federal government and the states,* [and was] meant to make sure the central authority didn't meddle with the customs of local jurisdictions."); James M. O'Neill, *Religion and Education under the Constitution* (New York: Harper and Brothers, 1949), 67-69, 79-83 (arguing that Jefferson's "wall" separated the federal government and one religion); Joseph M. Snee, "Religious Disestablishment and the Fourteenth Amendment," *Washington University Law Quarterly* 1954 (1954): 389 (arguing that Jefferson's "wall" affirmed the principle of federalism); Comment, "Jefferson and the Church-State Wall," 645, 656-659 (arguing that Jefferson's "wall" was a study in federalism, and the "wall" described in the Danbury letter was erected only against the federal government).

90. Jefferson, Second Inaugural Address, 4 March 1805, in *Life and Selected Writings of Jefferson,* 341. See Anson Phelps Stokes, *Church and State in the United States*, 3 vols. (New York: Harper and Brothers, 1950), 1:335 (stating that in this passage of the address Jefferson "doubtless had in mind particularly his well-known objection to presidential Thanksgiving Day proclamations").

91. Letter from Thomas Jefferson to the Reverend Samuel Miller, 23 January 1808, *The Writings of Thomas Jefferson,* ed. Andrew A. Lipscomb and Albert Ellery Bergh, library edition, 20 vols. (Washington, D.C.: Thomas Jefferson Memorial Association, 1904-1905), 11:428-430.

92. Arthur Gilbert argued that Bills 84 and 85 are evidence that "both Madison and Jefferson lent their weight to legislation that provided state sanction for religious morality in general." Gilbert, "Religious Freedom and Social Change in a Pluralistic Society: A Historical Review," in *Religion and the Public Order*, ed. Donald A. Giannella (Chicago: University of Chicago Press, 1964), 101-102.

93. *Report of the Revisors*, 60. The bill is reprinted in *Papers of Jefferson*, 2:556-558.

94. *Report of the Revisors*, 60; *Papers of Jefferson*, 2:556-557.

95. There is less evidence establishing Jefferson's direct authorship of Bill 86 than of the preceding four bills in the revised code. It is clear, however, that Jefferson authorized and endorsed the proposal given the dominant role he played in revising the laws of Virginia.

96. *Papers of Jefferson*, 2:558.

97. *Grand Rapids School District v. Ball*, 473 U.S. 373, 389-390 (1985).

98. For more on the Supreme Court's "symbolic union" analysis, see Theodore C. Hirt, "'Symbolic Union' of Church and State and the 'Endorsement' of Sectarian Activity: A Critique of Unwieldy Tools of Establishment Clause Jurisprudence," *Wake Forest Law*

Review 24 (1989): 823; Note, "Symbolic Union and the Establishment Clause," *Missouri Law Review* 53 (1989): 139.

99. *Everson*, 330 U.S. at 35 n. 15 (Rutledge, J., dissenting).

100. Of the many revised bills Jefferson drafted he considered his religious freedom bill the most important. When he penned his own epitaph, he noted his authorship of only this bill from the revised code among the achievements for which he wished to be remembered. Ford, ed., *The Works of Thomas Jefferson*, 12:483.

101. In his *Autobiography,* Jefferson recalled that the struggle to defend religious liberty in his native Commonwealth was the severest contest of his political career. Jefferson, *Autobiography,* 41.

102. Schachner, *Thomas Jefferson*, 1:154. Lance Banning offered a similar observation of Madison: "As Madison went on, instead, to even larger deeds, his magnificent 'Memorial' assumed a rightful place beside his friend's great statute [for religious freedom] among the documentary foundations of the libertarian tradition." Banning, "James Madison, the Statute for Religious Freedom, and the Crisis of Republican Convictions," in *Virginia Statute*, 130. See also Peterson, "Jefferson and Religious Freedom," 113 ("the Virginia Statute for Religious Freedom . . . is . . . a beacon of light and liberty to the world.").

103. Healey, *Jefferson on Religion in Public Education,* 135.

104. Gurley, "Thomas Jefferson's Philosophy and Theology," 234-235.

105. Miller, *The First Liberty*, 49.

106. See, for example, Thomas J. Curry, *The First Freedoms: Church and State in America to the Passage of the First Amendment* (New York: Oxford University Press, 1986), 148 ("In the same sheaf of bills that contained the statute on religious freedom, Madison included [Bill 85]. . . . [T]here can be little doubt that Madison personally disapproved of it; but the fact that he included it in the collection was significant. Such incidents proceeded from the habits of mind and unchallenged assumptions about society of a people overwhelmingly Protestant Christian."); Robert Boston, *Why the Religious Right is Wrong About Separation of Church and State* (Buffalo: Prometheus Books, 1993), 69-70 ("The history surrounding this bill [Bill 84] is fuzzy at best, and it's quite possible Madison sponsored it for political reasons. . . . Or Madison might simply have wanted to give the government some mechanism for punishing those who disrupted church services (a problem in some colonies). Madison may also have introduced it as part of a package of legislation providing a penal code for Virginia in the wake of the Revolution, intending to update it and remove the antiquated portions later. . . . Lastly, the bill could have been a youthful mistake taken before Madison's thinking on religious freedom jelled. Whatever the case, this incident is a minor blotch on Madison's otherwise impeccable credentials as a separationist."); Robert D. McAninch, "James Madison on Church and State Relations" (M.A. thesis, West Virginia University, 1970), 53, 56 ("Madison did indeed introduce [Bill 84] into the Assembly, but it was buried in a package of one-hundred and seventeen other bills. . . . There is little evidence to demonstrate that Madison was in agreement with the substance of bill number 84, as it was simply part of the revised code. . . . Madison may have chosen to remain silent on bill number 84 so as to not weaken the tide of opposition that he had produced against the General Assessment."); Robert Alley, "The Madison and Jefferson Blues," *Liberty* (January / February 1995): 18-19 (Madison and Jefferson sponsored bills they disliked as part of a political compromise to accomplish a greater good; the political climate in Virginia prohibited Jefferson and Madison from enacting the radical separationist measures they desired).

107. For a discussion on explanations for apparent inconsistencies in Jefferson's and Madison's church-state views, see Daniel L. Dreisbach, *Real Threat and Mere Shadow: Religious Liberty and the First Amendment* (Westchester, Ill.: Crossway Books, 1987), 107-111.

108. But cf. *Everson*, 330 U.S. at 41 (Rutledge, J., dissenting) ("Madison and his coworkers made no exceptions or abridgments to the complete separation they created.").

109. In their declining years, upon mature reflection, both Jefferson and Madison acknowledged that on occasion in the heat of political battle they made critical compromises on church-state matters. See, for example, Jefferson, *Autobiography,* 8-9 (Jefferson recounted that in May 1774, as a member of the House of Burgesses, he participated in drafting and enacting a "cooked up" resolution designating a "Day of Fasting, Humiliation, and Prayer" in order to excite public opposition to England); Dreisbach, *Real Threat and Mere Shadow,* 188-189, 152-153 (despite reservations about issuing religious day proclamations, Madison acknowledged in his "Detached Memoranda" that during the 1812 war with England he succumbed to congressional pressure to designate a day of public humiliation and prayer). Significantly, neither Jefferson nor Madison gave any indication that their authorship and sponsorship, respectively, of Bills 83 to 86 were motivated, in whole or in part, by political considerations rather than principle. Moreover, the legislative compromises some commentators allege were made by Jefferson and Madison are antithetical to the underlying separationist position the two Virginians purportedly embraced. It is implausible that if Jefferson and Madison were ardent separationists they would have acceded to such accommodationist compromises. Arguably, the inconsistencies in Bills 82 to 86 only emerge when the measures are viewed from a secular, strict separationist perspective.

110. See Gurley, "Thomas Jefferson's Philosophy and Theology," 227 (arguing that Jefferson "declared that the example of state executives in making religious pronouncements had influenced the presidents; however, he believed that what might be right for a state government would be wrong for the national government"); Adams and Emmerich, "A Heritage of Religious Liberty," 1586, 1607 (arguing that Jefferson's disparate actions on the state and federal levels can, perhaps, be reconciled by reference to the principle of federalism since Jefferson believed state governments, not the federal government, exercised a degree of civil authority in religious matters).

111. See George F. Will, "Person of the Millennium," *Washington Post*, 16 December 1990, K7; Ken Burns, "Man of the Millennium: What Thomas Jefferson Means Today," *USA Weekend,* 16 February 1997, 4.

112. See Cord, *Separation of Church and State*, xiii ("Separation of Church and State is probably the most distinctive concept that the American constitutional system has contributed to the body of political ideas."); Leo Pfeffer, "Freedom and Separation: America's Contribution to Civilization," *Journal of Church and State* 2 (1960): 100 (religion clauses are America's greatest contribution to civilization).

113. For an excellent study of the Jefferson image in American intellectual thought, see Merrill D. Peterson, *The Jefferson Image in the American Mind* (New York: Oxford University Press, 1960).

114. The "law office historian," imbued with the adversary ethic, selectively recounts facts, emphasizing data that supports the recorder's own prepossessions and minimizing significant facts that complicate or conflict with that bias.

115. Howe, *The Garden and the Wilderness,* 4.

Chapter 10

James Madison and the First Amendment Establishment of Religion Clause

Donald L. Drakeman

About one hundred federal and state court decisions have highlighted James Madison's influential role in crafting the sixteen words of the religion clauses of the First Amendment to the Constitution: "Congress shall make no law respecting an establishment of religion, or prohibiting the free exercise thereof." Struggling to come to terms with highly controversial twentieth-century issues of public policy and constitutional interpretation, many judges, including Supreme Court justices, have turned to our fourth president for guidance. Why? What relevance are Madison's two-century-old activities and writings for courts contemplating such modern phenomena as whether or not a state may pay for the cost of busing students to religious schools, especially when the constitutional era knew neither public schools nor buses?

Madison becomes involved because judges are not supposed to make up the law, or fashion public policy out of whole cloth; theoretically, that is the legislative branch's task. Rather, members of the judiciary are charged with (or, perhaps more accurately, have claimed, since early in the Republic,[1] responsibility for) interpreting the language of the Constitution in particular cases, thus putting themselves in the position of deciding what that great document says about buses and parochial schools. The Constitution, of course, says nothing at all about school buses, and that creates the problem for the judges. Some in an earlier era might have argued that the mere fact of constitutional silence should settle the issue; it is none of the courts' business, and obviously not a constitutional question, there being no "school bus" clause or "parochial school" proviso in the Bill of Rights. In the late twentieth century, however, the courts, especially the United States Supreme Court, have gone out of their way to look for constitutional issues, asserting federal jurisdiction over many aspects of the health, education, and welfare of United States citizens. Meanwhile, clever lawyers have convinced the judiciary that the word "Congress" in the First Amendment might really mean just about any form of government—federal, state, and local—and that use of state tax dollars for the cost of gas, tire changes, labor, and equipment involved in taking some children to religious schools could be a "law respecting an establishment of religion."

Having gone this far, the court is stuck. It would be hard pressed to say that the clear language of the establishment clause of the First Amendment commands a particular result on the bus issue; the language is anything but clear, as decades of litigation have amply demonstrated. Yet once the court has chosen to hear the case on the grounds that a constitutional issue is present, it must make some decision. Moreover, the court must also provide a supporting rationale that appears to be based on an interpretation of the Constitution rather than just saying "We are nine smart people who think this is a good decision." James Madison then is called to the rescue. In the school bus case, *Everson v. Board of Education* (1947),[2] the entire Supreme Court sought refuge in Madison and his efforts, with fellow Virginian Thomas Jefferson, to establish religious freedom in Virginia. Doing so gave the justices access to a trove of pre-constitutional documents and activities, including Jefferson's "Statute for Establishing Religious Freedom" and Madison's "Memorial and Remonstrance Against Religious Assessments," a petition written and circulated in 1785 to oppose a Virginia tax in support of "Teachers of the Christian Religion." Madison's petition appears to deal with something that sounds educational, but, unfortunately, does not touch on school buses.

Why choose James Madison rather than the great orator Patrick Henry or first president George Washington, both of whom appeared to support Virginia's bill to levy tax money for religious teachers? The reason is simple according to the Supreme Court justices—Madison endowed the First Amendment with Virginia's disestablishmentarian history by virtue of his personal role in the adoption of the establishment clause. In the words of Justice Wiley Rutledge, who wrote an often-cited dissenting opinion, "All the great instruments of the Virginia struggle for religious liberty. . . became warp and woof of our constitutional tradition, not simply by the course of history, but by the common unifying force of Madison's life, thought and sponsorship."[3] Madison thus is not just any founding father, but the one who brought the First Amendment to life, a fact the justices use to claim that his words and deeds have special authority. What better way to determine the intentions of the framers than to look to the "Father of the Constitution" and the author of the First Amendment? Madison's appeal in church-state cases is so strong that he has been consistently invoked from the Supreme Court's first serious encounter with the First Amendment religion clauses in *Reynolds v. United States* (1878), involving the prosecution of a Mormon for bigamy, to the recent *Rosenberger v. University of Virginia* (1995) case in which Justices David Souter and Clarence Thomas sparred over conflicting interpretations of Madison in deciding whether or not a public university could deny funding to a student-run Christian newspaper.[4]

The Supreme Court's reliance on Madison rests on a few critical issues of fact over which lawyers and historians have argued. For example, was the Supreme Court correct when it attributed authorship of the First Amendment to Madison? The historical record strongly suggests that the answer is no. Whether Madison did or did not write the establishment clause, is it reasonable to assume that the first Congress intended to erect a "wall of separation," in Jefferson's words, between religion and all governments? Again, the answer is no. Is there any manifest intent behind the First Amendment establishment clause that speaks definitively on modern church-state issues? Probably not. Can we, nevertheless, find a way to shed light on modern constitutional concerns by reflecting on Madison's roles in Virginia's disestablishment efforts and in handling church-state matters as president? Perhaps.

First Amendment Authorship

There has been relatively little controversy concerning Madison's authorship and sponsorship of the establishment clause, which is unfortunate because he neither wrote nor sponsored it. The legislative debate is remarkably short, breathtakingly so for the long-winded commentary it has spawned. If the existing records are assumed to be accurate (and they probably are not—Madison griped about the "mutilation and perversion" of the accounts by a newspaper reporter often described as drunken),[5] the entire debate in the House was remarkably brief and featured only a handful of the fifty-one members of Congress voting on the proposal. Nor is it particularly illuminating. As Leonard W. Levy has written, the "debate was sometimes irrelevant, usually apathetic and unclear. Ambiguity, brevity, and imprecision in thought and expression characterize the comments of the few members who spoke."[6]

Madison did, indeed, introduce into the first Congress a list of proposed amendments to the Constitution that were eventually shaped into a bill of rights, a document he had originally thought superfluous in light of the limited powers of the new federal government. Nevertheless, he had been convinced to make the proposals because some state ratifying conventions had requested or required the explicit protection of individual liberties. And so, on 8 June 1789, he proposed the following language:

> The civil rights of none shall be abridged on account of religious belief or worship, nor shall any national religion be established, nor shall the full and equal rights of conscience be in any manner, or on any pretext, infringed . . . . No State shall violate the equal rights of conscience.[7]

The non-establishment proposal submitted by Madison was almost identical to one debated but voted down at the Maryland convention ("there [shall] be no national religion established by law") and was quite different from the one first approved in Virginia, where Madison was involved in drafting proposed amendments, and later in North Carolina ("no particular religious sect or society ought to be favored or established, by law, in preference to others").[8]

Debate on these topics opened two months later on 15 August 1789, and somehow the word "national"—a politically charged term in the nascent republic—had been dropped. The comments from the members of Congress seem almost desultory. There was some discussion as to whether the provision was even worth having, giving Madison the chance to say exactly what the proposal meant to him. It did not seem to be particularly important. The records report, "[w]hether the words are necessary or not, he did not mean to say, but they had been required by some of the State Conventions." He took the words to mean that "Congress should not establish a religion, and enforce the legal observation of it by law, nor compel men to worship God in any manner contrary to their conscience."[9] Madison's focus thus seemed to be on prohibiting the federal Congress from establishing one or more religions, but neither he nor his colleagues shed any light on what they thought an establishment of religion was.

Samuel Livermore of New Hampshire noted that he was not satisfied with Madison's approach, but he thought that the first Congress had better things to do than debate a bill of rights, and "he did not wish them to dwell long on the subject." Nevertheless, he put forth the language his state's ratifying convention had proposed: "Congress shall make no laws touching religion, or infringing the rights of conscience."[10] Madison promptly withdrew his amendment, and Congress passed Livermore's by a vote of thirty-one to twenty. Sadly, for those interested in divining congressional intent, there is no record of the yeas and nays.

It is not clear whether Madison thought Livermore's formulation achieved essentially the same goals as his version, but he certainly raised no objection to the New Hampshire language. There may be a couple of potentially significant differences in wording, however. The Madison version under debate read "no religion shall be established by law" which might, under an especially broad reading, proscribe establishments at the state level, a result that would have been extremely unpopular in New Hampshire and Massachusetts which had well entrenched "standing orders," that is, state-supported religious establishments.[11] Madison seemed sensitive to this concern and offered to put "national" before "religion," which would emphasize the fact that the provision would not affect the states.[12] But Livermore's proposal more clearly stated that "Congress" would be barred from making laws "touching religion," thus appearing to take any possible jurisdiction on the subject of religion away from the federal legislature. Such a careful approach makes particular sense coming from Livermore since many at the Granite State's ratifying convention had been anxious to diminish the power of the new federal government but were also firmly in support of links between religion and the state. Many delegates had been agitated over the fact that the Constitution provided no religious test for federal office, risking the loss to the new government of the salutary effect of religion on morality. A fair reading of Livermore's proposal, especially in the light of its origins in New Hampshire, seems to be that Congress could act neither to support religion nor to eliminate existing links between state governments and religion. The country would be free from a national religious establishment while the states could do whatever they wanted on the subject of religion.

A couple of weeks later, on 20 August, the House returned to the establishment clause. Fisher Ames of Massachusetts proposed, and Congress agreed, that the clause be revised to read, "Congress shall make no law establishing religion." There is no record of any debate, and the Ames version passed, apparently without comment.[13] It is not clear why Ames proposed this change, although it is worth noting that the Commonwealth of Massachusetts maintained its establishment of religion until well into the nineteenth century. Thus, Ames was probably not motivated by an aversion to religious establishments in general, but sought language to prevent the Congress from creating a new federal establishment.

The Senate considered the House's proposed establishment clause in early September. The record is thin, and it appears that the following revised version was ultimately approved after the Senate considered alternate proposals resembling those suggested by the ratifying conventions in Virginia, North Carolina, and New York: "Congress shall make no law establishing articles of faith, or a mode of worship."[14] A House-Senate conference committee then met to resolve the differences, and one of the committee members was James Madison. The committee concurred on a final version of the establishment clause that resembled the House version drafted by Ames: "Congress shall make no law respecting an establishment of Religion."[15] The "respecting" language was new and its origin is unknown. The proposal that appears to most closely resemble the "respecting an establishment" language was Livermore's suggestion (which was previously passed by the House) that there be no law "touching" religion; in both cases, the wording appeared to carve out a subject matter—"religion" or "an establishment of religion"—that would be beyond the reach of Congress.

If there are any "fathers" of the establishment clause, they are Ames and Livermore as much as Madison, and the impetus for its final form was drawn as much from the pro-establishment New England states these men represented, as from Madison's disestablishmentarian Virginia. What does that tell us when it comes to twentieth-century issues of constitutional interpretation? Not much, really. The record of the first Congress (sparse as it may be) shows one thing clearly—that the Founding Fathers were not especially concerned about the establishment clause, pro or con. It generated little debate and none of it was spirited. Madison made a proposal to bar a "national establishment," which he was not sure was necessary, and he quickly withdrew it in favor of the New Hampshire language from Livermore, who said that he "did not wish to dwell long on the subject." The final version sounded most like Ames' language that was not the subject of any debate, and it is probably impossible to divine the intention of any of these "authors" of the establishment clause. It was obviously not an important issue. There was no credible movement espousing a federally established church, thus there was nothing for Congress to worry about. Judging by the role of New Englanders in this limited debate, we may see it as including an effort to protect state establishments from federal interference, hence Livermore's "touching religion" language or the final version prohibiting laws "respecting" an establishment of religion.

This analysis suggests that Supreme Court Justice Wiley Rutledge may have misread the history when he concluded that the "Virginia struggle for religious liberty thus became warp and woof of our constitutional tradition" as a result of the "common unifying force of Madison's life, thoughts and sponsorship."[16] Under Rutledge's approach, which seems to be that the establishment clause somehow codified the beliefs of its author, it would seem to be equally appropriate to read into the First Amendment the long-standing and close bonds between church and state fostered by the governments of Massachusetts and New Hampshire until decades after the first Congress adopted the bill of rights. It seems more appropriate, however, to see the establishment clause as the product of a natural coalition of those who disliked any religious establishment, such as Madison, and the possibly more numerous legislators who thought that the relationship of church and state was none of the *federal* government's business, with the discussions taking place in an environment in which no one was especially concerned about federal establishment issues at all. Even Madison, perhaps the most ardent foe of religious establishments to sit in the first Congress, did not propose to use the Constitution to disestablish state churches, although he and Livermore concurred on an amendment that would have made the "equal rights of conscience" clause applicable to the states, a proposal adopted by the House but voted down by the Senate.

Ultimately, the First Amendment's establishment clause served not to define what an establishment of religion was, but rather *who* should make governmental decisions about the relationship between church and state—and the answer was that the states would play that role. Evidence that James Madison concurred in this "jurisdictional" reading of the establishment clause is found in his comments on Thomas Jefferson's second inaugural speech. In reviewing a draft of the speech, Madison recommended the following language, which later became, with modest revisions, the president's final text: "religious exercises, could therefore be neither controuled nor prescribed by us. They have . . . been left as the Constitution found them, under the direction and discipline acknowledged within the several States."[17] If there was an important issue addressed in the adoption of the establishment clause, it was not how to separate church and state; rather, it was how decision-making on such issues should be apportioned between the states and the new federal government.

So how do we apply the wisdom of the founders to modern church-state cases? That would be a difficult question even if we limited it to exclusively federal issues such as military and congressional chaplains, national days of prayer, and the like. To further complicate matters, the Supreme Court has decided that the post-Civil War Fourteenth Amendment's "due process" clause caused the Bill of Rights to apply to state governments as well as the federal government, and has held that the word "Congress" in the establishment clause applies to state and local governments as well as the federal legislature.[18] Doing so seems to stand the establishment clause on its head. A provision apparently designed to ensure that local issues would be resolved locally is now being used to arbitrate at the federal level virtually all church-state questions.

During the Revolutionary era, Virginia had begun to sever ties with a state-sponsored Anglican church that had links to England, thanks to the efforts of

Madison, Jefferson, and others; at the same time, Samuel Livermore's New Hampshire and Fisher Ames' Massachusetts had well entrenched state churches strongly supportive of the patriot cause. In all cases, these practices were left, in Jefferson's (really Madison's) words, "as the Constitution found them," subject to state, not federal, control. Now, in the late twentieth century, the Supreme Court has decided that Virginia, Massachusetts, and New Hampshire are constitutionally required to abide by a single federal standard in church-state matters. Whatever we may think about that decision as a matter of public policy, it makes it difficult to hold up any particular bit of eighteenth-century history and call it the "warp and woof" of the establishment clause.

My reading of the legislative history of the establishment clause is not unique, but it appears to be a distinctly minority view in the vast literature on the topic of church and state in America. This is perplexing not because my argument is so persuasive but because there really is so little evidence to support the classic "warp and woof" position. Judges, lawyers, and even historians have been so anxious to infuse the establishment clause's vague language with intellectual content and a philosophical pedigree that they have held firmly to a view of history at odds with the preponderance of the facts. A revised view of the First Amendment's history thus may appear threatening because it raises a difficult question: If we reduce Virginia's disestablishmentarian impulses to the modest role they actually played in the adoption of the establishment clause, must we concomitantly revise our constitutional jurisprudence? An uncompromising devotee of the "original intent" school of interpretation might say so, but constitutional decision-making is often far more complicated than merely trying to read the minds of the framers. Perhaps instead we can take a renewed look at Madison as neither warp nor woof but as a thoughtful politician who struggled to come to terms with the complex issues of how religions and governments should interact.

James Madison on Establishment Issues

Madison's views may not necessarily have been written into the First Amendment (or at least not until the Supreme Court did so about two centuries after it was adopted), but his experiences in church-state matters may help illuminate some of the murky questions we continue to encounter. As president and as a craftsman of state and federal constitutions and laws, Madison grappled with a number of the kinds of issues we face today, and he was a thoughtful and articulate commentator on several areas of church and state interactions.

Perhaps the first lesson we can learn from Madison is how hard these issues are. They are often highly emotional issues about which thoughtful, well-educated people may hold diametrically opposing positions. In fact, the very same people may hold—or at least espouse—conflicting views in different contexts or simply at different times. Such inconsistency may result from the fact that we encounter church-state issues in the political realm where things that appear clear in theory become muddled in a complex web of interconnecting political issues and competing "factions" (to use a favorite word of Madison's).

Madison was hardly immune to these pressures. As a member of Congress, he served on the committee that selected the first congressional chaplain, a practice he later decried, calling it a "palpable violation of equal rights, as well as of Constitutional principles."[19] He voiced no concern when the Congress, in its first official act after adopting the Bill of Rights, passed a resolution asking President Washington to declare a "day of public thanksgiving and prayer, to be observed by acknowledging, with grateful hearts, the many signal favors of Almighty God," especially in that He gave them the opportunity to establish the Constitution.[20] During his presidency, Madison declared national days of prayer and fasting, a practice Jefferson had eschewed, though later in life he described himself as having been "disinclined" to do so, offering five separate arguments for the impropriety of the practice. Perhaps most surprisingly for the man who had labored strenuously and effectively to secure support for Jefferson's "Bill for Establishing Religious Freedom," Madison, in 1785, introduced into the Virginia legislature a bill endorsed and possibly written by Jefferson authorizing the governor, when the General Assembly was in recess, to declare a day of "public fasting and humiliation, or thanksgiving." On such occasions, "every minister of the gospel" was to "perform divine service and preach a sermon, or discourse, suited to the occasion in his church, on pain of forfeiting fifty pounds for every failure, not having a reasonable excuse."[21] Here were Jefferson and Madison, two of America's most ardent champions of religious liberty and dedicated disestablishmentarians, collaborating to fine preachers for not properly sermonizing when required to do so by the state government! Could Madison have somehow forgotten that he had written just a few months earlier that employing of "Religion as an engine of Civil policy" is "an unhallowed perversion of the means of salvation?"[22]

Madison is often venerated as the patron saint of those espousing a very strict separation between church and state for his carefully crafted "Memorial and Remonstrance" and his effective role in Virginia's formal disestablishment, but a number of his official executive and legislative acts ran counter to his brilliantly written position papers. Can we conclude that Madison, the great statesman, was a hypocrite on matters of church and state? That would not be fair to Madison. But the extent to which Madison permitted principle and practice to contrast so sharply in his own life demonstrates the extraordinary difficulty of resolving church-state issues. We need to remember that Madison was a politician trying to resolve difficult national issues that may have affected the success or failure of the American effort to succeed as an independent nation. Despite his second thoughts, President Madison twice acceded to congressional requests to have the government call on people to seek God's blessing on his beloved nation. During the dangerous days of the War of 1812, it was politically pragmatic to act on Congress' requests for national days of prayer, especially since Madison's relationship with Congress was often tenuous. Federalists, in fact, denounced Madison's proclamations as a trick designed to inspire public (and perhaps divine) support for the unpopular war.[23] In short, the transition from theory to practice in the political arena is highly complex, and even a highly principled leader like Madison found it necessary to bend (and maybe occasionally break from) his principles to achieve other political ends that he may have believed were more important at the time.

A second insight that may help explain some of Madison's apparent inconsistencies is that he seemed to treat religion very differently than he treated churches. Madison's views on religious belief were consistently reverent and respectful; for him, religious faith was "the duty which we owe to our Creator,"[24] and he believed that each person had to address the issues of faith and practice individually and free of compulsion. Religion was important to a vast number of Madison's contemporaries and constituents, and he reserved some of his strongest arguments to attack that "diabolical Hell conceived principle" of religious persecution and intolerance.[25] The "most valuable" proposal for the Bill of Rights, he swore, was the one that would have mandated religious freedom on both a federal and a state level,[26] and Madison deemed the equal right of conscience—and the duty owed by each person to the Creator—to be "precedent . . . to the claims of Civil Society" and an unalienable right.[27] Madison, then, took religious beliefs seriously, and as Madison biographer Ralph L. Ketcham has persuasively argued, Madison's commitment to the separation of church and state had its source in a reverence for religion, not from a contempt for beliefs that might wither without governmental support.[28]

In contrast, Madison was often highly suspicious of churches. While he may have occasionally blurred the line separating religion and government, he never deviated from his dedication to separating church and state, that is, the *institutions* of religion and government. At a young age, he wrote of the "pride, ignorance and knavery" of the priests of Virginia's established church and, as a Virginia legislator, he fought hard and successfully to separate church and state.[29] When he became president, he continued to take a very hard line when it came to governmental aid to churches. He vetoed the incorporation of a church in the federally controlled District of Columbia, arguing that it was an establishment of religion contrary to the Constitution. On the same grounds, he vetoed a bill setting aside land for a church in the new territory of Salem, Mississippi. As another Madison biographer, Irving Brant, has pointed out, there "was ample warrant for the legislation, in simple justice" because a surveyor's error had allowed the church to be mistakenly built on a piece of public land. Madison, however, considered it "a principle and precedent for the appropriation of funds of the United States for the use and support of religious societies" in violation of the establishment clause.[30] Later in life, he wrote that the "danger of silent accumulations and encroachments by Ecclesiastical Bodies [had] not sufficiently engaged attention in the U.S."[31] Madison then lumped churches together with "all corporations" whose power to accumulate property "in perpetuity" represented a risk to the nation, as the "growing wealth acquired by them never fails to be a source of abuses."[32] Madison's general aversion to wealthy and powerful institutions thus appeared to be a strong force in his disestablishmentarian efforts, especially since many examples in Europe and his native Virginia made a convincing case that churches were hardly immune to the potential for corruption and abuse inherent in any powerful organization. Reviewing the "fifteen centuries [that] the legal establishment of Christianity [had] been on trial," Madison's "Memorial and Remonstrance" rendered a guilty verdict of "pride and indolence in the Clergy, ignorance and servility in the laity, in both, superstition, bigotry and persecution."[33] Accordingly, Madison's respect for the rights of individuals to practice their religions did not lead him to endow religious institutions with any special privileges; to the contrary, he sought to diminish the possibility that churches would grasp political and economic power at the expense of individual liberties.

Another way to view Madison's apparent inconsistencies on the subject of religion and government is through an appreciation for the remarkably close connection in the American public's minds and hearts between God and country. The new American nation was full of people who believed in God and His continuing role in the history of mankind, and they typically saw the country as having a covenant with the Almighty and a special purpose in the divine plan, a faith shared by many Americans today.[34] From John Winthrop's "City upon a Hill" through the many appeals by Americans to God during the Revolution, by Abraham Lincoln and others during the Civil War, and even to the present day when politicians from Ronald Reagan to Colin Powell have claimed a national link with Divine plans, Americans have bonded religion and the Republic together no matter how much church may be officially separated from state in a formal or institutional sense. In Powell's recent words, "America has been established by divine providence to lead the world."[35] Supreme Court Justice William O. Douglas wrote in 1952 that "[w]e are a religious people whose institutions presuppose a Supreme Being," and for him it was a self-evident proclamation.[36] And so it was in the eighteenth century for Madison and other "enlightened" men, as well as for their countrymen. It was impossible to separate their religious beliefs and theological vocabulary from their political lives and visions, and they did not seek to do so. Madison lived his political life within this culture, and he occasionally participated in symbolic links between religion and the Republic, especially when it came to asking for God's blessing for the new nation. Note, for example, Madison's proclamation of 9 July 1812 in which he requested divine support for the country, appealing publicly to a shared spirituality he called "our holy religion":

> I do therefore recommend [a] day to be set apart for the devout purposes of rendering the Sovereign of the Universe and the Benefactor of Mankind the public homage due to His holy attributes; of acknowledging the transgressions which might justly provoke the manifestations of His divine displeasure; of seeking His merciful forgiveness and His assistance in the great duties of repentance and amendment, and especially of offering fervent supplications that in the present season of calamity and war He would take the American people under His peculiar care and protection.[37]

Yet, despite Madison's pious pronouncements joining God and country, he was adamant that the *institutions* of church and state be walled off from each other for their mutual benefit and for the protection of individual freedom. Any apparent inconsistencies in his actions and words remain in the interaction of religion and the Republic, not in the dealings of churches and governments.

In the twentieth century, we have seen the difficulty of deciding how far we really should separate religion and government. There have been relatively few disputes over direct ties between churches and state and federal governments. Tax dollars are not routed directly to the churches, and church officials do not have any special standing in the government. Rather, modern American church-state controversies have typically revolved around much more symbolic links between the country and religious faith: prayers in public schools, creches and menorahs on public property, invocations and benedictions at public events like graduations or legislative sessions. We are an increasingly diverse nation in almost every respect, but over ninety percent of Americans consistently profess a belief in God.[38] So many citizens continue to share "our holy religion," to use Madison's phrase (whatever it may mean), that there are few complaints even now as presidents have continued to declare national days of prayer. Madison's discomfort over such declarations notwithstanding, twentieth-century appeals to the Almighty retain the ringing cadences of what might be called "old time religion." Here are a few lines from a 1988 presidential proclamation:

> Let us [pray] for the love of God and His great goodness, in search of His guidance and the grace of repentance, in seeking His blessings, His peace, and the resting of His kind and holy hands on ourselves, our Nation, our friends in the defense of freedom, and all mankind, now and always.[39]

Two centuries after the First Amendment separated church and state at the federal level, the government has continued to ask each citizen to appeal for God's help in the affairs of state.

How can Madison help us make decisions about these kinds of links between God and country? On the issues of national days of prayer and legislative chaplains, we find Madison acting one way and arguing to the contrary, showing us how, perhaps, the steadfast principle of church-state separation might occasionally bend a bit in the face of political and cultural realities. This is not to say that these kinds of issues are unsolvable or that Madison is unable to help us. National days of prayer are probably not consistent with the notion of government keeping its hands off religion, as Madison wrote, but two centuries of continuous practice do not seem to have caused much harm since only a few church-state scholars and compulsive readers of the *Federal Register* even know about them.[40] Similarly, having a clergyman on the federal payroll solely to offer prayers in Congress looks to me like a violation of the "pure principle of religious freedom,"[41] as it did to Madison in his mature years, but, then again, our legislators need as much help as they can get. I would follow Madison's instincts to avoid these practices, partially on the grounds of principle, as Madison stated it, and partially on the issue of competence. Governments do some things well and others quite poorly. Religious faith and practice are profoundly important, and they are things that governments have never done particularly well, especially since official acts of piety tend either to be unfairly sectarian or so watered down that they appear equally inoffensive and uninspirational. If the American people want to pray, if legislators choose to fall on their knees and beg for divine help (or forgiveness), then by all means let them do so voluntarily at religious services, prayer breakfasts, and anywhere else they select. And we ought not to hound them out of the schools, legislative halls, and other government buildings on the grounds that it is unseemly to mix personal piety with public space. Many Americans are devoutly religious and we should not ask them to pretend that they are not.[42]

Madison seems much more clear on financial ties between churches and states; and the state and federal legislatures have rarely, if ever, proposed such formal establishments of religion, at least after the first few decades in the nineteenth century. The Supreme Court has, therefore, not been called on to invalidate laws made by Congress "respecting an establishment of religion" in what might be called the classical sense of the term "establishment" in which tax dollars are used to fill the churches' coffers.

This brings us back to the original question: Does the Constitution permit states to pay the cost of busing children to religious schools? The entire Supreme Court invoked Madison's views to try to settle this question, all swearing allegiance to a Madisonian separation of church and state; and the vote was five to four in favor of allowing the busing, with a strong dissenting contingent of justices. Not only did the justices differ sharply on their interpretations of the establishment clause, but they could not even agree on how Madison's views might apply to this kind of case. Whether or not he is the establishment clause's "warp and woof," we should be wary of trying to speculate about what Madison might do or say if he were confronted with these kinds of modern issues: it is hard enough for us to get a firm grip on what his position was vis-à-vis eighteenth-century questions. Madison was one of America's most thoughtful and principled statesmen to attempt to figure out how religion and government should interact with each other, and he was unable to maintain a clear and consistent position. We should not be surprised that neither the legislatures nor the courts have been any more successful in the last two hundred years.

Notes

The author would like to thank John F. Wilson, Christine Whelan, Brian Rokus, Brad Saft, and Lucie Kantrow for helpful comments on this chapter.

1. *Marbury v. Madison*, 5 U.S. (1 Cranch) 137, 177 (1803): "It is emphatically the province and duty of the judicial department to say what the law is." More recently, see *Cooper v. Aaron,* 358 U.S. 1, 18-19 (1958).

2. 330 U.S. 1 (1947).

3. 330 U.S. at 39 (Rutledge, J., dissenting).

4. *Reynolds v. United States*, 98 U.S. 145 (1879); *Rosenberger v. University of Virginia*, 132 L. Ed. 2d 700 (1995).

5. The House debates are recorded in the first volumes of *The Debates and Proceedings in the Congress of the United States*, ed. Joseph Gales, 42 vols. (Washington, D.C.: Gales and Seaton, 1834-56) [hereinafter *Annals of Congress*]. For a brief discussion on sources, see Leonard W. Levy, *The Establishment Clause: Religion and the First Amendment* (New York: Macmillan, 1986), 187-189; see also Marion Tinling, "Thomas Lloyd's Reports of the First Federal Congress," *William and Mary Quarterly*, 3d ser., 18 (October 1961): 519-545.

6. Levy, *The Establishment Clause*, 79.

7. *Annals of Congress,* 1:451-452 (8 June 1789); Madison, "Amendments to the Constitution," 8 June 1789, *The Papers of James Madison*, ed. Charles F. Hobson, Robert A. Rutland et al. (Charlottesville, Va.: University Press of Virginia, 1979), 12:201-202 [hereinafter *Papers of Madison*].

8. For the state ratification debates, see Bernard Schwartz, *The Bill of Rights: A Documentary History,* 2 vols. (New York: Chelsea House, 1971).

9. *Annals of Congress*, 1:758 (15 August 1789).

10. *Annals of Congress*, 1:759 (15 August 1789).

11. New Hampshire's constitution extolled "[m]orality and piety . . . rightly grounded on evangelical principles," and stipulated that the legislature was empowered to authorize towns "to make adequate provision at their own expense, for the support and maintenance of public protestant teachers of piety, religion and morality," a similar kind of establishment to the one that Madison had fervently opposed in his "Memorial and Remonstrance." See Jean Yarbrough, "New Hampshire: Puritanism and the Moral Foundations of America," in *Ratifying the Constitution*, ed. Michael Allen Gillespie and Michael Lienesch (Lawrence, Kans.: University Press of Kansas, 1989), 241.

12. *Annals of Congress*, 1:758 (15 August 1789).

13. *Annals of Congress*, 1:796 (20 August 1789). Irving Brant has suggested that "[i]t is probable that Madison wrote the Ames version" since it closely resembles remarks he had made on the floor and Ames had not been a proponent of a bill of rights, but Brant provides no supporting evidence. He does conclude, however, that Ames "would have been ready enough to co-operate in promoting a change which would both attain Madison's objective and relieve the fear of New Englanders that the constitutional amendment might interfere with their established state churches." Irving Brant, "Madison: On the Separation of Church and State," *William and Mary Quarterly*, 3d ser., 8 (January 1951): 15.

14. Helen E. Veit, Kenneth R. Bowling, and Charlene Bangs Bickford, eds., *Creating the Bill of Rights: The Documentary Record from the First Federal Congress* (Baltimore: Johns Hopkins University Press, 1991), 48 (14 September 1789).

15. *Creating the Bill of Rights*, 49 (24 September 1789).

16. *Everson*, 330 U.S. at 39 (Rutledge, J., dissenting). Chief Justice Richard Neely of the West Virginia Court of Appeals has suggested, in somewhat more colorful language, that the Supreme Court may be prone to such mistakes: "Lawyers . . . who take seriously recent U.S. Supreme Court historical scholarship as applied to the Constitution also probably believe in the Tooth Fairy and the Easter Bunny." Richard Neely, *How Courts Govern America* (New Haven, Conn.: Yale University Press, 1981), 18. Others have argued that Madison was not necessarily the dominant force in the adoption of the establishment clause. See, for example, Clifton B. Kruse, "The Historical Meaning and Judicial Construction of the Establishment of Religion Clause of the First Amendment," *Washburn Law Journal* 2 (Winter 1962): 65-144; Cushing Strout, *The New Heavens and New Earth: Political Religion in America* (New York: Harper and Row, 1974), 95-97; Daniel L. Dreisbach, *Real Threat and Mere Shadow: Religious Liberty and the First Amendment* (Westchester, Il.: Crossway Books, 1987), 60-62, 103-104, 266-267 n. 33. Nevertheless, as the relatively recent *Rosenberger* case demonstrates, the Supreme Court justices and many others continue to employ Madison as being especially representative of the founding fathers' attitudes about the separation of church and state.

17. James Morton Smith, ed., *The Republic of Letters: The Correspondence between Thomas Jefferson and James Madison 1776-1826*, 3 vols. (New York: W.W. Norton, 1995), 3:1364.

18. See, for example, *Everson*, 330 U.S. at 8, 14-15.

19. Elizabeth Fleet, ed., "Madison's 'Detached Memoranda,'" *William and Mary Quarterly*, 3d ser., 3 (October 1946): 558. Cf. Robert L. Cord, *Separation of Church and State: Historical Fact and Current Fiction* (New York: Lambeth Press, 1982), 23.

20. *Annals of Congress*, 1:949-950 (25 September 1789).

21. *The Papers of Thomas Jefferson*, ed. Julian P. Boyd, 27 vols. to date (Princeton, N.J.: Princeton University Press, 1950-) 2:556. See Daniel L. Dreisbach, "Thomas Jefferson and Bills Number 82-86 of the Revisions of the Laws of Virginia, 1776-1786: New Light on the Jeffersonian Model of Church-State Relations," *North Carolina Law Review* 69 (1990): 193 (noting that the bill did not pass).

22. Madison, "Memorial and Remonstrance," Papers of Madison, 8:301.

23. See Perry Miller, *The Life of the Mind in America* (New York: Harcourt Brace and World, 1965), 38.

24. Madison, "Memorial and Remonstrance," *Papers of Madison*, 8:299.

25. Letter from James Madison to William Bradford, 24 January 1774, *Papers of Madison*, 1:106.

26. *Annals of Congress*, 1:784 (17 August 1789); Madison, "Amendments to the Constitution," 17 August 1789, *Papers of Madison*, 12:344.

27. Madison, "Memorial and Remonstrance," *Papers of Madison*, 8:299.

28. Ralph L. Ketcham, "James Madison and Religion: A New Hypothesis," in *James Madison on Religious Liberty*, ed. Robert S. Alley (Buffalo, N.Y.: Prometheus Books, 1985), 192.

29. Letter from James Madison to William Bradford, 24 January 1774, *Papers of Madison*, 1:106.

30. Brant, "Madison: On the Separation of Church and State," 18.

31. Fleet, ed., "Madison's 'Detached Memoranda,'" 554.

32. Fleet, ed., "Madison's 'Detached Memoranda,'" 556.

33. Madison, "Memorial and Remonstrance," *Papers of Madison*, 8:301.

34. See, for example, John F. Wilson, *Public Religion in American Culture* (Philadelphia: Temple University Press, 1979), and Robert N. Bellah, *The Broken Covenant: American Civil Religion in Time of Trial* (New York: Seabury Press, 1975).

35. Kennedy Center Lecture, 1995, as quoted in Michael R. Gordon and Bernard E. Trainor, "Beltway Warrior," *New York Times Sunday Magazine*, 27 August 1995, 40.

36. *Zorach v. Clauson*, 343 U.S. 306, 313 (1952).

37. James D. Richardson, ed., *A Compilation of the Messages and Papers of the Presidents*, 20 vols. (New York: Bureau of National Literature, 1897), 2:498.

38. See *Religion in America* (Princeton, N.J.: Gallup Organization, 1987), 51.

39. President, Proclamation 5767, "National Day of Prayer," *Federal Register* 53, no. 24 (5 February 1988): 3327-28, microfiche.

42. In the words of novelist and former presidential speech writer Peter Benchley, whose protagonist had been asked to pen the presidential message announcing a national day of prayer, "Why bother with proclamations, period? Nobody ever reads them, let alone heeds them. The newspapers print them between the obituaries and the neuter-your-pet notices." Peter Benchley, Q Clearance (New York: Random House, 1986), 3.

41. Fleet, ed., "Madison's 'Detached Memoranda,'" 558.

42. For more along these lines, see Donald L. Drakeman, *Church-State Constitutional Issues: Making Sense of the Establishment Clause* (Westport, Conn.: Greenwood Press, 1991).

About the Contributors

Mark A. Beliles is cofounder and chairman of the board of directors of the Providence Foundation, an international Christian research and educational organization that focuses on religious history and its impact on culture. He is also pastor of Grace Covenant Church in Charlottesville, Virginia. Dr. Beliles is the author of *Thomas Jefferson's Abridgement of the Words of Jesus of Nazareth* (Providence Foundation, 1993) and coauthor of *America's Providential History* (Providence Foundation, 1989).

Robert L. Cord is Matthews Distinguished University Professor and professor of political science at Northeastern University in Boston. He is the author of numerous scholarly publications, including *Separation of Church and State: Historical Fact and Current Fiction* (Lambeth Press, 1982).

Donald L. Drakeman is the president of a biotechnology company and an adjunct professor of politics at Princeton University. He is the author of *Church-State Constitutional Issues: Making Sense of the Establishment Clause* (Greenwood Press, 1991), and coeditor of *Church and State in American History: The Burden of Religious Pluralism,* 2d ed. (Beacon Press, 1987). Dr. Drakeman has published articles in scholarly journals, including *Cardozo Law Review, Journal of Church and State*, *Rutgers Law Review*, and *Seton Hall University Law Review*.

Daniel L. Dreisbach is an associate professor of justice, law, and society at American University in Washington, D.C. He is the editor of *Religion and Politics in the Early Republic: Jasper Adams and the Church-State Debate* (University Press of Kentucky, 1996), and author of *Real Threat and Mere Shadow: Religious Liberty and the First Amendment* (Crossway Books, 1987). He has published articles in scholarly journals, including *American Journal of Legal History*, *Baylor Law Review*, *Journal of Church and State*, *North Carolina Law Review*, and *William and Mary Quarterly*.

Garrett Ward Sheldon is the John Morton Beaty Professor of Political and Social Sciences at the University of Virginia's College at Wise. Among his many publications are *Religion and Politics: Major Thinkers on the Relationship Between Church and State* (Peter Lang, 1990); *The History of Political Theory: Ancient Greece to Modern America* (Peter Lang, 1988); *The Political Philosophy of Thomas Jefferson* (Johns Hopkins University Press, 1991); *What Would Jefferson Say*? (Penguin, 1998); and the novel, *What Would Jesus Do?* (Broadman & Holman, 1993). In 1992 he won the Outstanding Faculty in Virginia Award.

Charles B. Sanford is an ordained minister who has served American Baptist, United Methodist, United Church of Christ, and Presbyterian churches in Vermont, New York, and Wisconsin. He is the author of *The Religious Life of Thomas Jefferson* (University Press of Virginia, 1984) and *Thomas Jefferson and His Library* (Archon Books, 1977).

Mary-Elaine Swanson is vice president of the American Christian History Institute and an associate of the Foundation for American Christian Education. She has written extensively on, and developed curricula for, the study of American history. She is the author of *The Education of James Madison: A Model for Today* (The Hoffman Center, 1994).

Thomas C. Thompson is an independent scholar currently conducting research on the portrayal of colonial and revolutionary history in motion pictures. He has published articles on the methodology of film and history and colonial agriculture, as well as on English legal history. Dr. Thompson has held positions at the University of California, Riverside; California State University at Los Angeles; and California State Polytechnic at San Luis Obispo.

Douglas L. Wilson is the Saunders Director of the International Center for Jefferson Studies at Monticello and Scholar in Residence at the University of Virginia. He is the editor of *Jefferson's Literary Commonplace Book* (Princeton University Press, 1989), published in the second series of *The Papers of Thomas Jefferson*. He has published numerous other books and articles on Thomas Jefferson and Abraham Lincoln.